Leslie A. O.

Cultural Diversity and Education

FOURTH EDITION

Cultural Diversity and Education

Foundations, Curriculum, and Teaching

James A. Banks

University of Washington, Seattle

Allyn and Bacon

Boston ■ London ■ Toronto ■ Sydney ■ Tokyo ■ Singapore

Vice President: *Paul A. Smith*
Senior Editor: *Traci Mueller*
Editorial Assistant: *Bridget Keane*
Executive Marketing Manager: *Lisa Kimball*
Editorial Production Service: *Grace Sheldrick, Wordsworth Associates*
Manufacturing Buyer: *Megan Cochran*
Cover Administrator: *Linda Knowles*
Electronic Composition: *Omegatype Typography, Inc.*

Library of Congress Cataloging-in-Publication Data

Banks, James A.
  Cultural diversity and education : foundations, curriculum, and teaching / James A. Banks.–4th ed.
    p. cm.
    Rev. ed. of: Multiethnic education. 3rd ed. c1994.
    Includes bibliographical references and index.
    ISBN   0–205–30865–1
    1. Minorities–Education–United States. 2. Multicultural education–United States. I. Banks, James A. Multiethnic Education. II. Title.

LC3731 .B365 2001

00-025849

To Lula, Cherry Ann, Rosie Mae, and Tessie Mae,
important women in my life,
and to Angela and Patricia,
with the hope that this book
will help to make their future world
better than ours

BRIEF CONTENTS

CONTENTS

3   Multicultural Education: Development, Goals, and Approaches   40

PREFACE

As cultural, ethnic, language, and religious diversity increases in the United States, the challenge of educating citizens to function effectively in a pluralistic democratic society deepens. The dream that drew millions of immigrants to these shores a century ago is still a powerful magnet. Most of the immigrants who come to the United States today, like those a century ago, are seeking better economic opportunities. However, the source of the nation's immigrants has changed substantially. Most of the 8.8 million immigrants who came to the U.S. between 1901 and 1910 were Europeans. Today, most of the immigrants who come to the U.S. are from nations in Asia and Latin America. These groups made up nearly three-fourths of the 7.6 million immigrants that settled in the United States between 1991 and 1998. The U.S. Census Bureau projects that ethnic groups of color in the United States will increase from 28 percent of the nation's population today to 47 percent in 2050.

The French demographer Jean-Claude Chenais observes that for the first time in history one nation contains all of the world's races, religions, and languages (cited in Riche, 2000). This rich diversity in the United States presents both an opportunity and a challenge. Diversity enriches the nation because it provides alternative ways to view the world and to solve societal problems. A major challenge faced by democratic pluralistic nations such as the U.S. is how to balance diversity and unity. A nation-state that denies individuals the opportunity to participate freely in their community cultures runs the risk of alienating them from the national civic culture. In order to create a shared civic community in which all groups participate and to which they have allegiance, steps must be taken to construct an inclusive national civic culture.

A major goal of multicultural education is to help students develop the knowledge, attitudes, and skills needed to participate effectively in their cultural communities and within the civic culture of the nation-state. To help students attain these goals, the school's curriculum and social structure must be substantially reformed and educators must acquire new knowledge and skills.

Cultural Diversity and Education: Foundations, Curriculum, and Teaching, Fourth Edition, is designed to help educators clarify the philosophical and definitional issues related to multicultural education, derive a clarified philosophical position, design and implement effective teaching strategies that reflect diversity, and develop sound guidelines for multicultural practices. *Cultural Diversity and Education* describes actions that educators can take to institutionalize multicultural ideas, concepts, and practices.

Readers familiar with the third edition of this book will note that this edition has been substantially revised. The broader scope of the book is one of its most significant changes. The previous editions focused largely on ethnic diversity. This edition gives more attention to other cultural groups. The broader scope of this book is most clearly evident in Chapters 7, 8, and 13. The "Stages of Ethnicity" have been broadened and reconceptualized as "The Stages of Cultural Identity" in

Chapter 7. Chapters 8 and 13 are new to this edition. Chapter 8 focuses on race, disability, and giftedness. Gender and educational equity is the subject of Chapter 13.

The significant changes in this edition necessitated that the title of this book be changed. *Multiethnic Education: Theory and Practice,* the title of this book for its three previous editions, no longer describes its contents. The new title, *Cultural Diversity and Education: Foundations, Curriculum, and Teaching,* more accurately reflects the book's content and focus.

Much of the text has been rewritten to make it more consistent with the needs of today's college and university students and also with current theory, research, and terminology. It is now possible to include the broader range of topics in three new chapters—8, 9, and 13. Part Three, "Knowledge Construction and School Reform," which consists of Chapters 8 and 9, is new to this edition. The citations and references throughout the book have been thoroughly revised and updated.

Cultural Diversity and Education: Foundations, Curriculum, and Teaching is divided into five parts. Parts One, Two, and Three focus on the foundations of multicultural education; Parts Four and Five focus on curriculum and teaching.

Part One discusses the dimensions, history, and goals of multicultural education. Conceptual and philosophical issues and problems related to education and cultural diversity are the focus of Part Two. The major research and programmatic paradigms related to cultural diversity and education are described. The philosophical and ideological issues related to diversity and education are also described in this part.

Part Three examines knowledge construction and school reform. It describes knowledge systems and paradigms that underlie school practices and pedagogy and the ways in which existing knowledge systems can be transformed. Curriculum and effective teaching strategies are discussed in the three chapters in Part Four. The curriculum issues and teaching strategies described in this part of the book focus on helping students learn how to construct knowledge, make reflective decisions, and participate in meaningful personal, social, and civic action. The first two chapters in Part Four include teaching units that illustrate how teachers can help students to acquire the knowledge, values, and skills they will need to become effective participants in a pluralistic, democratic society.

Gender and educational equity; language, culture, and education; prejudice reduction; and curriculum guidelines are discussed in the first two chapters in Part Five. The final chapter, which describes curriculum guidelines, also summarizes some of the major issues, problems, and recommendations presented in *Cultural Diversity and Education: Foundations, Curriculum, and Teaching,* Fourth Edition. The Appendix consists of a checklist, based on the Guidelines described in Chapter 16, that can help educators determine the extent to which their institutions reflect the diversity within their societies.

REFERENCE

Riche, M.F. (2000, June). America's diversity and growth: Signposts for the 21st century. *Population Bulletin, 55*: 38. Washington, DC: Population Reference Bureau.

Acknowledgments

I want to thank several colleagues who helped with the preparation of this edition. Ricardo L. García contributed Chapter 14. I wrote Chapter 16 with the following colleagues: Carlos E. Cortés, Geneva Gay, Ricardo L. García, and Anna S. Ochoa. My thanks to the following reviewers: Carlos F. Diaz, Florida Atlantic University; David H. Spain, University of Washington, Seattle; and Ricardo L. García, the University of Nebraska-Lincoln. Even though all the comments on the manuscript were helpful and informative, I assume total responsibility for the contents of this book.

I am grateful to the National Academy of Education for a Spencer Fellowship that supported my research for three years during the early part of my career. Many of the concepts I formulated during these years are incorporated into this and the previous editions of *Cultural Diversity and Education.* My former and present students at the University of Washington listened to and reacted to many of the ideas in this book as these ideas were formulated and refined.

Grace Sheldrick of Wordworth Associates has provided editorial-production assistance on my books for nearly two decades. I want to thank her again for her keen insights and professionalism.

I want to thank Cherry A. McGee Banks, a professor at the University of Washington, Bothell, for stimulating and supporting my intellectual growth for three decades and for perceptive and helpful reactions to the ideas in this book. My daughters, Angela and Patricia, have taught me about the essence of life and have given me renewed faith that humankind can create a better world.

I want to thank the following organizations and publishers for permitting me to draw freely from the publications noted that I authored:

Cassell, for a section from one of my chapters in James A. Banks & James Lynch (Eds.), *Multicultural Education in Western Societies.* (London: Holt, Rinehart and Winston, 1996), pp. 10–25.

The Centre for the Study of Curriculum and Instruction, The University of British Columbia, for "Reducing Prejudice in Students: Theory, Research and Strategies," in Kogila Moodley (Ed.), *Race Relations and Multicultural Education* (Vancouver: Centre for the Study of Curriculum and Instruction, the University of British Columbia, 1985), pp. 65–87.

The Faculty of Education, University of Birmingham (England), for "Ethnic Revitalization Movements and Education." *Educational Review,* Vol. 37, No. 2 (1985), pp. 131–139.

Heldref Publications for "Pluralism, Ideology and Curriculum Reform." *The Social Studies,* Vol. 67 (May–June, 1967), pp. 99–106.

Longman (a division of Pearson Education) for two figures from James A. Banks & Cherry A. McGee Banks (with Ambrose A. Clegg, Jr.). *Teaching Strategies for the Social Studies: Decision-Making and Citizen Action.* New York: Longman, 1999.

The National Council for the Social Studies for "Cultural Democracy, Citizenship Education, and the American Dream" (NCSS Presidential Address), *Social Education,* Vol. 47 (March, 1983), pp. 231–232; "Should Integration Be a Goal in a Pluralistic Society?" in Raymond Muessig (Ed.), *Controversial Issues in the Social Studies.*

Washington, DC: National Council for the Social Studies, 1975, pp. 197–228; with Carlos E. Cortés, Geneva Gay, Ricardo L. García, and Anna S. Ochoa, *Curriculum Guidelines for Multicultural Education* (Washington, DC: National Council for the Social Studies, 1992).

The State University of New York Press for "A Curriculum for Empowerment, Action, and Change." In Christine E. Sleeter (Ed.), *Empowerment through Multicultural Education* (pp. 125–141, ff. 311–313). Albany: State University of New York Press, 1991.

The University of Chicago Press for "The Social Studies, Ethnic Diversity and Social Change." From *Elementary School Journal,* Vol. 87 (May, 1987), pp. 531–543. Copyright 1987 by The University of Chicago Press. All rights reserved.

Macmillan Library Reference for a revised version of pages 464–466 of James A. Banks, "Multicultural Education: Its Effects on Students' Racial and Gender Role Attitudes." From *Handbook of Research on Social Studies Teaching and Learning* (James P. Shaver, Ed.). New York, Macmillan, 1991, pp. 464–466. Used with permission.

American Educational Research Association for "The Lives and Values of Researchers: Implications for Educating Citizens in a Multicultural Society." (AERA Presidential Address). *Educational Researcher,* Vol. 27 (No.7), October, 1998, pp. 4–17. Used with permission of AERA.

Chapter 8, for which I hold the copyright, was first published, in a slightly revised version, as "The Social Construction of Difference and the Quest for Educational Equality" in Ronald S. Brandt (Ed.), *Education in a New Era* (pp. 21–45) (2000 ASCD Yearbook). Washington, DC: Association for Supervision and Curriculum Development, 2000.

I also thank the American Association of University Women Foundation for giving me permission to reprint a section from this publication in Chapter 13: *Gender Gaps: Where Schools Still Fail Our Children.* New York: Marlowe & Co., 1998; pp. 4–8, 121–130. Used and adapted with permission.

James A. Banks

PART ONE

Dimensions, History, and Goals

Chapter 1
The Dimensions of Multicultural Education

Chapter 2
Multicultural Education: History and Revitalization Movements

Chapter 3
Multicultural Education: Development, Goals, and Approaches

Chapter 1 describes five dimensions of multicultural education conceptualized by the author: (1) content integration, (2) the knowledge construction process, (3) prejudice reduction, (4) an equity pedagogy, and (5) an empowering school culture and social structure. The need for each of these dimensions to be implemented in order to create comprehensive and powerful multicultural educational practices is described and illustrated.

Chapter 2 describes the development of educational reform movements related to cultural and ethnic diversity within an historical context. Historical developments related to ethnicity since the early 1900s, the intergroup education movement of the 1940s and 1950s, new immigrants in the United States, and the ethnic revival movements that have emerged in various Western societies since the 1960s are discussed. A typology that classifies the major phases of ethnic revitalization movements, particularly as they have developed in the United States and in other Western nation-states, is also presented in this chapter.

In Chapter 3 the historical development of multicultural education is described. The nature of multicultural education, its goals, current practices, problems, and promises are discussed. Four approaches to multicultural education are also described: The Contributions Approach, The Additive Approach, The Transformation Approach, and The Decision-Making and Social Action Approach.

CHAPTER

1

The Dimensions of Multicultural Education

The Aims and Goals of Multicultural Education

The heated discourse on multicultural education, especially in the popular press and among writers outside the field (Fullinwider, 1996; Graff, 1992; Sleeter, 1995; Taylor et al., 1994), often obscures the theory, research, and consensus among multicultural education scholars and researchers about the nature, aims, and scope of the field (Banks, 1995a; Gay, 1995). A major goal of multicultural education—as stated by specialists in the field—is to reform schools, colleges, and universities so that students from diverse racial, ethnic, and social-class groups will experience educational equality.

Another important goal of multicultural education is to give both male and female students an equal chance to experience educational success and mobility (Sadker & Sadker, 1994). Multicultural education theorists are increasingly interested in how the interaction of race, class, and gender influences education (Banks, 1997b; Cyrus, 1997). However, the emphasis that different theorists give to each of these variables varies considerably. Although there is an emerging consensus about the aims and scope of multicultural education, the variety of typologies, conceptual schemes, and perspectives within the field reflects its emergent status and the fact that complete agreement about its aims and boundaries has not been attained (Baker, 1994; Banks, 1997a; Garcia, 1998; Gay, 1994; Nieto, 1999).

There is general agreement among most scholars and researchers in multicultural education that for it to be implemented successfully, institutional changes must be made, including changes in the curriculum; the teaching materials; teaching and learning styles; the attitudes, perceptions, and behaviors of teachers and administrators; and in the goals, norms, and culture of the school (Banks & Banks, 1995). However, many school and university practitioners have a limited conception of multicultural education; they view it primarily as curriculum reform that involves changing or restructuring the curriculum to include content about ethnic groups, women, and other cultural groups. This conception of multicultural education is widespread because curriculum reform was the main focus when the movement first emerged in the 1960s and 1970s and because the multiculturalism discourse in the popular media has focused on curriculum reform and has largely ignored other dimensions and components of multicultural education (Hughes, 1993).

The Dimensions and Their Importance

If multicultural education is to become better understood and implemented in ways more consistent with theory, its various dimensions must be more clearly described, conceptualized, and researched. Multicultural education is conceptualized in this chapter as a field that consists of the five dimensions I have formulated (Banks, 1995a):

1. Content integration,
2. The knowledge construction process,
3. Prejudice reduction,
4. An equity pedagogy, and
5. An empowering school culture and social structure (see Figure 1.1).

Each of the five dimensions is defined and illustrated later in this chapter.

Educators need to be able to identify, to differentiate, and to understand the meanings of each dimension of multicultural education. *They also need to understand that multicultural education includes but is much more than content integration.* Part of the controversy in multicultural education results from the fact that many writers in the popular press see it only as content integration and as an educational movement that benefits only people of color. When multicultural education is conceptualized broadly, it becomes clear that it is for *all* students, and not just for low-income students and students of color (Banks, 1995a; May, 1999; Nieto, 1999). Research and practice will also improve if we more clearly delineate the boundaries and dimensions of multicultural education.

This chapter defines and describes each of the five dimensions of multicultural education. The knowledge construction process is discussed more extensively than the other four dimensions. The kind of knowledge that teachers examine and master will have a powerful influence on the teaching methods they create, on their interpretations of school knowledge, and on how they use student cultural knowledge. The knowledge construction process is fundamental in the implementation of multicultural education. It has implications for each of the other four dimensions— for example, for the construction of knowledge about pedagogy.

Limitations and Interrelationship of the Dimensions

The dimensions typology is an ideal-type conception. It approximates but does not describe reality in its total complexity. Like all classification schema, it has both strengths and limitations. Typologies are helpful conceptual tools because they provide a way to organize and make sense of complex and distinct data and observations. However, their categories are interrelated and overlapping, not mutually exclusive. Typologies are rarely able to encompass the total universe of ex-

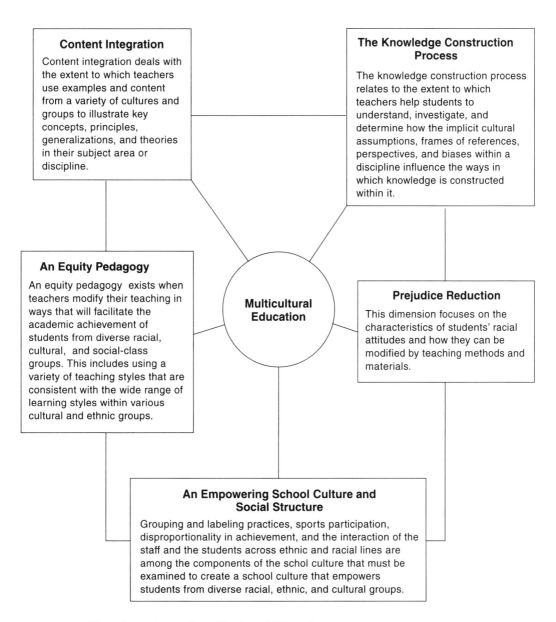

FIGURE 1.1   The Dimensions of Multicultural Education

isting or future cases. Consequently, some cases can be described only by using several of the categories.

The dimensions typology provides a useful framework for categorizing and interpreting the extensive and myriad literature on cultural diversity, ethnicity, and education. However, the five dimensions are conceptually distinct but highly interrelated. *Content integration,* for example, describes any approach that is used to integrate content about racial and cultural groups into the curriculum. The *knowledge construction process* describes a method in which teachers help students to understand how knowledge is created and how it reflects the experiences of various ethnic and cultural groups.

The Meaning of Multicultural Education to Teachers

A widely held and discussed idea among theorists is that in order for multicultural education to be effectively implemented within a school, changes must be made in the total school culture as well as within all subject areas, including mathematics and science (Secada, Fennema, & Adajian, 1995). Despite the wide acceptance of this basic tenet by theorists, it confuses many teachers, especially those in subject areas such as science and mathematics. This confusion often takes the form of resistance to multicultural education. I have been told by many teachers after a conference presentation on the characteristics and goals of multicultural education: "These ideas are fine for the social studies, but they have nothing to do with science or math. Science is science, regardless of the culture of the students."

This statement can be interpreted in a variety of ways. However, one way of interpreting it is as a genuine belief by a teacher who is unaware of higher-level philosophical and epistemological knowledge and issues in science or mathematics or who does not believe that these issues are related to schoolteaching (Harding, 1998). The frequency with which I have encountered this belief in staff development conferences and workshops for teachers has convinced me that the meaning of multicultural education must be better contextualized in order for the concept to be more widely understood and accepted by teachers and other practitioners, especially in such subject areas as mathematics and the sciences.

We need to better clarify the different dimensions of multicultural education and to help teachers see more clearly the implications of multicultural education for their own subject areas and teaching situations. The development of active, cooperative, and motivating teaching strategies that makes physics more interesting for students of color might be a more important goal for a physics teacher of a course in which few African American students are enrolling or successfully completing than is a search for ways to infuse African contributions to physics into the course. Of course, in the best possible world both goals would be attained. However, given the real world of the schools, we might experience more success in multicultural teaching if we set limited but essential goals for teachers, especially in the early phases of multicultural educational reform.

The development of a phase conceptualization for the implementation of multicultural educational reform would be useful. During the first or early phases, all teachers would be encouraged to determine ways in which they could adapt or modify their *pedagogy,* or teaching, to a multicultural population with diverse abilities, learning characteristics, and motivational styles. A second or later phase would focus on curriculum *content integration*. One phase would not end when another began. Rather, the goal would be to reach a phase in which all aspects of multicultural educational reform would be implemented simultaneously. Often in multicultural educational reform, the first focus is on content integration rather than on knowledge construction or pedagogy. A content-integration focus often results in many mathematics and science teachers believing that multicultural education has little or no meaning for them. The remainder of this chapter describes the dimensions of multicultural education with the hope that this discussion will help teachers and other practitioners determine how they can implement multicultural education in powerful and effective ways.

Contextualizing Multicultural Education

We need to do a better job of contextualizing the concept of multicultural education. When we tell practitioners that multicultural education implies reform in a discipline or subject area without specifying in detail the nature of that reform, we risk frustrating motivated and committed teachers because they do not have the knowledge and skills to act on their beliefs. Educators who reject multicultural education will use the "irrelevance of multicultural education" argument as a convenient and publicly sanctioned form of resistance and as a justification for inaction.

Many of us who are active in multicultural education have backgrounds in the social sciences and humanities. We consequently understand the content and process implications of multicultural education in these disciplines. A variety of programs, units, and lessons have been developed illustrating how the curriculum can be reformed and infused with multicultural perspectives, issues, and points of view from the social sciences and the humanities (Banks, 1997c; Derman-Sparks & Phillips, 1997). As students of society and of the sociology of knowledge, we also understand, in general ways, how mathematics and science are cultural systems that developed within social and political contexts (Harding, 1998).

Most mathematics and science teachers do not have the kind of knowledge and understanding of their disciplines that enables them to construct and formulate lessons, units, and examples that deal with the cultural assumptions, frames of references, and perspectives within their disciplines. Few teachers seem able to identify and describe the assumptions and paradigms that underlie science and mathematics (Kuhn, 1970). They often make such statements as "Math and science have no cultural contexts and assumptions. These disciplines are universal across cultures." Knowledge about the philosophical and epistemological issues and problems in science and mathematics, and the philosophy of science, is often limited to graduate seminars and academic specialists in these disciplines (Harding, 1998; Powell & Frankenstein, 1997).

Specialists and leaders in multicultural education, because of their academic backgrounds, have been able to identify the basic issues and problems in mathematics and science but have not, in my view, provided the field with the clarity, curriculum work, and examples of lessons that mathematics and science teachers need in order to view the content within their disciplines from multicultural perspectives. Some promising attempts have been made to develop multicultural materials for mathematics and science teachers (Secada, Fennema, & Adajian, 1995; Powell & Frankenstein, 1997). However, more work must be done in this area before most mathematics and science teachers can develop and implement a curriculum-content approach to multicultural education.

Multicultural education is a way of viewing reality and a way of thinking, and not just content about various ethnic and cultural groups. Much more important work needs to be done in order to provide teachers with the examples and specifics they need. In the meantime, we can help all teachers, including mathematics and science teachers, to conceptualize and develop an *equity* pedagogy (Banks, 1997a), a way of teaching that is not discipline-specific but that has implications for all subject areas and for teaching in general.

The Dimensions of Multicultural Education

Teachers can examine five dimensions of the school when trying to implement multicultural education. These dimensions, identified above, are summarized in Figure 1.1. They are defined and illustrated below.

Content Integration

Content integration deals with the extent to which teachers use examples and content from a variety of cultures and groups to illustrate key concepts, principles, generalizations, and theories in their subject area or discipline. The infusion of ethnic and cultural content into the subject area should be logical and not contrived. The widespread belief that content integration constitutes the whole of multicultural education might be an important factor that causes many teachers of subjects such as mathematics and science to view multicultural education as an endeavor primarily for social studies and language arts teachers.

More opportunities exist for the integration of ethnic and cultural content in some subject areas than in others. In the social studies, the language arts, music, and family and consumer sciences, there are frequent and ample opportunities for teachers to use ethnic and cultural content to illustrate concepts, themes, and principles. There are also opportunities to integrate the math and science curriculum with ethnic and cultural content (Addison-Wesley, 1992). However, these opportunities are not as apparent or as easy to identify as they are in subject areas such as the social studies and the language arts.

In the language arts, for example, students can examine the ways in which Ebonics (Black English) is both similar to and different from mainstream U.S. English (Perry & Delpit, 1998). The students can also study how African American oratory is used to engage the audience with the speaker. They can read and listen to speeches by such African Americans as Jesse Jackson, Barbara Jordan, and

Martin Luther King, Jr., when studying Ebonics and African American oratory (Foner & Branham, 1998). The importance of oral traditions in Native American cultures can also be examined. Personal accounts by Native Americans can be studied and read aloud (Hirschfelder, 1995).

The scientific explanation of skin color differences, the biological kinship of the human species, and the frequency of certain diseases among specific human groups are also content issues that can be investigated in science. The contributions to science made by cultures such as the Aztecs, the Egyptians, and the Native Americans are other possibilities for content integration in science (Bernal, 1987, 1991; Weatherford, 1988).

The Knowledge Construction Process

The knowledge construction process consists of the methods, activities, and questions teachers use to help students to understand, investigate, and determine how implicit cultural assumptions, frames of reference, perspectives, and biases within a discipline influence the ways in which knowledge is constructed. When the knowledge construction process is implemented in the classroom, teachers help students to understand how knowledge is created and how it is influenced by the racial, ethnic, and social-class positions of individuals and groups (Code, 1991; Harding, 1991). *Positionality* is the term used to describe the ways in which race, social class, gender, and other personal and cultural characteristics of knowers influence the knowledge they construct or produce.

In the Western empirical tradition, the ideal within each academic discipline is the formulation of knowledge without the influence of the researchers' personal or cultural characteristics (Myrdal, 1969). However, as critical theorists, scholars of color, and feminist scholars have pointed out, personal, cultural, and social factors influence the formulation of knowledge even when objective knowledge is the ideal within a discipline (Banks, 1996; Code, 1991; Collins, 1998). Often the researchers themselves are unaware of how their personal experiences and positions within society influence the knowledge they produce. Most mainstream U.S. historians were unaware of how their regional and cultural biases influenced their interpretation of the Reconstruction period until W. E. B. Du Bois (1935) published a study that challenged the accepted and established interpretations of that period.

It is important for teachers as well as students to understand how knowledge is constructed within all disciplines, including mathematics and science. Social scientists, as well as physical and biological scientists on the cutting edges of their disciplines, understand the nature and limitations of their fields. However, the disciplines are often taught to students as a body of truth not to be questioned or critically analyzed. Students need to understand, even in the sciences, how cultural assumptions, perspectives, and frames of references influence the questions that researchers ask and the conclusions, generalizations, and principles they formulate.

Students can analyze the knowledge construction process in science by studying how racism has been perpetuated in science by genetic theories of intelligence,

Darwinism, and eugenics (Gould, 1981; Harding, 1998). Scientists developed theories such as polygeny and crainiometry that supported and reinforced racist assumptions and beliefs in the eighteenth and nineteenth centuries (Hannaford, 1996; Gould, 1981). Although science has supported and reinforced institutionalized racism at various times and places, it has also contributed to the eradication of racist beliefs and practices. Biological theories and data that revealed the characteristics that different racial and ethnic groups share, and anthropological theory and research about the universals in human cultures, have contributed greatly to the erosion of racist beliefs and practices (Benedict, 1940; Boas, 1940).

Knowledge Construction and the Transformative Curriculum

The curriculum in the schools must be transformed in order to help students develop the skills needed to participate in the knowledge construction process. The transformative curriculum changes the basic assumptions of the curriculum and enables students to view concepts, issues, themes, and problems from diverse ethnic and cultural perspectives (Banks, 1996).

The transformative curriculum can teach students to think by encouraging them, when they are reading or listening to resources, to consider the author's purposes for writing or speaking, his or her basic assumptions, and how the author's perspective or point of view compares with that of other authors and resources. Students can develop the skills to analyze critically historical and contemporary resources by being given several accounts of the same event or situation that present different perspectives and points of view.

Teaching about Knowledge Construction and Production

Teachers can use two important concepts in U.S. history to help students to better understand the ways in which knowledge is constructed and to participate in rethinking, reconceptualizing, and constructing knowledge. *The New World* and *The European Discovery of America* are two central ideas that are pervasive in the school and university curriculum as well as within the popular culture. The teacher can begin a unit focused on these concepts with readings, discussions, and visual presentations that describe the archaeological theories about the peopling of the Americas nearly 40,000 years ago by groups that crossed the Bering Strait while hunting for animals and plants to eat. The students can then study about the Aztecs and other highly developed civilizations that developed in the Americas prior to the arrival of the Europeans in the fifteenth century.

After the study of the Native American cultures and civilizations, the teacher can provide the students with brief accounts of some of the earliest Europeans, such as Columbus and Cortés, who came to America. The teacher can then ask the students what they think the term *The New World* means, whose point of view it reflects, and to list other and more neutral words to describe the Americas (Bigelow & Peterson, 1998). The students could then be asked to describe *The European Discovery of America* from two different perspectives: (1) from the point of view of a Taino or Arawak Indian (Rouse, 1992) (the Tainos were living in the Caribbean when Columbus arrived there in 1492); and (2) from the point of view of an objective or neutral historian who has no particular attachment to either American Indian or European society.

The major objective of this lesson is to help students to understand knowledge as a *social construction* and to understand how concepts such as *The New World* and *The European Discovery of America* are not only ethnocentric and Eurocentric terms, but are also normative concepts that serve latent but important political purposes, such as to justify the destruction of Native American peoples and civilizations by Europeans such as Columbus and those who came after him (Stannard, 1992; Todorov, 1992; Zinn & Kirschner, 1995). *The New World* is a concept that subtly denies the political existence of Native Americans and their nations prior to the coming of the Europeans.

The goal of teaching knowledge as a social construction is neither to make students cynics nor to encourage them to desecrate European heroes such as Columbus and Cortés. Rather, the aim is to help students to understand the nature of knowledge and the complexity of the development of U.S. society and to understand how the history that becomes institutionalized within a society reflects the perspectives and points of views of the victors rather than of the vanquished. When viewed within a global context, the students will be able to understand how the creation of historical knowledge in the United States parallels the creation of knowledge in other democratic societies and is a much more open and democratic process than in totalitarian nation-states.

Another important goal of teaching knowledge as a construction process is to help students to develop higher-level thinking skills and empathy for the peoples who have been victimized by the expansion and growth of the United States. When diverse and conflicting perspectives are juxtaposed, students are required to compare, contrast, weigh evidence, and make reflective decisions. They are also able to develop an empathy and an understanding of each group's perspective and point of view. The creation of their own versions of events and situations, and new concepts and terms, also requires students to reason at high levels and to think critically about data and information.

Prejudice Reduction

The prejudice reduction dimension of multicultural education describes the characteristics of students' racial attitudes and strategies that can be used to help them develop more democratic attitudes and values. Researchers have been investigating the characteristics of children's racial attitudes since the 1920s (Lasker, 1929). This research indicates that most young children enter school with negative racial attitudes that mirror those of adults (Aboud, 1988; Stephan, 1999). Research also indicates that effective curricular interventions can help students develop more positive racial and gender attitudes (Banks, 1995b). Since the intergroup education movement of the 1940s and 1950s (Trager & Yarrow, 1952), a number of investigators have designed interventions to help students develop more positive racial attitudes and values (Slavin, 1995).

The Modification of Children's Racial Attitudes.   A comprehensive review of the research (Banks, 1993) identifies four types of intervention studies that have been conducted to help children develop more democratic racial attitudes and behaviors. These types are *reinforcement* studies, *perceptual differentiation* studies, *curricular intervention* studies, and studies that use *cooperative learning* activities and contact situations. This research indicates that teachers can help students develop more positive racial attitudes by designing and implementing well-planned and well-conceptualized curricular interventions.

In a series of laboratory studies conducted by Williams and Morland (1976) and their colleagues, researchers were able to reduce white bias in both African American and White children by using reinforcement procedures. In one study (Williams & Edwards, 1969), for example, the investigators showed the children a white horse and a black horse, and a white figure and a brown figure. The researchers were able to reduce white bias in the students by giving them positive reinforcement when they chose positive—rather than negative—adjectives to describe the black horse and the brown figure. Researchers using reinforcement techniques have found that when white bias is reduced using black and white animals and boxes, the changed attitudes are generalized to human figures and photographs. *It is important to point out that these interventions reduced but did not eliminate white bias in young children.*

Katz and Zalk (1978) examined the effects of four different interventions on the racial attitudes of second- and fifth-grade children high in prejudice. They were perceptual differentiation of minority group faces, increased positive interracial contact, vicarious interracial contact, and reinforcement of the color black. The perceptual differentiation treatment was based on the hypothesis that people find it more difficult to differentiate the faces of members of out-groups than to differentiate the faces of members of their own groups. It is not uncommon to hear a member of one racial group say that he or she has trouble telling members of another group apart. Katz and Zalk hypothesized that if they could teach children to better differentiate the faces of out-groups, prejudice would be reduced. Each of the four interventions was effective in reducing prejudice. However, the *vicarious contact* and *perceptual differentiation* treatments had the most long-term effects.

A number of curriculum intervention studies that use multicultural materials have been conducted. Trager and Yarrow (1952) found that first- and second-grade children who experienced a democratic, multicultural curriculum developed more positive racial attitudes than did students who experienced a traditional, mainstream curriculum. Litcher and Johnson (1969) found that multiethnic readers helped White second-grade children develop more positive racial attitudes. However, when they replicated the study using photographs (Litcher, Johnson, & Ryan, 1973), the children's attitudes were not significantly changed. The Litcher,

Johnson, and Ryan study highlights an important trend in the prejudice-reduction literature. Although curricular materials can help students develop more positive racial attitudes, successful intervention is a complicated process that is influenced by a number of factors, including the teacher's racial attitudes and skills, the length of the intervention, the classroom atmosphere, the ethnic and racial composition of the school and classroom, and the racial atmosphere and composition of the community.

Within the last three decades a number of researchers have studied the effects of cooperative learning on the academic achievement and racial attitudes of students from different racial and ethnic groups (Aronson & Gonzalez, 1988; Cohen, 1972; 1986; Slavin, 1979; 1995). This research has been heavily influenced by the theory developed by Allport (1954). Allport hypothesized that prejudice would be reduced if interracial contact situations have the following characteristics:

1. They are cooperative rather than competitive.
2. The individuals experience equal status.
3. The individuals have shared goals.
4. The contact is sanctioned by authorities such as parents, the principal, and the teacher.

The research on cooperative learning activities indicates that African American, Mexican American, and White students develop more positive racial attitudes and choose more friends from outside racial groups when they participate in group activities that have the conditions identified by Allport. Cooperative learning activities also have a positive effect on the academic achievement of students of color (Slavin, 1995).

Equity Pedagogy

An equity pedagogy exists when teachers modify their teaching in ways that will facilitate the academic achievement of students from diverse racial, cultural, ethnic, and gender groups (Banks, 1995a). Research indicates that teachers can increase the classroom participation and academic achievement of students from different ethnic and cultural groups by modifying their instruction so that it draws on their cultural and language strengths. In a study by Philips (1993) American Indian students participated more actively in class discussions when teachers used group-oriented participation structures that were consistent with their community cultures. Au (1980) and Tharp (1989), working in the Kamehameha Early Education Program (KEEP), found that both student participation and standardized achievement test scores increased when they incorporated teaching strategies consistent with the cultures of Native Hawaiian students and used the children's experiences in reading instruction.

Studies summarized by Darling-Hammond (1995) indicate that the academic achievement of students of color and low-income students increases when they have high quality teachers who are experts in their content specialization, pedagogy, and child development. She reports a significant study by Dreeben and Gamoran (1986). They found that when African American students received high quality instruction their reading achievement was as high as that of White students. The quality of instruction, not the race of the students, was the significant variable.

Research and theories developed by Ladson-Billings (1994), Delpit (1995), and Heath (1983) indicate that teachers can improve the school success of students if they are knowledgeable about the cultures, values, language, and learning characteristics of their students. Research indicates that cooperative—rather than competitive—teaching strategies help African American and Mexican American students to increase their academic achievement as well as help all students, including White mainstream students, to develop more positive racial attitudes and values (Aronson & Gonzalez, 1988).

An Empowering School Culture and Social Structure

This dimension of multicultural education involves restructuring the culture and organization of the school so that students from diverse racial, ethnic, and gender groups will experience equality. This variable must be examined and addressed by the entire school staff, including the principal and support staff. It involves an examination of the latent and manifest culture and organization of the school to determine the extent to which it fosters or hinders educational equity.

The four dimensions of multicultural education discussed above, *content integration, the knowledge construction process, prejudice reduction*, and an *equity pedagogy,* each deal with an aspect of a cultural or social system—the school. However, the school can also be conceptualized as one social system, which is larger than its interrelated parts, such as its formal and informal curriculum, teaching materials, counseling program, and teaching strategies. When conceptualized as a *social system*, the school is viewed as an institution that "includes a social structure of interrelated statuses and roles and the functioning of that structure in terms of patterns of actions and interactions" (Theodorson & Theodorson, 1969, p. 395). The school can also be conceptualized as a cultural system with a specific set of values, norms, ethos, and shared meanings.

Among the variables that need to be examined in order to create a school culture that empowers students from diverse cultural groups are grouping practices (Wheelock, 1992), labeling practices, sports participation, and whether there are ethnic turfs that exists in the cafeteria or in other parts of the school (Tatum, 1997). The behavior of the school staff must also be examined in order to determine the subtle messages it gives the students about racial, ethnic, cultural, and social-class diversity. Testing practices, grouping practices, tracking, and gifted programs often contribute to ethnic and racial inequality within the school (Sapon-Shevin, 1994).

A number of school reformers have used a systems approach to reform the school in order to increase the academic achievement of low-income students and students of color. There are a number of advantages to approaching school reform from a holistic perspective. To implement any reform in a school effectively, such as effective prejudice reduction teaching, changes are required in a number of other school variables. Teachers, for example, need more knowledge and need to examine their racial and ethnic attitudes; consequently, they need more time as well as a variety of instructional materials. Many school reform efforts fail because the roles, norms, and ethos of the school do not change in ways that will make the institutionalization of the reforms possible.

The *effective* school reformers is one group of change agents that has approached school reform from a systems perspective. Brookover and Erickson (1975) developed a social-psychological theory of learning, which states that students internalize the conceptions of themselves that are institutionalized within the ethos and structures of the school. Related to Merton's (1968) self-fulfilling prophecy, this theory states that student academic achievement will increase if the adults within the school have high expectations for students, clearly identify the skills they wish them to learn, and teach those skills to them.

Research by Brookover and his colleagues (Brookover et al., 1979; Brookover & Lezotte, 1979) indicates that schools populated by low-income students within the same school district vary greatly in student achievement levels. Consequently, Brookover attributes the differences to variations in the school's social structure. He calls the schools in low-income areas that have high academic achievement *improving* schools. Other researchers, such as Edmonds (1986) and Lezotte (1993), call them *effective* schools (Levine & Lezotte, 1995).

Comer and his colleagues (Comer, Haynes, Joyner, & Ben-Avie, 1996) have developed a structural intervention model that involves changes in the social-psychological climate of the school. The teachers, principal, and other school professionals make collaborative decisions about the school. The parents also participate in the decision-making process. The data collected by Comer and his colleagues indicate that this approach has been successful in increasing the academic achievement of low-income, inner-city African American students.

Summary

This chapter describes the goals of multicultural education and its five dimensions. The dimensions are designed to help practicing educators to understand the different aspects of multicultural education and to enable them to implement it comprehensively. The dimensions help educators understand, for example, that content integration is only one important part of comprehensive multicultural education.

The dimensions discussed in this chapter are (1) *content integration,* (2) *the knowledge construction process,* (3) *prejudice reduction,* (4) *an equity pedagogy,* and (5) *an empowering school culture and social structure.* Content integration deals with the extent to which teachers use examples and content from a variety of cultures and groups to illustrate key concepts, principles, generalizations, and theories in their subject area or discipline. The knowledge construction process relates to the extent to which teachers help students to understand, investigate, and determine how the implicit cultural assumptions, frames of references, perspectives, and biases within a discipline influence the ways in which knowledge is constructed within it.

In the prejudice reduction dimension, teachers help students develop more positive attitudes toward different racial and ethnic groups. Research indicates that most young children come to school with negative racial attitudes that mirror those of adults. It also indicates that the school can help students develop more positive intergroup attitudes and beliefs. An equity pedagogy exists when teachers modify their teaching in ways that will facilitate the academic achievement of students from diverse racial, cultural, gender, and social-class groups. This includes using a variety of teaching styles and approaches that are consistent with the wide range of learning styles within various cultural and ethnic groups.

Another important dimension of multicultural education is a school culture and social structure that promotes gender, racial, and social-class equality. To implement this dimension, the culture and organization of the school must be restructured in a collaborative process that involves all members of the school staff.

REFERENCES

Aboud, F. (1988). *Children and Prejudice.* New York: Basil Blackwell.

Addison-Wesley Publishing Company. (1992). *Multiculturalism in Mathematics, Science, and Technology: Readings and Activities.* Menlo Park, CA: Author.

Allport, G. W. (1954). *The Nature of Prejudice.* Cambridge, MA: Addison-Wesley.

Aronson, E., & Gonzalez, A. (1988). Desegregation, Jigsaw, and the Mexican-American Experience. In P. A. Katz & D. A. Taylor (Eds.), *Eliminating Racism: Profiles in Controversy* (pp. 301–314). New York: Plenum Press.

Au, K. (1980). Participation Structures in a Reading Lesson with Hawaiian Children. *Anthropology and Education Quarterly, 11*(2), 91–115.

Baker, G. (1994). *Planning and Organizing for Multicultural Instruction* (2nd ed). Menlo Park, CA: Addison-Wesley.

Banks, J. A. (1993). Multicultural Education for Young Children: Racial and Ethnic Attitudes and Their Modification. In B. Spodek (Ed.), *Handbook of Research on the Education of Young Children* (pp. 236–250). New York: Macmillan.

Banks, J. A. (1995a). Multicultural Education: Historical Development, Dimensions, and Practice. In J. A. Banks & C. A. M. Banks (Eds.), *Handbook of Research on Multicultural Education* (pp. 3–24). New York: Macmillan.

Banks, J. A. (1995b). Multicultural Education: Its Effects on Students' Ethnic and Gender Role Attitudes. In J. A. Banks & C. A. M. Banks (Eds.), *Handbook of Research on Multicultural Education* (pp. 617–627). New York: Macmillan.

Banks, J. A. (1996). *Multicultural Education, Transformative Knowledge and Action: Historical and Contemporary Perspectives.* New York: Teachers College Press.

Banks, J. A. (1997a). *Educating Citizens in a Multicultural Society.* New York: Teachers College Press.

Banks, J. A. (1997b). Multicultural Education: Characteristics and Goals. In J. A. Banks & C. A. M. Banks (Eds.), *Multicultural Education: Issues and Perspectives* (3rd ed.) (pp. 3–31). Boston: Allyn and Bacon.

Banks, J. A. (1997c). *Teaching Strategies for Ethnic Studies* (6th ed.). Boston: Allyn and Bacon.

Banks, J. A., & Banks, C. A. M. (Eds.). (1995). *Handbook of Research on Multicultural Education.* New York: Macmillan.

Benedict. R. (1940). *Race, Science and Politics.* New York: Modern Age Publishers.

Bernal, M. (1987, 1991). *Black Athena: The Afro-Asiatic Roots of Classical Civilization*, Vols. 1–2. New Brunswick, NJ: Rutgers University Press.

Bigelow, B., & Peterson, B. (Eds.). (1998). *Rethinking Columbus: The Next 500 Years.* Milwaukee: Rethinking Schools.

Boas, F. (1940). *Race, Language, and Culture.* New York: Macmillan.

Brookover, W. B., Beady, C., Flood, P., Schweitzer, J., & Wisenbaker, J. (1979). *School Social Systems and Student Achievement: Schools Can Make a Difference.* New York: Praeger.

Brookover, W. B., & Erickson, E. (1975). *Sociology of Education.* Homewood, IL: Dorsey.

Brookover, W. B., & Lezotte, L. W. (1979). *Changes in School Characteristics Coincident with Changes in Student Achievement.* East Lansing: Institute for Research on Teaching, College of Education, Michigan State University.

Code, L. (1991). *What Can She Know? Feminist Theory and the Construction of Knowledge.* Ithaca, NY: Cornell University Press.

Cohen, E. G. (1972). Interracial Interaction Disability. *Human Relations, 25,* 9–24.

Cohen, F. G. (1986). *Designing Groupwork: Strategies for the Heterogeneous Classroom.* New York: Teachers College Press.

Collins, P. H. (1998). *Fighting Words: Black Women and the Search for Justice.* Minneapolis: University of Minnesota Press.

Comer, J. P., Haynes, N. M., Joyner, E. T., & Ben-Avie, M. (Eds.). (1996). *Rallying the Whole Village: The Comer Process for Reforming Education.* New York: Teachers College Press.

Cyrus, V. (Ed.). (1997). *Experiencing Race, Class, and Gender in the United States.* Mountain View, CA: Mayfield.

Darling-Hammond, L. (1995). Inequality and Access to Knowledge. In J. A. Banks & C. A. M. Banks (Eds.), *Handbook of Research on Multicultural Education* (pp. 465–483). New York: Macmillan.

Delpit, L. (1995). *Other People's Children: Cultural Conflict in the Classroom.* New York: The New Press.

Derman-Sparks, L., & Phillips, C. B. (1997). *Teaching/Learning Anti-Racism.* New York: Teachers College Press.

Dreeben, R., & Gamoran, A. (1986). Race, Instruction, and Learning. *American Sociological Review, 51* (5), 660–669.

Du Bois, W. E. B. (1935). *Black Reconstruction.* New York: Harcourt, Brace.

Edmonds, R. (1986). Characteristics of Effective Schools. In U. Neisser (Ed.), *The School Achievement of Minority Children* (pp. 93–104). Hillsdale, NJ: Lawrence Erlbaum.

Foner, P. S., & Branham, R. J. (Eds.). (1998). *Lift Every Voice: African American Oratory 1787–1900.* Tuscaloosa: The University of Alabama Press.

Fullinwider, R. K. (Ed.). (1996). *Public Education in a Multicultural Society: Policy, Theory, Critique.* New York: Cambridge University Press.

Garcia, R. L. (1998). *Teaching for Diversity.* Bloomington, IN: Phi Delta Kappa Educational Foundation.

Gay, G. (1994). *At the Essence of Learning: Multicultural Education.* West Lafayette, IN: Kappa Delta Pi.

Gay, G. (1995). Curriculum Theory and Multicultural Education. In J. A. Banks & C. A. M. Banks (Eds.), *Handbook of Research on Multicultural Education* (pp. 25–43). New York: Macmillan.

Gould, S. J. (1981). *The Mismeasure of Man.* New York: Norton.

Graff, G. (1992). *Beyond the Culture Wars: How Teaching the Conflicts Can Revitalize American Education.* New York: Norton.

Hannaford, I. (1996). *Race: The History of an Idea in the West.* Baltimore: The John Hopkins University Press.

Harding, S. (1991). *Whose Science? Whose Knowledge? Thinking from Women's Lives.* Ithaca, NY: Cornell University Press.

Harding, S. (1998). *Is Science Multicultural? Postcolonialisms, Feminisms, and Epistemologies.* Bloomington: Indiana University Press.

Heath, S. B. (1983). *Ways with Words: Language, Life, and Work in Communities and Classrooms.* New York: Cambridge University Press.

Hirschfelder, A. (Ed.). (1995). *Native Heritage: Personal Accounts by American Indians 1790 to the Present.* New York: Macmillan.

Hughes, R. (1993). *Culture of Complaint: The Fraying of America.* New York: Oxford University Press.

Katz, P. A., & Zalk, S. R. (1978). Modification of Children's Racial Attitudes. *Developmental Psychology, 14,* 447–461.

Kuhn, T. S. (1970). *The Structure of Scientific Revolutions* (2nd ed., enlarged). Chicago: The University of Chicago Press.

Ladson-Billings, G. (1994). *The Dreamkeepers: Successful Teachers of African American Children.* New York: Jossey-Bass.

Lasker, B. (1929). *Race Attitudes in Children.* New York: Holt, Rinehart & Winston.

Levine, D. U., & Lezotte, L. W. (1995). Effective Schools Research. In J. A. Banks & C. A. M. Banks (Eds.), *Handbook of Research on Multicultural Education* (pp. 525–547). New York: Macmillan.

Lezotte, L. W. (1993). Effective Schools: A Framework for Increasing Student Achievement. In J. A. Banks & C. A. M. Banks (Eds.), *Multicultural Education: Issues and Perspectives* (2nd ed.) (pp. 303–316). Boston: Allyn and Bacon.

Litcher, J. H., & Johnson, D. W. (1969). Changes in Attitudes toward Negroes of White Elementary School Students after Use of Multiethnic Readers. *Journal of Educational Psychology, 60,* 148–152.

Litcher, J. H., Johnson, D. W., & Ryan, E. L. (1973). Use of Pictures of Multiethnic Interaction to Change Attitudes of White Elementary School Students toward Blacks. *Psychological Reports, 33,* 367–372.

May, S. (Ed.). (1999). *Critical Multiculturalism: Rethinking Multicultural and Antiracist Education.* Philadelphia: Falmer Press.

Merton, R. K. (1968). *Social Theory and Social Structure.* (1968 enlarged ed.) New York: The Free Press.

Myrdal, G. (1969). *Objectivity in Social Research.* Middletown, CT: Wesleyan University Press.

Nieto, S. (1999). *The Light in Their Eyes: Creating Multicultural Learning Communities.* New York: Teachers College Press.

Perry, T., & Delpit, L. (Eds.). (1998). *The Real Ebonics Debate: Power, Language, and the Education of African-American Children.* Boston: Beacon Press.

Philips, S. U. (1993). *The Invisible Culture: Communication in Classroom and Community on the Warm Springs Indian Reservation.* Prospects Heights, IL: Waveland Press. (originally published 1983)

Powell, A. B., & Frankenstein, M. (Eds.). (1997). *Ethnomathematics: Challenging Eurocentrism in Mathematics Education.* Albany: State University of New York Press.

Rouse, I. (1992). *The Tainos: Rise and Decline of the People Who Greeted Columbus.* New Haven: Yale University Press.

Sadker, M. P., & Sadker, D. M. (1994). *Failing at Fairness: How America's Schools Cheat Girls.* New York: Scribner's.

Sapon-Shevin, M. (1994). *Playing Favorites: Gifted Education and the Disruption of Community.* Albany: State University of New York Press.

Secada, W. G., Fennema, E., & Adajian, L. B. (Eds.). (1995). *New Directions for Equity in Mathematics Education.* New York: Cambridge University Press.

Slavin, R. E. (1979). Effects of Biracial Learning Teams on Cross-Racial Friendships. *Journal of Educational Psychology, 71,* 381–387.

Slavin, R. E. (1995). Cooperative Learning and Intergroup Relations. In J. A. Banks & C. A. M. Banks (Eds.), *Handbook of Research on Multicultural Education* (pp. 628–634). New York: Macmillan.

Sleeter, C. E. (1995). An Analysis of the Critiques of Multicultural Education. In J. A. Banks & C. A. M. Banks (Eds.), *Handbook of Research on Multicultural Education* (pp. 81–94). New York: Macmillan.

Stannard, D. E. (1992). *American Holocaust: Columbus and the Conquest of the New World.* New York: Oxford University Press.

Stephan, W. (1999). *Reducing Prejudice and Stereotyping in Schools.* New York: Teachers College Press.

Tatum, B. D. (1997). *"Why Are All the Black Kids Sitting Together in the Cafeteria?" And Other Conversations about Race.* New York: Basic Books.

Taylor, C., et al. (1994). *Multiculturalism: Examining the Politics of Recognition.* Princeton, NJ: Princeton University Press.

Tharp, R. G. (1989). Culturally Compatible Education: A Formula for Designing Effective Classrooms. In H. T. Trueba, G. Spindler, & L. Spindler (Eds.), *What Do Anthroplogists Have to Say about Dropouts?* (pp. 51–66). New York: Falmer Press.

Theodorson, G. A., & Theodorson, A. G. (1969). *A Modern Dictionary of Sociology.* New York: Barnes & Noble.

Todorov, T. (1992). *The Conquest of America: The Question of the Other.* New York: Harper.

Trager, H. G., & Yarrow, M. R. (1952). *They Learn What They Live: Prejudice in Young Children.* New York: Harper & Brothers.

Weatherford, J. (1988). *Indian Givers: How the Indians of the Americas Transformed the World.* New York: Fawcett Columbine.

Wheelock, A. (1992). *Crossing the Tracks: How "Untracking" Can Save America's Schools.* New York: The New Press.

Williams, J. E., & Edwards, C. D. (1969). An Exploratory Study of the Modification of Color and Racial Concept Attitudes in Preschool Children. *Child Development, 40,* 737–750.

Williams, J. E., & Morland, J. K. (1976). *Race, Color, and the Young Child.* Chapel Hill: The University of North Carolina Press.

Zinn, H., & Kirshner, G. (1995). *A People's History of the United States: The Wall Charts.* New York: The New Press.

2 Multicultural Education: History and Revitalization Movements

The Rise of Nativism

Most of the European immigrants who came to North America before 1890 were from nations in Northern and Western Europe, such as the United Kingdom, Germany, Sweden, and Switzerland. Although conflicts developed between these various immigrant groups, the English dominated the social, economic, and political life in North America by the 1700s. As the twentieth century approached and new waves of immigrants began to arrive in the United States from Southern, Central, and Eastern Europe, the immigrants from Northern and Western Europe began to perceive themselves as the old immigrants and rightful inhabitants of the nation. They saw the new immigrants as a threat to U.S. civilization and to its democratic tradition. Sharp and often inaccurate distinctions were made between the new and old immigrants.

A movement called *nativism* arose to stop the flood of the new immigrants from arriving in the United States (Bennett, 1988). The nativists pointed out that the new immigrants were primarily Catholics, whereas the old immigrants were mainly Protestants. A strong element of anti-Catholicism became an integral part of the nativistic movement.

Because of their Catholicism, cultural differences, and competition for jobs with the old immigrants and native-born Americans, the new immigrants became the victims of blatant nativism. Suspicion and distrust of all foreigners became widespread near the turn of the century. The outbreak of the Great War in Europe in 1914 greatly increased the suspicion and distrust of immigrant groups in the United States and further stimulated nativistic feelings and groups. Nativism swept through the United States during World War I. Nativists argued for 100 percent Americanism and said that America should be for "Americans." The new immigrant groups tried desperately but unsuccessfully to prove their national loyalty.

Nativism and Education

The public schools, colleges, and universities usually perpetuate the dominant ideologies and values that are promoted and embraced by the powerful groups within society (Apple, 1996). Reflecting the prevailing goals of the nation as articulated by its powerful political and economic leaders, the schools and colleges promoted and embraced Americanization and blind loyalty to the nation and also showed a distrust of foreigners and immigrant groups during the turn of the century and World War I periods.

The teaching of German and other foreign languages was prohibited in many schools. German books in school libraries were sometimes burned. Some schools prohibited the playing of music by German composers in music classes and in school assemblies (Jones, 1992). In this atmosphere of virulent nativism, government-sponsored propaganda, and emphasis on blind patriotism and Americanization, the idea of cultural pluralism in education would have been alien and perhaps viewed as seditious and un-American.

The Melting Pot

The assimilationist ideology, pervasive near the turn of the century and during World War I, was embodied and expressed in the play *The Melting Pot.* This play, written by the English Jewish author Israel Zangwill, opened in New York City in 1908. It became a tremendous success. The great ambition of the play's composer-protagonist, David Quixano, was to create an American symphony that would personify his deep conviction that his adopted land was a nation in which all ethnic differences would mix and from which a new person, superior to all, would emerge.

What in fact happened, however, was that most of the immigrant and ethnic cultures stuck to the bottom of the mythical melting pot. Anglo-Saxon culture remained dominant; other ethnic groups had to give up many of their cultural characteristics in order to participate fully in the nation's social, economic, and political institutions (Jones, 1992).

However, cultural influence was not in one direction only. Although the Anglo-Saxon Protestant culture became and remained dominant in the United States, other ethnic groups, such as the Germans, the Irish, Indians, and African Americans, influenced the Anglo-Saxon culture just as the Anglo-Saxon culture influenced the culture of these groups. However, the Anglo-Saxon Protestant culture has had the most cogent influence on U.S. culture (Stewart & Bennett, 1991). This influence has been in many cases positive. The American ideals of human rights, participatory democracy, and separation of church and state are largely Anglo-Saxon contributions to U.S. civilization (Adler & Van Doren, 1977).

The American school, like other American institutions, embraced Anglo-conformity goals. Two major goals were to rid ethnic groups of their ethnic traits and to force them to acquire Anglo-Saxon values and behavior. In 1909 Ellwood Patterson Cubberley (1909), the famed educational leader, clearly stated a major goal of the common schools:

> Everywhere these people [immigrants] tend to settle in groups or settlements, and to set up here their national manners, customs, and observances. Our task is to break

up these groups or settlements, to assimilate and amalgamate these people as part of our American race, and to implant in their children, as far as can be done, the Anglo-Saxon conception of righteousness, law and order, and popular government, and to awaken in them a reverence for our democratic institutions and for those things in our national life which we as a people hold to be of abiding *worth.* (pp. 15–16)

The Call for Cultural Pluralism

In the early years of the twentieth century, a few philosophers and writers, such as Horace Kallen (1924), Randolph Bourne (1916), and Julius Drachsler (1920), strongly defended the rights of the immigrants living in the United States. They rejected the assimilationist argument made by leaders such as Cubberley. They argued that a political democracy must also be a cultural democracy, and that the thousands of Southern, Eastern, and Central European immigrant groups had a right to maintain their ethnic cultures and institutions in U.S. society. They used a "salad bowl" argument, maintaining that each ethnic culture would play a unique role in U.S. society but would also contribute to the total society. They argued that ethnic cultures would enrich U.S. civilization. They called their position *cultural pluralism* and said it should be used to guide public and educational policies.

The arguments of the cultural pluralists were a cry in the wilderness. They fell largely on deaf ears. Most of the nation's political, business, and educational leaders continued to push for the assimilation of the immigrant and indigenous racial and ethnic groups. They felt that only in this way could a unified nation be made out of so many different ethnic groups with histories of wars and hostilities in Europe. The triumph of the assimilationist forces in U.S. life was symbolized by the Immigration Acts of 1917 and 1924.

The Immigration Act of 1917, designed to halt the immigration of Southern, Central, and Eastern European groups, such as Poles, Greeks, and Italians, required immigrants to pass a reading test in order to enter the United States. When this act passed but failed to reduce the number of immigrants from these nations enough to please the nativists, they pushed for and succeeded in getting another act passed, the Immigration Act of 1924. This second act drastically limited the number of immigrants that could enter the United States from all European nations except those in Northern and Western Europe. It ended the era of massive European immigration to the United States and closed a significant chapter in U.S. history.

Ethnic Education between the Two World Wars

Mainstream U.S. leaders and educators generally ignored the voices advocating pluralistic policies in the early years of the twentieth century. However, because of the tremendous ethnic and cultural diversity within the United States, rarely is there consensus within our society on any important social or educational issue. Consequently, while individuals who dominated educational policy usually embraced the assimilationist ideology and devoted little time and energy to the education of the nation's ethnic minority groups, other U.S. leaders, researchers, and educators engaged in important discussions about the education of the nation's ethnic minorities, formulated educational policy related to ethnic groups, and did important research on American ethnic communities (Weinberg, 1977). Ironically, however, often the policy formulated by those deeply concerned about the education of ethnic minorities was assimilationist oriented. This orientation indicated the extent to which the assimilationist ideology had permeated U.S. life and thought. However, there were always a few educational leaders who advocated pluralism.

Policies and programs in ethnic education did not suddenly arise during the ethnic revitalization movements of the 1960s and 1970s. These developments evolved gradually over a long period. It is true, however, that they became more intense during various historical periods, usually because of heightened racial consciousness and concern stimulated by events such as racial conflicts and tensions. The evolutionary character of multicultural education in the United States can be illustrated by a brief discussion of the educational policies related to Native Americans, African Americans, and Mexican Americans between the two great world wars. The education of other ethnic groups, such as Jewish Americans, Italian Americans, and Puerto Rican Americans, could also be used to illustrate the evolutionary nature of multicultural education (Fass, 1989). However, the choice of these first three ethnic groups can in part be justified by the fact that educational policy and programs related to them stimulated enduring and controversial discussions that still continue.

Native American Education

How Native Americans should be educated has evoked a continuing debate since the late 1800s (Adams, 1995; Lomawaima, 1994; Szasz, 1974; 1988). Since the 1920s, educational policy for Native Americans has vacillated from strong assimilationism to self-determination and cultural pluralism. The landmark Meriam Report, issued in 1928, recommended massive reforms in Native American education (Meriam, 1928). The Report recommended that Indian education be tied more closely to the community, to the building of day schools in the community, and to the reform of boarding schools. It also recommended that the curriculum in Indian schools be changed to reflect Indian cultures and the needs of local Indian communities (Szasz, 1974). The 1969 U.S. Senate Report on Indian Education (1969), called the Kennedy Report, stated that many of the reforms recommended by the Meriam Report had not been attained.

African American Education

Developments in the education of African Americans were both active and controversial in the decades between the war years. Carter G. Woodson, an African American historian who received a doctorate from Harvard in 1912, did seminal research and work on Black history and Black education (Roche, 1996). Woodson founded, with others, the Association for the Study of Negro Life and History in

1915 (now the Association for the Study of Afro-American Life and History, Inc.). This organization was founded to sponsor and encourage research in African American history and to disseminate this research to scholars and teachers in predominantly African American schools and colleges. The Association started two important publications—*The Journal of Negro History* and *The Negro History Bulletin*. Woodson began Negro History Week in 1926 to commemorate milestones in African American history. In 1976, this annual commemoration was changed to National Afro-American History Month, which is observed during February.

African American educational policy became very controversial within the Black community. Booker T. Washington and W. E. B. Du Bois set forth sharply contrasting views about directions for African American education. Washington, a former slave and the most influential African American leader of his time, believed that African American students needed a practical, industrial education (Harlan, 1972; Washington, 1901). He implemented his ideas at Tuskegee Institute in Tuskegee, Alabama. Du Bois, the noted African American scholar and educational philosopher, received his Ph.D. from Harvard in 1895. He believed that a "talented tenth" should be educated for leadership in the African American community. The talented tenth, he argued, should study the classics, political philosophy, and other academic subjects (Du Bois, 1961).

Mexican American Education

During the 1930s and 1940s, considerable attention was focused on the education of Mexican Americans by scholars and educators concerned with their educational plight. Most educators during this period viewed the school as an agency for the acculturation of Mexican American students (Moreno, 1999). Carter and Segura (1979) described Mexican American education during the 1930s:

> School programs for Chicano children during the 1930s emphasized vocational training and manual-arts training; learning of English; health and hygiene; and adoption of American core values such as cleanliness, thrift and punctuality. Segregation, especially in the early grades, was regularly recommended and commonly established. It was inexplicably argued that Americanization could best be accomplished by keeping foreigners out of contact with Americans. (p. 17)

The voices speaking for the education of Mexican Americans during the 1930s and 1940s, however, were not unanimous. George I. Sanchez (Murillo, 1996), a pioneer Mexican American educator and scholar, urged educators to consider the unique cultural and linguistic characteristics of Mexican American students when planning and implementing educational programs for them.

The Intergroup-Education Movement

Social, political, and economic changes caused by World War II stimulated a curriculum movement related to cultural and ethnic diversity that became known as *intergroup education* (C. A. M. Banks, 1996). World War II created many job opportunities in northern cities. Many African Americans and Whites left the South during the war years in search of jobs. More than 150,000 African Americans left the South each year in the decade between 1940 and 1950 and settled in northern cities (Lemann, 1991). In such northern cities as Chicago and Detroit conflict developed between African Americans and Whites as they competed for jobs and housing. Racial conflict also occurred in the Far West. Mexican Americans and Anglos clashed in "zoot-suit" riots in Los Angeles during the summer of 1943. These racial conflicts and tensions severely strained race relations in the nation.

Racial tension and conflict were pervasive in northern cities during the war years. In 1943, race riots took place in Los Angeles, Detroit, and in the Harlem district of New York City. The most destructive riot during the war broke out in Detroit on a Sunday morning in June 1943. More southern migrants had settled in Detroit during this period than in any other city in the United States. The Detroit riot raged for more than thirty hours. When it finally ended, thirty-four persons were dead and property worth millions of dollars had been destroyed. The Detroit riot stunned the nation and stimulated national action by concerned African American and White citizens.

A major goal of intergroup education was to reduce racial and ethnic prejudice and misunderstandings (Taba, Brady, & Robinson, 1952). Activities designed to reduce prejudice and to increase interracial understanding included the teaching of isolated instructional units on various ethnic groups, exhortations against prejudice, organizing assemblies and cultural get-togethers, disseminating information on racial, ethnic, and religious backgrounds, and banning books considered stereotypic and demeaning to ethnic groups. A major assumption of the intergroup-education movement was that factual knowledge would develop respect and acceptance of various ethnic and racial groups (Taba & Wilson, 1946). Unlike the ethnic studies movement of the late 1960s, however, the emphasis in the intergroup education movement of the 1940s and 1950s was neither on strong cultural pluralism nor on maintaining or perpetuating strong ethnic loyalties.

Two important national projects were implemented to actualize the goals of intergroup education. The Intergroup Education in Cooperating Schools project, directed by Hilda Taba, was designed to effect changes in elementary and secondary schools (Taba, Brady, & Robinson, 1952). The other project, the College Study in Intergroup Relations, was sponsored by the American Council on Education and directed by Lloyd Allen Cook (1950). The College Study project was the first cooperative effort in the United States to improve the intercultural component of teacher education. Twenty-four colleges with teacher education programs participated in this project from 1945 to 1949.

The Intergroup-Education Movement Ends

The intergroup education movement and its related reforms failed to become institutionalized within most U.S. schools, colleges, and teacher-training institutions. This statement should not be interpreted to mean that the movement did not benefit our society and educational institutions. Cook (1947) has noted the tremendous influence the College Study projects had on the individuals who participated in them. The action and research projects undertaken in the College Study contributed to our practical and theoretical knowledge about race relations and about intervention efforts designed to influence attitudes and behavior. The basic idea of the College Study was a sound one that merits replication: teacher training institutions formed a consortium to develop action and research projects to effect change.

It is also true that many individual teachers and professors, and probably many individual school and teacher training institutions, continued some elements of the reforms related to intergroup education after the national movement faded. By the 1960s, however, when racial tension intensified in the nation and race riots again sprang up, few U.S. schools and teacher education institutions had programs and curricula that dealt adequately with the study of racial and ethnic relations. However, most predominantly African American schools and colleges were teaching Black studies and were responding in other ways to many of the unique cultural characteristics of African American students.

As we consider ways to institutionalize reforms related to multicultural education, it is instructive to consider why the reforms related to intergroup education failed to become institutionalized in most U.S. schools and colleges. The reforms related to the movement failed to become institutionalized, in part, for the following six reasons:

1. Most mainstream U.S. educators never internalized the ideology and major assumptions on which intergroup education was based.

2. Most mainstream U.S. society never understood how the intergroup education movement contributed to the major goals of the U.S. common schools.

3. Most U.S. educators saw intergroup education as a reform project for schools that had open racial conflict and tension and not for what they considered their smoothly functioning and nonproblematic schools.

4. Racial tension in the cities took more subtle forms in the 1950s. Consequently, most U.S. educators no longer saw the need for action designed to reduce racial conflict and problems.

5. Intergroup education remained on the periphery of mainstream educational thought and developments and was financed primarily by special funds. Consequently, when the special funds and projects ended, the movement largely faded.

6. The leaders of the intergroup education movement never developed a well-articulated and coherent philosophical position that revealed how the intergroup education movement was consistent with the major goals of the U.S. common schools and with American creed values such as equality, justice, and human rights.

Assimilation Continues and Helps to Shape a Nation

Despite the intergroup education reforms of the 1940s and 1950s, assimilationist forces and policies dominated U.S. life from about the turn of the century to the beginning of the 1960s. The assimilationist ideology was not seriously challenged during this long period, even though there were a few individuals, such as Marcus Garvey in the 1920s, who championed separatism and ethnic pluralism (Clarke, 1974). These lone voices were ignored or silenced.

Most minority as well as dominant group leaders saw the assimilation of U.S. ethnic groups as the proper societal goal. Social scientists and reformers during this period were heavily influenced by the writings of Robert E. Park, the eminent U.S. sociologist who had once worked as an informal secretary for Booker T. Washington (Shils, 1991). Park believed that race relations proceeded through four inevitable stages: *contact, conflict, accommodation,* and *assimilation* (Park & Burgess, 1924). The most reform-oriented social scientists and social activists embraced assimilation as both desirable and inevitable within a democratic pluralistic nation such as the United States.

The assimilationist policy shaped a nation from millions of immigrants and from diverse Native American groups. The United States did not become an ethnically Balkanized nation; this could have happened. The assimilationist idea also worked reasonably well for ethnic peoples who were White. However, it did force many of them to become marginal individuals and to deny family and heritage (Brodkin, 1999; Dershowitz, 1997; Jacobson, 1998). This situation should not be taken lightly, for denying one's basic group identity is a very painful and psychologically unsettling process. However, most, but not all, White ethnic groups in the United States have been able, in time, to climb up the economic and social ladders (Alba, 1990; Waters, 1990).

The New Pluralism

The assimilationist idea has not worked nearly as well for people of color. This is what African Americans realized by the early 1960s. The unfulfilled promises and dreams of the assimilationist idea were major causes of the Black civil rights movement of the 1960s. By the late 1950s and early 1960s, discrimination in such areas as employment, housing, and education, combined with rising expectations, caused African Americans to lead an unprecedented fight for their rights, which became known as the Black civil rights movement.

Many African Americans who had become highly assimilated were still unable to participate fully in many mainstream U.S. institutions. African Americans were still denied many opportunities because of their skin color (Edwards & Polite, 1992; Landry, 1987). They searched for a new ideal. Many endorsed some form of cultural pluralism. An idea born during the turn of the century was refashioned to fit the hopes, aspirations, and dreams of disillusioned and alienated people of color in the 1960s.

African Americans demanded more control over the institutions in their communities and also demanded that all institutions, including the schools, more accurately reflect their ethnic cultures. They demanded more African American teachers and administrators for their youths, textbooks that reflected African American history and culture, and that schools become more sensitive to African American culture (Harding, 1990).

Educational institutions, at all levels, began to respond to the Black civil rights movement. The apparent success of the Black civil rights movement caused other ethnic groups of color on the margins of society, such as Mexican Americans, Asian Americans, and Puerto Ricans, to make similar demands for political, economic, and educational changes.

Mexican American studies (Gutierrez, 1995) and Asian American (Aguilar-San Juan, 1994) studies courses that paralleled Black studies courses emerged. The reform movements initiated by the groups of color caused many White ethnic groups that had denied their ethnic cultures to proclaim ethnic pride and to push for the insertion of more content about White ethnic groups into the curriculum (Novak, 1971). This movement became known as the *new pluralism.* In a sense, the African American civil rights movement legitimized ethnicity, and other ethnic groups that felt victimized began to search for their ethnic roots and to demand more group and human rights. The civil rights movement initiated by African Americans stimulated groups such as women, people with disabilities, and gay rights advocates to push strongly for their rights and entitlements.

The New Immigrants

Since the Immigration Reform Act of 1965 became effective in 1968, the United States has experienced its largest wave of immigrants since the beginning of the twentieth century. Nearly 80 percent (78.6 percent) more immigrants entered the United States in the decade between 1971 and 1980 than had entered in the years between 1951 and 1960. Immigration to the United States continued at a rapid pace between 1981 and 1988. Nearly 5 million (4,710,700) immigrants settled in the United States during this period (U.S. Bureau of the Census, 1991). During the 1990s more than 1 million immigrants settled in the United States each year (Martin & Midgley, 1999). More than 8 million made the U.S. their home during this decade.

Not only has the number of immigrants entering the United States increased by leaps and bounds since 1968, but the characteristics of the immigrants have also changed dramatically. In the decade between 1951 and 1960, most of the immigrants to the United States came from Europe (about 59.3 percent). However, between 1971 and 1980, Europeans made up only 18 percent of the legal immigrants who settled in the United States. The European percentage of the immigrants to the United States continued to decline during the 1980s. Between 1981 and 1988, they made up 10.8 percent of U.S. legal immigrants (U.S. Bureau of the

Census, 1991). The percentage of European immigrants settling in the U.S. between 1981 and 1996 increased slightly to 11.7 percent, largely reflecting the significant increase in immigrants from nations in the former Soviet Union (U.S. Bureau of the Census, 1998).

Most immigrants to the United States from the 1970s through the 1990s came from Asian and Latin American nations, such as the Philippines, Korea, China, and Mexico. A significant number of people from the war-torn nations of Indochina sought refuge in the United States when communists gained control of their homelands. By 1990 almost 1 million Vietnamese were living in the United States.

The wave of new immigrants to the United States from non-European nations, and the relatively low birthrate among Whites compared to that of most groups of color, are having a significant influence on U.S. society, particularly on its demographic characteristics. The new wave of immigrants to the United States has hastened the decline in the relative proportion of the White population in the United States. This decline began as early as 1900. Between 1900 and 1980 the White proportion of the U.S. population declined from 87.7 percent to 83.1 percent. During the same time, the proportion of non-Whites in the United States increased from 12.3 percent of the population in 1900 to 16.9 percent in 1980 (Momeni, 1984).

In the year 2000, the U.S. population was approximately 275 million people, about 72 percent of whom were non-Hispanic Whites. African Americans made up 12 percent of the population; Hispanics 11 percent, Asian and Pacific Islanders 4 percent; and American Indians, Aleuts, and Eskimos 1 percent (Martin & Midgley, 1999). The U.S. Census projects that the nation's population will reach 394 million in 2050, and that non-Hispanic Whites will make up 53 percent of the population (Martin & Midgley, 1999). People of color are projected to make up about 47 percent of the population in 2050. It is often inaccurately reported that Whites will be a minority by 2050. However, U.S. Census projections indicate that they will still be a slight majority.

The new immigrants, along with the diversity of indigenous U.S. ethnic groups, are having a tremendous influence on the nation's schools, colleges, universities, and other institutions. Students of color made up 35 percent of the students enrolled in public schools in grades one through twelve in 1995 (U.S. Department of Education, 1998). This was an 11 percent increase from 1976. The increase was due primarily to the increase in the percentage of Latino students. Demographers project that students of color will make up about 46 percent of the nation's school-age youths by the year 2020 (Pallas, Natriello, & McDill, 1989). In some urban school districts, more than fifty different languages are spoken (Teachers of English to Speakers of Other Languages, 1997).

Because the characteristics of the students in U.S. schools are changing substantially and because most teachers are female, White, middle-class, and speak only English, conflict often develops between the home and the school and between teachers and students (Delpit, 1995; Ladson-Billings, 1994). The schools have been reluctant to adapt their curricular and teaching styles to make them more consistent with the needs of students of color, low-income students, and language minority students. In many schools that have multiethnic and multilanguage populations, the curriculum, teaching, and motivational techniques remain Anglocentric and monolingual.

Racial and ethnic problems are major sources of conflict in many U.S. schools, particularly in urban areas. Disproportionality in achievement, discipline, and dropout rates between mainstream students and students of color is a significant source of tension in most urban school districts. The parents blame teachers and administrators; the school blames the home and the student's culture.

As long as the achievement gap between African Americans and Whites and Anglos and Latinos is wide, ethnic conflicts and tension in schools will continue. Improving the academic achievement of students of color and of low-income students, and developing and implementing a multicultural curriculum that reflects the cultures, experiences, and perspectives of diverse groups, will help reduce the racial conflict and tension in U.S. schools and will increase the academic achievement of all students.

Ethnic Revitalization Movements: A Phase Typology

The ethnic revival movements in the United States echoed throughout the world as groups such as the Jamaicans in the United Kingdom, the Australian Aborigines, and the Moluccans and Surinamese in the Netherlands demanded more social, political, and educational equality in their societies (Cropley, 1983; Eldering & Kloprogge, 1989). In both the United States (Banks & Banks, 1995) and the United Kingdom (Figueroa, 1995; May, 1999) multicultural education has created tremendous debate over goals. However, the two nations appear to be in different phases of ethnic revitalization and consequently in different stages of debate.

This section describes a typology that attempts to outline the major phases of the development of ethnic revitalization movements in Western societies. The typology is a preliminary ideal-type construct and constitutes a set of hypotheses based on the existing and emerging theory and research and on my study of ethnic behavior in several Western nations. Because it is drawn primarily from ethnic events in the United States, it might be less generalizable in other nations. Observers in other nations must determine the extent to which the typology is valid in their societies. This typology is presented to stimulate discussion and analysis and to help educators better interpret ethnic events in Western nations.

I am conceptualizing ethnic revitalization as consisting of four major phases: *a precondition phase; a first or early phase; a later phase;* and *a final phase* (see Table 2.1). The typology is an ideal-type construct and should be considered as dynamic and multifaceted rather than as static and one-dimensional. The divisions between the phases are blurred rather than sharp. One phase does not end abruptly and another begins; rather, the phases blend and overlap. As with any ideal-type typology, the phases approximate reality rather than directly describe it. No actual ethnic movement exemplifies each characteristic of the four phases.

TABLE 2.1   **Phases in the Development of Ethnic Revitalization Movements**

The Precondition Phase

This phase is characterized by the existence of a history of colonialism, imperialism, racism, an institutionalized democratic ideology, and efforts by the nation-state to close the gap between democratic ideals and societal realities. These events create rising expectations among victimized ethnic groups that pave the way for ethnic protest and a revitalization movement.

The First Phase

This phase is characterized by ethnic polarization, an intense identity quest by victimized ethnic groups, and single-causal explanations. An effort is made by ethnic groups to get racism legitimized as a primary explanation of their problems. Both radical reformers and staunch conservatives set forth single-causal explanations to explain the problems of victimized ethnic groups.

The Later Phase

This phase is characterized by meaningful dialogue between victimized and dominant ethnic groups, multiethnic coalitions, reduced ethnic polarization, and the search for multiple-causal explanations for the problems of victimized ethnic groups.

The Final Phase

Some elements of the reforms formulated in the earlier phases become institutionalized during this phase. Other victimized cultural groups echo their grievances, thereby expanding and dispersing the focus of the ethnic reform movement. Conservative ideologies and policies become institutionalized during this phase, thus paving the way for the development of a new ethnic revitalization movement.

Ethnic Revitalization: The Precondition Phase

Ethnic revitalization movements usually arise within societies that have a history of imperialism, colonialism, and institutionalized racism. Groups with particular ethnic, racial, and cultural characteristics are denied equality and structural inclusion into the nation-state. These societies also have a national democratic ideology stating that equality and justice should exist for all individuals and groups within the nation-state. The first phase of revitalization begins when the nation-state takes steps to close the gap between its democratic ideals and the inequality institutionalized within it.

The attempt to improve the conditions of marginalized groups—usually stimulated by action taken by these groups—creates rising expectations and hope and causes these groups to perceive their current condition as intolerable. The ethnic revitalization movement is born out of the hope and rising expectations created by the nation-state when it attempts to eliminate some of its most blatant forms of institutionalized racism and discrimination. The desegregation of the armed forces and state universities after World War II and the *Brown* v. *Board of Education* Supreme Court decision (1954), which made *de jure* school segregation illegal, were key events in the United States that stimulated the birth of the civil rights movement of the 1960s and 1970s.

Ethnic Revitalization: The First Phase

In the first phase of ethnic revitalization, positions are sharply drawn, and ardent, single-causal explanations tend to predominate, controversy is bitter, and the debate tends to take the form of "us and them"—you are either for us or with them. Racism is usually the major issue in the debate during the early stages of ethnic revitalization because it has usually not been previously acknowledged as an important component of the society. It is during the early stages of ethnic revitalization that groups that perceive themselves as oppressed or as victims of racism force the dominant society to acknowledge that racism is institutionalized within it.

The debate between radical reformers and conservative defenders of the status quo remains stalemated and single-focused until the existence of racism is acknowledged by the dominant group and meaningful steps are taken to eliminate it. Until this acknowledgment occurs in official statements, policies, and actions, radical reformers continue to perceive racism as the single cause of the social, economic, and educational problems of excluded ethnic groups. Radical reformers will not search for or find more complex variables that explain the problems of victimized ethnic groups until mainstream leaders acknowledge the existence of institutionalized racism. In other words, institutionalized racism must become legitimized as an explanation, and serious steps must be taken to eliminate it, before an ethnic revitalization movement can reach a phase in which other explanations will be accepted by radical reformers who articulate the interests of groups that are victims of institutionalized racism.

During the early phase of ethnic revitalization, ethnic groups, in their efforts to shape new identities and to legitimize their histories and cultures, often glorify those histories and cultures and emphasize the ways their people have been oppressed by the dominant group and mainstream society. This early combination of protest and ethnic polarization must be understood within a broad social and political context. Groups that perceive themselves as oppressed and that internalize the dominant society's negative stereotypes and myths about themselves are likely to express strong in-group feelings during the early stages of ethnic revitalization. They also attempt to shape a new identity. During this phase the group is also likely to reject outside ethnic and racial groups, to romanticize its past, and to view contemporary social and political conditions quite subjectively.

An ethnic group in the early stage of revitalization is also likely to demand that the school curriculum portray a romanticized version of its history (to compensate for past omissions and errors) and to emphasize how the group has been victimized by other ethnic and racial groups. Extremely negative sanctions are directed against members of the ethnic group who do not endorse a strong ethnic position. Consequently, little fruitful dialogue is likely to take place either within or between different ethnic groups. Members of both the "oppressed" and the "oppressive" groups remain ardent in their positions during the first phase of revitalization.

Educational institutions tend to respond to the first phases of ethnic revitalization with quickly conceptualized and hurriedly formulated programs designed primarily to silence ethnic protest rather than to contribute to equality and to the structural inclusion of ethnic groups into society. In both the United States and the United Kingdom, many early programs related to ethnic groups were poorly conceptualized and were implemented without careful and thoughtful planning. Such programs are usually attacked and eliminated during the later phases of ethnic revitalization when the institutionalization of ethnic programs and reforms begins. Their weakness becomes the primary justification for their elimination. When such programs were attacked and eliminated in the United States, many careful and sensitive observers noted that they had been designed to fail.

The Rise of Antiegalitarian Ideology and Research

The ideology and research that radical reformers develop during the early stage of ethnic revitalization do not go unchallenged. An ideological war takes place between radical reformers and conservatives who defend the status quo. While radical and liberal reformers develop ideology and research to show how the ethnic groups' major problems are caused by institutionalized racism and the wider society (Gans, 1995; Kinchelole, Steinberg, & Gresson III, 1996), antiegalitarian advocates and researchers develop an ideology and research stating that the failure of ethnic groups in school and society is due to their own inherited and socialized characteristics (Herrnstein & Murray, 1994; Murray, 1984). *Both radical and conservative scholars tend to develop single-causal theories and explanations during the early phase of ethnic revitalization.* The theories and explanations developed by radical theorists tend to focus on racism and other problems in society (Gans, 1995), whereas theories and explanations developed by conservative researchers usually focus on the characteristics of ethnic students themselves, such as their genetic characteristics and their family socialization (Herrnstein & Murray, 1994; Murray, 1984).

Radical reformers use the research and theory developed by antiegalitarian researchers as evidence to support their arguments that racism is pervasive and institutionalized within the society and that it has permeated much of the research done at some of the nation's most prestigious universities.

Ethnic Revitalization: The Later Phase

During the later phase of ethnic revitalization, ethnic groups search for multiple rather than single causes for their problems; racism as an explanation becomes legitimized but is recognized as only one important cause of the problems of ethnic groups; ethnic rhetoric and polarization lessen; and ethnic groups form coalitions and jointly articulate their grievances.

During the first phase of ethnic revitalization, many researchers and intellectuals who feel committed to ethnic equality but who do not agree with radical reformers on many issues do not freely express their views in public forums because they fear being called racists. These individuals begin to express their views and opinions freely during the later phase of ethnic revitalization (Jencks & Phillips, 1998; Wilson, 1996). This now becomes possible because emotions cool, thus enabling individuals who disagree to engage in fruitful dialogue without accusations and epithets.

In the United States, a group of conservative intellectuals has emerged who argue that they are committed to ethnic equality and that their views represent another valid way for ethnic groups to attain structural inclusion (Chavez, 1991; D'Souza, 1995; Glazer, 1997; Steele, 1990). In general, these intellectuals favor few government intervention programs and encourage ethnic groups to establish businesses and to compete in the market economy of the United States. This group of intellectuals, the neoconservatives, has been highly visible and influential in the national press and has evoked tremendous controversy, especially among ethnic scholars and leaders (Steinfels, 1979). Only a few of these scholars, however, are ethnic minorities (Chavez, 1991; D'Souza, 1995; Steele, 1990).

Nation-states facilitate the movement from early to later phases of ethnic revitalization by making symbolic concessions to ethnic groups, such as African American studies programs, the hiring of ethnics in highly visible positions, the establishment of affirmative action policies, and the creation of a middle-class ethnic elite that serves as visible proof that "ethnics can make it" (Carter, 1991). The ethnic elite plays a very important role in moving the nation-state from the early to the later phase of ethnic revitalization. They develop counter arguments to radical reformers, teach balanced and scholarly ethnic studies courses, and search for complex explanations for the causes of the social, economic, and political problems of ethnic groups (Carter, 1991; Wilson, 1996).

Ethnic Revitalization: The Final Phase

During the final phase of ethnic revitalization, many of the reforms born during the early and later phases become institutionalized within the schools and other institutions. Other groups that perceive themselves as oppressed also begin to echo the grievances of ethnic groups and thus broaden the scope of the reform movement. Women, people with disabilities, and other groups articulate their problems and make their special case for entitlements (Banks & Banks, 1997). Conflict tends to develop between these groups and ethnic groups because they compete for the same scarce resources.

Institutions such as the state and federal government, universities, and schools begin to view these groups as a collectivity and to respond to their needs with single programs, projects, and legislation. When women and people with disabilities began to argue their case for inclusion into the school curriculum in the United States, schools created *multicultural education,* which combined content and information about these diverse groups into a single program. The United States federal government established affirmative action programs designed to help both ethnic minorities and women gain more access to jobs and education.

The final phase of ethnic revitalization is a process that does not end until diverse ethnic and racial groups experience structural inclusion and equality within the nation-state. Consequently, the final phase of ethnic revitalization has not ended in the United States, the United Kingdom, Australia, or Canada because ethnic groups of color are still only partially included within the structures of these societies. Even when ethnic groups attain *inclusion* into institutions, they do not necessarily experience *equality.* Many middle-class African Americans in the United States are discovering, for example, that when they gain *access* to mainstream U.S. institutions they do not necessarily experience *equality* within them (Feagin & Sikes, 1994).

At the same time that the United States is experiencing the final phase of ethnic revitalization, social, political, and economic events are developing that are paving the way for a new ethnic revival that may have many of the same characteristics of the ethnic movement in the 1960s and 1970s. A conservative government and national atmosphere are engendering the kind of alienation, hostility, and poverty that gave rise to ethnic revival movements during the 1960s and 1970s.

Several indicators of the rise of a new ethnic revitalization movement were evident in the United States as the twenty-first century began. They included the significance of the Afrocentric movement (Asante, 1990), the significant number of second-generation middle-class African American youths who are enrolling in predominantly Black colleges and universities, and the ethnic and cultural expressions among young people within groups such as Asian Americans, Mexican Americans, and American Indians. The attacks on affirmative action and bilingual education and the ethnic violence that was directed toward groups of color and Jewish Americans in the late 1990s were reactions by the mainstream White community to the quests by ethnic groups for inclusion, cultural legitimacy, and political power.

The situation in the United States as the twenty-first century began indicates that ethnic revitalization movements are cyclical rather than linear. Once an ethnic revival movement has occurred within a nation-state, social, political, and economic conditions tend to arise that give birth to new revivals. As ethnic revitalization movements reach their later and final phases—as in the United States today— events tend to evoke new ones. Ethnic revitalization movements will continue to reemerge in Western democratic societies until racial and ethnic groups attain structural inclusion and equality in their nation-states and societies.

Ethnic Revitalization: Educational Implications

To help nations move from early to later phases of ethnic revitalization, educational institutions at all levels should help minority and majority group students to interpret accurately the current phase of the ethnic revival movement and to respond to it in ways that will help ethnic students satisfy their psychological and academic needs.

During the early phase of ethnic revitalization (such as existed in the United Kingdom in the 1980s), the school should help legitimize racism as a valid explanation of societal realities in the nation-state. Educators who refuse to validate racism as an explanation or to take serious steps to eliminate it will extend the early phase of ethnic revitalization and alienate many ethnic students and radical reformers. Educators who insist, during the early stage of an ethnic revival movement, that the problems of ethnic groups are caused by more complicated variables than racism may be accurate in their views, but they are not dealing with the subjective reality of marginalized ethnic groups of color. *Racism is the most important or only significant variable for these groups because their daily experiences validate this reality.* When educational and other institutions have validated racism as an important explanation of the problems of ethnic groups of color and have taken meaningful steps to eliminate it, then other causes of their problems can be legitimately explored and validated.

Multiple-causal theories that explain the problems of ethnic groups are developing and becoming legitimate in the United States. Even though racism is still regarded as an important and cogent variable in U.S. society, a few African American scholars, such as Wilson (1996), Patterson (1997), and Ogbu (1995), are trying to determine how such variables as class, culture, and values influence the achievement and experiences of ethnic groups. However, the writings of these scholars of color have created considerable controversy and debate within both minority and majority communities. In general, their writings are less controversial among mainstream White groups than among people of color.

Summary

A large wave of immigrants from Southern, Central, and Eastern Europe entered the United States between 1890 and 1917. The Europeans who already lived in the United States during this period were primarily from Northern and Western Europe. Because of their cultural differences, Catholicism, and competition for jobs with native-born Americans, a nativistic movement arose to halt the immigration of the new immigrants. Nativism became widespread throughout the United

States and influenced the nation's institutions, including the schools. The outbreak of World War I in Europe greatly increased nativistic expressions within the larger society and the schools. The schools tried to make the immigrants 100 percent Americans and to exclude all elements of foreignness from the curriculum.

A few philosophers and writers, such as Horace Kallen, Randolph Bourne, and Julius Drachsler, defended the immigrants' rights, stating that cultural democracy should exist in a democratic nation such as the United States. The arguments of these writers, however, influenced few U.S. leaders.

Most institutions within U.S. society, including the schools, remained assimilationist-oriented between World Wars I and II and devoted little serious attention to the educational needs and problems of students of color. However, a number of U.S. educational and scholarly leaders formulated policy and programs for educating students of color during this period. The educational developments in Native American, African American, and Mexican American education between the two wars illustrate the evolutionary nature of ethnic education in the United States.

The intergroup education movement grew out of the social developments that emerged in response to World War II. Conflict and riots developed in U.S. cities as African Americans and Whites and Anglos and Mexican Americans competed for housing and jobs. The intergroup education movement tried to reduce interracial tensions and to further intercultural understandings. Developments in intergroup education took place at the elementary, secondary, and college levels. The intergroup education movement, itself only mildly pluralistic, did not seriously challenge the assimilationist ideology in U.S. life. When the ethnic revitalization movements of the 1960s and 1970s and related educational reform movements emerged, the intergroup education movement had largely faded.

Since 1968, the United States has experienced a major wave of new immigrants primarily from nations in Latin America and Asia. These new immigrants have had a major influence on the social, economic, and educational institutions in the United States. Schools, colleges, and universities are trying to respond to the ethnic, cultural, and language diversity they are now experiencing. However, they face many challenges, including tight budgets and a conservative political climate.

Other Western nation-states, such as the United Kingdom, France, Canada, and Australia, have also become more ethnically diverse since World War II. The ethnic minorities within these societies face problems similar to their counterparts in the United States. Multicultural education has emerged within these nations to respond to the unique needs, problems, and aspirations of ethnic minorities.

Since the 1960s, a series of ethnic revitalization movements have arisen in the various Western nation-states. This chapter presents a typology that describes the major phases of ethnic revitalization movements, particularly as they have developed in the United States and the United Kingdom. The major phases of ethnic revitalization movements can be identified, even though they acquire unique and different characteristics in the various nation-states. Different nation-states are also in different phases of ethnic revitalization.

Nation-states can facilitate the movement from early to later phases of ethnic revitalization by implementing educational policies and programs that promote the integration of structurally excluded ethnic groups into the mainstream society. A curriculum that reflects the cultures, ethos, and experiences of the diverse groups within a nation will reduce ethnic polarization and weaken ethnic revival movements.

REFERENCES

Adams, D. W. (1995). *Education for Extinction: American Indians and the Boarding School Experience 1875–1928.* Lawrence: University Press of Kansas.

Adler, M. J., & Van Doren, C. (Eds.). (1977). *Great Treasure of Western Thought.* New York: R. R. Bowker.

Aguilar-San Juan, K. (Ed.). (1994). *The State of Asian America: Activism and Resistance in the 1990s.* Boston: South End Press.

Alba, R. D. (1990). *Ethnic Identity: The Transformation of White America.* New Haven, CT: Yale University Press.

Apple, M. W. (1996). *Cultural Politics and Education.* Buckingham, England: Open University Press.

Asante, M. K. (1990). *Kemet, Afrocentricity, and Knowledge.* Trenton, NJ: Africa World Press.

Banks, C. A. M. (1996). The Intergroup Education Movement. In J. A. Banks (Ed.), *Multicultural Education, Transformative Knowledge, and Action* (pp. 251–277). New York: Teachers College Press.

Banks, J. A., & Banks, C. A. M. (Eds.). (1995). *Handbook of Research on Multicultural Education.* New York: Macmillan.

Banks, J. A., & Banks, C. A. M. (Eds.). (1997). *Multicultural Education: Issues and Perspectives* (3rd. ed.). Boston: Allyn and Bacon.

Bennett, D. H. (1988). *The Party of Fear: From Nativist Movements to the New Right in American History.* Chapel Hill: The University of North Carolina Press.

Bourne, R. S. (1916). Trans-National America. *The Atlantic Monthly, 118,* 95.

Brodkin, K. (1999). *How Jews Became White Folks and What That Says about Race in America.* New Brunswick, NJ: Rutgers University Press.

Carter, S. L. (1991). *Reflections of an Affirmative Action Baby.* New York: Basic Books.

Carter, T. P., & Segura, R. D. (1979). *Mexican Americans in School: A Decade of Change.* New York: College Entrance Examination Board.

Chavez, L. (1991). *Out of the Barrio.* New York: Basic Books.

Clarke, J. H. (Ed.), with the assistance of A. J. Garvey. (1974). *Marcus Garvey and the Vision of Africa.* New York: Vintage Books.

Cook, L. A. (1947). Intergroup Education. *Review of Educational Research, 17,* 266–278.

Cook, L. A. (Ed.). (1950). *College Programs in Intergroup Relations.* Washington, DC: American Council on Education.

Cropley, A. J. (1983). *The Education of Immigrant Children.* London: Croom Helm.

Cubberley, E. P. (1909). *Changing Conceptions of Education.* Boston: Houghton Mifflin.

Delpit, L. D. (1995). *Other People's Children: Cultural Conflict in the Classroom.* New York: The New Press.

Dershowitz, A. M. (1997). *The Vanishing American Jew.* New York: Little Brown.

Drachsler, J. (1920). *Democracy and Assimilation.* New York: Macmillan.

D'Souza, D. (1995). *The End of Racism: Principles for a Multicultural Society.* New York: The Free Press.

Du Bois, W. E. B. (1961). *The Souls of Black Folk.* New York: Fawcett Publications. (published originally in 1903.)

Edwards, A., & Polite C. K. (1992). *Children of the Dream: The Psychology of Black Success.* New York: Doubleday.

Eldering, L., & Kloprogge, J. (Eds.). (1989). *Different Cultures, Same School: Ethnic Minority Children in Europe.* Berwyn, PA: Swets North America.

Fass, P. S. (1989). *Outside In: Minorities and the Transformation of American Education.* New York: Oxford University Press.

Feagin, J. R., & Sikes, M. P. (1994). *Living with Racism: The Black Middle-Class Experience.* Boston: Beacon Press.

Figueroa, P. (1995). Multicultural Education in the United Kingdom: Historical Development and Current Status. In J. A. Banks & C. A. M. Banks

(Eds.), *Handbook of Research on Multicultural Education* (pp. 778–800). New York: Macmillan.

Gans, H. J. (1995). *The War against the Poor: The Underclass and Antipoverty Policy.* New York: Basic Books.

Glazer, N. (1997). *We Are All Multiculturalists Now.* Cambridge, MA: Harvard University Press.

Gutierrez, R. A. (1995). Historical and Social Science Research on Mexican Americans. In J. A. Banks & C. A. M. Banks (Eds.), *Handbook of Research on Multicultural Education* (pp. 203–222). New York: Macmillan.

Harding, V. (1990). *Hope and History: Why We Must Share the Story of the Movement.* Maryknoll, NY: Orbis Books.

Harlan, L. R. (1972). *Booker T. Washington: The Making of a Black Leader, 1856–1901.* New York: Oxford University Press.

Herrnstein, R. J., & Murray, C. (1994). *The Bell Curve: Intelligence and Class Structure in American Life.* New York: The Free Press.

Jacobson, M. F. (1998). *Whiteness of a Different Color: European Immigrants and the Alchemy of Race.* Cambridge, MA: Harvard University Press.

Jencks, C., & Phillips, M. (Eds.). (1998). *The Black-White Test Score Gap.* Washington, DC: Brookings Institution Press.

Jones, M. A. (1992). *American Immigration* (2nd ed). Chicago: The University of Chicago Press.

Kallen, H. M. (1924). *Culture and Democracy in the United States.* New York: Boni and Liveright.

Kincheloe, J. L., Steinberg, S. R., & Gresson, A. D. III (Eds.). (1996). *Measured Lies: The Bell Curve Examined.* New York: St. Martin's Press.

Ladson-Billings, G. (1994). *The Dreamkeepers: Successful Teachers of African American Children.* San Francisco: Jossey-Bass.

Landry, B. (1987). *The New Black Middle Class.* Berkeley: The University of California Press.

Lemann, N. (1991). *The Promised Land: The Great Migration and How It Changed America.* New York: Knopf.

Lomawaima, K. T. (1994). *They Called It Prairie Light: The Story of the Chilocco Indian School.* Lincoln: University of Nebraska Press.

Martin, P., & Midgley, E. (1999). *Immigration to the United States.* Washington, DC: Population Reference Bureau.

May, S. (Ed.). (1999). *Critical Multiculturalism: Rethinking Multicultural and Antiracist Education.* Philadelphia: Falmer Press.

Meriam, L. (Ed.). (1928). *The Problem of Indian Administration.* Baltimore: The Johns Hopkins University Press.

Momeni, J. A. (1984). *Demography of Racial and Ethnic Minorities in the United States: An Annotated Bibliography with a Review Essay.* Westport, CT: Greenwood Press.

Moreno, J. F. (Ed.). (1999). *The Elusive Quest for Equality: 150 Years of Chicano/Chicana Education.* Cambridge, MA: Harvard Educational Review.

Murillo, N. (1996). George I. Sanchez and Mexican American Educational Practice. In J. A. Banks (Ed.), *Multicultural Education, Transformative Knowledge, and Action* (pp. 129–140). New York: Teachers College Press.

Murray, C. (1984). *Losing Ground: American Social Policy, 1950–1980.* New York: Basic Books.

Novak, M. (1971). *The Rise of the Unmeltable Ethnics: Politics and Culture in the Seventies.* New York: Macmillan.

Ogbu, J. U. (1995). Understanding Cultural Diversity and Learning. In J. A. Banks & C. A. M. Banks (Eds.), *Handbook of Research on Multicultural Education* (pp. 582–593). New York: Macmillan.

Pallas, A. M., Natriello, G., & McDill, E. L. (1989). The Changing Nature of the Disadvantaged Population: Current Dimensions and Future Trends. *Educational Researcher, 18,* 16–22.

Park, R. E., & Burgess, E. (1924). *Introduction to the Science of Sociology.* Chicago: The University of Chicago Press.

Patterson, O. (1997). *The Ordeal of Integration: Progress and Resentment in America's "Racial" Crisis.* Washington, DC: Civitas/Counterpoint.

Roche, A. M. (1996). Carter G. Woodson and the Development of Transformative Scholarship. In J. A. Banks (Ed.), *Multicultural Education, Transformative Knowledge, and Action* (pp. 91–114). New York: Teachers College Press.

Shils, E. (Ed.). (1991). *Remembering the University of Chicago: Teachers, Scientists, and Scholars.* Chicago: The University of Chicago Press.

Steele, S. (1990). *The Content of Our Character.* New York: St. Martin's.

Steinfels, P. (1979). *The Neoconservatives: The Men Who Are Changing America's Politics.* New York: Simon & Schuster.

Stewart, E. C., & Bennett, M. J. (1991). *American Cultural Patterns: A Cross-Cultural Perspective* (rev. ed.). Yarmouth, ME: Intercultural Press.

Szasz, M. C. (1974). *Education and the American Indian: The Road to Self-Determination, 1928–1973.* Albuquerque: University of New Mexico Press.

Szasz, M. C. (1988). *Indian Education in the American Colonies, 1607–1783.* Albuquerque: University of New Mexico Press.

Taba, H., Brady, E. H., & Robinson, J. T. (1952). *Intergroup Education in Public Schools.* Washington, DC: American Council on Education.

Taba, H., & Wilson, H. E. (1946). Intergroup Education through the School Curriculum. *Annals of the American Academy of Political and Social Science, 244*, 19–25.

Teachers of English to Speakers of Other Languages. (1997). *ESL Standards for Pre–K-12 Students.* Alexandria, VA: Author.

U.S. Bureau of the Census. (1991). *Statistical Abstract of the United States: 1991* (111th ed.). Washington, DC: U.S. Government Printing Office.

U.S. Bureau of the Census. (1998). *Statistical Abstract of the United States: 1998* (118th ed.). Washington, DC: U.S. Government Printing Office.

U.S. Department of Education, National Center for Education Statistics. (1998). *The Condition of Education, 1998.* Washington, DC: U.S. Government Printing Office.

U.S. Senate, Report of the Committee on Labor and Public Welfare, Special Subcommittee on Indian Education. (1969). *Indian Education. A National Tragedy–A National Challenge.* 91st Congress, 1st Session. Washington, DC: U.S. Government Printing Office.

Washington, B. T. (1901). *Up from Slavery: An Autobiography.* New York: Doubleday and Company.

Waters, M. C. (1990). *Ethnic Options: Choosing Identities in America.* Berkeley: University of California Press.

Weinberg, M. (1977). *A Chance to Learn: A History of Race and Education in the United States.* New York: Cambridge University Press.

Wilson, W. J. (1996). *When Work Disappears: The World of the New Urban Poor.* New York: Knopf.

3 Multicultural Education: Development, Goals, and Approaches

The Emergence of Multicultural Education

In the United States, as well as in other Western nations such as the United Kingdom, Canada, Australia, France, and the Netherlands, the emergence of multicultural education has been a gradual and evolutionary process. This chapter describes multicultural education as it developed in the United States.

Multicultural education has also developed in a related but not identical way in the other Western nation-states (Allan & Hill, 1995; Moodley, 1995). Educational developments in nations such as the United Kingdom, Canada, and Australia are often similar to developments in the United States. However, these developments often occur at different times and reflect the cultural, political, and historical context of the nation in which they occur. In both the United States and Australia in the late 1980s, for example, pluralism was strongly challenged by a call for national cohesion and identity. In the United States, however, the call for nationalism occurred when a new wave of immigrants was settling in the nation. Australia, like the United Kingdom, had severely restricted new immigration (Allan & Hill, 1995).

Phase I: Monoethnic Courses

When the Black civil rights movement began in the mid-1960s in the United States, African Americans demanded that the schools and other institutions respond more adequately to their needs and aspirations. They called for more Black teachers for African American youths, community control of Black schools, and the rewriting of textbooks to make them more accurately reflect African American history and culture. They also demanded African American studies courses. During the 1970s, ethnic minorities, such as African Americans, Asians in the United Kingdom, and Canadian Indians, also demanded that educational institutions within their societies respond more directly and positively to their needs and goals.

In time, other ethnic groups in the United States, such as Mexican Americans and American Indians, made demands on schools and colleges similar to those made by African Americans. These institutions responded by establishing courses on specific ethnic groups, such as African American history and literature, and Mexican American history and literature. This phase in the development of multicultural education can be considered Phase I. It was characterized by monoethnic courses, the assumption that only a member of an ethnic group should teach a course on that group, and a focus on White racism and on how Whites have oppressed ethnic groups of color. A pervasive assumption made during Phase I ethnic studies courses was that Black studies were needed only by African American students and that Asian American studies were needed only by Asian American students.

Phase II: Multiethnic Studies Courses

As more and more ethnic groups in the United States, including White ethnic groups such as Jewish Americans and Polish Americans, began to demand separate courses and the inclusion of their histories and cultures in the curriculum, schools and colleges began to offer multiethnic studies courses that focus on several ethnic cultures and view the experiences of ethnic groups from comparative perspectives. Courses such as Ethnic Minority Music and The History and Culture of Minorities in the United States are taught from comparative perspectives.

We can call the multiethnic studies phase of the development of multicultural education Phase II. Ethnic studies courses became more global, conceptual, and scholarly during this period. They also became less politically oriented and began to explore diverse points of view and interpretations of the experiences of ethnic groups in the United States. The recognition emerged and grew that ethnic studies should be designed for all students, and not just for students who were members of particular ethnic groups. Two basic assumptions of multiethnic studies courses are that ethnic groups have had both similar and different experiences in the United States and that a comparative study of ethnic cultures can result in useful concepts, generalizations, and theories.

Phase III: Multiethnic Education

As ethnic studies became more global and widespread, more and more educators began to recognize that even though reforming the course of study in schools and colleges was necessary, it was not sufficient to result in effective educational reform. The negative attitudes of many teachers made their use of new ethnic materials and teaching strategies ineffective and in some cases harmful. Educators also began to recognize that ethnic studies courses alone could not enable students such as African Americans, Latinos, and Native Americans to achieve at levels comparable with the achievement levels of most mainstream White students.

Research emerged that indicated how students of color are often placed in low academic tracts because of middle-class and Anglo-biased IQ tests (Oakes, 1985) and how students who speak a first language other than standard Anglo-American English often fail to achieve in school, in part, because of their language differences (August & Hakuta, 1998; Ovando & Collier, 1998). Studies that documented the affects of teacher attitudes on student achievement, attitudes, and behavior were published (Kleinfeld, 1975; Rist, 1970). Research also revealed the negative attitudes and interactions that teachers often have with low-income students and students of color (Rist, 1970).

These recognitions and studies convinced many educators involved in the education of students of color that ethnic studies courses and materials, no matter how soundly conceptualized and taught, could not by themselves bring about the kind of substantial educational reform needed to enable students from diverse racial and ethnic groups to experience educational equality. In other words, educators began to realize that ethnic studies were necessary but not sufficient to bring about effective educational reform and equity. Educators began to call for a more broadly conceptualized kind of educational reform, with a focus on the total school environment. Educators began to view the total school as the unit of change, and not just any one variable within the educational environment, such as materials or teaching strategies. This more broadly conceptualized reform movement became known as *multiethnic education,* which emerged as Phase III in the development of pluralistic education.

Phase IV: Multicultural Education

Some educators became interested in an educational reform movement that would deal not only with the educational problems of low-income students and students of color but also with the educational problems of cultural groups such as women, people with disabilities, religious groups, different social class groups, and regional groups such as Appalachian Whites. This broader reform movement is known as *multicultural education,* which is Stage IV of the development of pluralistic education (Banks & Banks, 1995; Grant, 1999).

Multicultural education became the preferred concept in many educational institutions, in part because the concept enabled schools, colleges, and universities to pool limited resources and thus to focus on a wide range of groups rather than to limit their focus to racial and ethnic minorities (Banks & Banks, 1995). The *Standards* published by the National Council for Accreditation of Teacher Education (NCATE) (1999) require teacher-education institutions to implement components, courses, and programs in multicultural education. The NCATE multicultural standards, first published as a part of the council's general standards in 1977, have been revised and reissued through the years. NCATE is now developing performance-based standards, which will be published early in the new century. Multicultural standards will be an integral part of these standards (National Council for the Accreditation of Teacher Education, 1999).

Many educators support the multicultural education concept but are concerned that the focus of the movement may become so broad and global that the issues of *racism* and *racial discrimination,* important concerns of pluralistic education in the 1960s when it emerged, might become lost or de-emphasized (Gay, 1995). Another problem with multicultural education is that the boundaries of the field are so broad that it is often difficult to determine which cultural groups are the primary focus or concern in a particular curriculum, publication, or conference. Some authors use the term *multicultural education* to refer to groups of color and to language minority groups (Baker, 1994; Nieto, 1999). Increasingly, however, the term is being used to refer to education related to race, class, gender, social class, exceptionality, and to the interaction of these variables (Banks & Banks, 1997; Grant, 1999).

A Caveat

Because of the historical and evolutionary way in which Phases I through IV of multicultural education is discussed above, the reader may understandably conclude that when Phase II emerged Phase I disappeared. This is not what in fact has happened or is happening. As Figure 3.1 illustrates, when Phase II emerged, Phase I continued, although perhaps in a modified form and on a more limited scale. The earlier phases also begin to take on some characteristics of the newly emerging phases. Phase I types of ethnic studies courses became more conceptual and scholarly when Phase II of multicultural education began to emerge. The assumption also grew that an academically qualified individual, regardless of his or her ethnic group membership, could effectively teach an ethnic studies course on any ethnic group.

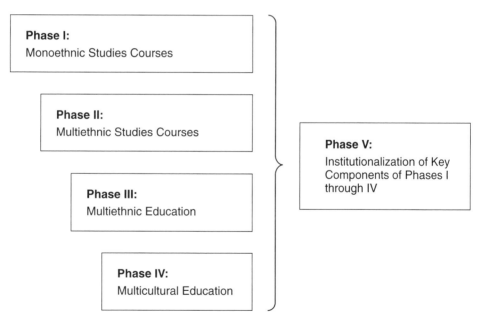

FIGURE 3.1 The Evolution of Multicultural Education
This figure illustrates how the earlier phases of multicultural education continue to exist when new phases of the movement emerge. However, when the new phases emerge, the earlier phases tend to assume some of the characteristics of the newer phases and to continue on a more limited scale.

Phase V: The Institutionalization Process

I am conceptualizing Phase V of the development of multicultural education as the institutionalization of the key and most effective components of Phases I through IV. Phase V is a *process* that is slowly occurring. Elements of multicultural education are beginning to permeate the curriculum and the total educational environment. However, this process is necessarily a slow one that requires strong support and commitment from boards of education, administrators, and teachers. It took several centuries for the current historical periods (e.g., the Middle Ages, the Renaissance, the European Discovery of America) to be conceptualized and institutionalized. As we try to reconceptualize world and U.S. history and literature, it is reasonable to expect this process to take considerable time and to require continuing effort and commitment by everyone involved in the educational process. Figure 3.2 summarizes the historical development of multicultural education as discussed in this and the previous chapters.

The Goals of Multicultural Education

Multicultural education is a reform movement designed to make major curricular and structural changes in the education of students in schools, colleges, and universities. Multicultural education theorists believe that many school practices related to race and ethnicity are harmful to students and reinforce many ethnic stereotypes and discriminatory practices in Western societies.

Multicultural education assumes that ethnicity, race, culture, and language diversity are salient parts of the United States and other Western societies. It also assumes that ethnic, cultural, and language diversity is a positive element in a society because it enriches a nation and increases the ways in which its citizens can perceive and solve personal and public problems. Ethnic, cultural, and language diversity also enriches a society because it provides individuals with more opportunities to experience other cultures and thus to become more fulfilled as human beings. When individuals are able to participate in a variety of ethnic cultures, they are more able to benefit from the total human experience.

Individuals who know, participate in, and see the world from only their unique cultural and ethnic perspectives are denied important parts of the human experience and are culturally and ethnically encapsulated. Fred M. Hechinger, in the foreword to *The Shortchanged Children of Suburbia* (Miel, with Kiester, 1967), tells an anecdote about an economically and culturally encapsulated child:

> The story is told about a little girl in a school near Hollywood who was asked to write a composition about a poor family. The essay began: "This family was very poor. The Mommy was poor. The Daddy was poor. The brothers and sisters were poor. The maid was poor. The nurse was poor. The butler was poor. The cook was poor. And the chauffeur was poor." (p. 5)

Culturally and ethnically encapsulated individuals are also unable to know fully and to see their own cultures because of their cultural and ethnic blinders.

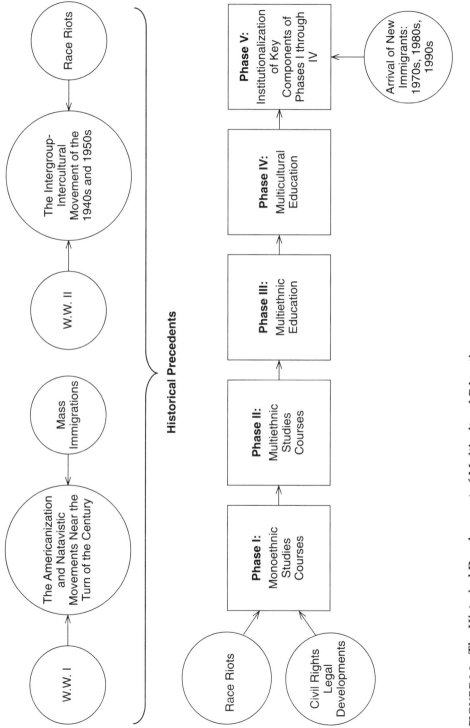

Historical Precedents

FIGURE 3.2 The Historical Development of Multicultural Education
This figure illustrates the societal and historical forces that resulted in the development of the reforms related to multicultural education.

We can get a full view of our own cultures and behaviors only by viewing them from the perspectives of other racial and ethnic cultures. Just as a fish is unable to appreciate the uniqueness of his aquatic environment, so are many mainstream students unable to see and fully appreciate the uniqueness of their cultural characteristics (Howard, 1999). A key goal of multicultural education is to help individuals gain greater self-understanding by viewing themselves from the perspectives of other cultures.

Multicultural education attempts to acquaint each ethnic and cultural group with the unique cultures of other ethnic groups. It also tries to help ethnic group members see that other ethnic cultures are just as meaningful and valid as their own. Multicultural education assumes that with acquaintance and understanding, respect might follow.

Another major goal of multicultural education is to provide students with cultural and ethnic alternatives. Both the Anglo-American student and the Filipino American student should be provided with cultural and ethnic options in the school. Historically, the U.S. school curriculum has focused primarily on the culture of Anglo Americans. The school was, and often is, primarily an extension of the Anglo-American student's home and community culture and often did not present students with cultural, ethnic, and language alternatives.

The Anglocentric curriculum, which still exists to varying degrees in most U.S. schools, has harmful consequences for both Anglo-American students and students of color, such as African Americans and Mexican Americans. By teaching Anglo-American students only about their own culture, the school is denying them the richness of the music, literature, values, life-styles, and perspectives that exist among such ethnic groups as African Americans, Puerto Ricans in the United States, and Asian Americans. Anglo-American students should know that African American literature is uniquely enriching, and that groups such as Native Americans and Mexican Americans have values that they may freely embrace. Many of the behaviors and values within these ethnic groups may help White mainstream students to enrich their personal and public lives.

The Anglocentric curriculum negatively affects the student of color because he or she may find the school culture alien, hostile, and self-defeating. Most ethnic minority communities are characterized by some values, institutions, behavior patterns, and linguistic traits that differ in significant ways from those within the dominant society and in the schools (Heath, 1983; Ladson-Billings, 1994; Philips, 1983). Because of the negative ways in which ethnic students and their cultures are often viewed by educators, many of these students do not attain the skills they need to function successfully within the wider society (Heath, 1983; Shade, Kelly, & Oberg, 1997).

One major goal of multicultural education is to provide all students with the skills, attitudes, and knowledge they need to function within their community culture and the mainstream culture, as well as within and across other ethnic cultures (Banks, 1997). The Anglo-American student should be familiar with Black English; the African American student should be able to speak and write standard English and to function successfully within mainstream U.S. institutions.

Another major goal of multicultural education is to reduce the pain and discrimination the members of some ethnic and racial groups experience in the schools and in the wider society because of their unique racial, physical, and cultural characteristics. Groups such as Filipino Americans, Mexican Americans, Asians in the United Kingdom, and Chinese Canadians often deny their ethnic identity, ethnic heritage, and family in order to assimilate and participate more fully in the social, economic, and political institutions of their societies (Rodriguez, 1982). Individuals who are Polish Canadians, Jewish Americans, and Italian Australians also frequently reject parts of their ethnic cultures when trying to succeed in school and in society. Schools often force members of these groups to experience "self-alienation" in order to succeed. This is a high price to pay for educational, social, and economic mobility.

When individuals are forced to reject parts of their ethnic cultures in order to experience success, problems are created for both individuals and society. Ethnic peoples of color, such as African Americans and Chinese Canadians, experience special problems because no matter how hard they try to become like Anglos most of them cannot totally succeed because of their skin color.

Some African Americans become very Anglo-Saxon in speech, ways of viewing the world, and in their values and behavior. These individuals become so Anglicized that we might call them "Afro-Saxons." However, such individuals may still be denied jobs or the opportunities to buy homes in all-White neighborhoods because of their skin color (Feagin & Sikes, 1994). They may also become alienated from their own ethnic communities and families in their attempts to act and be like White mainstream Americans. These individuals may thus become alienated from both their ethnic cultures and the mainstream Anglo culture. Social scientists call such individuals *marginal* persons.

Individuals who belong to such groups as Jewish Americans and Italian Australians may also experience marginality when they attempt to deny their ethnic heritages and to become Anglo-Americans or Anglo-Australians. Although they can usually succeed in looking and acting like Anglos, they are likely to experience a great deal of psychological stress and identity conflict when they deny and reject family and their ethnic languages, symbols, behaviors, and beliefs (Dershowitz, 1997). Ethnicity plays a cogent role in the socialization of ethnic group members; ethnic characteristics are a part of the basic identity of many individuals. When such individuals deny their ethnic cultures, they are rejecting an important part of self (Crocker, Major, & Steele, 1998).

Marginal ethnic group members are likely to be alienated citizens who feel that they do not have a stake in society (Banks, 1997). Individuals who deny and/or reject their basic group identity, for whatever reasons, are not capable of becoming fully functioning and self-actualized persons. Such individuals are more likely than other people to experience political and social alienation. It is in the best interest of a political democracy to protect the rights of all citizens to maintain allegiances to their ethnic groups and cultural communities (Flores & Benmayor, 1997; Kymlicka, 1995). Research has demonstrated that individuals are quite capable of maintaining allegiance to both their ethnic group and the nation-state

(Apter, 1977). Social science research also indicates that individuals have a need for basic group identities, even in highly modernized societies (Isaacs, 1975).

Another important goal of multicultural education is to help students master essential literacy, numeracy, thinking, and perspective-taking skills. Multicultural education assumes that multicultural content can help students master important skills in these areas. Multicultural readings and data, if taught effectively, can be highly motivating and meaningful.

Research indicates that students are more likely to master skills when the teacher uses content that deals with significant human problems and issues that relate directly to their lived experiences, identities, hopes, dreams, and struggles (Lee, 1993). Students are also more likely to master skills when they study content and problems related to the world in which they live. Students in most Western nations live in societies in which ethnic problems are real and salient. Many students live within communities in which racial and ethnic tension are salient and are important parts of their lives.

Content related to ethnicity in Western societies and to the ethnic communities in which many students live is significant and meaningful to students, especially to those who live and go to school within racially segregated communities. Research indicates that racial and ethnic segregation is increasing within U.S. schools (Orfield, Eaton et al., 1996). Social-class segregation is also increasing within the wider society. Social class and race are frequently highly interrelated in U.S. society.

Cross-Cultural Competency

A key goal of multicultural education is to help students develop cross-cultural competency. However, those of us working in multicultural education have not clarified, in any adequate way, the minimal level of cross-cultural competency we consider appropriate and/or satisfactory for teacher education students or for elementary and high school students. Nor have we developed valid and reliable ways to assess levels of cross-cultural competency. I think we know what questions to raise about cross-cultural functioning. However, we need to devote considerable time and intellectual energy to answering these questions.

Is the Anglo-American student, for example, who eats a weekly meal at an authentic Mexican American restaurant and who has no other cross-ethnic contacts during the week functioning cross-culturally? Most of us would probably agree that the act of eating at an ethnic restaurant, in and of itself, is not an instance of meaningful cross-cultural behavior. However, if the Anglo-American student, while eating at the Mexican American restaurant, understands and shares the ethnic symbols in the restaurant, speaks Spanish while in the restaurant, and communicates and interacts positively and comfortably with individuals within the restaurant who are culturally Mexican American, then he or she would be functioning cross-culturally at a meaningful level.

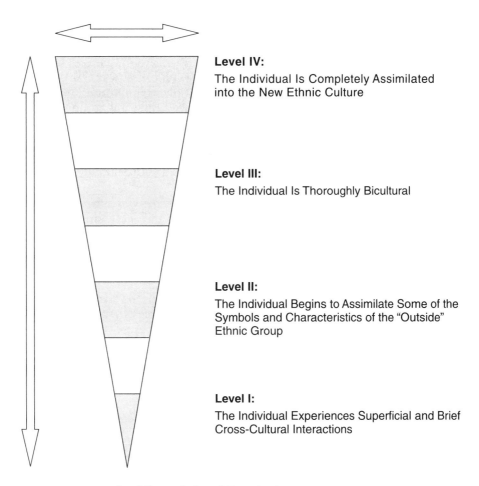

FIGURE 3.3   Levels of Cross-Cultural Functioning
This figure presents a conceptualization of levels of cross-cultural competency.
Cross-cultural functioning can range from Level I (brief and superficial contacts with
another ethnic culture) to Level IV (in which the individual totally culturally
assimilates into a new ethnic culture and consequently becomes alienated from his
or her own ethnic culture).

Levels of Cross-Cultural Functioning

I have developed a typology that conceptualizes levels of cross-cultural functioning. Educators need to determine which of these levels are desirable and practical
for most students to attain. The typology is presented in Figure 3.3.

Level I of cross-cultural functioning consists primarily of superficial and
brief cross-cultural encounters, such as eating occasionally at a Chinese American

restaurant or speaking to the Jewish neighbor who lives across the street when you meet her in the street. Level II of cross-cultural functioning occurs when the individual begins to have more meaningful cross-cultural contacts and communications with members of other ethnic and cultural groups. He or she begins to assimilate some of the symbols, linguistic traits, communication styles, values, and attitudes that are normative within the outside cultural group.

Level III of cross-cultural functioning occurs when the individual is thoroughly bicultural and is as comfortable within the adopted culture as he or she is within his or her primordial or first culture. Each of the two cultures is equally meaningful to the bicultural individual. The bicultural individual is bilingual and is adept at cultural-switching behavior.

Level IV of cross-cultural functioning occurs when the culturally oriented individual has been almost completely resocialized and assimilated into the foreign or host culture. This process occurs, for example, when the African American individual becomes so highly culturally assimilated (in terms of behavior, attitudes, and perceptions) into the Anglo-American culture that he or she is for all sociological purposes an Afro-Saxon.

Most multicultural education theorists do not see Level I or Level IV of cross-cultural functioning as desirable goals of multicultural education. Most would probably opt for Level II or Level III or for some point between these two levels. I should quickly point out that this typology of levels is an ideal-type conceptualization and that continua exist both between and within the levels.

Multicultural Education: Nature and Promises

Multicultural education reaches far beyond ethnic studies or the social studies. It is concerned with modifying the total educational environment so that it better reflects the ethnic and cultural diversity within a society. This modification includes not only studying ethnic cultures and experiences but also making institutional changes within the school so that students from diverse ethnic groups have equal educational opportunities and the school promotes and encourages ethnic, cultural, and language diversity.

Multicultural education also seeks to create and perpetuate a unified nation-state and culture. While respecting and recognizing diversity, it seeks to create a nation-state in which the values of diverse groups and cultures are reflected. Multicultural education seeks to actualize the idea of *e pluribus unum,* that is, to create a society of diverse people united within a framework of overarching democratic values. The best way to create a unified nation-state in which all groups have strong national identities and allegiances is to structurally include them into the nation-state and the society.

Multicultural education is designed for all students, of all races, ethnic groups, and social classes, and not just for schools that have racially and ethnically mixed populations. A major assumption theorists make is that multicultural education is needed as much if not more by students who are middle-class members of the dominant, mainstream group as it is by marginalized students of color.

Because multicultural education is a very broad concept that implies total school reform, educators who want their schools to become multicultural must examine their total school environment to determine the extent to which it is mono-ethnic and promotes dominant group hegemony. These educators then must take appropriate steps to create and sustain a multicultural educational environment. The ethnic and racial composition of the school staff, its attitudes, the formalized and hidden curricula, the teaching strategies and materials, the testing and counseling programs, and the school's norms are some of the factors that must reflect ethnic diversity within the multicultural school. Figure 3.4 illustrates these and other variables of the school environment that must be reformed in order to make the school multicultural.

The reform must be systemwide or systemic to be effective. Multicultural education is consistent with the notion of *systems thinking* discussed by Senge (1990). To

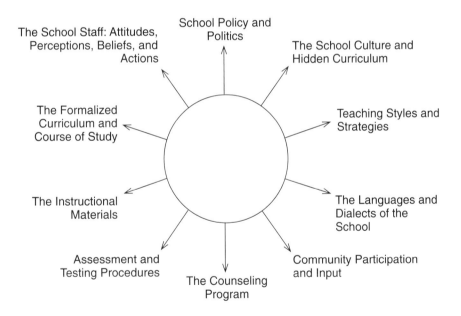

FIGURE 3.4 The Total School Environment
In this figure, the total school environment is conceptualized as a system that consists of a number of major identifiable variables and factors, such as the school culture, school policy and politics, and the formalized curriculum and course of study. In the idealized multicultural school, each variable reflects ethnic pluralism. Even though any one factor may be the focus of initial school reform, changes must take place in each factor in order to create and sustain an effective multicultural educational environment.

implement multicultural education effectively, the school, college, or university must be conceptualized as a system with highly interrelated components and elements. Each part interacts with and affects the others. Consequently, a change in any one element in the system affects all of the other elements.

Any one of the factors in Figure 3.4 may be the initial focus for school reform, but changes must take place in all of the major school variables in order for multicultural education to be successfully implemented. We learned from the ethnic studies movement of the 1960s that few substantial changes take place when you simply give teachers multicultural materials but do not provide educational opportunities that enable them to acquire new conceptual frameworks for viewing Western society and culture.

The unit of change must be the total school environment rather than any one element, such as materials, teaching strategies, the testing program, or teacher training. Teacher education and empowerment are essential, but other changes must take place in the school environment in order to reform the school. Many teachers attain new insights, materials, and multicultural teaching strategies during summer workshops. They are eager to try them in their schools. However, these teachers often become very discouraged when they return to their schools, where traditional norms toward ethnic and cultural diversity often exist and where they frequently receive no institutional support from their administrators or peers. Without such support, teachers with new skills and insights give up and revert to their old behaviors and attitudes.

Linking Multicultural and Global Education: Promises

The curriculum should help students develop the knowledge, attitudes, and skills needed to function within various cultures in their own society. However, because we live in a highly interdependent world society, the school should also help students develop the attitudes and competencies needed to function within cultures outside of their nation-state. Because of their interrelationships and shared goals, educators should try to relate multicultural and global education more effectively.

A linkage would help reduce curriculum fragmentation and contribute to important student learning in cultural studies (Diaz, Massialas, & Xanthopoulos, 1999). If students develop the ability to view events and situations from the perspectives of ethnic groups in their nation-state, they will be better able to view events within other nations from the perspectives of the major participants in these events. Students who are able to relate positively to and function within a variety of cultures within their own nation are also more likely to function successfully in foreign cultures than are individuals who view domestic ethnic cultures as exotic and strange. We can reduce nonreflective nationalism and ethnocentrism in students by helping them become more multiculturally literate and competent citizens in their nation-state.

Linking Multicultural and Global Education: Problems

We should attempt to link and relate multicultural and global education even though each reform movement has unique characteristics that should be respected and maintained in any linkage efforts. *We should not assume that multicultural education and global education are identical.* This assumption creates problems and intensifies existing ones. Some educators confuse studying about the countries of origin of ethnic groups with the study of these groups in their nation-states. They assume, for example, that when they are teaching about Mexico they are teaching about Mexican Americans.

Other teachers ignore domestic ethnic groups and teach only about their original homelands. Some U.S. teachers are more comfortable teaching about Mexicans who live in Mexico or about Africans than they are teaching about Mexican Americans or African Americans who live in their own communities. They will therefore teach about Mexico and Africa but will rarely teach content related to Mexican Americans and African Americans. Teaching about distant lands is apparently less threatening to some teachers than is teaching about ethnic cultures, problems, and conflicts within their own community. Special ways to solve this problem should be discussed in any attempts to link multicultural and global education.

Even though multicultural and global education should be joined and related, each reform movement has unique contributions to make to educating students to be effective citizens in a pluralistic democratic society. These unique qualities should be maintained and recognized in any linkage attempts. Ethnic minority cultures within a nation should not be confused with national cultures in other nations.

Linking Multicultural and Global Education by Helping Students Develop Interrelated Identifications

Despite some problems that may emerge, linking multicultural and global education can result in important learning outcomes if proper precautions are taken. Multicultural and global education are related because of the similarity in the skills, attitudes, and behaviors that both reform movements are trying to help students develop. Both multicultural and global education have as major goals helping students develop *cross-cultural competency* (the knowledge, attitudes, and skills needed to function in diverse cultural settings) and helping students develop the ability to view events, situations, and problems from the perspectives of different ethnic and nationality groups.

Multicultural and global education are related in still another important way: students can develop clarified and reflective global identifications only after they have developed clarified and reflective *ethnic* and *national* identifications. The next section of this chapter discusses the need for the school curriculum to help students develop three interrelated identifications: *ethnic, national, and global.*

Ethnic, National, and Global Identifications

Identification is "a social-psychological process involving the assimilation and internalization of the values, standards, expectations, or social roles of another person or persons…into one's behavior and self-conception" (Theodorson & Theodorson, 1969, pp. 194–195). When an individual develops an identification with a particular group, he or she "internalizes the interests, standards, and role expectations of the group" (Theodorson & Theodorson, 1969, p. 195). Identification is an evolving, dynamic, complex, and ongoing process and not a static or unidimensional conceptualization. All individuals belong to many different groups and consequently develop multiple group identifications. Students have a gender identification, a family identification, a racial identification, as well as identifications with many other formal and informal groups.

A major assumption of this chapter is that all students come to school with ethnic identifications, whether the identifications are conscious or unconscious. Many Anglo-American students are consciously aware of their national identifications as Americans, but they are not consciously aware that they have internalized the values, standards, norms, and behaviors of the Anglo-American ethnic group (Alba, 1990). Students who are African Americans, Jewish Americans, Mexican Americans, and Italian Americans are usually consciously aware of both their ethnic and national identifications. However, many students from all ethnic groups come to school with confused, unexamined, and nonreflective ethnic and national identifications and with almost no global identification or consciousness.

Identity is a concept that relates to all that we are. Societal quests for single, narrow definitions of nationalism have prevented many students from getting in touch with that dimension of their identity that relates to ethnicity. Ethnic identification for many students is a very important part of their personal identity. The individual who has a confused, nonreflective, or negative ethnic identification lacks one of the essential ingredients for a healthy and positive personal identity.

The school should help students develop three kinds of highly interrelated identifications that are of special concern to multicultural educators: an *ethnic*, a *national*, and a *global* identification. These identifications should be *clarified, reflective,* and *positive.* Individuals who have *clarified* and *reflective* ethnic, national, and global identifications understand how these identifications developed; they also are able to examine their ethnic group, nation, and world thoughtfully and objectively and to understand both the personal and public implications of these identifications.

Individuals who have *positive* ethnic, national, and global identifications evaluate their ethnic, national, and global communities highly and are proud of these identifications. They have both the desire and competencies needed to take actions that will support and reinforce the values and norms of their ethnic, national, and global communities. Consequently, the school should not only be concerned about helping students develop reflective ethnic, national, and global identifications, but it should also help them acquire the cross-cultural competencies (which consist of knowledge, attitudes, and skills) needed to function effectively within their ethnic, national, and world communities.

Ethnic Identification

The school within a pluralistic democratic nation should help ethnic students develop clarified, reflective, and positive ethnic identifications. This does not mean that the school should encourage or force ethnic minority students who have identifications with the mainstream ethnic group or who have identifications with several ethnic groups to give up these identifications. However, it does mean that the school will help all students develop an understanding of their ethnic group identifications, objectively examine their ethnic groups, better understand the relationship between their ethnic groups and other ethnic groups, and learn the personal and public implications of their ethnic group identifications and attachments.

A positive and clarified ethnic identification is of primary importance to students in their first years of life. However, rather than help students develop positive and reflective ethnic identifications, historically the school and other social institutions have taught ethnic minority students to be ashamed of their ethnic affiliations and characteristics (Greenbaum, 1974). Social and public institutions have forced many individuals who are Polish American, Italian Australian, and Jewish Canadian to experience self-alienation and desocialization and to reject family heritages, cultures, and languages. Many members of these ethnic groups have denied important aspects of their ethnic cultures and have changed their names in order to attain full participation within their society. Many ethnic individuals consciously denied their family heritages and languages in order to attain social, economic, and educational mobility. However, within a pluralistic democratic society individuals should not have to give up all of their meaningful ethnic traits and attachments in order to attain structural inclusion into society. In democratic, pluralistic nation-states, individuals should be free to publicly affirm their ethnic, cultural, and gender identities (Flores & Benmayor, 1997).

National Identification

The school should also help each student acquire a clarified, reflective, and positive national identification and related cross-cultural competencies. Each student should develop a commitment to national democratic ideals, such as human dignity, justice, and equality (Banks, 1997). The school should also help students acquire the attitudes, beliefs, and skills they need to become effective participants in the nation-state and the civic culture. Thus, the development of social participation skills and activities should be major goals of the school curriculum within a democratic pluralistic nation. Students should be provided opportunities for social participation activities whereby they can take action on issues and problems that are consistent with democratic values. Citizenship education and social participation activities are integral parts of a sound school curriculum (Banks & Banks, with Clegg, 1999).

National identification and related citizenship competencies are important for all citizens, regardless of their ethnic group membership and ethnic affiliations. National identification should be acknowledged and promoted in all educational programs related to ethnicity and education. However, individuals can have a wide range of cultural and linguistic traits and characteristics and still be reflective and effective citizens of their nation-states (Flores & Benmayor, 1997; Kymlicka, 1995).

Individuals can have ethnic allegiances and characteristics and yet endorse overarching and shared national values and ideals as long as their ethnic values and behaviors do not violate or contradict democratic values and ideals. *Educational programs should recognize and reflect the multiple identifications students are developing.* I believe students can develop a reflective and positive national identification only after they have attained reflective, clarified, and positive ethnic identifications. This is as true for Anglo-American students as it is for Jewish American, African American, or Italian American students. Often, mainstream individuals do not view themselves as an ethnic group. However, sociologically they have many of the same traits and characteristics of other ethnic groups, such as a sense of peoplehood, unique behavioral values and norms, and unique ways of perceiving the world (Alba, 1990; Gordon, 1964).

Mainstream students who believe that their ethnic group is superior to other ethnic groups and who have highly ethnocentric and racist attitudes do not have clarified, reflective, and positive ethnic identifications (Howard, 1999). Their ethnic identifications are based on the negative characteristics of other ethnic groups and have not been reflectively and objectively examined. Many mainstream and other ethnic individuals have ethnic identifications that are nonreflective and unclarified. It is not possible for students with unreflective and totally subjective ethnic identifications to develop positive and reflective national identifications because ethnic ethnocentrism is inconsistent with such democratic values as human dignity, freedom, equality, and justice.

Ethnic group individuals who have historically been victims of discrimination must develop positive and reflective ethnic identifications before they will be able to develop clarified national identifications. It is difficult for Polish American or Jewish Australian students to support the rights of other ethnic groups or the ideals of the nation-state when they are ashamed of their own ethnicity or feel their ethnic group is denied basic civil rights and opportunities.

Global Identification

It is essential that we help students to develop clarified, reflective, and positive ethnic and national identifications. However, because we live in a global society in which the solutions to the world's problems require the cooperation of all the nations of the world, it is also important for students to develop global identifications and the knowledge, attitudes, and skills needed to become effective and influential citizens in the world community (Anderson, 1990; Diaz, Massialas, & Xanthopoulos, 1999). Most students have rather conscious identifications with their communities and nation-states, but they often are only vaguely aware of their status as world citizens. Most students do not have a comprehensive understanding of the full implications of their world citizenship.

There are many complex reasons that most students often have little awareness or understanding of their status as world citizens and rarely think of themselves as citizens of the world (Banks, 1997). This lack of awareness results partly from the fact that most nation-states focus on helping students to develop nationalism rather than to understand their role as citizens of the world. The teaching of nationalism often results in students' learning misconceptions, stereotypes, and myths about other nations and acquiring negative and confused attitudes toward them.

Students also have limited awareness of their roles as world citizens because of the nature of the world community itself. The institutions that attempt to formulate policies for the international community or for groups of nations—such as the United Nations, the Organization of African Unity, and the Organization of American States—are usually weak because of their inability to enforce their policies and recommendations, because of the strong nationalism manifested by their members, and because the international community does not have an effectively mobilized and politically efficacious constituency. Strong nationalism makes most international bodies weak and largely symbolic.

Students find it difficult to view themselves as members of an international community not only because such a community lacks effective governmental bodies, but also because very few heroes or heroines, myths, symbols, and school rituals are designed to help students develop an attachment to and identification with the global community. It is difficult for students to develop identifications with a community that does not have heroes, heroines, and rituals in which they can participate and benefits that can be identified, seen, and touched. We thus must identify and/or create international heroes, heroines, and school rituals to help students develop global attachments and identifications.

When educators attempt to help students develop more sophisticated international understanding and identification, they often experience complex problems. It is difficult to gain public support for programs in international education because many parents view global education as an attempt to weaken national loyalty and undercut nationalism. Many teachers are likely to view global education as an add-on to an already crowded curriculum and thus to assign it a low priority. Some teachers, like many of their students, have misconceptions about and negative attitudes toward other nations that they are likely to perpetuate in the classroom.

Goals for Global Education

When formulating goals and teaching strategies for global education, educators should be aware of the societal and instructional constraints. However, they should realize that it is vitally important for students to develop a sophisticated understanding of their roles in the world community (Anderson, 1990). Students should also understand how life in their communities influences other nations and the cogent influences that international events have on their daily lives. Global education should have as major goals helping students develop an understanding of the interdependence among nations in the modern world, clarified attitudes toward other nations, and a reflective identification with the world community.

The Need for a Delicate Balance of Identifications

Strong nationalism that is nonreflective will prevent students from developing reflective and positive global identifications. Nonreflective and unexamined ethnic identifications and attachments may prevent the development of a cohesive nation and a unified national ideology. Thus, while we should help students to develop reflective and positive ethnic identifications, we must also help them to clarify and strengthen their national identifications—which means that they will develop and internalize such democratic values as justice, human dignity, and equality.

Students need to develop a delicate balance of ethnic, national, and global identifications and attachments. In the past, however, educators have often tried to develop strong national identifications by repressing ethnicity and making ethnic students ashamed of their ethnic roots and families. Schools taught ethnic youths shame, as William Greenbaum (1974) has compassionately written. This is an unhealthy and dysfunctional approach to building national solidarity and reflective nationalism and to shaping a nation in which all of its citizens endorse its overarching values such as democracy and human dignity and yet maintain a sense of ethnic pride and identification.

I hypothesize that ethnic, national, and global identifications are developmental in nature and that an individual can attain a healthy and reflective national identification only when he or she has acquired a healthy and reflective ethnic identification; and that individuals can develop a reflective and positive global identification only after they have a realistic, reflective, and positive national identification (see Figure 3.5).

Individuals can develop a commitment to and an identification with a nation-state and the national culture only when they believe that they are a meaningful and important part of that nation and that it acknowledges, reflects, and values their culture and them as individuals. A nation that alienates and does not meaningfully and structurally include an ethnic group into the national culture runs the risk of creating alienation within that ethnic group and of fostering separatism and separatist movements and ideologies. Students will find it very difficult if not impossible to develop reflective global identifications within a nation-state that perpetuates a nonreflective and blind nationalism.

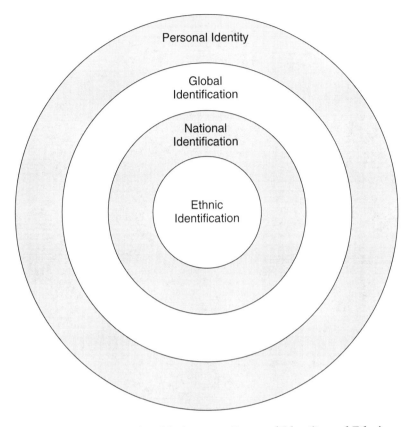

FIGURE 3.5   The Relationship between Personal Identity and Ethnic, National, and Global Identifications
Personal identity is the "I" that results from the lifelong binding together of the many threads of a person's life. These threads include experience, culture, and heredity, as well as identifications with significant others and many different groups, such as one's ethnic group, one's nation, and the global community.

The Stages of Cultural Identity: A Typology

A typology of the stages of cultural identity (which includes ethnic identity) that describes the developmental nature of cultural, national, and global identifications and clarification is presented in Chapter 7. This typology assumes that individuals can be classified according to their cultural identities. This typology, as summarized in Figure 3.6, illustrates the hypothesis that students must have clarified and positive cultural and ethnic identifications (Stage 3) before they can attain clarified and reflective national and global identifications (Stages 5 and 6).

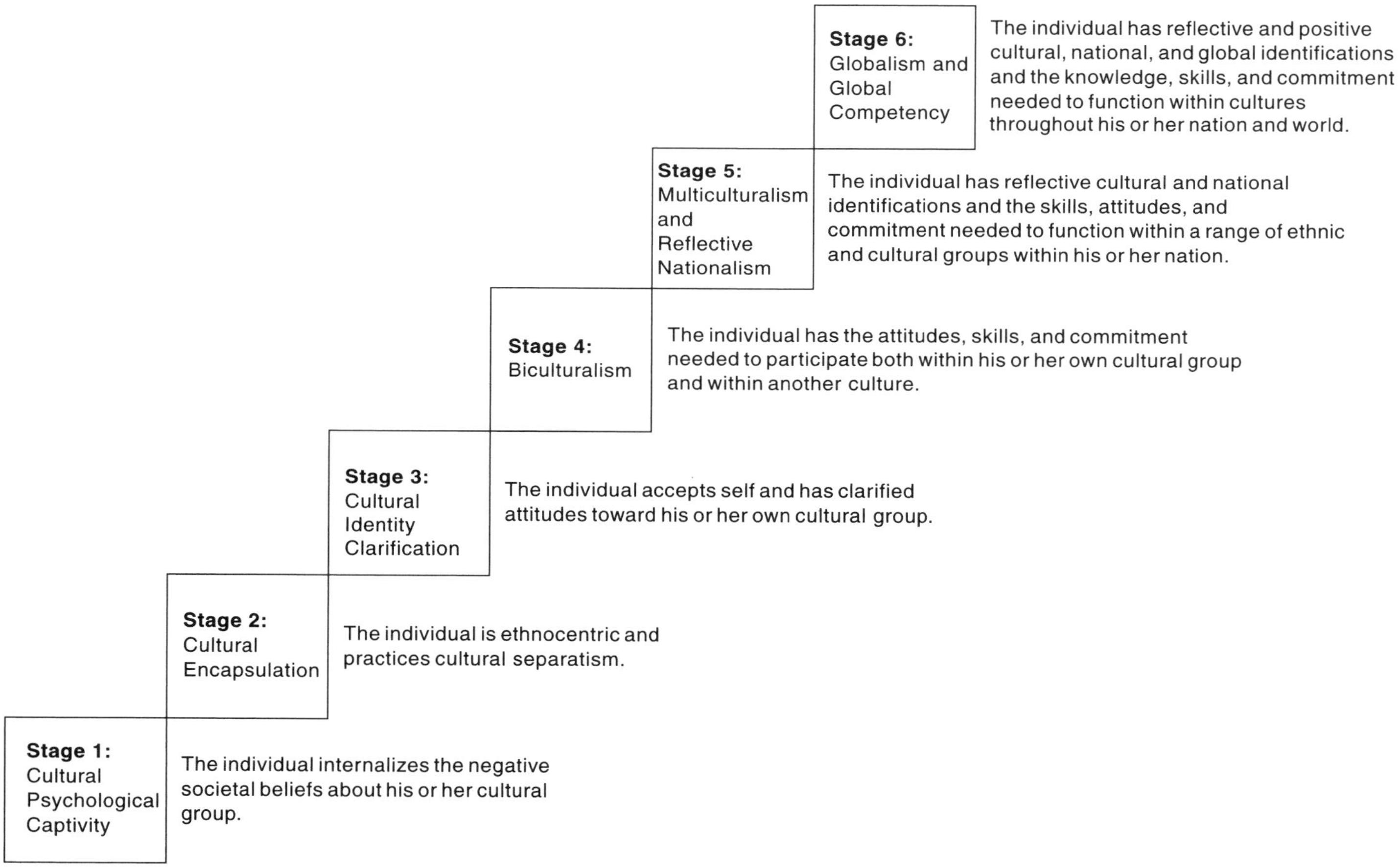

Stage 6:
Globalism and
Global
Competency

The individual has reflective and positive cultural, national, and global identifications and the knowledge, skills, and commitment needed to function within cultures throughout his or her nation and world.

Stage 5:
Multiculturalism
and
Reflective
Nationalism

The individual has reflective cultural and national identifications and the skills, attitudes, and commitment needed to function within a range of ethnic and cultural groups within his or her nation.

Stage 4:
Biculturalism

The individual has the attitudes, skills, and commitment needed to participate both within his or her own cultural group and within another culture.

Stage 3:
Cultural
Identity
Clarification

The individual accepts self and has clarified attitudes toward his or her own cultural group.

Stage 2:
Cultural
Encapsulation

The individual is ethnocentric and practices cultural separatism.

Stage 1:
Cultural
Psychological
Captivity

The individual internalizes the negative societal beliefs about his or her cultural group.

FIGURE 3.6   The Stages of Cultural Identity: A Typology
This figure illustrates the author's hypothesis that students must have clarified and positive cultural identifications (Stage 3) before they can attain reflective and positive national and global identifications (Stages 5 and 6).

Approaches to Multicultural Curriculum Reform

The school curriculum must be reformed in order to help students to develop clarified ethnic, national, and global identifications. Four approaches to the integration of ethnic content into the curriculum, which are described below, have evolved since the 1960s. The higher-level approaches, such as the Transformation Approach and the Decision-Making Approach, can best help students to develop the identifications needed to function effectively in pluralistic democratic societies.

The Contributions Approach

The Contributions Approach to integration is one of the most frequently used and is often used extensively during the first phase of an ethnic revival movement. This approach is characterized by the addition into the curriculum of ethnic heroes who are selected using criteria similar to those used to select mainstream heroes for inclusion into the curriculum. The mainstream curriculum remains unchanged in terms of its basic structure, goals, and salient characteristics.

The Heroes and Holidays Approach is a variant of the Contributions Approach. In this approach, ethnic content is limited primarily to special days, weeks, and months related to ethnic events and celebrations. Cinco de Mayo, Martin Luther King's Birthday, and African American History Week are examples of ethnic days and weeks that are celebrated in the schools. During these celebrations, teachers involve students in lessons, experiences, and pageants related to the ethnic groups being commemorated. When this approach is used, the class studies little or nothing about the ethnic groups before or after the special event or occasion.

The Contributions Approach is the easiest approach for teachers to use to integrate the curriculum with ethnic content. However, it has several serious limitations. Students do not attain a global view of the role of ethnic and cultural groups in U.S. society. Rather, they see ethnic issues and events primarily as an addition to the curriculum, and consequently as an appendage to the main story of the development of the nation and to the core curriculum in the language arts, the social studies, the arts, and to other subject areas. The teaching of ethnic issues with the use of heroes, holidays, and contributions also tends to gloss over important concepts and issues related to the victimization and oppression of ethnic groups and their struggles against racism and for power. Issues such as racism, poverty, and oppression tend to be evaded in the Contributions Approach to curriculum integration. The focus, rather, tends to be on success and the validation of the Horatio Alger myth that every American who is willing to work hard can go from rags to riches and pull himself or herself up by the bootstrap.

The Contributions Approach often results in the trivialization of ethnic cultures, the study of their strange and exotic characteristics, and the reinforcement of stereotypes and misconceptions. When the focus is on the contributions and unique aspects of ethnic cultures, students are not helped to understand them as complete and dynamic wholes.

The Ethnic Additive Approach

Another important approach to the integration of ethnic content to the curriculum is the addition of content, concepts, themes, and perspectives to the curriculum without changing its basic structure, purposes, and characteristics. The Additive Approach is often accomplished by the addition of a book, a unit, or a course to the curriculum without changing it substantially.

The Additive Approach allows the teacher to put ethnic content into the curriculum without restructuring it, which takes substantial time, effort, training, and rethinking of the curriculum and its purposes, nature, and goals. The Additive Approach can be the first phase in a more radical curriculum reform effort designed to restructure the total curriculum and to integrate it with ethnic content, perspectives, and frames of reference. However, this approach shares several disadvantages with the Contributions Approach. Its most important shortcoming is that it usually results in the viewing of ethnic content from the perspectives of mainstream historians, writers, artists, and scientists because it does not involve a restructuring of the curriculum. The events, concepts, issues, and problems selected for study are selected using Mainstream-Centric and Eurocentric criteria and perspectives. When teaching a unit such as *The Westward Movement* in a fifth-grade U.S. history class, the teacher may integrate her unit by adding content about the Lakota (Sioux) Indians. However, the unit remains mainstream centric and focused because of its perspective and point of view. A unit called *The Westward Movement* is mainstream and Eurocentric because it focuses on the movement of European Americans from the eastern to the western part of the United States. The Lakota Indians were already in the West and consequently were not moving West. The unit might be called *The Invasion from the East* from the point of view of the Lakota. An objective title for the unit might be *Two Cultures Meet in the Americas.*

The Additive Approach also fails to help students to view society from diverse cultural and ethnic perspectives and to understand the ways in which the histories and cultures of the nation's diverse ethnic, racial, cultural, and religious groups are inextricably bound.

The Transformation Approach

The Transformation Approach differs fundamentally from the Contributions and Additive Approaches. This approach changes the basic assumptions of the curriculum and enables students to view concepts, issues, themes, and problems from several ethnic perspectives and points of view. The key curriculum issue involved in the Transformation Approach is not the addition of a long list of ethnic groups, heroes, and contributions, but the infusion of various perspectives, frames of reference, and content from various groups that will extend students' understandings of the nature, development, and complexity of U.S. society. When students are studying the Revolution in the British colonies, the perspectives of the Anglo Revolutionaries, the Anglo Loyalists, African Americans, Indians, and the British are essential for them to attain a thorough understanding of this significant event in U.S. history. Students must study the various and sometimes divergent meanings of the Revolution to these diverse groups to fully understand it.

When studying U.S. history, language, music, arts, science, and mathematics, the emphasis should not be on the ways in which various ethnic and cultural groups have contributed to mainstream U.S. society and culture. The emphasis, rather, should be on how the common U.S. culture and society emerged from a complex synthesis and interaction of the diverse cultural elements that originated within the various cultural, racial, ethnic, and religious groups that make up U.S. society. One irony of conquest is that those who are conquered often deeply influence the cultures of the conquerors.

The Decision-Making and Social Action Approach

This approach includes all of the elements of the Transformation Approach but adds components that require students to make decisions and to take actions related to the concept, issue, or problem they have studied in the unit. In this approach, students study a social problem, such as "What actions should we take to reduce prejudice and discrimination in our school?" They gather pertinent data, analyze their values and beliefs, synthesize their knowledge and values, and identify alternative courses of action, and finally decide what, if any, actions they will take to reduce prejudice and discrimination in their school. Major goals of the Decision-Making and Social Action Approach are to teach students thinking and decision-making skills, to empower them, and to help them acquire a sense of political efficacy.

Mixing and Blending the Approaches

The four approaches to the integration of ethnic and cultural content into the curriculum that I have described are often mixed and blended in actual teaching situations. One approach, such as the Contributions Approach, can also be used as a vehicle to move to other and more intellectually challenging approaches, such as the Transformation and the Decision-Making and Social Action Approaches. It is not realistic to expect a teacher to move directly from a highly mainstream-centric curriculum to one that focuses on decision-making and social action. Rather, the move from the first to the higher levels of ethnic content integration into the curriculum is likely to be gradual and cumulative (see Figure 3.7).

Multicultural Education and Educational Reform

Changing the school so that it reflects the ethnic diversity within a society provides a tremendous opportunity to implement the substantial curriculum reforms that are essential, such as conceptual teaching, interdisciplinary approaches to the study of social issues, value inquiry, and providing students with opportunities to become involved in social action and social participation activities. Thus, multicultural education can serve as a vehicle for general and significant educational reform. This is probably its greatest promise. We can best view multicultural education as a process

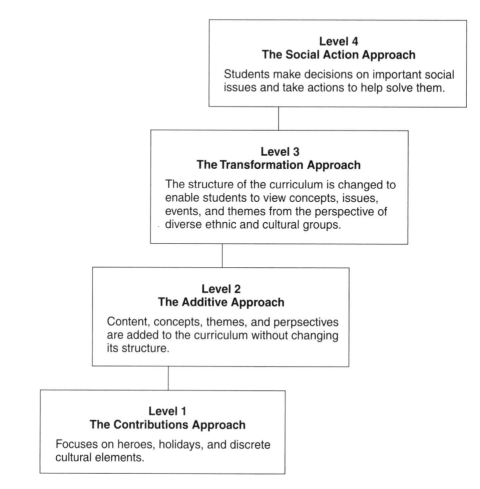

FIGURE 3.7   Banks's Approaches to Multicultural Curriculum Reform

as well as a reform movement that will result in a new type of schooling that will present novel views of the human experience and will help students to acquire the knowledge, skills, and commitments needed to make their societies and the world more responsive to the human condition.

Summary

Multicultural education has had an evolutionary development in the United States and in the other major Western nations, such as the United Kingdom, Canada, Australia, France, and Sweden (Allan & Hill, 1995; Banks & Banks, 1995;

Moodley, 1995). The development of multicultural education since the 1960s can be conceptualized in the five phases presented in this chapter. This chapter also describes major goals for multicultural education, including (1) helping students gain a greater self-understanding by viewing their cultures from the perspectives of other ethnic groups; (2) providing students with cultural and ethnic alternatives; (3) helping students attain cross-cultural competency; (4) helping students master essential literacy, numeracy, and thinking skills; and (5) helping students to develop clarified and reflective ethnic, national, and global identifications. The curriculum must be reformed to help students to develop clarified identifications. The higher-level approaches, such as the Transformation Approach and the Decision-Making and Social Action Approach, can best help to attain these goals.

Educators should attempt to link and relate multicultural and global education because of the common goals these two educational reform movements are trying to help students attain and because of the widespread fragmentation in the school curriculum. Because both multicultural and global education have unique contributions to make to the general education of students and because they are in many ways distinct, efforts made to link multicultural and global education should maintain the uniqueness of each reform movement. Educators should also take special precautions to ensure that domestic ethnic cultures in a nation are not confused with the cultures of nations that are the original homelands of ethnic groups.

During their socialization, students develop multiple group identifications. The school should help students develop three kinds of identifications that are of special concern to multicultural educators: an *ethnic,* a *national,* and a *global* identification.

Multicultural education includes but is much more comprehensive than ethnic studies or curriculum reform related to ethnicity. Multicultural education is concerned with modifying the total school environment so that students from diverse ethnic and cultural groups will experience equal educational opportunities. Educators must reform their total educational environments in order to implement powerful multicultural education.

REFERENCES

Alba, R. D. (1990). *Ethnic Identity: The Transformation of White America.* New Haven: Yale University Press.

Allan, R., & Hill, B. (1995). Multicultural Education in Australia: Historical Development and Current Status. In J. A. Banks & C. A. M. Banks (Eds.), *Handbook of Research on Multicultural Education* (pp. 763–777). New York: Macmillan.

Anderson, L. (1990). A Rationale for Global Education. In K. A. Tye (Ed.), *Global Education: From Thought to Action* (pp. 13–34). Arlington, VA: Association for Supervision and Curriculum Development.

Apter, D. E. (1977). Political Life and Cultural Pluralism. In M. M. Tumin & W. Plotch (Eds.), *Pluralism in a Democratic Society* (pp. 58–91). New York: Praeger.

August, D., & Hakuta, K. (Eds.). (1998). *Educating Language-Minority Children.* Washington, DC: National Academy Press.

Baker, G. C. (1994). *Planning and Organizing for Multicultural Instruction* (2nd ed.). Menlo Park, CA: Addison-Wesley.

Banks, J. A. (1997). *Educating Citizens in a Multicultural Society.* New York: Teachers College Press.

Banks, J. A., & Banks, C. A. M. (Eds.). (1995). *Handbook of Research on Multicultural Education*. New York: Macmillan.

Banks, J. A., & Banks, C. A. M. (Eds.). (1997). *Multicultural Education: Issues and Perspectives* (3rd ed.). Boston: Allyn and Bacon.

Banks, J. A., & Banks, C. A. M. (with Clegg, A. A., Jr.). (1999). *Teaching Strategies for the Social Studies* (5th ed.). New York: Longman.

Crocker, J., Major, B., & Steele, C. (1998). Social Stigma. In D. T. Gilbert, S. T. Fiske, & G. Lindzey (Eds.), *The Handbook of Social Psychology* (Vol. 2, pp. 504–553). New York: McGraw-Hill.

Dershowitz, A. M. (1997). *The Vanishing American Jew*. New York: Little Brown.

Diaz, C. F., Massialas, B. G., & Xanthopoulos, J. A. (1999). *Global Perspectives for Educators*. Boston: Allyn and Bacon.

Feagin, J. R., & Sikes, M. P. (1994). *Living with Racism: The Black Middle-Class Experience*. Boston: Beacon Press.

Flores, W. V., & Benmayor, R. (Eds.). (1997). *Latino Cultural Citizenship*. Boston: Beacon Press.

Gay, G. (1995). Curriculum Theory and Multicultural Education. In J. A. Banks & C. A. M. Banks (Eds.), *Handbook of Research on Multicultural Education* (pp. 25–43). New York: Macmillan.

Gordon, M. M. (1964). *Assimilation in American Life: The Role of Race, Religion, and National Origins*. New York: Oxford University Press.

Grant, C. A. (Ed.). (1999). *Multicultural Research: A Reflective Engagement with Race, Class, Gender, and Sexual Orientation*. Philadelphia: Falmer Press.

Greenbaum, W. (1974). America in Search of a New Ideal: An Essay on the Rise of Pluralism. *Harvard Educational Review, 44*, 411–440.

Heath, S. B. (1983). *Ways with Words: Language, Life and Work in Communities and Classrooms*. New York: Cambridge University Press.

Howard, G. (1999). *We Can't Teach What We Don't Know: White Teachers, Multiracial Schools*. New York: Teachers College Press.

Isaacs, H. R. (1975). Basic Group Identity: The Idols of the Tribe. In N. Glazer & D. P. Moynihan (Eds.), *Ethnicity: Theory and Experience* (pp. 29–52). Cambridge, MA: Harvard University Press.

Kleinfeld, J. (1975). Effective Teachers of Eskimo and Indian Students. *School Review, 83*, 301–344.

Kymlicka, W. (1995). *Multicultural Citizenship: A Liberal Theory of Minority Rights*. New York: Oxford University Press.

Ladson-Billings, G. (1994). *The Dreamkeepers: Successful Teachers of African American Children*. San Francisco: Jossey-Bass.

Lee, C. D. (1993). *Signifying as a Scaffold for Literary Interpretation: The Pedagogical Implications of an African American Genre*. Urbana, IL: National Council of Teachers of English.

Miel, A., with Kiester, E., Jr. (1967). *The Shortchanged Children of Suburbia*. New York: American Jewish Committee.

Moodley, K. A. (1995). Multicultural Education in Canada: Historical Development and Current Status. In J. A. Banks & C. A. M. Banks (Eds.), *Handbook of Research on Multicultural Education* (pp. 801–820). New York: Macmillan.

National Council for the Accreditation of Teacher Education. (1999). NCATE Releases Draft Elementary Standards for Field Review. [http://www.ncate.org/specfoc/elemrel.htm].

Nieto, S. (1999). *The Light in Their Eyes: Creating Multicultural Communities*. New York: Teachers College Press.

Oakes, J. (1985). *Keeping Track: How Schools Structure Inequality*. New Haven: Yale University Press.

Orfield, G., Eaton, S. E., & Associates. (1996). *Dismantling Desegregation: The Quiet Reversal of Brown v. Board of Education*. New York: The New Press.

Ovando, C. J., & Collier, V. P. (1998). *Bilingual and ESL Classrooms: Teaching in Multicultural Contexts* (2nd ed.). New York: McGraw-Hill.

Philips, S. U. (1983). *The Invisible Culture: Communication in Classroom and Community on the Warm Spring Indian Reservation*. New York: Longman.

Rist, R. C. (1970). Student Social Class and Teacher Expectations: The Self-Fulfilling Prophecy in Ghetto Education. *Harvard Educational Review, 40*, 411–451.

Rodriguez, R. (1982). *Hunger of Memory: The Education of Richard Rodriguez*. Boston: David Godine.

Senge, P. M. (1990). *The Fifth Discipline: The Art and Practice of the Learning Organization*. New York: Doubleday/Currency.

Shade, B. J., Kelly, C., & Oberg, M. (1997). *Creating Culturally Responsive Classrooms*. Washington, DC: American Psychological Association.

Theodorson, G. A., & Theodorson, A. G. (1969). *A Modern Dictionary of Sociology*. New York: Barnes and Noble Books.

White, J. L., & Parham, N. (1990). *The Psychology of Blacks: An Afro-American Perspective* (2nd ed.). Englewood Cliffs, NJ.: Prentice-Hall.

PART TWO

Conceptual and Philosophical Issues

Part Two discusses and analyzes some of the major conceptual and philosophical issues and problems related to education and diversity. It is necessary to formulate precise and valid concepts and to formulate sound philosophical beliefs and positions before effective educational programs related to cultural and ethnic diversity can be implemented. The four chapters in Part Two are interrelated by their focus on significant conceptual and philosophical issues and their policy, curriculum, and teaching implications.

The major concepts related to ethnic and cultural diversity, such as culture, ethnic group, and multicultural education, are described in Chapter 4. The components of culture identified in this chapter are essential for understanding the complex aspects of race, ethnicity, and culture in modernized societies. Chapter 5 presents major paradigms related to culture, race, and ethnicity that have developed in various Western nation-states.

Chapter 6 describes and clarifies the major philosophical issues and concepts related to education and diversity. Educators and social scientists with divergent and conflicting ideological positions are recommending a range of educational programs and practices. This chapter presents a typology for classifying ideologies related to education and diversity and proposes a multicultural ideology to guide reform in schools, colleges, and universities. The ways in which the curriculum can be designed to reflect the cultural identities of students are described in Chapter 7.

4 Culture, Ethnicity, and Education

A wide range of concepts has emerged to describe the educational programs and practices related to ethnic, cultural, and language diversity. These concepts reflect the many different and often conflicting goals, approaches, and strategies related to education and diversity. Concepts such *as multicultural education, critical multiculturalism* (Kanpol & McLaren, 1995), *intercultural education,* and *antiracist education* are sometimes used interchangeably and at other times to describe different but interrelated programs and practices.

The major concepts in multicultural education need to be more clearly defined (Grant & Ladson-Billings, 1997). Concept clarification within this area is needed so that objectives can be more clearly delineated and strategies for attaining them more appropriately designed. Concepts are very important because they influence research questions, methods, findings, programs, and evaluation strategies.

This chapter defines and delineates the boundaries of some of the major concepts related to education and cultural diversity and suggests their different programmatic and policy implications. This conceptual analysis is designed to help educators at all levels better clarify, specify, and evaluate goals related to cultural, ethnic, and language diversity (Garcia, 1999).

Multicultural Education

Multicultural education is one of the most frequently used concepts to describe diversity in education today, not only in the United States but also in such nations as Australia, the United Kingdom, and Canada. However, the term *intercultural education,* rather than *multicultural education,* is frequently used on the European continent (Batelaan, 1997). Researchers and policy makers who prefer intercultural to multicultural education contend that intercultural implies an education that promotes interaction among different cultures whereas multicultural does not. However, intercultural education is rarely used outside of Europe.

The use of multicultural education varies widely in different school districts and in the educational literature. Sometimes it is used synonymously with ethnic studies; at other times it is used to describe the education of students of color. It is necessary to discuss the meaning of culture in order to describe what multicultural education suggests theoretically since *culture* is the root of the word *multicultural* and thus of the term *multicultural education.*

The Meaning of Culture

There are many different definitions of culture, but no single definition that all social scientists would heartily accept (Barnard & Spencer, 1996). Some definitions, however, are fairly widely accepted. Sir E. B. Taylor (1871) formulated a highly influential definition of culture in 1871: "Culture or civilization, taken in its wide ethnographic sense, is that complex whole which includes knowledge, belief, art, morals, law, custom, and any other capabilities and habits acquired by man as a member of society" (p. 1). Today, Taylor's definition is not popular among social scientists because they believe it is not a very helpful guide for research. They think the definition is too broad and lacks sufficient boundaries. Kuper (1999) has written a lively account of the long quest by anthropologists to construct an acceptable definition of culture.

In a comprehensive study of the definitions of culture published in 1952, Alfred L. Kroeber and Clyde Kluckhohn report more than 160. They concluded that most social scientists agreed that "culture consists of patterns, explicit and implicit, of and for behavior acquired and transmitted by symbols, constituting the distinctive achievements of human groups, including their embodiments in artifacts; the essential core of culture consists of traditional (i.e., historically derived and selected) ideas and especially attached values" (p. 161).

In their summary definition of culture, Kroeber and Kluckhohn, like most social scientists today, emphasize the intangible, symbolic, and ideational aspects of group life as the most important aspects of culture. Some social scientists go so far as to exclude material objects (artifacts) from their definition of culture (Theodorson & Theodorson, 1969). Even social scientists who view tangible or material objects as a part of culture believe that the interpretation of these objects and the rules governing their use constitute the essence of culture and not the artifacts themselves.

Some social scientists distinguish between *society* and *culture.* These social scientists "reserve the word society for the observable interactions among people, and the word culture for the intangible symbols, rules, and values that…people use to define themselves" (Dimen-Schein, 1977, p. 23).

Culture as Symbols and Interpretations

Symbolic anthropologists, such as Clifford Geertz and David Schneider, view culture as primarily *symbols and meanings.* In a famous and highly influential essay, "Thick Description: Toward an Interpretive Theory of Culture," Geertz (1973) presents his definition of culture:

> The concept of culture I espouse…is essentially a semiotic one. Believing, with
> Max Weber, that man is an animal suspended in webs of significance he himself

has spun, I take culture to be those webs, and the analysis of it to be therefore not an experimental science in search of law but *an interpretive one in search of meaning.* (p. 5) [emphasis added]

Geertz (1973) illustrates his symbolic interpretation of culture and his concept of thick description in a classic ethnographic account that uses thick description to describe a Balinese cockfight. Writes Geertz, "Anthropological writings are themselves interpretations" (p. 15).

Culture as a Strategy for Survival

Culture is sometimes defined as a strategy or program for survival. In this view of culture, it is created when human groups try to satisfy their survival needs. Bullivant (1984), who views culture as a *survival strategy,* states that culture is not static, but is subject to the circumstances (environment) in which a society finds itself. He describes three kinds of environments to which human groups respond when creating culture: the *geographical* environment, the *social* environment, and the *metaphysical* environment. Bullivant (1984) defines culture as "an interdependent and patterned system of valued traditional and current public knowledge and conceptions, embodied in behaviors and artifacts, and transmitted to present and new members, both symbolically and non-symbolically, which a society has evolved historically and progressively modifies and augments, to give meaning to and cope with its definitions of present and future existential problems" (p. 4).

The Characteristics of Cultures

Most social scientists view culture as consisting primarily of the symbolic, ideational, and intangible aspects of human societies (Kuper, 1999). Even when they view artifacts and material objects as being a part of culture, most social scientists regard culture as the way people interpret, use, and perceive such artifacts and material objects. It is the values, symbols, interpretations, and perspectives that distinguish one people from another in modernized societies and not artifacts, material objects, and other tangible aspects of human societies. Both the Japanese and the Americans use the automobile, but how they organize the making of it and how they interpret it within their societies may differ considerably and thus constitute an essential component of their respective cultures.

Cultures are dynamic, complex, and changing. However, in the schools, cultures often are perceived as static, unchanging, and fragmented. Concepts such as "American Indian culture" and "African American culture" often imply static, unchanging life-styles. Native Americans are often described in misleading ways, such as living in tepees. One result of such perceptions and descriptions is the perpetuation of stereotypes about different ethnic, cultural, and racial groups.

Cultures are also systems; they must be viewed as wholes, not as discrete and isolated parts. Any change in one aspect of a culture affects all of its components. For example, the large number of women who entered the work force in the 1970s and 1980s has influenced how women view themselves, how men view women, and the family socialization of children. Many more children today are in childcare facilities at a much younger age than was the case in the 1950s, when fewer women in the United States worked outside the home.

Gilligan (1982) describes caring, interconnection, and sensitivity to the needs of other people as dominant values among women and of the female microculture in the United States. Most of the research she cites was done with women socialized before the women's rights movement of the 1960s and 1970s. Increased women's rights during the 1980s and 1990s probably had a significant influence on their values, particularly those related to caring and interconnection.

Culture, Macroculture, and Microcultures

The concept of culture as formulated by most social scientists does not deal with variations within the national culture or the smaller cultures within it. However, when dealing with multicultural education, it is necessary to discuss cultural variation within the national culture because multicultural education focuses on equal educational opportunities for different groups within the national culture. Two related concepts can help us deal with cultural variations within the national culture. We can call the national or shared culture of the nation-state or society the big culture, or *macroculture.* The smaller cultures that constitute it can be called *microculture.*

Every nation-state has overarching values, symbols, and ideations shared to some degree by all microcultures. Various microcultural groups within the nation, however, may mediate, interpret, reinterpret, perceive, and experience these overarching national values and ideals differently. Figure 4.1 shows the relationship between microcultures and the national macroculture.

The national, overarching ideals, symbols, and values can be described for various nation-states. Myrdal (1944), the Swedish economist, identifies values such as justice, equality, and human dignity as overarching values in the United States. He calls these values the American Creed. Myrdal also describes the "American Dilemma" as an integral part of U.S. society. This dilemma results from the fact that even though most U.S. citizens internalize American Creed values, such as justice and human dignity, they often violate them in their daily behavior. Myrdal concludes that a tremendous gap exists between American ideals and American realities. Other U.S. overarching values include the Protestant work ethic, individualism as opposed to a group orientation, distance, and materialism and material progress (Stewart & Bennett, 1991).

The Variables and Components of Culture

As indicated in the previous section, most social scientists today emphasize the intangible components of culture, such as symbols, values, ideations, and ways of in-

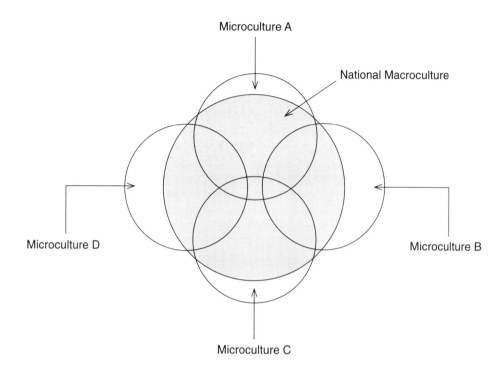

FIGURE 4.1 Microcultures and the National Macroculture

terpreting reality. I have identified six major cultural elements or components that are useful for interpreting the behavior of students and teachers and for teaching about various microcultural groups in Western nation-states. Figure 4.2 shows the elements and components of cultures discussed in the following sections.

Values and Behavioral Styles

Values are abstract, generalized principles of behavior to which members of society attach a high worth or regard. Individuals acquire their values during socialization. Values are one of the most important elements of cultures and microcultures that distinguish one group from another. Values influence behavior and also how people perceive their environment.

Each nation-state has national values that are to some extent shared by all of its microcultural groups; it also has other important values that distinguish one microcultural group from another. In their research on the cognitive styles of students, Ramírez and Castañeda (1974) found that Mexican American and Anglo-American students, as groups, had some different values that are revealed in their cognitive styles or approaches to learning. They found that Mexican Americans tend to be field-sensitive whereas Anglo-Americans are more field-independent.

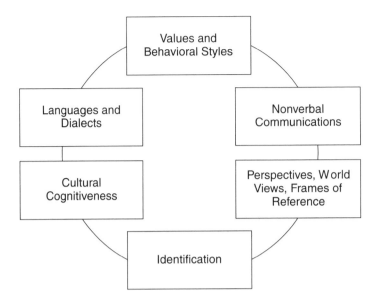

FIGURE 4.2   Elements and Components of Culture
These components of culture, which can be conceptualized as
distinct, exist within a holistic and highly interrelated system.

Field-sensitive students prefer to work with other people to achieve a goal; field-independent students prefer to work independently. Field-sensitive and field-independent learners also differ in other important ways.

Research on women has revealed that men and women exhibit some significant differences in value orientations. As pointed out previously, individualism is very important to men, whereas relationships, caring, and interconnection tend to be more important to women. Women also experience more problems with competitive achievement and more "fear of success" than do men (Belenky et al., 1986; Horner, 1972).

Languages and Dialects

Languages and dialects are important components of culture. How people view and interpret the world is reflected in their language. Within most nation-states, people speak the national language (or lingua franca) plus many variations of the national language as well as other languages. In the United States, people speak many different varieties of English, including Black English and English with Southern and Eastern regional accents. The first language for many Americans is not English but Spanish, Korean, Chinese, or Vietnamese. The United States Census indicated that 14 percent of school-age youths spoke a first language at home other than English in 1990 (U.S. Bureau of the Census, 1998). People in nations such as the United Kingdom, Australia, and Canada also speak many different dialects and languages in addition to the shared national language or languages. Canada has two national languages, English and French. Many other languages are also spoken in Canada. Cultural differences are both reflected and perpetuated by languages and dialects.

Nonverbal Communications

The way people communicate nonverbally is an important part of culture. How people look at each other and what the particular looks mean often vary within and across different microcultural groups within a society. Philips (1983), in her study of Native Americans on the Warm Spring Indian Reservation in Oregon, describes how the communication styles of Indian students and their Anglo teachers—both verbal and nonverbal—differ and often conflict. Nonverbal communication often reveals latent but important components of a culture or microculture. Looking an older person directly in the eye is considered offensive in some U.S. microcultures.

Cultural Cognitiveness

Cultural cognitiveness occurs when individuals or a group are aware of and think about their culture or microculture as unique and distinct from other cultures or microcultures within a society. Cultural cognitiveness involves the process of knowing, including both awareness and judgment.

Cultural cognitiveness differs from cultural identification. An individual may have a strong identification with a culture but little awareness of it as a unique culture, distinct from others. Conversely, an individual may have strong cultural cognitiveness or awareness but little identification with his or her microculture. An individual with strong cultural awareness may be a staunch assimilationist who tries to escape most or all of the symbols of his or her culture.

Perspectives, World Views, and Frames
of Reference

Certain perspectives, points of view, and frames of reference are normative within each culture and microcultural group. Cultures are epistemological communities. This does not mean that every individual within a particular cultural or microcultural group endorses a particular point of view or perspective. It does mean, however, that particular views and perspectives occur more frequently within some microcultural groups than do others or within the macroculture. Japanese American perspectives on their World War II internment, African American perspectives on the civil rights movement of the 1960s, and women's perspectives on caring, independence, and individuation (Gilligan, 1982) are perspectives held by microcultural groups that differ from perspectives within other microcultural groups and within the macroculture.

Identification

When an individual identifies with his or her cultural or microcultural group, he or she feels a part of the group; internalizes its goals, interests, and aspirations; and also internalizes its values and standards. An individual's level of identification with his or her cultural group can vary greatly, from practically no identification to almost total identification. An individual African American, Jewish American, or Jamaican in the United Kingdom may have a weak or a strong identification with his or her ethnic group.

Microcultural Groups and Individuals

Individuals are not just African American or White, male or female, or middle or working class. Even though we discuss variables such as race/ethnicity, gender, social class, and exceptionality (member of a special population, such as having a disability or being gifted) as separate variables, individuals belong to these groups at the same time (see Figure 4.3). Each variable influences the behavior of individuals. The influence of these variables is rarely singular; they often interact to influ-

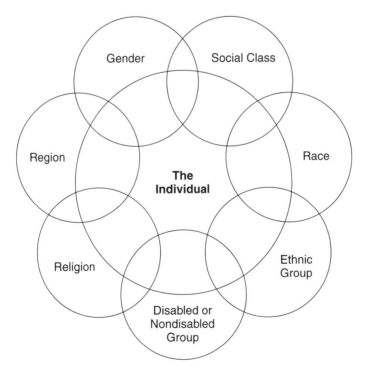

FIGURE 4.3   Individuals Belong to Many Different Microcultural Groups

ence the behavior of individuals. Gilligan (1982) points out that women are less oriented toward individuation than are men. African American culture tends to be more group oriented than is the mainstream U.S. culture. A reasonable hypothesis is that African American women are even less oriented toward individuation than are White women.

Figure 4.4 illustrates how four major variables—race/ethnicity, gender, social class, and exceptionality—influence student behavior both singly and interactively. The figure also shows that many other variables, which are not identified, also simultaneously influence student behavior.

Multicultural Education: Nature and Limitations

Multicultural education suggests a type of education concerned with creating educational environments in which students from a variety of microcultural groups such as race/ethnicity, gender, social class, regional groups, and people with disabilities experience educational equality. The problems of these various groups are highlighted and compared. The total school environment is reformed so that it promotes respect and equity for a wide range of microcultural groups. Multicultural education, conceptualized in this way, is based on the assumption that such concepts as prejudice, discrimination, and identity conflicts are common to diverse microcultural groups.

A generic focus within a school reform effort, such as multicultural education, can make a substantial contribution to the education of students in a diverse society. However, school reform efforts should go beyond the level of generic multicultural education and focus on the unique problems that women, African Americans,

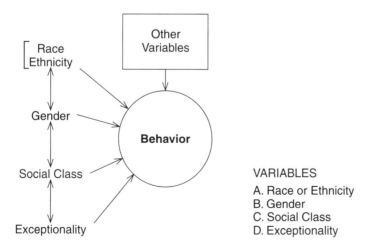

FIGURE 4.4   **Multicultural Subvariants**

people with disabilities, and other victimized cultural groups experience in the United States and in other nations. Many problems these groups face are unique and require specialized analyses and strategies. In addition to a powerful generic multicultural education, educational interventions that focus on the specific problems and issues of ethnic groups of color and language minority groups are essential (Fordham, 1996; Moreno, 1999).

Multicultural education is a popular concept because it is often interpreted to mean combining the problems of people of color, women, and other marginalized groups. Public and school policies that are based primarily on this combining process will prove ineffective and perhaps detrimental to all of the groups concerned. Because of the unique problems of each ethnic and racial group, educational institutions should implement targeted educational interventions to complement and strengthen generic multicultural education. These concepts are complementary but not interchangeable.

Because multicultural education is a very broad and inclusive concept, and because it focuses on *cultural differences,* it is not an adequate concept to guide research and policy decisions on problems related to students of color and language minority students. It is not clear from the literature on multicultural education, for example, which groups constitute the target populations in educational reform. Multicultural education also does not deal adequately with the ways in which the needs of the various microcultural groups conflict, interact, and intersect.

Multicultural education theorists sometimes imply that cultural differences and cultural ethnocentrism are the major causes of intergroup tensions and conflicts. *However, racial problems are often more significant in intergroup relations than are cultural differences* (Jones, 1997; Stephan, 1999). Multicultural education is a useful concept in that it enables the educational reformer to focus on a range of marginalized and victimized groups within society. This is the strength of the concept and is probably why it has so many supporters among practitioners.

Multicultural education is not a sufficient concept. Concepts such as *race, racism,* and *power* must become integral parts of effective school reform efforts. Sexism, for example, is very important when dealing with gender issues just as the concepts of race and racism are important for individuals researching or designing educational policy for people of color. Concepts such as ethnic studies, women studies, and bilingual education are needed to support and enhance the concept of multicultural education. *Critical multicultural education* tries to make power, race, and critical theory issues significant components of multicultural education (Kanpol & McLaren, 1995).

The Nature of an Ethnic Group

An ethnic group is a microcultural group with several distinguishing characteristics. Social scientists do not completely agree on one definition of ethnic group. However, we can define an ethnic group as a group that shares a common ancestry, culture, history, tradition, and sense of peoplehood. An ethnic group is primarily an involuntary group, although identification with the group may be optional (Banks et al., 1992).

This definition suggests that Anglos in the United States and Australia, and the British and French in Canada, are ethnic groups. Pakistanis in the United Kingdom and Mexicans in the United States are ethnic minority groups, a specific type of ethnic group. Members of an ethnic minority group have unique physical and/or cultural characteristics that enable members of other groups to identify its members easily, often for purposes of discrimination (Banks, 1997).

Types of Ethnic Groups

There are different types of ethnic groups. Each type is an involuntary group whose members share a sense of peoplehood and an interdependence of fate. A *cultural* ethnic group is an ethnic group that shares a common set of values, experiences, behavioral characteristics, and linguistic traits that differ substantially from other ethnic groups within society. Individuals usually gain membership in such a group not by choice but through birth and early socialization. Individuals who are members of cultural ethnic groups are likely to take collective and organized actions to support public policies that will enhance the survival of the group's culture and ethnic institutions. Members of cultural ethnic groups also pass on the symbols, language, and other components of the cultural heritage to the next generation. The individual's ethnic cultural heritage is a source of pride and group identification.

An *economic* ethnic group is an ethnic group that shares a sense of group identity and sees its economic fate tied together. Individual members of the group feel that their economic fate is intimately tied to the economic future of other members of the group. The members of an economic ethnic group respond collectively to societal issues they perceive as critical to determining their economic status, and they work together to influence policies and programs that will benefit the economic status of the group. The individual within an economic ethnic group tends to feel that taking individual actions to improve his or her economic status is likely to be ineffective as long as the economic status of the ethnic group is not substantially improved.

A *political* ethnic group is an ethnic group that has a sense of shared political interests and a feeling of political interdependence. The group responds to political issues collectively and tries to promote those public policies and programs that will enhance the interests of its members as a group. Groups that are political ethnic groups are also usually economic ethnic groups because politics and economics are tightly interwoven in a society. Thus, we can refer to those ethnic groups that work to influence political and economic policies that will benefit their collectivities as *ecopolitical ethnic groups.*

A *holistic* ethnic group is an ethnic group that has all of the characteristics of the various types of ethnic groups that we have described in their purest forms. Thus, a holistic ethnic group is an involuntary group of individuals who share a sense of peoplehood and an interdependence of fate, a common sense of identity, and common behavioral characteristics. Its members respond collectively to economic and political issues and try to promote public programs and policies that will further the interests of the group as a whole. African Americans and Mexican Americans closely approach the holistic ethnic group. Native Americans, Puerto Ricans in the United States, and Asian Americans are each acquiring more characteristics of a holistic ethnic group as the political maturity and collective political action of these groups increase.

Ethnic Group: A Multidimensional Concept

The definitions of ethnic groups discussed above suggest that all people in modernized, culturally pluralistic nation-states are members of ethnic groups. Within a modernized society, however, almost no individuals are totally ethnic, because ethnic characteristics within a modernized society are mediated by technology, acculturation, the physical amalgamation of ethnic groups, and other aspects of modernization. Thus, the appropriate question to ask is not whether an individual is ethnic, but to what extent he or she is ethnic.

Ethnic group membership is a multidimensional concept. The previous discussion and Figure 4.2 identify six major components of culture. These same major variables exist within an ethnic group, which is one type of microcultural group. These separate variables within an ethnic group, although highly interrelated, are conceptually distinct and can be identified. An individual's level of ethnic behavior and characteristics can be determined by ascertaining the extent to which he or she has behavior and characteristics that reflect these ethnic variables.

The Relationship between Physical Characteristics and Ethnic Behavior

It is very important to realize that ethnic behavior and characteristics should not be confused with an individual's biological characteristics and physical traits. It is true that a close relationship often exists between an individual's biological traits and his or her ethnic and cultural characteristics. In premodern societies, there was usually a 100 percent correlation between an individual's biological "ethnic" group and his or her cultural characteristics. This relationship exists to some extent today. Most African Americans, for example, have some "Black" cultural characteristics.

However, some African Americans have so few cultural traits that are Black and so little identification with African Americans as an ethnic group that we might call them Afro-Saxons. This same situation exists for many highly assimilated and upwardly mobile members of ethnic groups such as Mexican Americans, Italian Australians, and Canadian Indians. Americans with an Italian surname may be so totally culturally assimilated in terms of their values, behaviors, and perceptions that they are culturally not Italian Americans but Anglo-Americans. An individual

American who has one-eighth each German, Australian, Romanian, Algerian, Chilean, Scotch, Italian, and Korean ancestry, and whose parents did not provide any conscious ethnic influence, is not necessarily without an ethnic identification or ethnic behavior. He or she is most likely culturally an Anglo-American who has an identification with Anglo-Americans as an ethnic group. This identification with Anglo-Americans may be conscious or unconscious. Most frequently, this type of individual will have an unconscious identification with Anglo-Americans as an ethnic group and will offer a self-description as "merely an American."

The Variables of Ethnic Group Behavior

The six major variables of culture identified in Figure 4.2 can be used to conceptualize and determine the level of ethnic behavior of individuals or groups and the level of cross-cultural competency (see Table 4.1). Each of these variables can be conceptualized as existing on a continuum. Measurement techniques can be structured to determine the level of ethnic behavior and traits possessed by individual members of ethnic groups. This multidimensional conceptualization of ethnic behavior can help students understand that an individual may be highly ethnic linguistically but highly assimilated in terms of ethnic values and perspectives. This multidimensional conceptualization of ethnic group can also help students to better understand the complex nature of ethnic group life in Western societies and to mitigate some of the serious and damaging misconceptions about ethnic groups that are pervasive within the schools and the larger society.

The last variable of ethnic group behavior identified in Table 4.1 is the individual's psychological identification with his or her ethnic group. This variable is called *ethnicity*. It is one of the most important variables of ethnic group behavior within a modernized society. In some cases, ethnicity may be the only significant variable of ethnic group behavior possessed by highly assimilated and upper-status members of ethnic groups within a modernized democratic society.

Ethnic Studies

Ethnic studies can be defined as the scientific and humanistic study of the histories, cultures, and experiences of ethnic groups within a society. It includes but is not limited to a study of ethnic minority groups, such as Chinese Canadians, Australian Aborigines, British Jamaicans, and African Americans. Ethnic studies refers primarily to the objectives, methods, and materials that make up the courses of study within schools and other educational institutions. It constitutes one essential component of multicultural education. Since the 1960s, many attempts have been made in nations such as the United States, Canada, the United Kingdom, and Australia to infuse ethnic studies into school and university curricula.

The concept of ethnic studies suggests that a wide variety of ethnic groups are studied within a comparative framework. Students are helped to develop concepts,

TABLE 4.1   **Matrix for Conceptualizing and Assessing Cross-Cultural Behavior**

Variables	Understandings and Behavior	Levels of Competency
		1 2 3 4 5 6 7
Values and Behavioral Styles	The ability to understand and interpret values and behavioral styles that are normative within the ethnic group.	◄─────────────►
	The ability to express values behaviorally that are normative within the ethnic group.	
	The ability to express behavioral styles and nuances that are normative within the ethnic group.	
Languages and Dialects	The ability to understand, interpret, and speak the dialects and/or languages within the ethnic culture.	◄─────────────►
Nonverbal Communications	The ability to understand and accurately interpret the nonverbal communications within the ethnic group.	◄─────────────►
	The ability to communicate accurately nonverbally within the ethnic group.	
Cultural Cognitiveness	The ability to perceive and recognize the unique components of one's ethnic group that distinguished it from other microcultural groups within the society and from the national macroculture.	◄─────────────►
	The ability to take actions that indicate an awareness and knowledge of one's ethnic culture.	
Perspectives, World Views, and Frames of Reference	The ability to understand and interpret the perspectives, world views, and frames of reference normative within the ethnic group.	◄─────────────►
	The ability to view events and situations from the perspectives, world views, and frames of reference normative within the ethnic group.	
Identification	The ability to have an identification with one's ethnic groups that is subtle and/or unconscious.	◄─────────────►
	The ability to take overt actions that show conscious identification with one's ethnic group.	

generalizations, and theories that they can use to better understand a range of human behavior (Banks, 1997). Modernized ethnic studies programs are not only comparative and conceptual but are also interdisciplinary and cut across subject matter lines. Thus, within a globally conceptualized ethnic studies program, teachers of the humanities, the communication arts, and the sciences incorporate ethnic content into the total curriculum. Ethnic content is not reserved for special days, occasions, or courses.

Even though specialized courses such as African American studies, Asian studies, and Canadian Indian studies can help attain specified curricular objectives, a major goal of curriculum reform should be to infuse ethnic content into the core or general curriculum that all students experience. Ethnic content should be for all students, not just for those who are members of ethnic minority groups.

Race as a Factor in Intergroup Problems

Multicultural education assumes that the intergroup problems in Western nation-states are primarily cultural rather than racial. Widespread cultural assimilation has taken place among ethnic minorities in nations such as the United States and Canada, especially among people who are upwardly mobile. Some research indicates that the values, goals, and aspirations of lower-class African American youths are strikingly similar to those of middle-class Whites in the United States (Valentine, 1971). Thus, even though significant cultural differences exist between Anglo-Americans and most ethnic minorities in the United States, Anglo-Americans and ethnic minorities in the United States share many cultural characteristics. When cultural differences are minimized, conflict between non-White minorities and Whites frequently occurs. The cause of most of this conflict is often racial rather than cultural. Gordon (1964) seriously questions the extent of cultural pluralism in the United States:

> Structural pluralism…is the major key to the understanding of the ethnic makeup of American society, while cultural pluralism is the minor one.… The most salient fact…is the maintenance of structurally separate subsocieties of the three major religious and the racial and quasi-racial groups, and even vestiges of the nationality groups, along with a massive trend toward acculturation of all groups…to American culture patterns. (p. 159)

The cultural and ethnic differences among racial groups must be reflected in educational programs designed to reduce intergroup tension and to foster interracial understanding. Overemphasis on cultural differences and cultural pluralism, however, may divert attention from *racial differences* and hostility. We err seriously when we try to understand ethnic conflict in the schools by focusing exclusively on cultural differences between dominant ethnic groups and ethnic minorities. Racism and racial conflict were very evident in the United States and throughout the world when the twenty-first century began.

If we develop educational programs and policies designed to make students more accepting of cultural differences but fail to deal seriously with problems caused by racial differences, we will not solve our basic intergroup problems (Stephan, 1999). This is especially true because widespread cultural assimilation is taking place in Western societies, and thus cultural differences between ethnic minorities and dominant ethnic groups will probably be less significant in the future than they are today.

Education for Ethnic and Racial Diversity

Concepts and terms related to ethnicity are the most useful and appropriate for conceptualizing the problems related to the education of ethnic minorities. Most definitions of ethnicity focus on the culture and race of immigrants and immigrant descendant groups. We must concentrate on both variables when designing programs to reduce interethnic and interracial conflict. In his study of definitions of ethnicity, Isajiw (1974) found that culture was the second most frequently mentioned attribute of ethnicity, and race (and physical characteristics) was the fourth. Other frequently occurring attributes included common national or geographic origin, religion, language, sense of peoplehood, common values, separate institutions, and minority or subordinate status. In his definition of ethnic group Gordon (1964) emphasizes the importance of race.

Both racial and cultural differences must be reflected in educational programs designed to reduce intergroup conflict and misunderstanding. *Many of our efforts, however, must focus directly on reducing institutional, individual, and cultural racism* because racial differences, and not more generalized cultural differences, are the causes of the most serious psychological problems that students of color often experience in the schools and in society (Jones, 1997; Stephan, 1999).

The relationship between racism and the rejection of the cultures of people of color by dominant groups must also be considered when formulating educational policy to reduce interethnic conflict. Racism is a major reason that many Whites perceive and evaluate the cultures of people of color negatively. Intergroup problems frequently arise not because of the nature of the cultural differences between Whites and people of color, but because of the race of the individual or group who exhibits the specific cultural characteristics. The language of low-income people in the United States is often ridiculed, while the speech of White Boston Brahmins, which is as much a dialect as Black English, is frequently admired by Anglo-Americans. In the 1950s, Mexican American children were often prohibited from speaking Spanish in many schools in the Southwest (U.S. Commission on Civil Rights, 1974). However, when Spanish was spoken by Whites it was usually viewed as a useful and esteemed language. This kind of racism can be called *cultural racism.*

Because we need to focus our attention on variables related to both race and culture, and the complex interactions and relationships between these two major variables, *racism* must be an integral and essential part of powerful multicultural education (Montagu, 1997; Omi & Winant, 1994). The insights and knowledge from critical race theory can inform educators about the complex and insidious ways racism is embedded in U.S. institutions, including schools, colleges, and universities (Crenshaw, Gotanda, Peller, & Thomas, 1995; Delgado, 1995). Educational theorists such as Tate and Ladson-Billings have used insights, analyses, and findings from critical theory to inform educational theory and practice (Ladson-Billings & Tate, 1995; Tate, 1997).

Reducing Racial Conflict

A number of basic issues and problems related to race, ethnicity, and education warrant immediate and decisive action. A top priority should be to implement programs and practices designed to modify the negative racial attitudes of students. Research indicates that children are aware of racial differences at an early age and often express negative racial attitudes (Aboud, 1988; Ramsey, 1998). Research further suggests that the racial attitudes of students tend to become more negative and crystallized as they grow older if deliberate efforts are not made to influence them (Aboud, 1988; Stephan, 1999).

To modify the racial attitudes of students successfully, experiences designed to influence the racial feelings and perceptions of teachers must be implemented. The attitudes, behavior, and the perceptions of classroom teachers have a profound impact on the social atmosphere of the school and the attitudes of students. Teachers are even more important than the materials they use because the ways in which they present material highly influence how they are viewed by students. Teachers must be strongly committed to a racially tolerant school atmosphere before such a setting can be created and maintained.

Unfortunately, research indicates that many teachers display negative attitudes and behavior toward low-income students and students of color. Research indicates that many teachers, in both subtle and overt ways, communicate negative feelings to students of color and have a disproportionate number of negative verbal and nonverbal interactions with them (Haberman, 1996; Irvine, 1990; Zeichner & Hoeft, 1996).

Research indicates that teacher in-service education is essential if we are going to reduce institutional racism in the school setting (Garcia, 1996). In-service education for teachers and other school personnel must have at least three major objectives: (1) to help teachers gain a new conceptualization of the history and culture of their societies; (2) to help them confront their own racial feelings, which can be a painful process and, if not handled competently, can be destructive and unsettling; and (3) to help them to conceptualize and develop teaching techniques that will enhance the academic achievement of students from diverse racial, ethnic, and language groups. It is essential that teachers clarify their racial feelings before they can contribute positively to the reduction of racial prejudice in students and function effectively within multicultural and multi-language schools and classrooms.

The school can also help reduce cultural racism and ethnocentrism by maximizing the cultural options of mainstream youths and helping them break out of their ethnic encapsulations (Donaldson, 1996). These youths need to learn that there are other ways of being, of feeling, and of perceiving. Most individuals are socialized within ethnic enclaves, where they learn one basic life-style. Consequently, they assume that their way is the only way, or that it is the only legitimate cultural style. Other life-styles seem strange, different, and exotic. Most individuals of color are forced to function within the dominant culture. However, many mainstream individuals are never required to function within other ethnic cultures. The school should provide all students with opportunities to become familiar with other races, life-styles, and cultures and should help students develop multicultural literacy and become more knowledgeable and sophisticated about other cultures and groups. Most people are ignorant about ethnic cultures other than their own.

Mainstream youths should be taught that they have cultural options. We severely limit the potentiality of students when we merely teach them aspects of their own cultures. Anglo-American students should realize that using Black English is one effective way to communicate; that Native Americans have values, beliefs, and life-styles that may be functional for them; and that alternative ways of behaving and of viewing the universe are practiced within the United States that they can freely embrace. By helping mainstream students view the world beyond their limited racial, ethnic, cultural, and language perspectives, we will enrich them as human beings and enable them to live more productive and fulfilling lives.

Summary

A wide range of concepts are used to describe programs and practices related to ethnic, cultural, and racial diversity in Western societies. The proliferation of concepts in part reflects the ideological conflicts in multicultural education and the emergent status of educational reform related to ethnic and cultural diversity. Concepts related to diversity must be better clarified before pluralistic educational reforms and research can be more effectively designed and implemented.

This chapter examines the major concepts in the field, such as culture, multicultural education, and ethnic studies. I have tried to clarify the meanings of these concepts and to describe their policy implications.

The issues and problems related to race and education are complex and difficult to diagnose and solve. Many variables influence the relationship between people of color and Whites, such as socioeconomic status, ethnicity, values, languages, and behavioral patterns. Variables related to culture and ethnicity will remain important in explaining interactions among racial groups as long as the groups are socialized within different ethnic communities and have negative attitudes toward the cultural differences exhibited by other racial groups.

However, a focus on ethnic and cultural variables should not divert attention from the role of individual and institutional racism in Western societies. Racism is the basic cause of many of the serious psychological problems that people of color experience in the schools and in the larger society. The interaction of race and culture also explains many interracial problems. Individuals and groups frequently respond negatively to specific cultural behaviors because they are exhibited by racially stigmatized ethnic minorities.

Effective educational policy and programs must be based on research and theory that focus on both race and culture and on the complex interactions between these two major variables, such as socioeconomic status. Programs that focus exclusively on cultural differences are not likely to lead to positive interracial interactions and understandings. An exclusively culture approach is also limited by the extensive degree to which cultural assimilation has taken place in Western societies. Race, however, cannot totally explain interethnic problems because significant cultural differences exist among some minority cultures and mainstream cultures in the various Western societies.

Because of the complexity of the problem, we need to examine multiple variables when trying to determine causes and to devise effective educational programs related to race and education. Further research and analyses are needed to clarify the relationship between culture and race in explaining interracial problems and conflict. Race must be an essential part of powerful and effective multicultural education.

REFERENCES

Aboud, F. (1988). *Children and Prejudice*. Cambridge, MA: Basil Blackwell.

Banks, J. A. (1997). *Teaching Strategies for Ethnic Studies*. (6th ed.). Boston: Allyn and Bacon.

Banks, J. A., Cortés, C., Gay, G., Garcia, R., & Ochoa, A. (1992). *Curriculum Guidelines for Multicultural Education* (rev. ed.). Washington, DC: National Council for the Social Studies.

Barnard, A., & Spencer, J. (Eds.). (1996*). Encyclopedia of Social and Cultural Anthropology*. New York: Routledge.

Batelaan, P. (Ed.). (1997). *European Journal of Intercultural Studies, 8* (1), 5–115 (published by Carfax, Oxfordshire, England).

Belenky, M. F., Clinchy, B. M., Goldberger, N. R., & Tarule, J. M. (1986). *Women's Ways of Knowing: The Development of Self, Voice, and Mind*. New York: Basic Books.

Bullivant, B. M. (1984). *Pluralism: Cultural Maintenance and Evolution*. Clevedon, Avon, England: Multilingual Patterns Ltd.

Crenshaw, K., Gotanda, N., Peller, G., & Thomas, K. (Eds.). (1995). *Critical Race Theory: The Key Writings That Formed the Movement*. New York: The New Press.

Delgado, R. (Ed.). (1995). *Critical Race Theory: The Cutting Edge*. Philadelphia: Temple University Press.

Dimen-Schein, M. (1977). *The Anthropological Imagination*. New York: McGraw-Hill.

Donaldson, K. B. M. (1996). *Combating Racism in United States Schools*. Westport, CT: Praeger.

Fordham, S. (1996). *Blacked Out: Dilemmas of Race, Identity, and Success at Capital High*. Chicago: The University of Chicago Press.

Garcia, E. (1996). Preparing Instructional Professionals for Linguistically and Culturally Diverse Students. In J. Sikula, T. J. Buttery, & E. Guyton (Eds.), *Handbook of Research on Teacher Education* (2nd ed.) (pp. 802–813). New York: Macmillan.

Garcia, E. (1999). *Student Cultural Diversity: Understanding and Meeting the Challenge*. Boston: Houghton Mifflin.

Geertz, C. (1973). *The Interpretation of Cultures*. New York: Basic Books.

Gilligan, C. (1982). *In a Different Voice: Psychological Theory and Women's Development*. Cambridge, MA: Harvard University Press.

Gordon, M. M. (1964). *Assimilation in American Life*. New York: Oxford University Press.

Grant, C. A., & Ladson-Billings, G. (1997). *Dictionary of Multicultural Education.* Phoenix: Oryx Press.

Haberman, M. (1996). Selecting and Preparing Culturally Competent Teachers for Urban Schools. In J. Sikula, T. J. Buttery, & E. Guyton (Eds.), *Handbook of Research on Teacher Education* (pp. 747–801). New York: Macmillan.

Horner, M. S. (1972). Toward an Understanding of Achievement-Related Conflicts in Women. *Journal of Social Issues, 28,* 157–176.

Irvine, J. J. (1990). *Black Students and School Failure: Policies, Practices, and Prescriptions.* New York: Praeger.

Isajiw, W. W. (1974). Definitions of Ethnicity. *Ethnicity, 1,* 111–124.

Jones, J. M. (1997). *Race and Racism* (2nd ed.). New York: McGraw-Hill.

Kanpol, B., & McLaren, P. (Eds.). (1995). *Critical Multiculturalism: Uncommon Voices in a Common Struggle.* Westport, CT: Bergin & Garvey.

Kroeber, A. L., & Kluckhohn, C. (1952). *Culture: A Critical Review of Concepts and Definitions.* New York: Vintage Books.

Kuper, A. (1999). *Culture: The Anthropologists' Account.* Cambridge, MA: Harvard University Press.

Ladson-Billings, G., & Tate, W. F. (1995). Toward a Critical Theory of Education. *Teachers College Record, 97,* 47–68.

Montagu, A. (1997). *Man's Most Dangerous Myth: The Fallacy of Race* (6th ed.). Walnut Creek, CA: AltaMira Press.

Moreno, J. F. (Ed.). (1999). *The Elusive Quest for Equality: 150 Years of Chicano/Chicana Education.* Cambridge, MA: Harvard Educational Review.

Myrdal, G., with R. Sterner, & A. Rose. (1944). *An American Dilemma: The Negro Problem and Modern Democracy.* New York: Harper and Row.

Omi, M., & Winant, H. (1994). *Racial Formation in the United States: From the 1960s to the 1990s.* New York: Routledge.

Philips, S. U. (1983). *The Invisible Culture.* New York: Longman.

Ramírez, M. III, & Castañeda, A. (1974). *Cultural Democracy, Bicognitive Development and Education.* New York: Academic Press.

Ramsey, P. G. (1998). *Teaching and Learning in a Diverse World: Multicultural Education for Young Children* (2nd ed.). New York: Teachers College Press.

Stephan, W. (1999). *Reducing Prejudice and Stereotyping in Schools.* New York: Teachers College Press.

Stewart, E. C., & Bennett, M. J. (1991). *American Cultural Patterns: A Cross-Cultural Perspective.* Yarmouth, ME: Intercultural Press.

Tate, W. F. IV. (1997). Critical Race Theory and Education: History, Theory, and Implications. In M. W. Apple (Ed.), *Review of Research in Education* (Vol. 22), pp. 195–247. Washington, DC: American Educational Research Association.

Taylor, E. B. (1871). *Primitive Culture* (Vol. 1). London: John Murray.

Theodorson, G. A., & Theodorson, A. G. (1969). *A Modern Dictionary of Sociology.* New York: Barnes and Noble.

U.S. Bureau of the Census (1998). *Statistical Abstract of the United States: 1998* (118th ed). Washington, DC: U.S. Government Printing Office.

U.S. Commission on Civil Rights. (1974). *Toward Quality Education for Mexican Americans,* Report VI. Washington, DC: Author.

Valentine, C. A. (1971). Deficit, Difference, and Bicultural Models of Afro-American Behavior. *Harvard Educational Review, 41,* 137–157.

Zeichner, K. M., & Hoeft, K. (1996). Teacher Socialization for Cultural Diversity. In J. Sikula, T. J. Buttery, & E. Guyton (Eds.), *Handbook of Research on Teacher Education* (2nd ed.) (pp. 525–547). New York: Macmillan.

5 Race, Diversity, and Educational Paradigms

The academic and social problems that low-income students and students of color experience in the schools have been discussed widely during the last two decades. The academic achievement of students of color, such as Japanese Americans and Chinese Americans, exceeds that of Whites (Lee, 1998). However, the academic achievement of most other groups of students of color in the United States is considerably below that of Whites (Deyhle & Swisher, 1997; Miller, 1995; Nettles & Perna, 1997; Pang & Cheng, 1998; Suárez-Orozco & Suárez-Orozco, 1995).

The percentage of individuals within a group who has graduated from college is an important index of that group's educational attainment. In 1997, 23 percent of all Americans 25 years or older had completed four years of college or more. The percentages for Asians and Pacific Islanders and for White Americans were 42.2 percent and 24.6 percent, respectively. The percentages for African Americans, Mexican Americans, Puerto Rican Americans and Cuban Americans were 13.3 percent, 7.5 percent, 10.7 percent, and 19.7 percent, respectively (U.S. Bureau of the Census, 1998). The percentage for Asian and Pacific Islanders is considerably higher than the one for Whites. However, the percentages for other groups of color is considerably below the percentage for Whites. Table 5.1 shows high school and college completion rates for these groups.

Ethnic minority students in other Western nations, such as the West Indians in the United Kingdom and the Metis in Canada, also achieve below their mainstream peers (Moodley, 1992).

A wide range of educational reforms designed to increase equality for students from diverse ethnic, racial, and social-class groups has been implemented. These various educational reforms have emanated from concepts, theories, and paradigms based on different and often conflicting assumptions, values, and goals. This chapter identifies, describes, and critically analyzes the major concepts and paradigms that have been used to explain the low academic achievement of ethnic, racial, and low-income students; the educational programs and practices that exemplify these concepts and paradigms; and their values and assumptions. The chapter also describes how extensively single-factor paradigms are used to guide educational research and practice and their limitations. It then briefly outlines a multifactor, *holistic* theory of multicultural education that can be used to guide educational practice and research.

TABLE 5.1   **Educational Attainment for Selected Ethnic Groups, 1997, in Percent, for Persons 25 Years Old and Over**

	Total	White	Black	Asian and Pacific Islander	Mexican American	Puerto Rican American	Cuban American
Completed 4 years high school or more	82.1	83.0	74.9	84.9	48.6	61.1	65.2
Completed 4 years of college or more	23.9	24.6	13.3	42.2	7.5	10.7	17.7

Source: U.S. Bureau of the Census (1998). *Statistical Abstract of the United States: 1998* (118th ed.). Washington, DC: U.S. Government Printing Office, p. 167.

The Nature of Paradigms

Kuhn (1970) uses the term *paradigm* to describe the "entire constellation of beliefs, values, techniques, and so on shared by members of a given [scientific] community" (p. 15). The laws, principles, explanations, and theories of a discipline are also part of its paradigm. Kuhn argues that during the history of a science, new paradigms arise to replace older ones. He calls this phenomenon a "scientific revolution." Kuhn refers primarily to natural science disciplines and draws most of his examples from the natural sciences. It is not clear, in the Kuhnian sense, whether social science has developed true paradigms because of the paucity of universal laws, principles, and theories in social science and because social science is characterized by many competing systems of explanations. Writes Kuhn (1970), "It remains an open question what parts of social science have yet acquired such paradigms at all. History suggests that the road to a firm research consensus is extraordinarily arduous" (p. 15).

Barnes (1982), building on Kuhn's work, defines a paradigm as "an existing scientific achievement, a specific concrete *problem-solution* which has gained universal acceptance throughout a scientific field as a valid procedure, and as a model of valid procedure for pedagogic use" (p. 17). He writes further that

> the culture of an established natural science is passed on in the form of paradigms. The central task of the teacher is to display them. The central task of the students is to assimilate them, and to acquire competence in their routine use.... *Scientific training...demands acceptance of the existing orthodoxy in a given field.* Accordingly, it tends to avoid anything which might undermine or offer an alternative to that orthodoxy. [emphasis added] The history of a field, wherein are found radically variant concepts, problems and methods of problem-solution, is either ignored, or is systematically rewritten as a kind of journey toward, and hence a legitimation of, present knowledge. (pp. 18–19)

Multicultural Education Paradigms

The word *paradigm* in this chapter describes an interrelated set of facts, concepts, generalizations, and theories that attempt to explain human behavior or social phenomena and that imply policy and action. A paradigm, which is also a set of explanations, has specific goals, assumptions, and values that can be described. Paradigms compete with one another in the arena of ideas and public policy.

The various problem-solutions or paradigms in multicultural education, like other systems of explanations, have many of the characteristics of paradigms discussed by Kuhn and Barnes, although they are *quasi* or *partial* paradigms in the Kuhnian sense. The *cultural deprivation, language,* and *radical* paradigms in multicultural education constitute constellations of beliefs, values, and techniques and are shared by members of a given scientific community. These conceptions are also problemsolutions that have gained acceptance as valid procedures and explanations.

Each paradigm, such as the cultural deprivation, the language, and the radical, demands acceptance of its orthodoxy and tends to avoid concepts, explanations, and theories that might offer an alternative view or explanation. Each paradigm is also a *partial* theory that provides an incomplete explanation of social reality (Merton, 1968). *Each paradigm is perspectivistic and emanates from specific values, assumptions, and conceptions of the good society.* Paradigms both mirror and perpetuate specific ideologies and lead to different educational policies and practices. Some paradigms, such as the cultural deprivation and the genetic, support dominant ethnic group hegemony and inequality; others, such as the radical and racism, imply reconstruction of the political and economic systems so that excluded ethnic and social-class groups can experience equality.

Response Paradigms: The Schools React to Ethnic Revitalization Movements

When we examine the development of ethnic revitalization movements in Western democratic nations, such as the United States, Canada, the United Kingdom, and Australia, and the responses that educational institutions have made to them, we can identify and describe specific types and patterns of institutional responses. These patterns and prototypical responses are called *paradigms* in this chapter. These paradigmatic responses do not necessarily occur in a linear or set order in any particular nation, although some of them tend to occur earlier in the development of ethnic revitalization movements than do others. Thus, the response paradigms relate in a general way to the phases of ethnic revitalization movements described in Chapter 2. The ethnic additive and self-concept development paradigms, for example, tend to arise during the first or early phase of an ethnic revitalization movement. Single-explanation paradigms tend to emerge before multiple explanation ones. Single-explanation paradigms usually emerge during the first phase of ethnic revitalization, but multiple-explanation paradigms usually do not emerge or become popular until the later phase.

A sophisticated neoconservative paradigm tends to develop during the final phase of ethnic revitalization, when the groups that are trying to institutionalize pluralism begin to experience success and those committed to *assimilationism* and to defending the status quo begin to fear that the pluralistic reformers might institutionalize a new ideal and create new goals for the nation-state.

A number of response paradigms develop when ethnic revitalization movements emerge (see Table 5.2). These multicultural education paradigms might develop within a nation at different times or they may coexist at the same time. Each paradigm is likely to exist in some form in a nation that has experienced an ethnic revitalization movement. However, only one or two are likely to be dominant at any particular time. The leaders and advocates of particular paradigms compete to make their paradigms the most popular in academic, government, and school settings. Proponents of paradigms that can attract the most government and private support are likely to become the prevailing voices for multicultural education within a particular time or period.

Sometimes one dominant paradigm replaces another, and something akin to what Kuhn calls a *scientific revolution* takes place (Kuhn, 1970). However, what happens more frequently is that a new paradigm will emerge that challenges an older one but does not replace it. During the late 1960s in the United States, the cultural deprivation paradigm dominated the theory, research, and practice related to educating low-income students and students of color (Bereiter & Engelmann, 1966). This paradigm was seriously challenged by the cultural difference paradigm in the 1970s (Baratz & Baratz, 1970). The cultural difference paradigm did not replace the cultural deprivation paradigm; rather, the two paradigms coexisted. However, the cultural deprivation paradigm lost much of its influence and legitimacy, especially among most scholars of color (Banks, 1997).

The cultural deprivation paradigm was reborn during the late 1980s and early 1990s in the form of a new concept, "at risk" (Cuban, 1989). The at-risk paradigm coexists with other paradigms, such as the cultural difference, language, and radical paradigms. However, it became popular in part because it is a funding category for state and federal funding agencies.

The Ethnic Additive and Self-Concept Development Paradigms

Often the first phase of a school's response to an ethnic revitalization movement consists of the infusion of bits and pieces of content about ethnic groups into the curriculum, especially into courses in the humanities, the social studies, and the language arts. Teaching about ethnic heroes and celebrating ethnic holidays are salient characteristics of the ethnic additive paradigm.

This paradigm usually emerges as the first one for a variety of reasons. It develops in part because ethnic groups usually demand the inclusion of their heroes, holidays, and contributions into the curriculum during the first phase of ethnic revitalization. This paradigm also emerges because during the early phase of ethnic revitalization teachers usually have little knowledge about marginalized ethnic

TABLE 5.2 Multicultural Education Paradigms

Paradigm	Major Assumptions	Major Goals	School Programs and Practices
Ethnic Additive	Ethnic content can be added to the curriculum without reconceptualizing or restructuring it.	To integrate the curriculum by adding special units, lessons, and ethnic holidays to it.	Special ethnic studies units; ethnic studies classes that focus on ethnic foods and holidays; units on ethnic heroes.
Self-Concept Development	Ethnic content can help increase the self-concept of ethnic minority students. Ethnic minority students have low self-concepts.	To increase the self-concepts and academic achievement of ethnic minority students.	Special units in ethnic studies that emphasize the contributions ethnic groups have made to the making of the nation; units on ethnic heroes.
Cultural Deprivation	Many poor and ethnic minority youths are socialized within homes and communities that prevent them from acquiring the cognitive skills and cultural characteristics needed to succeed in school.	To compensate for the cognitive deficits and dysfunctional cultural characteristics that many poor and ethnic minority youths bring to school.	Compensatory educational experiences that are behavioristic and intensive, e.g., Head Start and Follow Through programs in the United States.
Language	Ethnic and linguistic minority youths often achieve poorly in school because instruction is not conducted in their mother tongue.	To provide initial instruction in the child's mother tongue.	Teaching English as a Second Language programs; bilingual-bicultural education programs.
Racism	Racism is the major cause of the educational problems of non-White ethnic minority groups. The school can and should play a major role in eliminating institutional racism.	To reduce personal and institutional racism within the schools and the larger society.	Prejudice reduction; antiracist workshops and courses for teachers; antiracist lessons for students: an examination of the total environment to determine ways in which racism can be reduced, including curriculum materials, teacher attitudes, and school norms.

(continued)

TABLE 5.2   Continued

Paradigm	Major Assumptions	Major Goals	School Programs and Practices
Radical	A major goal of the school is to educate students so they will willingly accept their social-class status in society. The school cannot help liberate victimized ethnic and cultural groups because it plays a key role in keeping them oppressed. Lower-class ethnic groups cannot attain equality within a class-stratified capitalist society. Radical reform of the social structure is a prerequisite of equality for poor and minority students.	To raise the level of consciousness of students and teachers about the nature of capitalist, class-stratified societies; to help students and teachers develop a commitment to radical reform of the social and economic systems in capitalist societies.	
Genetic	Lower-class and ethnic minority youths often achieve poorly in school because of their biological characteristics. Educational intervention programs cannot eliminate the achievement gap between these students and majority-group students because of their different genetic characteristics.	To create a meritocracy based on intellectual ability as measured by standardized aptitude tests.	Ability-grouped classes; use of IQ tests to determine career goals for students; different career ladders for students who score differently on standardized tests.
Cultural Pluralism	Schools should promote ethnic identifications and allegiances. Educational programs should reflect the characteristics of ethnic students.	To promote the maintenance of groups; to promote the liberation of ethnic groups; to educate ethnic students in a way that will not alienate them from their home cultures.	Ethnic studies courses that are ideologically based; ethnic schools that focus on the maintenance of ethnic cultures and traditions.

Paradigm	Major Assumptions	Major Goals	School Programs and Practices
Cultural Difference	Minority youths have rich and diverse cultures that have values, languages, and behavioral styles that are functional for them and valuable for the nation-state.	To change the school so it respects and legitimizes the cultures of students from diverse ethnic groups and cultures.	Educational programs that reflect the learning styles of ethnic groups, that incorporate their cultures when developing instructional principles, and that integrate ethnic content into the mainstream curriculum.
Assimilationism	Ethnic minority youths should be freed of ethnic identifications and commitments so they can become full participants in the national culture. When schools foster ethnic commitments and identifications, this retards the academic growth of ethnic youths and contributes to the development of ethnic tension and Balkanization.	To educate students in a way that will free them of their ethnic characteristics and enable them to acquire the values and behavior of the mainstream culture.	A number of educational programs are based on assimilationist assumptions and goals, such as cultural deprivation programs, most Teaching English as a Second Language programs, and the mainstream curriculum in most Western nations. Despite the challenges they received during the 1970s, the curricula in the Western nations are still dominated by assimilationist goals and ideologies.

groups. It is much easier for them to add isolated bits of information about ethnic groups to the curriculum and to celebrate ethnic holidays than to meaningfully integrate ethnic content into the curriculum or to restructure the curriculum. Thus, African American History Month, American Indian Day, and Asian and Afro-Caribbean feasts and festivals become a part of the curriculum.

The ethnic additive paradigm also arises early because educational institutions tend to respond to the first phase of ethnic revitalization with quickly conceptualized and hurriedly formulated programs that are designed primarily to silence ethnic protest rather than to contribute to equality and to the structural inclusion of ethnic groups into society (Hu-DeHart, 1995). In each of the major Western nations, many early programs related to ethnic groups were poorly conceptualized and were implemented without careful and thoughtful planning. Such programs are usually attacked and eliminated during the later phases of ethnic revitalization, when the institutionalization of ethnic programs and reforms begins. The weaknesses of these early programs become the primary justification for their elimination. When such programs were attacked and eliminated in the United States in the 1980s many careful and sensitive observers stated that they had been designed to fail.

Two other major goals that educators express during the first phase of ethnic revitalization are to raise the self-concepts of students of color and to increase their racial pride. These goals develop because leaders of ethnic movements try to shape new and positive ethnic identities and because educators assume that members of ethnic groups who have experienced discrimination and structural exclusion have negative self-concepts and negative attitudes toward their own racial and ethnic groups. Much of the social science research before the 1960s reinforced this belief (Clark, 1963; Cross, 1991). Some leaders of ethnic movements also express it. Many educators assume that students need healthy self-concepts in order to do well in school. They also assume that content about ethnic heroes and holidays will enhance the self-concepts and academic achievements of ethnic groups (Asante, 1991). Stone has described some of the serious limitations of the self-concept paradigm (Stone, 1981).

Implications for School Practice

The ethnic additive and self-concept development paradigms often result in policies and school practices that require no fundamental changes in the views, assumptions, and institutional practices of teachers and administrators. These paradigms often lead to the trivialization of ethnic cultures by well-meaning teachers (Moodley, 1995). The emphasis is usually on the life-styles of ethnic groups rather than on reform of the social and political systems so that the opportunities and life chances of low-income students and students of color can be substantially improved (Giroux & McLaren, 1994; McLaren, 1997). Policy that emanates from the ethnic additive and self-concept development paradigms often results in educators doing little more than adding into the curriculum isolated bits of ethnic content designed to enhance the self-concepts of students of color. A fundamental rethinking of the total curriculum does not take place because the assumption is made that only students of color need to study ethnic content. Much of the ethnic studies curricula in the schools, especially during the early phase of ethnic revitalization movements, reflects the ethnic additive and self-concept development paradigms.

The Cultural Deprivation Paradigm

Cultural deprivation theories, programs, and research often develop during the first phase of an ethnic revitalization movement. Cultural deprivation theorists assume that low-income students do not achieve well in school because of family disorganization, poverty, and the lack of effective concept acquisition, and also because of other intellectual and cultural deficits these students experience during their first years of life (Keddie, 1973). Cultural deprivation theorists assume that a major goal of school programs for so-called culturally deprived students is to provide them with cultural and other experiences that will compensate for their cognitive and intellectual deficits. Cultural deprivation theorists believe that low-income students can learn the basic skills taught in the schools but that these skills must often be taught using intensive, behaviorally oriented instruction (Bereiter & Engelmann, 1966).

Programs based on cultural deprivation theory, such as most of the compensatory education programs in the United States, are structured in such a way that they require students to make major changes in their behavior. Teachers and other educators are required to make few changes in their behavior or in educational institutions. Such programs also ignore the cultures that students bring to school and assume that low-income students and students of color are culturally deprived or disadvantaged. Some of these programs in the United States have been able to help low-income students and students of color to experience achievement gains, but these gains are often not maintained as the students progress through the grades.

Implications for School Practice

Teachers and administrators who accept the cultural deprivation paradigm often blame the victims for their problems and academic failure (Gordon, 1999; Ryan, 1971). These educators argue that low-income students and students of color often do poorly in school because of their cultural and social-class characteristics, not because they are ineffectively taught. They believe that the school is severely limited in what it can do to help these students to achieve because of the culture into which they are socialized.

School programs based on the cultural deprivation paradigm try to alienate students from their first cultures because these cultures are regarded as the primary reason students from specific cultural groups are not achieving well in school. Students are forced to choose between commitment to their first cultures and educational success.

Educational programs and practices based on the cultural deprivation paradigm reflect and perpetuate the status quo and dominant group hegemony, ideology, and values. They do not question the extent to which dominant group values, assumptions, and societal practices keep low-income students and students of color marginalized and prevent them from becoming empowered and structurally integrated into mainstream society.

The Language Paradigm

Often during the early stage of ethnic revitalization, or when a large number of immigrants settle in a nation and enroll in the schools, educators view the problems of these groups as resulting primarily from their language or dialect differences. When the West Indians and Asians first enrolled in British schools in significant numbers in the 1960s, many British educators believed that if they could solve the language problems of these youths the students would experience academic success in British schools. British educators' early responses to the problems of immigrant children were thus almost exclusively related to language (Figueroa, 1995). Special programs were set up to train teachers and to develop materials for teaching English as a second language to immigrant students. French educators also viewed the problems of the North African and Asian students in their schools in the late 1970s as primarily language-related (Banks, 1978).

In the United States, the educational problems of Puerto Ricans and Mexican Americans are often assumed to be rooted in language (Genesee, 1994; Minami & Kennedy, 1991). Some supporters of bilingual education in the United States argued during the 1970s that if the language problems of these students were solved, they would experience academic success in the schools. As bilingual programs were established in the United States, educators began to realize that many other factors, such as social class, learning styles, and motivation, were also important variables that influenced the academic achievement of Latino ethnic groups in the United States.

The experiences with programs based on the language paradigm in the Western nations teach us that an exclusive language approach to the educational problems of ethnic and immigrant groups is insufficient. Languages are integral parts of cultures. Consequently, any attempt to educate students effectively from diverse language and cultural groups must be comprehensive in scope and must focus on variables in the educational environment other than language. An exclusive language approach is unlikely to help language minority students attain educational parity with mainstream students.

The Racism Paradigm

Sometime early during an ethnic revitalization movement, groups of color and their liberal allies usually state that institutionalized racism is the only or most important cause of the problems of ethnic groups in school and society (Lee, 1998). This claim by ethnic minorities usually evokes a counterclaim by those who defend the status quo, and an intense debate ensues. This debate usually takes place during the first phase of ethnic revitalization, when ethnic polarization and tension are high. The debate between those who claim that racism is the cause of the problems of ethnic groups and those who deny this claim is usually not productive because each side sets forth extreme and competing claims.

A major goal of the racism advocates is not so much to convince other people that racism does, in fact, cause all of the problems of marginalized ethnic groups. Rather, their goals are to legitimize racism as a valid explanation and to convince leaders and people who defend the status quo that racism is a historic and institutionalized part of Western societies. The debate between radical reformers and conservative defenders of the status quo remains stalemated and single-focused until the dominant group acknowledges the existence of racism and takes meaningful steps to eliminate it. Until this acknowledgment is made in official statements, policies, and actions, radical reformers will continue to state that racism is the single cause of the social, economic, and educational problems of marginalized ethnic groups.

Radical reformers will not search for or find more complex paradigms that explain the problems of marginalized ethnic groups until mainstream leaders acknowledge the existence of institutionalized racism. In other words, institutionalized racism must become legitimized as an explanation, and serious steps must be taken to eliminate it before an ethnic revitalization movement can reach a phase in which other paradigms will be accepted by radical reformers who articulate the interests of groups that are victims of institutionalized racism. Societies and nations are not successful in making the racism paradigm less popular until official bodies and leaders validate it, acknowledge that racism exists in the society, and take visible and vigorous steps to eliminate it, such as enacting legislation that prevents discrimination and hiring minorities for influential jobs in the public and private sectors.

The Radical Paradigm

A radical paradigm tends to develop during the early or later stage of ethnic revitalization. It usually has a critical theory or reproductionist orientation (Giroux & McLaren, 1994; McLaren, 1997). The other paradigms assume that the school can successfully intervene and help students of color and low-income students attain social and political equality, but the radical paradigm assumes that the school is part of the problem and plays a key role in keeping ethnic groups oppressed. Thus, it is very difficult for the school to help liberate oppressed groups because one of its central purposes is to educate students so that they will willingly accept their assigned status in society. A primary role of the school is to reproduce the current social-class, economic, and political structures.

The radical paradigm stresses the limited role that schools can play to eliminate racism and discrimination and to promote equality for low-income students. Jencks (Jencks, et al., 1972) believes that the schools have limited effects on income distribution and on equality. He argues that the most effective way to bring about equality for low-income citizens is to equalize incomes directly rather than to rely on the schools to bring about equality in the adult life of students. He suggests that the schooling route is much too indirect and will most likely result in failure. Bowles and Gintis (1976) wrote a neo-Marxist critique of schools in the United States that documents in considerable detail how schools reinforce the social-class stratification within society and make students politically passive and content with their social-class status.

The radical paradigm argues that multicultural education is a palliative to keep excluded and oppressed groups such as African Americans from rebelling against a system that promotes structural inequality and institutionalized racism. The radical critics contend that multicultural education does not deal with the real reasons that ethnic and racial groups are oppressed and victimized. It avoids any serious discussion of class, institutionalized racism, power, and capitalism (McCarthy, 1990). Multicultural education, argue the radical critics, diverts attention from the real problems and issues. They argue that we need to focus on the institutions and structures of society rather than on the characteristics of low-income students or on cultural differences.

One shortcoming of the radical paradigm is that by focusing on the power of social, economic, and political structures, it does not give sufficient attention to the agency evidenced by students and teachers. Teachers and students are not totally victimized by the social, political, and economic structures. They evidence agency and empowerment. Working-class youths, as Willis (1977) points out in his classic study, evidence agency in school and in society, often in ways that contribute to their marginalized status.

Theorists such as McLaren (1997) and Sleeter and McLaren (1995) are reconstructing and rethinking multicultural education so that it will deal more directly with issues of power, racism, and economic inequality. They call their work "critical multiculturalism." Anti-racism (Lee, 1998), which is a concept used more frequently in Canada and Europe than in the United States, focuses on the ways in which racism promotes structural inequality of groups who are victimized by racism. Each of these projects can contribute to a stronger and more powerful multicultural education.

Responding to the Radical Critics

Multicultural theorists need to study seriously the critics of the field, evaluate their arguments for soundness and validity, and incorporate their ideas that will contribute to the main goals of multicultural education. These goals include reforming the total school environment so that students from diverse racial, ethnic, and cultural groups will experience educational equality. Realistically, goals for multicultural education must be limited. Educators have little control over the wider society or over students when they leave the classroom. Educators can teach students the basic skills and can help them to develop more democratic attitudes by creating school and classroom environments that promote cultural democracy.

However, schools alone cannot eliminate racism and inequality in the wider society. They can reinforce democratic social and political movements that take place beyond the school walls and thus contribute in important ways to the elimination of institutional racism and structural inequality. The multicultural curriculum can give students keen insights into racism and inequality within their societies and thus help them develop a commitment to social change.

Multicultural theorists need to think seriously about the radical arguments that multicultural education is a palliative to contain ethnic rage and that it does not deal seriously with the structural inequalities in society and with such important concepts as racism, class, structural inequality, and capitalism. During the early stages of multicultural education in the United States, when it focused primarily on teaching the cultures and histories of ethnic groups of color, the attention devoted to concepts such as racism and structural inequality was salient. Yet, as the ethnic studies movement expanded to include more and more ethnic groups and eventually to include feminist issues and other cultural groups, increasingly less attention was devoted to racism and to the analysis of power relationships.

The radical critique of multicultural education—and the group of theorists who are constructing "critical multiculturalism"—should stimulate multicultural educators to devote more attention to such issues as racism, power relationships, and structural inequality. The radical writers are accurate when they argue that racism and structural inequality are the root causes of many problems of low-income groups and groups of color in modernized Western nations such as the United States and the United Kingdom. However, multicultural educators must live with the contradiction that they are trying to promote democratic and humane reforms within schools, which are institutions that often reflect and perpetuate some of the salient antidemocratic values pervasive within the wider society.

Contradiction is an integral part of social, economic, and political change. The school itself is contradictory, because it often expounds democratic values while at the same time contradicting them. Thus, the radical scholars overstate their case when they argue that the schools merely perpetuate and reproduce the inequalities in society. The influence of the schools on individuals is neither as unidimensional nor as cogent as some radical critics claim. The school, both explicitly and implicitly, teaches both democratic and antiegalitarian values, just as the wider society does. Thus, the schools, like the society of which they are a part, create the kind of moral dilemma for people that Gunnar Myrdal (1944) described when he studied U.S. race relations in the 1940s. Myrdal believed that this moral dilemma made social change possible because most Americans felt a need to make the democratic ideals they inculcated and societal practices more consistent.

The Genetic Paradigm

The ideology and research developed by radical reformers do not go unchallenged. An ideological war takes place between radical reformers and conservatives who defend the status quo. While radical and liberal reformers develop ideology and research to show how the major problems of ethnic groups are caused by institutionalized racism and capitalism, antiegalitarian advocates and researchers develop an ideology and research stating that the failure of ethnic groups in school and society is due to their own inherited or socialized characteristics.

Both radical reformers and conservative scholars tend to develop single-causal paradigms during the early phase of ethnic revitalization. The paradigms developed by radical theorists tend to focus on racism and other structural and institutional problems in society, and those developed by conservative researchers usually focus on the characteristics of marginalized students themselves, such as their genetic characteristics and their family socialization.

In the United States the most popular antiegalitarian theories focus on the genetic characteristics of African American and low-income students; these theories were developed by such researchers as Jensen (1969), Shockley (1972), and Herrnstein (1971). Jensen argues that the genetic makeup of African Americans is the most important reason that compensatory educational programs, designed to increase the IQ of African American students, have not been more successful. Shockley developed a theory about the genetic inferiority of African Americans that is less accepted by the academic community than is Jensen's.

In 1971, Herrnstein published his controversial article, which argued that social class reflects genetic differences, in *Atlantic Monthly,* a widely circulated and highly respected popular magazine. In this article, as well as in his book published in 1973, Herrnstein focused on the relationship between social class and IQ, and not on race and IQ. In their influential and controversial book published in 1994, *The Bell Curve,* Herrnstein and Murray also devoted most of the book to a discussion of social class and IQ. However, two of the book's 22 chapters focused of race and IQ. The press focused on these two chapters. The work became widely interpreted as a book primarily about race and IQ. It greatly harmed the quest for equality by African Americans. Educators not committed to educational equality for low-income students and students of color often embrace the genetic paradigm. They use it as an alibi for educational neglect.

Implications for School Practice

The assumption that IQ and other tests of mental ability can accurately measure innate mental ability is institutionalized and perpetuated within the schools (Gordon, 1999). Students are assigned to academic tracks based on their performance on tests of mental ability and on other factors such as teacher recommendations and grades. A highly disproportionate number of low-income students and students of color are assigned to lower-ability tracks. Assignment to lower academic tracks actualizes the self-fulfilling prophecy (Merton, 1968). Research by Oakes and Guiton (1995) documents how teacher expectations of students vary in different kinds of tracks. Students in higher academic tracks are expected to learn more and are consequently taught more; those in lower tracks are expected to learn less and are consequently taught less.

The tracking system, which is widespread within U.S. schools, perpetuates social-class and ethnic inequality and teaches students to be content with their social-class status. The genetic paradigm is used to support and justify the tracking system. It perpetuates dominant ethnic group hegemony, inequality, and class and ethnic stratification. Darling-Hammond (1995) has described the relationship between quality of teaching and student achievement. Her research indicates that high quality teaching is positively related to high student achievement, rather than to the cultural and racial characteristics of students.

Competing Paradigms

Particularly during the later stage of ethnic revitalization, when aspects of ethnic diversity are being implemented within the schools, an intense clash of ideologies and paradigms is likely to occur between people committed to ethnic pluralism

CHAPTER 5 / Race, Diversity, and Educational Paradigms **103**

and people who endorse assimilationism and are committed to preserving the status quo. The language paradigm (which often includes a call for bilingual education), the racism paradigm, and the radical paradigm are especially likely to evoke strong responses from assimilationists, who are committed to developing strong national commitments and identifications. In the United States, the call for bilingual education and the federal legislation and court decisions that promoted it stimulated one of the most acid educational debates in recent history (Garcia, 1999).

A cultural pluralism paradigm tends to emerge during the first phase of ethnic revitalization. It maintains that a major goal of the schools should be to help students develop commitments and attachments to their ethnic groups so they can participate in the liberation of those groups. Cultural pluralists believe that ethnicity and ethnic cultures have a significant influence on the socialization of students and thus should strongly influence the formulation of educational policies and programs (Asante, 1991).

As the ethnic revitalization movement develops, more moderate paradigms emerge, such as the cultural difference and bicultural paradigms. The cultural difference paradigm maintains that low-income students and students of color often do not achieve well in school not because they have a deprived culture, but because their cultures are different from the culture of the school. The school should therefore modify the educational environment in order to make it more consistent with the cultures of low-income students and students of color. If this is done, the students will experience academic gains in the school.

Assimilationists often oppose such pluralist programs as bilingual education and ethnic studies because, they argue, these programs prevent students from learning the skills needed to become effective citizens of the nation-state and from developing strong national loyalties. They also argue that pluralist educational programs promote ethnic attachments and loyalties that contribute to ethnic conflict, polarization, and stratification. Assimilationists maintain that the primary goal of the school should be to socialize students so that they attain the knowledge, attitudes, and skills needed to become effective citizens of their nation-states (Appiah, 1996). During the final phases of ethnic revitalization, assimilationist paradigms tend to become increasingly conservative. In the United States during the 1980s assimilationism developed into a neoconservative ideology that was strongly nationalistic and reactionary (Steinfels, 1979).

The Need for a Multifactor Paradigm and Holism

A number of single-factor paradigms attempt to explain why low-income students and students of color often do poorly in school. Proponents of these paradigms often become ardent in their views, insisting that one major variable explains the problem of marginalized students and that their educational problems can be solved if major policies are implemented related to a specific explanation or paradigm.

Many existing reforms in multicultural education, such as compensatory education and bilingual programs, are based on single-factor paradigms. Proponents of the ethnic additive and self-concept development paradigms believe that ethnic content and heroes can help low-income students and students of color increase their academic achievement; cultural deprivation proponents view cultural enrichment as the most important variable influencing academic achievement; radical scholars often view the school as having little possibility of significantly influencing the life-chances of low-income students and students of color.

Experiences in the major Western nations within the last three decades teach us that the academic achievement problems of students of color and low-income students are too complex to be solved with reforms based on single-factor paradigms and explanations (Moodley, 1992). Education is broader than schooling, and many problems that ethnic minority students experience in the schools reflect the problems in the wider society. The radical critique of schooling is useful because it helps us see the limitations of formal schooling. However, the radical paradigm is limited because it gives us few concrete guidelines about what *can* be done after we have acknowledged that schools are limited in their ability to bring about equality for low-income students and students of color. This paradigm also underestimates the agency of teachers and students.

When designing reform strategies, we must be keenly sensitive to the limitations of formal schooling. However, we must also be tenacious in our faith that the school can play a limited but cogent role in bringing about equal educational opportunities for low-income students and students of color, and in helping all students to develop cross-cultural understandings and competencies (Darling-Hammond, 1997; Gordon, 1999; Wang & Gordon, 1994). To design school programs that will effectively help students of color to increase their academic achievement and will help all students develop multicultural literacy and cross-cultural competency, we must conceptualize the school as a system in which all major variables and components are highly interrelated. *A holistic paradigm, which conceptualizes the school as an interrelated whole, is needed to guide educational reform.*

Viewing the school as a social system can help us derive an idea of school reform that can help students of color and low-income students to increase their academic achievement and help all students develop more democratic attitudes and values. Although our theory and research about multicultural education is limited and developing (Banks, 1995), both research and theory indicate that educators can successfully intervene to help students increase their academic achievement and develop more democratic attitudes and values (Ross, Smith, Casey, & Slavin, 1995; Schofield, 1995).

Conceptualizing the school as a social system suggests that we must formulate and initiate a change strategy that reforms the total school environment in order to implement multicultural education successfully. Reforming any one variable, such as curriculum materials or the formal curriculum, is necessary but not sufficient. Multicultural and sensitive teaching materials are ineffective in the hands of teachers who have negative attitudes toward different ethnic and cultural groups. Such teachers are not likely to use multicultural materials or to use them in a detrimental way when they do. Thus, helping teachers and other members of the school staff develop democratic attitudes and values is essential when implementing multicultural programs and experiences.

When formulating plans for multicultural education, educators should conceptualize the school as a microculture that has norms, values, roles, statuses, and goals like other cultural systems. The school has a dominant culture and a variety of subcultures. Almost all classrooms in Western societies are multicultural because European American students, as well as African American and Latino students, are socialized within diverse cultures. Teachers in schools in Western societies also come from many different ethnic groups and cultures. Although they may be forgotten and repressed, many teachers were socialized in cultures other than the mainstream one. The school is a microculture in which the cultures of students and teachers meet. *The school should be a cultural environment in which acculturation takes place: both teachers and students should assimilate some of the views, perceptions, and ethos of each other as they interact* (see Figure 5.1). Both teachers and students will be enriched by this process, and the academic achievement of students from diverse cultures will be enhanced because their cosmos and ethos will be reflected and legitimized in the school.

Historically, schools in Western societies have had assimilation rather than acculturation as their major goal. The students were expected to acquire the dominant culture of the school and society, but the school neither legitimized nor assimilated parts of the student's culture. Assimilation and acculturation are different in important ways. Assimilation involves the complete elimination of cultural differences and differentiating group identifications. When acculturation occurs, a culture is modified through contact with one or more other cultures but maintains its essence (Theodorson & Theodorson, 1969).

Both acculturation and accommodation should take place in today's schools in Western democratic societies. *When accommodation occurs, groups with diverse cultures maintain their separate identities but live in peaceful interaction.* However, in order for successful accommodation to take place, various ethnic and cultural groups must have equal status and share power (Cohen & Lotan, 1995). It is essential that schools in Western democracies acculturate students rather than foster tight ethnic boundaries because all students, including low-income students and students of color, must develop the knowledge, attitudes, and skills needed to become successful citizens of their cultural communities, their nation-states, and the global world community.

Summary

The achievement of most ethnic minority students is far below that of mainstream students in the major Western nations, such as the United States, Canada, the United Kingdom, and Australia. Groups such as Mexicans in the United States, Indians and

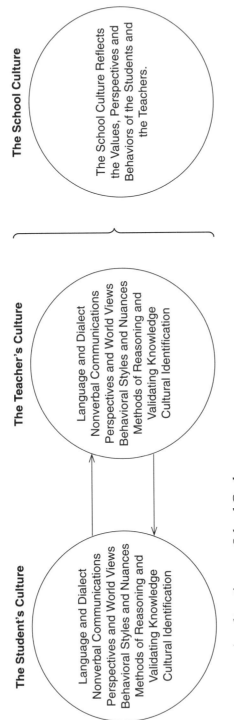

The School Culture

The School Culture Reflects the Values, Perspectives and Behaviors of the Students and the Teachers.

The Teacher's Culture

Language and Dialect
Nonverbal Communications
Perspectives and World Views
Behavioral Styles and Nuances
Methods of Reasoning and
Validating Knowledge
Cultural Identification

The Student's Culture

Language and Dialect
Nonverbal Communications
Perspectives and World Views
Behavioral Styles and Nuances
Methods of Reasoning and
Validating Knowledge
Cultural Identification

FIGURE 5.1 Acculturation as a School Goal
When the student assimilates elements of the teacher's culture and the teacher assimilates elements of the student's culture, the school culture becomes a synthesized cultural system that reflects the cultures of all of its participants.

Metis in Canada, Jamaicans in the United Kingdom, and the Australian Aborigines have academic achievement scores far below those of dominant mainstream groups in their societies. A number of explanations have been formulated to posit why the academic achievement of these students is below that of their mainstream peers. The various explanations—called *paradigms* in this chapter—have been formulated at different times in the various Western nations. These paradigms are based on different assumptions and values and imply different policy, action, and educational programs.

This chapter describes ten major paradigms: ethnic additive, self-concept development, cultural deprivation, language, racism, radical, genetic, cultural pluralism, cultural difference, and assimilationism. Single-factor paradigms often dominate policy and research discussions in multicultural education. However, multifactor paradigms must be used to guide educational reform and practice if educational institutions are to promote equality and help all students develop the knowledge, attitudes, and skills needed to function effectively in a culturally diverse society and world.

REFERENCES

Appiah, K. A. (1996). Culture, Subculture, Multiculturalism: Educational Options. In R. K. Fullinwider (Ed.), *Public Education in a Multicultural Society* (pp. 65–89). New York: Cambridge University Press.

Asante, M. K. (1991). The Afrocentric Idea in Education. *The Journal of Negro Education, 60,* 170–180.

Banks, J. A. (1978). Multiethnic Education across Cultures: United States, Mexico, Puerto Rico, France, and Great Britain. *Social Education, 42,* 177–185.

Banks, J. A. (1995). Multicultural Education: Historical Development, Dimensions, and Practice. In J. A. Banks & C. A. M. Banks (Eds.), *Handbook of Research on Multicultural Education* (pp. 3–25). New York: Macmillan.

Banks, J. A. (1997). *Educating Citizens in a Multicultural Society.* New York: Teachers College Press.

Baratz, S. S., & Baratz, J. C. (1970). Early Childhood Intervention: The Social Science Base of Institutional Racism. *Harvard Educational Review, 40,* 29–50.

Barnes, B. (1982). *T. S. Kuhn and Social Science.* New York: Columbia University Press.

Bereiter, C., & Engelmann, S. (1966). *Teaching Disadvantaged Children in the Preschool.* Englewood Cliffs, NJ: Prentice-Hall.

Bowles, S., & Gintis, H. (1976). *Schooling in Capitalist America.* New York: Basic Books.

Clark, K. B. (1963). *Prejudice and Your Child.* Boston: Beacon Press.

Cohen, E. G., & Lotan, R. A. (1995). Producing Equal-Status Interaction in the Heterogeneous Classroom. *American Educational Research Journal, 32* (1), 99–120.

Cross, W. E. (1991). *Shades of Black: Diversity in African-American Identity.* Philadelphia: Temple University Press.

Cuban, L. (1989). The "At-Risk" Label and the Problem of Urban School Reform. *Phi Delta Kappan, 70* (10), 780–801.

Darling-Hammond, L. (1995). Inequality and Access to Knowledge. In J. A. Banks & C. A. M. Banks (Eds.), *Handbook of Research on Multicultural Education* (pp. 465–483). New York: Macmillan.

Darling-Hammond, L. (1997). *The Right to Learn: A Blueprint for Creating Schools That Work.* San Francisco: Jossey-Bass.

Deyhle, D., & Swisher, K. (1997). Research in American Indian and Alaska Native Education: From Assimilation to Self-Determination. In M. W. Apple (Ed.), *Review of Research in Education* (Vol. 22), (pp. 113–194). Washington, DC.: American Educational Research Association.

Figueroa, P. (1995). Multicultural Education in the United Kingdom: Historical Development and Current Status. In J. A. Banks & C. A. M. Banks

(Eds.), *Handbook of Research on Multicultural Education* (pp. 778–800). New York: Macmillan.

Garcia, E. E. (1999). Chicanos/as in the United States: Language, Bilingual Education, and Achievement. In J. F. Moreno (Ed.), *The Elusive Quest for Equality: 150 Years of Chicano/Chicana Education* (pp. 141–168). Cambridge, MA: Harvard Educational Review.

Genesee, F. (Ed.). (1994). *Educating Second Language Children.* New York: Cambridge University Press.

Giroux, H. A., & McLaren, P. (Eds.). (1994). *Between Borders: Pedagogy and the Politics of Cultural Studies.* New York: Routledge.

Gordon, E. W. (1999). *Education and Justice: A View from the Back of the Bus.* New York: Teachers College Press.

Herrnstein, R. J. (1971). I.Q. *Atlantic Monthly, 228,* 43–64.

Herrnstein, R. J., & Murray, C. (1994). *The Bell Curve: Intelligence and Class Structure in American Life.* New York: The Free Press.

Hu-DeHart, E. (1995). Ethnic Studies in U.S. Higher Education: History, Development, and Goals. In J. A. Banks & C. A. M. Banks (Eds.), *Handbook of Research on Multicultural Education* (pp. 696–707). New York: Macmillan.

Jencks, C. et al. (1972). *Inequality: A Reassessment of the Effect of Family and Schooling in America.* New York: Basic Books.

Jensen, A. R. (1969). How Much Can We Boost IQ and Scholastic Achievement? *Harvard Educational Review, 39,* 1–123.

Keddie, N. (1973). *The Myth of Cultural Deprivation.* Baltimore: Penguin Books.

Kuhn, I. S. (1970). *The Structure of Scientific Revolutions* (2nd ed.). Chicago: University of Chicago Press.

Lee, E. (1998). Anti-Racist Education: Pulling Together to Close the Gaps. In E. Lee, D. Menkart, & M. Okazawa-Rey, M. (Eds.), *Beyond Heroes and Holidays* (pp. 26–34). Washington, DC.: Network of Educators on the Americas.

Lee, S. M. (1998). Asian Americans: Diverse and Growing. *Population Bulletin, 53*(2), 1–40. Washington, DC.: Population Reference Bureau.

McCarthy, C. (1990). *Race and Curriculum.* New York: Falmer Press.

McLaren, P. (1997). *Revolutionary Multiculturalism: Pedagogies of Dissent for the New Millennium.* Boulder, CO: Westview.

Merton, R. K. (1968). *Social Theory and Social Structure* (enlarged ed.). New York: The Free Press.

Miller, L. S. (1995). *An American Imperative: Accelerating Minority Educational Advancement.* New Haven, CT: Yale University Press.

Minami, M., & Kennedy, B. P. (Eds.). (1991). *Language Issues in Literacy and Bilingual/Multicultural Education,* Reprint Series #22. Cambridge, MA: Harvard Educational Review.

Moodley, K. A. (Ed.). (1992). *Beyond Multicultural Education: International Perspectives.* Calgary, Alberta: Detselig Enterprises Ltd.

Moodley, K. A. (1995). Multicultural Education in Canada: Historical Development and Current Status. In J. A. Banks & C. A. M. Banks (Eds.), *Handbook of Research on Multicultural Education* (pp. 763–777). New York: Macmillan.

Myrdal, G. (1944). *An American Dilemma: The Negro Problem and Modern Democracy.* New York: Harper & Row.

Nettles, M. T., & Perna, L. W. (1997). *The African American Education Data Book,* Vol. II: *Preschool through High School Education.* Fairfax, VA: Frederick D. Patterson Research Institute.

Oakes, J., & Guiton, G. (1995). Matchmaking: The Dynamics of High School Tracking Decisions. *American Educational Research Journal, 32*(1), 3–33.

Pang, V. O., & Cheng L. L. (Eds.). (1998). *Struggling to Be Heard: The Unmet Needs of Asian Pacific American Children.* Albany: State University of New York Press.

Ross, S. M., Smith, L. J., Casey, J., & Slavin, R. E. (1995). Increasing the Academic Success of Disadvantaged Children: An Examination of Alternative Early Intervention Programs. *American Educational Research Journal, 32*(4), 773–800.

Ryan, W. (1971). *Blaming the Victim.* New York: Vintage Books.

Schofield, J. W. (1995). Improving Intergroup Relations among Students. In J. A. Banks & C. A. M. Banks (Eds.), *Handbook of Research on Multicultural Education* (pp. 635–646). New York: Macmillan.

Shockley, W. (1972). Dysgenics, Geneticity, Raceology: A Challenge to the Intellectual Responsibility of Educators. *Phi Delta Kappan, 53,* 297–307.

Sleeter, C. E., & McLaren, P. L. (Eds.). (1995). *Multicultural Education, Critical Pedagogy, and the Politics of Difference.* Albany: State University of New York Press.

Steinfels, P. (1979). *The Neoconservatives: The Men Who Are Changing America's Politics.* New York: Simon & Schuster.

Stone, M. (1981). *The Education of the Black Child in Britain: The Myth of Multiracial Education.* Glasgow: Fontana.

Suárez-Orozco, C., & Suárez-Orozco, M. (1995). *Transformations: Migration, Family Life, and Achievement Motivation among Latino Adolescents.* Stanford, CA: Stanford University Press.

Theodorson, G. A., & Theodorson, A. G. (1969). *A Modern Dictionary of Sociology.* New York: Barnes and Noble.

U.S. Bureau of the Census. (1998). *Statistical Abstract of the United States: 1998* (118th ed.). Washington, DC.: US. Government Printing Office.

Wang, M. C., & Gordon, E. W. (Eds.). (1994). *Educational Resilience in Inner-City America: Challenges and Prospectus.* Hillside, NJ: Lawrence Erlbaum.

Willis, P. (1977). *Learning to Labor: How Working Class Kids Get Working Class Jobs.* New York: Columbia University Press.

6 Pluralism, Ideology, and Educational Reform

Since the 1960s, educational institutions throughout the United States and other Western nations have implemented a variety of reforms related to diversity. Some of the reforms have been successful. Others have experienced problems that result from ideological conflicts and contested concepts. A number of important questions concerning the relationship between education and diversity have not been satisfactorily clarified or resolved. Concept clarification and more consensus are needed to implement more powerful and successful reforms.

A key question is: *How should public institutions such as schools, colleges and universities relate to diversity?* Should public institutions promote, remain neutral to, or ignore the cultural and ethnic characteristics of its students and diversity within society? Many educational leaders believe that educational institutions should not ignore diversity but should implement curricular reforms related to it. However, little agreement exists about what kinds of reforms should be initiated and about how they can best be implemented (Gutmann, 1994; Smelser & Alexander, 1999).

Views on diversity and schools, colleges, and universities range from beliefs that diversity should be an integral and salient part of the curriculum to cautions that too much emphasis on diversity might be harmful to the national culture and promote divisiveness (D'Souza, 1995; Gutmann, 1994; King, 1995; Schuman & Olufs, 1995; Smelser & Alexander, 1999). Views on diversity and education reflect different ideologies and have conflicting implications for policy and practice. These ideologies and their implications need to be uncovered and made explicit.

This chapter identifies two major ideological positions related to diversity and education that are evident in Western nations such as the United States, the United Kingdom, Canada, Australia, and the Netherlands (Gillborn, 1995; Moodley, 1992; Partington, 1998; Sarup, 1991; Troyna, 1993). The major assumptions and arguments of these positions are discussed and their limitations for educational reform are identified. The chapter then describes an ideological position that reflects both major ideologies and argues that it can best guide policy, practice, and reform. The final part of this chapter discusses the implications of this ideology—called the *multicultural ideology*—for educational policy and practice.

It is very important for the reader to realize that the ideological positions identified and described are ideal-type concepts. As pointed out in Chapter 9, an ideal-type idea does not define any specific case, but it is intended to help us describe, compare, discuss, and sharpen our observations. The two major positions in their ideal forms do not accurately describe the views of any particular writer or theorist. However, various views on diversity can be roughly classified using a continuum that has the two ideologies, in their ideal forms, at the extreme ends. The two major positions are the *cultural pluralist* ideology and the *assimilationist* ideology.

The Cultural Pluralist Ideology

The cultural pluralist ideology has been formulated in different societies and takes various forms (Asante, 1991; Gordon, 1995; Sarup, 1991). The pluralist makes assumptions about the nature of pluralistic democratic societies, the function of the ethnic group in socializing the individual, and the responsibility that the individual members of a marginalized ethnic group have to its liberation struggle. The pluralist also makes assumptions about research, learning, teacher education, and the goals of educational reform.

The pluralist argues that cultural and ethnic identities are very important in pluralistic Western societies. Western nation-states, according to the pluralist, consist of competing cultural and ethnic groups, each of which champions its own economic and political interests. It is extremely important, argues the pluralist, for individuals to develop a commitment to their cultural and ethnic group, especially if that group is oppressed by more powerful groups within society. The energies and skills of each member of a cultural or ethnic group are needed to help in that group's liberation struggle. Each individual member of the group has a moral obligation to join the liberation struggle. Thus, the pluralist stresses the rights of the group over the rights of the individual. The pluralist also assumes that a cultural or ethnic group can attain inclusion and full participation within a society only when it can bargain from a powerful position and when it has closed ranks within (Carmichael & Hamilton, 1967; Cruse, 1967).

The pluralist views the cultural or ethnic group as extremely important in the socialization of the individual within a modernized society. It is within their own particular cultural groups that individuals develop their languages, lifestyles, and values. They also experience important primary group relationships and attachments. The cultural community also serves as a supportive environment for individuals and helps to protect them from the harshness and discrimination they might experience in the wider society. The cultural community thus provides individuals with a sense of identity and psychological support, both of which are extremely important within a modernized society controlled primarily by one dominant group. The pluralist believes that community cultures are very important and that public institutions, such as schools, colleges, and universities, should actively promote the interests of the various cultural and ethnic groups in its policies and practices.

The pluralist makes assumptions about research that differ from those made by the assimilationist. The pluralist assumes that the cultures of students of color are not disadvantaged, deviant, or deficient; rather, they are well ordered and highly structured but different from each other and from the mainstream, dominant culture (Smitherman, 1999). Thus, the pluralist uses a culture difference model when researching ethnic and cultural groups, whereas the assimilationist researcher uses a deficit model or a genetic model. Because of their different research assumptions, the cultural pluralist researcher and the assimilationist researcher frequently derive different, and often conflicting, research conclusions. A number of researchers who are multiculturalists have used the cultural difference model extensively in their research studies on ethnic groups and have done a great deal to legitimize it within the social science and educational communities (Delpit, 1995; Suárez-Orozco & Suárez-Orozco, 1995).

The cultural pluralist also assumes that students of color have unique learning styles and that the school curriculum and teaching strategies should be revised to be more consistent with the cultural, cognitive and learning styles of students (Boykin, 1994; Gay, 2000; Hale, 1994; Shade, Kelly, & Oberg, 1997).

Pluralists, because of their assumptions about the importance of the ethnic and cultural group in the lives of students, believe the curriculum should be revised to reflect the cognitive styles, cultural history, and present experiences of cultural groups, especially students of color. The cultural pluralist believes that if the school, college, and university curriculum were more consistent with the experiences of cultural groups, the learning and adjustment problems that students of color experience in the education would be greatly reduced. Thus, the cultural pluralist argues that learning materials should be culture-specific and that a goal of the curriculum should be to help the students function more successfully within their community culture. The curriculum focuses on events from the points of view of specific ethnic groups (Asante, 1991; Gordon, 1995). It should promote cultural and ethnic attachments and allegiances and help students gain the skills and commitments needed to participate in civic action to help empower their cultural group.

The Assimilationist Ideology

The assimilationist thinks that the pluralist greatly exaggerates the extent of cultural differences in Western societies. However, the assimilationist does not deny that cultural and ethnic differences exist within Western societies or that ethnicity is very important to some groups. However, the assimilationist and the pluralist interpret ethnicity in Western societies differently. The assimilationist tends to see ethnic attachments as fleeting and temporary within a modernized world (Patterson, 1977; Schlesinger, 1991). Ethnicity, argues the assimilationist, wanes or disappears under the impact of modernization. The assimilationist believes that ethnicity is more important in developing societies than in highly modernized societies and that it crumbles under the forces of modernization and democratization (Apter, 1977). The assimilationist views the modernized state as universalistic rather than characterized by strong ethnic allegiances and attachments (D'Souza, 1995; Patterson, 1977).

Not only do assimilationists view ethnicity as inconsistent with modernized societies, they believe that strong ethnic attachments are dysfunctional in a modernized civic community. Assimilationists believe that the ethnic group promotes group rights over the rights of the individual and that the individual must be freed of ethnic attachments in order to have choices within society. The assimilationist believes that ethnic attachments and affiliation harm the goals of a modern nation-state. Ethnicity, argues the assimilationist, promotes divisions, exhumes ethnic conflicts, and leads to the Balkanization of society. The assimilationist sees integration as a societal goal in a modernized state and not ethnic segregation and separatism.

The assimilationist thinks that the best way to promote the goals of society and to develop commitments to democratic ideals is to promote the full socialization of all individuals and groups into the shared national civic culture. Every society, argues the assimilationist, has national values, ideologies, and norms to which each member of society must develop commitments if it is to function successfully and smoothly. In the United States, these values are embodied in the American Creed and in such documents as the United States Constitution and the Declaration of Independence (Ravitch, 1990). Each society also has a set of common skills and abilities that every successful member of society should master. In the United States these skills include speaking and writing the English language (Porter, 1990).

The primary goal of the school, like other publicly supported institutions, should be to socialize individuals into the common culture and enable them to function more successfully within it. At best, the school should take a position of benign neutrality in matters related to the ethnic attachments of its students (Glazer, 1977). If ethnicity and ethnic attachments are to be promoted, this should be done by private institutions like the church, the community club, and the private school.

The Assimilationist Ideology and Education

Like the cultural pluralists, the assimilationists make assumptions about research related to students of color. Their conclusions reflect their assumptions. Assimilationists assume that cultural groups with characteristics that cause their members to function unsuccessfully in the common culture are deficient, deprived, and pathological and lack needed functional characteristics. Researchers who embrace an assimilationist ideology usually use the genetic, cultural deprivation, or at-risk research models and theories when studying low-income students and students of color (Bereiter & Engelmann, 1966; Herrnstein & Murray, 1994, Richardson, 1990).

The assimilationist learning theorist assumes that learning styles are rather universal across cultures (such as the stages of cognitive development identified by Piaget) and that certain socialization practices, such as those exemplified among middle-class Anglo-Americans, enhance learning, whereas other early socialization practices, such as those found within most lower-class groups, retard students' abilities to conceptualize and to develop the verbal and cognitive abilities needed for school success. Consequently, assimilationist learning theorists often recommend that low-income students enter compensatory educational programs at increasingly early ages.

The assimilationist believes that curriculum materials and teaching styles should relate primarily to the national civic culture. Emphasis should be on the shared culture within the nation-state because all citizens must learn to participate in a civic culture that requires universal skills and competencies. Emphasis on cultural and ethnic differences might promote division and fail to facilitate socialization into the shared civic culture of the nation-state. The school's primary mission within a democratic society should be to socialize youths into the national civic culture.

The curriculum should stress the commonality of the heritage all people share in the nation-state. It should also help students develop a commitment to the shared national culture and the skills to participate in civic action designed to make the practices in a society more consistent with its ideals. The school should develop within students a critical acceptance of the goals, assumptions, and possibilities of democratic nation-states.

Attacks on the Assimilationist Ideology

Chapter 2 discusses how the assimilationist ideology has historically dominated U.S. intellectual and social thought. In other Western societies, such as Australia and Canada, social and public policy has also been most heavily influenced historically by the assimilationist ideology. Multicultural educational policies were not developed in Canada and Australia until the 1970s. The United States still does not have an official multicultural policy, although a number of legal cases and some federal legislation directly or indirectly support education related to cultural and ethnic diversity.

The United States became home for millions of European immigrants from the late nineteenth century to the first decades of the twentieth century. These immigrants came from many different nations. The assimilationist ideology became dominant in the United States in the attempt to forge one nation and civic community from so many different cultures and groups (Graham, 1995). The assimilationist ideology and its related policies were successful in forming one nation and including European Americans into its structure. However, it was much less successful with ethnic groups of color, which are still to a great extent marginalized in the U.S. society.

During the early decades of the twentieth century, writers such as Horace Kallen (1924), Randolph Bourne (1916), and Julius Drachsler (1920) set forth the concepts of cultural pluralism and cultural democracy, thereby challenging assimilationist policies and practices. When the ethnic revival movements emerged in the various Western societies in the 1960s and 1970s, the assimilationist ideology experienced one of its most serious challenges in the history of Western nation-states.

Since the 1960s in the various Western nation-states, a number of transformative scholars and researchers have challenged the assimilationist ideology and the practices associated with it (Gordon, 1995; King, 1995; Ladner, 1973; Partington, 1998; Sarup, 1991). The rejection of the assimilationist ideology by transformative scholars of color and leaders is historically very significant. This rejection represents a major break from tradition within ethnic groups, as Glazer (1977) observes. Traditionally, most intellectuals and social activists, particularly in the United States, have supported assimilationist policies and have believed that assimilation was needed to participate fully in mainstream society. Historically, there have been a few separatists among African Americans and other ethnic groups in the United States. However, these leaders have represented a cry in the wilderness. Significant, too, is the fact that many White liberal writers and researchers also began to attack the assimilationist ideology and the practices associated with it in the 1960s. This criticism represented a major break from White liberal tradition in the United States (Baratz & Shuy, 1969; Labov, 1970).

Writers and researchers of color attacked the assimilationist ideology for many reasons. They viewed it as a weapon of dominant groups designed to marginalize their cultures and to undercut political mobilization. These writers also viewed it as a racist ideology that justified damaging school and societal practices that victimized students of color. Many people of color also lost faith in the assimilationist ideology because they had become very disillusioned with what they perceived as its unfulfilled promises. The rise of ethnic awareness and ethnic pride also contributed to the rejection of the assimilationist ideology by many people of color in the 1960s. Many spokespersons and writers of color searched for an alternative ideology and endorsed some version of cultural pluralism. They viewed the pluralist ideology as much more consistent with the liberation of marginalized ethnic groups than the assimilationist ideology.

A Critique of the Pluralist and Assimilationist Ideologies

Although both the pluralist and assimilationist positions make some useful assumptions and set forth arguments that educators need to consider seriously as they attempt to revise the school, college, and university curriculum, neither ideology, in its ideal form, is sufficient to guide educational reform. The pluralist ideology is useful because it informs us about the importance of culture and ethnicity within a society and the extent to which ethnic groups determine the life chances of individuals. The assumptions the pluralist makes about the nature of the cultures of ethnic groups, the learning styles of students of color, and the importance of ethnic identity to many students are also useful to educators.

However, the pluralist exaggerates the extent of cultural pluralism within modern societies and fails to give adequate attention to the fact that high levels of cultural (if not structural) assimilation has taken place in societies such as the United States. Gordon (1964), who seriously questions the extent of cultural pluralism in U.S. society, writes: "Structural pluralism...is the major key to the understanding of the ethnic makeup of American society, while cultural pluralism is the minor one" (p. 159).

Exaggerating the extent of cultural differences between and among groups might be as detrimental for school policy as ignoring those that are real. The pluralist also fails to pay adequate attention to the fact that most members of ethnic groups in modern societies participate in a wider and more universal culture than the ones in which they have their primary group attachments. Thus, the pluralist appears reluctant to prepare students to cope adequately with the real world beyond the ethnic community. The cultural pluralist also has not clarified, in any meaningful way, the kind of relationship that should exist between competing ethnic groups that have different allegiances and conflicting goals and commitments. In other words, the pluralist has not adequately conceptualized how a strongly pluralistic nation will maintain an essential degree of societal cohesion.

The assimilationist argues that the school within a common culture should socialize youths so they will be effective participants within that culture and will develop commitments to its basic values, goals, and ideologies. The assimilationist also argues that the schools should help students attain the skills that will enable them to become effective and contributing members of the nation-state in which they live. It is important for educators to realize that most societies expect the schools to help socialize youths so they will become productive members of the nation-state and develop strong commitments to the idealized societal values. Educators should keep the broad societal goals in mind when they reform the curriculum of the nation's schools, colleges, and universities.

However, the assimilationist makes a number of highly questionable assumptions and promotes educational practices that often hinder the success of students socialized within ethnic communities that have cultural characteristics quite different from those of the school. The assimilationist's assumption that learning styles are universalistic rather than to some extent culture-specific is questionable (Hale, 1994; Shade, Kelly, & Oberg, 1997). The assumption that all students can learn equally well from teaching materials that reflect only the cultural experiences of the majority group is also questionable and possibly detrimental to students with strong ethnic identities and attachments (Spencer, 1990).

When assimilationists talk about the common culture, most often they mean the mainstream national culture and are ignoring the reality that most Western societies are made up of many different ethnic and cultural groups, each of which has some unique cultural characteristics that are part of the shared national culture. Educators should seriously examine the common culture concept and make sure that the view of the common national culture promoted in the schools, colleges, and universities is not racist, sexist, ethnocentric, or exclusive, but is multicultural and reflects the ethnic and cultural diversity within society. These kinds of questions need to be discussed: *Who defines the common culture? Whom does the definition benefit? Whom does it harm?*

The common culture needs to be redefined with broad participation by different cultural, ethnic, and language groups. The transformed idea of the common culture should reflect the social realities within the nation, not a mythical, idealized view.

The Multicultural Ideology

Because neither the cultural pluralist nor the assimilationist ideology can adequately guide educational reform within educational institutions, we need a different ideology that reflects both positions and yet avoids their extremes. We also need an ideology that is more consistent with the realities in Western societies. I call this position the *multicultural ideology.* It is found near the center of our continuum, which has the cultural pluralist and the assimilationist ideologies at the extreme ends (see Table 6.1).

The multicultural ideology has not historically been a dominant ideology in Western societies such as the United States and Australia. However, the experiences of some ethnic groups in the United States, the Jews being the most salient example, are highly consistent with the multicultural vision of society. Although the multicultural ideology is less theoretically developed than the other two positions, it, like the other ideologies, makes a number of assumptions about the nature of modernized society; about what a nation's goals should be; and about research, learning, teacher education, and the school curriculum.

The multicultural theorist thinks that the cultural pluralist exaggerates the importance of the ethnic group in the socialization of the individual and that the assimilationist greatly understates the role of cultural and ethnic groups in Western societies and in the lives of individuals. Thus, multicultural theorists believe that both the pluralist and the assimilationist have distorted views of societal realities. They assume that even though the ethnic group and the ethnic community are very important in the socialization of individuals, individuals are also strongly influenced by the common national culture during their early socialization, even if they never leave the ethnic community. A nation's common culture influences every member of society through such institutions as the school, the mass media, the courts, and the technology that its citizens share. Thus, conclude multicultural theorists, even though ethnic groups have some unique cultural characteristics, all groups in a society share many cultural characteristics and values. As more and more members of ethnic groups become upwardly mobile, ethnic group characteristics become less important—but they do not disappear. Many ethnic group members who are highly culturally assimilated maintain separate ethnic institutions and symbols (Gordon, 1964).

The multicultural theorist sees neither separatism (as the pluralist does) nor total integration (as the assimilationist does) as ideal societal goals, but rather envisions an open society, in which individuals from diverse cultural, ethnic, and social-class groups have equal opportunities to function and participate. In an open society, individuals can take full advantage of the opportunities and rewards within all social, economic, and political institutions without regard to their own ancestry or ethnic identity. They can also participate fully in the society while preserving their distinct ethnic and cultural traits and are able "to make the maximum number of voluntary contacts with others without regard to qualifications of ancestry, sex, or class" (Sizemore, 1972, p. 281).

TABLE 6.1   Ideologies Related to Ethnicity and Pluralism in Western Societies

The Cultural Pluralist Ideology ←—	The Multicultural Ideology —→	The Assimilationist Ideology
Separatism	Open society; Multiculturalism	Total integration
Primordial Particularistic	Universalized-primordialism	Universalistic
Minority emphasis	Minorities and majorities have rights.	Majoritarian emphasis
Groups rights are primary.	Limited rights for the group and the individual	Individual rights are primary.
Common ancestry and heritage unifies.	Ethnic attachments and ideology of common civic culture compete for allegiances of individuals.	Ideology of the common culture unifies.
Research Assumption Ethnic minority cultures are well ordered, highly structured, but different (language, values, behavior, etc.).	*Research Assumption* Ethnic minority cultures have some unique cultural characteristics; however, minority and majority groups share many cultural traits, values, and behavior styles.	*Research Assumption* Subcultural groups with characteristics that make its members function unsuccessfully in the common culture are deprived, pathological, and lack needed functional characteristics.
Cultural difference research model	Bicultural research model	Social pathology research model and/or genetic research model
Minorities have unique learning styles.	Minorities have some unique learning styles but share many learning characteristics with other groups.	Human learning styles and characteristics are universal.
Curriculum Use materials and teaching styles that are culture specific. The goal of the curriculum should be to help students function more successfully within their own ethnic cultures and help liberate their ethnic groups from oppression.	*Curriculum* The curriculum should respect the ethnicity of the child and use it in positive ways; the goal of the curriculum should be to help students learn how to function effectively within the common culture, their ethnic culture, and other ethnic cultures.	*Curriculum* Use materials and teaching styles related to the common culture; the curriculum should help the students develop a commitment to the common civic culture and its idealized ideologies.
Teachers Minority students need skilled teachers of their same race and ethnicity for role models, to learn more effectively, and to develop more positive self-concepts and identities.	*Teachers* Students need skilled teachers who are very knowledgeable about and sensitive to their ethnic cultures and cognitive styles.	*Teachers* A skilled teacher who is familiar with learning theories and is able to implement those theories effectively is a good teacher for any group of students, regardless of their ethnicity, race, or social class. The goal should be to train good teachers of students.

In the multicultural, open society envisioned by the multicultural theorist, individuals would be free to maintain their ethnic identities. They would also be able and willing to function effectively within the common culture and within and across other ethnic cultures. Individuals would be free to act in ways consistent with the norms and values of their ethnic groups as long as they did not conflict with the overarching national idealized values, such as justice, equality, and human dignity. All members of society would be required to conform to these values. *These values would be the unifying elements of the culture that would maintain and promote societal cohesion.*

Because of their perceptions of the nature of Western societies and their vision of the ideal society, multicultural theorists believe that the primary goal of the curriculum should be to help students learn how to function more effectively within their own community or ethnic culture, within the mainstream national culture, and within other cultural and ethnic communities. However, multicultural theorists feel strongly that during the process of education the school should not alienate students from their cultural and ethnic attachments but should help them to clarify their cultural and ethnic identities and make them aware of other cultural and ethnic alternatives.

The multicultural theorist believes that the curriculum should reflect the cultures of various cultural and ethnic groups *and* the shared national culture. Students need to study all of these cultures in order to become effective participants and decision-makers in a democratic pluralistic nation. The school curriculum should respect the community culture and knowledge of students and use them in positive ways. However, the students should be given options regarding their political choices and the actions they take regarding their cultural and ethnic attachments. The school should not force students to be and feel ethnic if they choose to free themselves of ethnic attachments and allegiances.

The multicultural theorist also assumes that some groups of students do have some unique learning styles, although they share many learning characteristics with other students. Educators should be knowledgeable about the aspects of their learning styles that are unique so they can better help students from different cultural and ethnic groups attain more success within the school and in the larger society.

Even though the multicultural ideology can best guide educational reform and school policy, difficult questions regarding the relationship between the school and the student's ethnic culture are inherent within this position. The multicultural theorist argues, for example, that the school should reflect both the student's ethnic culture and the common societal culture. These four questions emerge: How does the individual function within two cultures that sometimes have contradictory and conflicting norms, values, and expectations? What happens when the ethnic cultures of the students seriously conflict with the goals and norms of public institutions like the school? Do the institutions change their goals? If so, what goals do they embrace? The assimilationist solves this problem by arguing that the student should change to conform to the expectations and norms of public institutions.

Although I support the multicultural ideology and have presented my proposals for curriculum reform within that ideological framework (Banks, 1997), it is very difficult to resolve satisfactorily all the difficult questions inherent within this ideology. However, public institutions such as schools, colleges and universities can and should allow cultural group members to practice their culture-specific behaviors as long as they do not conflict with the major goals of these institutions. One of the school's major goals is to teach students to read, to write, to compute, and to think. The school cannot encourage cultural or ethnic behavior if it prohibits students from learning basic skills. On the other hand, some students might be able to learn to read more easily from culturally sensitive readers than from Anglocentric reading materials.

The Societal Basis for the Multicultural Ideology

Both the assimilationist and cultural pluralist ideologies emanate from misleading and/or incomplete analyses of the nature of ethnicity in modernized societies such as the United States. The assimilationist ideology in the United States derives primarily from two conceptualizations of ethnicity in U.S. society: *Anglo-conformity* and the *melting pot.* The cultural pluralist ideology emanates from a conceptualization of ethnicity in U.S. society called *cultural pluralism.* I summarize these conceptualizations and indicate why each is an inadequate and/or misleading conceptualization. I then present my own analysis of ethnicity in U.S. society— called *multiple acculturation*—and explain how it is consistent with the multicultural ideology.

Anglo-conformity suggests that ethnic groups gave up their cultural attributes and acquired those of Anglo-Saxon Protestants. This concept describes a type of unidirectional assimilation. The *melting pot,* long embraced as an ideal in U.S. society and culture, suggests that the various ethnic cultures in the United States were mixed and synthesized into a new culture, different from any of the original ethnic cultures. *Cultural pluralism* suggests, at least in its extreme form, that the United States is made up of various ethnic subsocieties, each of which has a set of largely independent norms, institutions, values, and beliefs.

Each conceptualization presents major problems when one views the reality of ethnicity and race in the United States. The Anglo-conformity conceptualization suggests that Anglo-Saxons were changed very little in the United States and that other ethnic groups did all of the changing. This conceptualization is incomplete, unidirectional, and static. The melting pot conceptualization is inaccurate and misleading because human cultures are complex and dynamic and do not melt like iron. Consequently, the melting pot is a false and misleading metaphor.

The strong cultural pluralist conceptualization denies the reality that there is a universal U.S. culture that every American, regardless of ethnic group, shares to a great extent. This culture includes American Creed values as *ideals,* American English, a highly technological and industrialized civilization, a capitalistic economy, and a veneration of materialism and consumption. Hofstadter (1963) argues convincingly that anti-intellectualism is another key component in the universal U.S. culture. This is not to deny that there are important subcultural variants within the different ethnic subsocieties in the United States or that there are many ethnic specific characteristics in U.S. ethnic communities. These ethnic specific variables are discussed later in this chapter.

Gordon (1964) believes that structural pluralism best describes the ethnic reality in U.S. society. According to Gordon, the ethnic groups in the United States have experienced high levels of cultural assimilation, but the nation is characterized by structural pluralism. In other words, ethnic groups are highly assimilated culturally (into the mainstream Anglo-American culture) but have separate ethnic subsocieties, such as African American fraternities, Jewish social clubs, and Chicano theaters.

Multiple Acculturation

Even though Gordon's (1964) notion of structural pluralism is helpful and deals more adequately with the complexity of ethnic diversity in modern U.S. society than do the other three concepts, I believe that the term *multiple acculturation* more accurately describes how the universal U.S. culture was and is forming than does the concept of cultural assimilation. The White Anglo-Saxon Protestant (WASP) culture was changed in the United States, as were the cultures of Africans and of Asian immigrants. African cultures and Asian cultures influenced and changed the WASP culture, just as the WASP culture influenced and modified African and Asian cultures. What was experienced in the United States, and what is still occurring, is multiple acculturation and not a kind of unidirectional type of cultural assimilation whereby the African American culture was influenced by the WASP culture and not the other way around.

The general or universal culture in the United States resulted from this series of multiple acculturations. This culture is still in the process of formation and change (see Figure 6.1). The universal U.S. culture is not just a WASP culture but contains important elements of the wide variety of ethnic cultures that are and/or were part of U.S. society. Those ethnic cultural elements that became universalized and part of the general U.S. culture have been reinterpreted and mediated by the unique social, economic, and political experiences in the United States. *It is inaccurate and misleading to refer to the universal U.S. culture as a WASP culture.*

This notion of U.S. culture has been and often is perpetuated in the school and university curriculum. It is, of course, true that the White Anglo-Saxon Protestants have had a greater influence on the mainstream U.S. culture than has any other single ethnic group. However, we can easily exaggerate the WASP influence on the general U.S. culture. European cultures were greatly influenced by African and Asian cultures before the European explorers started coming to the Americas in the fifteenth century (Bernal, 1987, 1991; Van Sertima, 1988). The earliest British immigrants borrowed heavily from the American Indians on the East coast and probably would not have survived if they had not assimilated Indian cultural components and used some of their farming methods and tools (Weatherford, 1988).

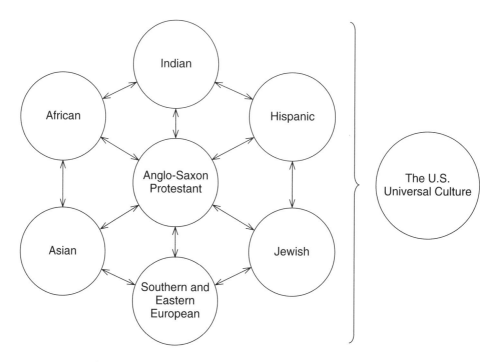

FIGURE 6.1   The Development of U.S. Culture
This figure illustrates how the U.S. universal culture developed through a process conceptualized as *multiple acculturation.* The Anglo-Saxon Protestant culture had the greatest influence on the development of U.S. culture, and each of the various ethnic cultures influenced the Anglo culture and was influenced by it. Each culture was also influenced by and influenced the others. These complex series of acculturations, which were mediated by the U.S. experience and the U.S. sociocultural environment, resulted in the universal U.S. culture. This process is still taking place today.

Ethnic Subsocieties and Nonuniversalized Cultural Components

Figure 6.1 describes the development of U.S. culture by emphasizing multiple acculturation and how ethnic cultural elements became universalized. Other U.S. ethnic realities are not shown in Figure 6.1. These realities include the significant number of ethnic cultural elements that have not become universalized (that are still shared primarily by ethnic subgroups) and the separate ethnic institutions and groups that constitute ethnic subsocieties within the larger U.S. society and culture. The sociocultural environment for most Americans is consequently bicultural. Almost every American participates both within the universal U.S. culture and society as well as within his or her ethnic subsociety. Like other U.S. ethnic groups, there is a subsociety within the WASP culture that has cultural elements not universal or shared by the rest of society. Patterson (1977) believes that this is a small subsociety in which few individuals participate and that most WASP cultural elements have become universalized:

> With the exception of small pockets such as the New England Brahmin elite, the vast majority of WASPs have abandoned the ethnic specificities of their original culture in favor of the elite version of the American universal culture. (p. 167)

Nonuniversalized ethnic cultural characteristics and ethnic subsocieties are realities in contemporary U.S. society. These cultural elements and subsocieties play an important role in the socialization of many individuals and help members of ethnic groups to satisfy important needs. Figure 6.2 illustrates the relationship between the universal U.S. culture and ethnic subsocieties.

Sharing Power

Ideological resistance is probably the major reason that multicultural education has not become more institutionalized, although it has made and is making significant inroads into the curriculum and structures of schools, colleges, and universities. One important implication of my analysis is that educators with conflicting ideologies about diversity need to have dialogue. However, power sharing must also take place if dialogue is to be meaningful. Powerful groups that now dominate educational policy and decisions, such as the Western traditionalists, must be willing to share power with marginalized and less powerful groups before a multicultural ideology can be institutionalized and educational policy shaped that reflects the experiences and interests of the diverse groups that make up the United States.

Historically in the United States, educational policy for powerless and structurally excluded ethnic groups, such as African Americans and Mexican Americans, has been made by powerful Anglo-American groups that controlled the educational system (Apple, 1996; Bowles & Gintis, 1976; Katz, 1975). As pointed out in Chapter 2, an Anglocentric education alienates students of color from their ethnic cultures and frequently fails to help them attain the attitudes, skills, and abilities needed to function effectively within the mainstream society and within other ethnic subsocieties.

Powerless and marginalized groups, such as Puerto Ricans in the United States and African Americans, must participate in shaping educational policy in order for educational reforms related to ethnic diversity to become institutionalized within the U.S. educational system (Walsh, 1991). The groups that exercise power in the U.S. educational establishment design and run the schools so that they reflect their ideology, assumptions, values, and perspectives. The assimilationists who control much of the popular culture and public opinion often see pluralism as a threat to the survival of the United States as they envision it. Ways must be devised for marginalized ethnic groups to gain power in education and to participate in major educational decisions that affect the education of their youths.

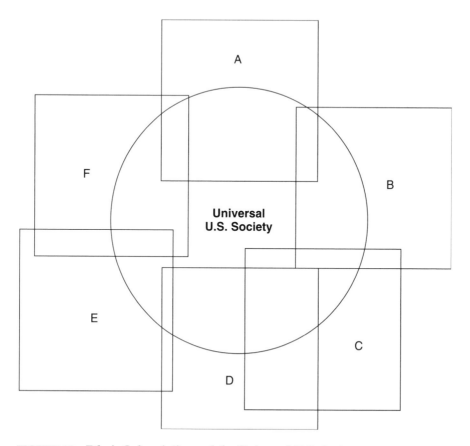

FIGURE 6.2   Ethnic Subsocieties and the Universal U.S. Society
In this figure, the universal U.S. society is represented by the circle. This culture is shared by all ethnic groups within the United States. A, B, C, D, E, and F represent ethnic subsocieties that consist of unique ethnic institutions, values, and cultural elements that are nonuniversalized and shared primarily by members of specific ethnic groups.

Only in this way will a philosophy of multiculturalism become institutionalized within education and will education become legitimate from the perspectives of the diverse groups that make up the nation.

Summary

Educational institutions in the various Western nations, stimulated by social forces and supported by private and public agencies, are implementing a wide variety of educational reforms related to diversity in their societies. However, there is widespread disagreement about what these reforms should be designed to attain and about the proper relationship that should exist between schools, colleges, and universities and the cultural identities of students. Educators and social scientists who embrace divergent ideologies are recommending conflicting educational policies and programs.

We can think of these varying ideologies as existing on a continuum, with the cultural pluralist position at one extreme end and the assimilationist position at the other. I argue that neither of these ideologies, in their ideal forms, can effectively guide educational policy in pluralistic democratic societies. Rather, educational policy can best be guided by an eclectic ideology that reflects both the cultural pluralist position and the assimilationist position, but that avoids their extremes. I call this the *multicultural ideology.*

The second part of this chapter discusses the multicultural ideology and describes how it derives from an accurate analysis of ethnic and race relations in the United States. The assimilationist ideology, which most mainstream educators in the United States embrace, derives from two misleading and incomplete conceptions of the nature of ethnicity in the United States: Anglo-conformity and the melting pot. Structural pluralism and multiple acculturation accurately describe the nature of group life in the United States. The multicultural ideology derives from these conceptions of ethnicity and race in the United States. In order for the multicultural ideology to be institutionalized within the nation's schools, colleges, and universities powerful mainstream groups must share power with less powerful groups.

REFERENCES

Apple, M. W. (1996). *Cultural Politics and Education.* Buckingham, England: Open University Press.

Apter, A. (1977). Political Life and Pluralism. In M. M. Tumin & W. Plotch (Eds.), *Pluralism in a Democratic Society* (pp. 59–81). New York: Praeger.

Asante, M. K. (1991). The Afrocentric Idea in Education. *The Journal of Negro Education, 60,* 170–180.

Banks, J. A. (1997). *Educating Citizens in a Multicultural Society.* New York: Teachers College Press.

Baratz, J. C., & Shuy, R. (Eds.). (1969). *Teaching Black Children to Read.* Washington, DC: Center for Applied Linguistics.

Bereiter, C., & Engelmann, S. (1966). *Teaching Disadvantaged Children in the Preschool.* Englewood Cliffs, NJ: Prentice-Hall.

Bernal, M. (1987, 1991). *Black Athena: The Afroasiatic Roots of Classical Civilization,* Vols. 1 & 2. New Brunswick, NJ: Rutgers University Press.

Bourne, R. S. (1916). Trans-National America. *The Atlantic Monthly, 118,* 95.

Bowles, S., & Gintis, H. (1976). *Schooling in Capitalist America: Educational Reform and the Contradictions of Economic Life.* New York: Basic Books.

Boykin, A. W. (1994). Afrocultural Expression and Its Implications for Schooling. In E. R. Hollins, J. E. King, & W. C. Hayman (Eds.), *Teaching Diverse Populations: Formulating a Knowledge Base* (pp. 243–256). Albany: State University of New York Press.

Carmichael, S., & Hamilton, C. V. (1967). *Black Power: The Politics of Liberation in America.* New York: Vintage Books.

Cruse, H. (1967). *The Crisis of the Negro Intellectual.* New York: William Morrow.

Delpit, L. (1995). *Other People's Children: Cultural Conflict in the Classroom.* New York: The New Press.

Drachsler, J. (1920). *Democracy and Assimilation.* New York: Macmillan.

D'Souza, D. (1995). *The End of Racism: Principles for a Multiracial Society.* New York: The Free Press.

Gay, G. (2000). *Power Pedagogy: Culturally Responsive Teaching for Ethnically Diverse Learners.* New York: Teachers College Press.

Gillborn, D. (1995). *Racism and Antiracism in Real Schools.* Philadelphia: Open University Press.

Glazer, N. (1977). Cultural Pluralism: The Social Aspect. In M. M. Tumin & W. Plotch (Eds.),

Pluralism in a Democratic Society (pp. 3–24). New York: Praeger.

Gordon, B. M. (1995). Knowledge Construction, Competing Critical Theories, and Education. In J. A. Banks & C. A. M. Banks (Eds.), *Handbook of Research on Multicultural Education* (pp. 184–199). New York: Macmillan.

Gordon, M. M. (1964). *Assimilation in American Life: The Role of Race, Religion, and National Origins.* New York: Oxford University Press.

Graham, P. A. (1995). Assimilation, Adjustment, and Access: An Antiquarian View of American Education. In D. Ravitch & M. A. Vinovskis (Eds.), *Learning from the Past* (pp. 3–24). Baltimore, MD: The John Hopkins University Press.

Gutmann, A. (Ed.). (1994). *Multiculturalism: Examining the Politics of Recognition.* Princeton, NJ: Princeton University Press.

Hale, J. E. (1994). *Unbank the Fire: Visions for the Education of African American Children.* Baltimore, MD: The Johns Hopkins University Press.

Herrnstein, R. J., & Murray, C. (1994). *The Bell Curve: Intelligence and Class Structure in American Life.* New York: The Free Press.

Hofstadter, R. (1963). *Anti-Intellectualism in American Life.* New York: Vintage.

Kallen, H. M. (1924). *Culture and Democracy in the United States.* New York: Boni and Liveright.

Katz, M. B. (1975). *Class, Bureaucracy, and Schools: The Illusion of Educational Change in America* (expanded ed.). New York: Praeger.

King, J. E. (1995). Culture-Centered Knowledge: Black Studies, Curriculum Transformation, and Social Action. In J. A. Banks & C. A. M. Banks (Eds.), *Handbook of Research on Multicultural Education* (pp. 265–290). New York: Macmillan.

Labov, W. (1970). The Logic of Nonstandard English. In F. Williams (Ed.), *Language and Poverty: Perspectives on a Theme* (pp. 153–189). Chicago: Markham Publishing Company.

Ladner, J. A. (Ed.). (1973). *The Death of White Sociology.* New York: Vintage.

Moodley, K. A. (Ed.). (1992). *Beyond Multicultural Education: International Perspectives.* Calgary: Detselig.

Partington, G. (1998). *Perspectives on Aboriginal and Torres Strait Islander Education.* Katoomba, NSW, Australia: Social Science Press.

Patterson, O. (1977). *Ethnic Chauvinism: The Reactionary Response.* New York: Stein & Day.

Porter, R. P. (1990). The Disabling Power of Ideology: Challenging the Basic Assumptions of Bilingual Education. In G. Imhoff (Ed.), *Learning in Two Languages* (pp. 19–37). New Brunswick, NJ: Transaction Publishers.

Ravitch, D. (1990). Multiculturalism: E Pluribus Plures. *The American Scholar, 54,* 337–354.

Richardson, V. (1990). At-Risk Programs: Evaluation and Critical Inquiry. In K. A. Sirotnik (Ed.), *Evaluation and Social Justice: Issues in Public Education,* No. 45. San Francisco: Jossey-Bass.

Sarup, M. (1991). *Education and the Ideologies of Racism.* Stoke-on-Trent, England: Trentham Books.

Schlesinger, A. R., Jr. (1991). *The Disuniting of America: Reflections on a Multicultural Society.* Knoxville, TN: Whittle Direct Books.

Schuman, D., & Olufs, D. (1995). *Diversity on Campus.* Boston: Allyn and Bacon.

Shade, B. J., Kelly, C., & Oberg, M. (1997). *Creating Culturally Responsive Classrooms.* Washington, DC: American Psychological Association.

Sizemore, B. A. (1972). Is There a Case for Separate Schools? *Phi Delta Kappan, 53,* 281–284.

Smelser, N. J., & Alexander, J. C. (Eds.). (1999). *Diversity and Its Discontents.* Princeton, NJ: Princeton University Press.

Smitherman, G. (1999). *Talkin That Talk: Language, Culture, and Education in African America.* New York: Routledge.

Spencer, M. B. (1990). Development of Minority Children: An Introduction. *Child Development, 61,* 267–269.

Suárez-Orozco, C., & Suárez-Orozco, M. (1995). *Transformations: Migration, Family Life, and Achievement Motivation among Latino Adolescents.* Stanford, CA: Stanford University Press.

Troyna, B. (1993). *Racism and Education.* Philadelphia: Open University Press.

Van Sertima, I. V. (Ed.). (1988). *Great Black Leaders: Ancient and Modern.* New Brunswick, NJ: Africana Studies Department, Rutgers University.

Walsh, C. E. (Ed.). (1991). *Pedagogy and the Struggle for Voice: Issues of Language, Power, and Schooling for Puerto Ricans.* New York: Bergin & Garvey.

Weatherford, J. (1988). *Indian Givers: How the Indians of the Americas Transformed the World.* New York: Fawcett Columbine.

7 The Stages of Cultural Identity: Implications for Curriculum Reform

In the 1970s, I taught ethnic studies courses in the teacher education program at the University of Washington. I noticed that identification with their ethnic groups, assimilation levels, ethnic behaviors, and militancy varied widely among students within the same ethnic groups. Some of my African American students, for example, confined most of their interactions within Black communities both on and off campus, whereas others lived in predominantly White suburbs and had few African American friends. Some of my Jewish students identified strongly with Israel and felt politically and culturally connected with it; others did not. Some of my Latino students were fluent in both English and Spanish, whereas others spoke only English and were uncomfortable when people expected or implied that they should be Spanish speakers.

My teaching experiences, readings, and observations of ethnic behaviors caused me to seriously question theories, concepts, and paradigms that indicated that ethnic groups such as African Americans, Puerto Ricans in the United States, and American Indians could be described with a set of generalized descriptions, such as "The Negro Personality" (Karon, 1958), that African Americans have negative self-racial attitudes (Clark, 1963), or that the "culture of poverty" can be used to describe Puerto Ricans (Lewis, 1965).

My teaching, research (1984), and other scholarly work (Banks, 1997) suggested that the experiences of ethnic groups in the United States had to be described with less global and more nuanced and complex conceptions, paradigms, and explanations. I believed that explanations that revealed the intricate diversity within ethnic groups were needed. Consequently, I developed the *Stages of Ethnicity Typology* (Banks, 1976) to help teachers, practitioners, and scholars conceptualize and observe the diversity within ethnic groups.

Use of the Typology in Research

The Stages of Ethnicity typology resonated with many scholars and practitioners. It has been used in a number of research studies and as a teaching tool in classrooms. Ford (1979) developed an instrument to measure the first five of the stages. Her study demonstrated that teachers are spread into the five stages that I hypothesized. The sixth stage of the typology was developed after the Ford study was completed.

Tomlinson (1995; 1996) used the typology in several studies of reading instruction to determine how curriculum goals are related to it and to help teachers with instruction. She writes:

> Banks' typology and curriculum goals have been useful in assisting…teachers with the delicate maneuverings in addressing critical issues of ethnic identity development that often remain overlooked when units of multicultural literacy instruction are attempted. (1996, p. 18)

Bean, Readence, and Mallette (1996) and Mallette, Bean, and Readence (1998) have used the typology in research to guide discussions of multiethnic literature. They describe the usefulness of the typology: "Using [it] as a frame for discussing multiethnic young-adult literature produced vibrant and lengthy discussions" (p. 197).

Expanding the Typology to Include Nonethnic Cultural Groups

I have expanded the typology to make it more inclusive. However, *ethnic groups are still included within the typology because an ethnic group is a type of cultural group.* Consequently, researchers doing work with the typology as "Stages of Ethnicity" can proceed with their work. However, my hope is that practitioners and researchers working with other cultural groups, such as gender groups, language groups, social-class groups, and groups with different sexual orientations, will use the typology in their teaching and research.

During the decades since I created the typology, I have noticed in my teaching, observations, and reading how other cultural groups exemplify the stages I first identified in the ethnicity typology. During the early stage of the feminist movement, for example, I observed how some newly turned feminists resented women who tried to both pursue a professional career and fulfill a nurturing role in their homes. I have also observed how some bilingual individuals insisted that speaking their first language is essential for being an authentic member of the ethnic or cultural group. In my multicultural classes in recent years, I have observed some of my gay students arguing that all gay people should "come out," or they are contributing to the marginalization of gay people. These kinds of behaviors exemplify *cultural encapsulation;* that is, individuals reject or ostracize members of their group whose behavior is inconsistent with what they think is needed to be authentic and legitimate group members.

Defining Cultural Groups and Cultural Identity

Chapter 4 presents several definitions of culture. These definitions indicate that *culture* consists of a shared symbols, meanings, values, and behaviors. Members of a cultural group usually interpret symbols and behaviors in similar ways. They also view themselves as a collective with a sense of connectedness. I am defining *cultural identity* as an individual's subjective conception of self in relationship to a cultural group (Reber, 1985).

The sense of connectedness that individuals have with their cultural group is often manifested as "us" and "them" feelings, perceptions, and behaviors. Whenever in-groups and out-groups form, stereotypes, prejudice, and discrimination develop. Social psychological theory and research, known as the *minimal group paradigm,* indicate that when mere categorization develops, individuals favor the in-group over the out-group and discriminate against out-group members (Rothbart & John, 1993; Smith & Mackie, 1995). This can occur in situations without prior historical conflict and animosity, competition, physical differences, or any kind of important difference.

Individuals belong to many different cultural groups (See Figure 4.1, page 73). *However, their level of identity with a particular cultural group varies greatly and is contextual.* A Chicana who is Catholic and a feminist may find that her Catholic cultural identity is more important to her in some settings and situations and that her feminist identity is more important in others. Sometime she will find that her cultural identities conflict.

Religious, gender, sexual orientation, regional (such as Appalachia), *exceptionality* (such as deaf culture), *socioeconomic,* and *language* groups are important cultural groups to which students in our schools, colleges, and universities belong. The teaching and learning of students can be impeded when a group to which they have a strong identity and attachment is marginalized within the school and in the curriculum. Some students enter school with unresolved issues related to one or more of the cultural groups to which they belong. This can also impede teaching and learning. Consequently, it is important for teachers to be aware of the groups to which students have strong identifications, especially if these group attachments are causing learning and behavioral problems in schools.

The cultural groups to which students belong can influence the basis for categorization and the formation of in-group and out-groups, especially within an institutional context in which cultural groups have differential status and power. Low-status cultural groups become stigmatized and marginalized. Latinos for whom Spanish is the first language often become a low-status group in their classroom and school. Members of low-status cultural groups are likely to experience some form of cultural psychological captivity and cultural encapsulation.

Language is an important cultural marker. It is often the basis for the creation and maintenance of cultural group identities. Language is an important part of an individual's identify and is often a significant factor in determining in-group and out-group status and perceptions. Languages are often symbols of group boundaries and the sources of intergroup conflicts and tensions (Giles, 1997; Isaacs, 1992), as are the other cultural groups mentioned above, such as groups formed on the basis of sexual orientation, exceptionality, religion, and region.

Social Groups and Cultural Groups

Students should discuss questions such as these when studying cultural groups: When does a social group become a cultural group? Are groups based on factors such as gender, sexual orientation, region, exceptionality, and social class *cultural groups*? What are the essential attributes of a cultural group? Are some groups, such as those based on gender, better described as *quasi-cultural groups* rather than as true cultural groups? Quasi means "having some but not all of the features of" a category (Flexner & Hauck, 1987, p. 1,581).

These questions should be discussed openly and freely in the democratic classroom. They are interesting and important teaching questions in part because they do not have conclusive or fixed answers. Students should participate in the discussions that social scientists are having about important concepts such as culture, diversity, and multiculturalism (Smelser & Alexander, 1999). Culture has a variety of meanings in anthropology (Kuper, 1999). Consequently, it is difficult to use a rigid category for determining a cultural group.

Gender as a Cultural Group

The case for gender as a cultural group is complex. Middle-class White males and middle-class White females are raised in the same families and communities and share many cultural characteristics. However, a number of researchers and writers have described the different values, symbols, and behaviors of such women and men. During the last two decades most of this work has focused on women. However, during the 1990s a number of popular books were published that focus on the culture, socialization, and problems of boys and men.

The books that focus on boys and men may have been partly stimulated by the large number of books dealing with women published from the 1970s to the 1990s. A number of these books were written for the popular market and were best-sellers. *Real Boys: Rescuing Our Sons from The Myths of Boyhood* (Pollack, 1998) was on the *New York Times* Best Seller List. *The Wonder of Boys: What Parents, Mentors and Educators Can Do to Shape Boys into Exceptional Men* by Michael Gurian (1996) was also a best-selling book. Gurian (1999) has written a number of books about boys, including *The Good Son: Shaping the Moral Development of Our Boys and Young Men.* Bly (1990) describes male initiation and the role of the mentor in *Iron John: A Book about Men.* Publications by Gibbs (1988) and Kunjufu (1986) focus on the special problems and experiences of African American boys.

McIntosh (1997) describes White male privilege and the ways in which women and groups of color experience unequal status in U.S. society. The ways in which communication differs among men and women and the communication problems this creates in their relationships are described by Tannen (1990). Gilligan (1982) focuses on the ways in which the values of men and women differ. She describes men as autonomous and women as interconnected. Gilligan states that women value relationships, connectedness, and caring more than men do.

The most interesting work on the culture of women within the last two decades has focused on epistemology and the construction of knowledge. Feminist scholars have described the ways in which knowledge is grounded in the researcher's *positionality*, meaning the ways in which gender, race, social class and other characteristics of the knower influence the construction and production of knowledge. In her book *What Can She Know? Feminist Theory and the Construction of Knowledge,* Code (1991) raises this question: "Is the sex of the knower epistemologically significant?" She answers this question in the affirmative because of the ways in which gender influences how knowledge is constructed, interpreted, and institutionalized within U.S. society. Belenky et al. (1986), Harding (1991), and Goldberger et al. (1996) have described the ways in which women's ways of knowing differ from the ways that men know. They describe how women produce unique perspectives on reality because of their position in the social and economic structure. Collins (1990) describes the unique perspective of Black women, which she calls the "outsider within" standpoint or perspective. Maher and Tetreault (1994) have studied the unique characteristics of classrooms in which a feminist pedagogy is used.

Scholarship on Other Cultural Groups

Lower-Class Culture

The literature on various cultural groups within the United States has grown significantly within the last two decades. There is a well-established literature on the lower class that dates back to at least 1890, when *How the Other Half Lives* by Jacob Riis (1957) was published. A more contemporary example is *The Other America* by Michael Harrington, published in 1962. Lewis's (1965) *La Vida: A Puerto Rican Family in the Culture of Poverty* is a controversial example of this genre (Rodriquez, 1995). Valentine (1968) wrote an insightful critique of the "culture of poverty" concept. Since the 1990s, social scientists have used the term *underclass,* rather than *culture of poverty* to describe the culture of the nation's urban poor. William Julius Wilson (1996), a highly respected sociologist, uses this concept in his insightful and compassionate study of the urban poor in Chicago, *When Work Disappears: The World of the New Urban Poor.* Jencks and Peterson (1991) have edited *The Urban Underclass.* As with all concepts, we have to be aware of and sensitive to the extent to which the concepts we use liberate or oppress the groups being described.

Gay Culture

A rich literature on gay culture and gay studies has been developing within the last decade. Examples of books in this genre are *Gay Culture in America,* edited by Herdt (1992); *Coming on Strong: Gay Politics and Culture,* edited by Shepherd and Wallis (1989); and *Coming out in College,* edited by Rhoads (1994). *The Harvard Educational Review* published a special issue, "Lesbian, Gay, Bisexual, and Transgender People and Education," in 1996.

Deaf Culture

The literature on deaf culture is also developing. Titles include *The Deaf Way: Perspectives from the International Conference on Deaf Culture,* edited by Erting et al.

(1994); and *Deaf in America: Voices from a Culture,* edited by Padden and Humphries (1988). Padden and Humphries describe why the deaf community constitutes a culture: "A large population, established patterns of cultural transmission, and a common language: these are all basic ingredients for a rich and inventive culture" (p. 9).

Ethnic Culture

The literature on ethnic groups and ethnic identity is extensive. A comprehensive discussion and review of racial identity models developed by researchers such as Helms and Cross are in a book edited by Helms (1990). Helms has developed racial identity theories and measures for African Americans and Whites. She further discusses these issues in a book with Cook (Helms & Cook, 1999). Cross (1991) describes Black identity development in these stages:

> *Pre-encounter* (stage 1) depicts the identity to be changed; *Encounter* (stage 2) isolates the point at which the person feels compelled to change; *Immension-Emersion* (stage 3) describes the vortex of identity change; and *Internalization and Internationalizaiton-Commitment* (stages 4 and 5) describe the habituation and internalization of the new identity. (p. 190) [emphasis in original]

Phinney and Rotheram (1987) have edited an excellent collection of papers on the development of ethnic identity among youth of color.

Assumptions about Students

When planning multicultural experiences for students, we tend to assume that cultural groups are monolithic and have rather homogeneous needs and characteristics. We often assume, for example, that individual members of ethnic minority groups, such as Jewish Americans and African Americans, have intense feelings of ethnic identity and a strong interest in learning about the experiences and histories of their ethnic cultures. Educators also frequently assume that the self-images and academic achievement of students of color will be enhanced if they are exposed to a curriculum that focuses on the heroic accomplishments and deeds of these groups and that highlights the ways in which ethnic groups have been victimized by the mainstream society.

Cultural Groups Are Complex and Dynamic

These kinds of assumptions are highly questionable and have led to some disappointments and serious problems in programs and practices related to diversity. In designing multicultural experiences for students, we need to consider seriously the psychological needs and characteristics of students and their emerging and changing cultural identities. Cultural groups are not monolithic but are dynamic and complex.

Many of our curriculum development and teacher education efforts are based on the assumption that cultural groups are static and unchanging. However, cultural groups are highly diverse, complex, and changing entities. Cultural identity, like other cultural characteristics, is also complex and changing among group members. Thus there is no one cultural identity among African Americans, women, deaf students, or gay students that we can identify, as social scientists have sometimes suggested, but many complex and changing identities among them.

Essentializing occurs when groups are viewed as having a few characteristics that can be easily identified and described. To say that Mexican Americans are "field sensitive" and that Anglo Americans are "field independent" is an example of essentializing. Characteristics such as field sensitive and field independent are found within all ethnic and cultural groups, although they may have a higher frequency within some groups than others. In their classic study, Ramírez and Castañeda (1974) found that rural and less assimilated Mexican Americans tend to be more field sensitive in their learning and cultural styles than Anglo Americans. However, this finding has often been misinterpreted and misused in schools.

During the 1960s and 1970s a number of social scientists stated that African Americans had confused racial identities and ambivalent, negative attitudes toward their own ethnic group (Clark, 1963). The typology I developed, however, suggests that only a segment of African Americans can be so characterized and that those African Americans are functioning at Cultural Identity Stage 1. Kardiner and Ovesey (1951) wrote a classical social pathology interpretation of the African American personality.

Researchers such as Cross (1991) and Spencer (1985) have developed concepts, theories, and research that seriously challenge the negative self-concept hypothesis. These researchers make a useful distinction between *personal identity* (self-concept, self-esteem) and *group identity,* or reference group orientation. In a series of pioneering studies, Spencer (1982, 1984) has marshaled significant support for the postulate that young African American children are able to distinguish their personal identity from their group identity, can have high self-esteem and yet express a White bias, and that the expression of a White bias results from a cognitive process that enables young children to perceive accurately the norms and attitudes toward Whites and African Americans that are institutionalized within society.

Effective educational programs should help students explore and clarify their cultural identities. To do this, teachers must recognize and respond sensitively and skillfully to the complex cultural identities and characteristics of the students in their classrooms. Teachers should learn how to facilitate the cultural identity quests among students and help them become effective and able participants in the common civic and national culture.

An important challenge for teachers is to determine the most important cultural groups for individual students. This can be a challenging and difficult task.

An African American student within a predominantly White school and classroom may show little interest in African American literature and history and may
seek out few African American children in the school. The student may want to
associate with Blacks and to learn about African American culture, but may feel
that the school environment marginalizes Blackness and views Blacks getting
together negatively. The student's behavior may be an attempt to experience
equal-status in the school, rather than to avoid experiences with African American
culture and people.

The Stages of Cultural Identity: A Typology

To reflect the myriad and emerging cultural identities among teachers and students, we must attempt to identify these identities and to describe their curricular
and teaching implications. The description of a typology that attempts to outline
the basic stages of the development of cultural identity among individuals follows. The typology is a preliminary ideal-type construct in the Weberian sense
and constitutes a set of hypotheses based on the existing and emerging theory and
research and on the author's study of cultural behavior.

This typology is presented to stimulate research and the development of concepts and theory related to culture, ethnicity, and language. Two other purposes of
the typology are to suggest preliminary guidelines for teaching about cultural diversity in schools, colleges, and universities, and also to help students and teachers
to function effectively at increasingly higher stages of cultural identity.

Stage 1: Cultural Psychological Captivity

During this stage, the individual absorbs the negative ideologies and beliefs about
his or her cultural group that are institutionalized within the society. Consequently, he or she exemplifies cultural self-rejection and low self-esteem. The individual is ashamed of his or her cultural group and identity during this stage and
may respond in a number of ways, including avoiding situations that bring contact with other cultural groups or striving aggressively to become highly culturally assimilated. Conflict develops when the highly assimilated psychologically
captive individual is denied structural assimilation or total societal participation.

Individuals who are members of groups that have historically been victimized by discrimination, such as Polish Americans, the deaf, and gays, as well as
members of highly visible and stigmatized racial groups, such as African Americans and Chinese Canadians, are likely to experience some form of cultural psychological captivity. The more that a cultural group is stigmatized and rejected by
the mainstream society, the more likely are its members to experience some form
of psychological captivity. Thus, individuals who are members of the mainstream
cultural or ethnic group within a society are the least likely individuals to experience cultural psychological captivity.

Stage 2: Cultural Encapsulation

Stage 2 is characterized by cultural encapsulation and cultural exclusiveness, including voluntary separatism. The individual participates primarily within his or her own cultural community and believes that his or her cultural group is superior to other groups. Many individuals within Stage 2, such as many Anglo-Americans, have internalized the dominant societal myths about the superiority of their group and the innate inferiority of other ethnic groups. Many individuals who are socialized within all-White suburban communities in the United States and who live highly ethnocentric and encapsulated lives can be described as Stage 2 individuals. Alice Miel (with Kiester, 1967) describes these kinds of individuals in *The Short-changed Children of Suburbia.*

The characteristics of Stage 2 are most extreme among individuals who suddenly begin to feel that their cultural group and its way of life, especially its privileged and ascribed status, are being threatened by other groups. This phenomenon could be observed when White male privilege was challenged when women successfully competed with them for high-level jobs in business and in the professions during the 1980s and 1990s. This development may explain, in part, what pundits have dubbed the "angry White male." Extreme forms of this stage are also manifested among individuals who have experienced psychological captivity (Stage 1) and who have recently discovered their cultural identity. This new cultural consciousness is usually caused by a cultural revitalization movement. This type of individual, like the individual who feels that the survival of his or her cultural group is threatened, is likely to express intensely negative feelings toward outside groups.

However, individuals who have experienced cultural psychological captivity and who have newly discovered their cultural consciousness tend to have highly ambivalent feelings toward their own cultural group and try to confirm, for themselves, that they are proud of their cultural group. Consequently, strong and verbal rejection of out-groups usually takes place. Out-groups are regarded as enemies and, in extreme manifestations of this stage, are viewed as planning genocidal efforts to destroy their group. Many of the members of the Skinheads state that Blacks and Jews are trying to destroy them and that they are behaving defensively when they target Jews and Blacks for ethnic and racial violence.

The individual's cultural connectedness is escalated and highly exaggerated. The individual within this stage of cultural identity tends to reject strongly members of his or her cultural group who are regarded as assimilationist-oriented and liberal, who do not endorse the rhetoric of separatism, or who openly socialize with members of outside groups, especially with members of groups that are regarded as low-status and stigmatized in society.

The Stage 2 individual expects members of the cultural group to show strong overt commitments to the liberation struggle of the group or to the protection of the group from outside and "foreign" groups. The individual often endorses a separatist ideology. Members of outside cultural groups are likely to regard Stage 2 individuals as bigots or extremists. As these individuals begin to question some of the basic assumptions of their culture and to experience less ambivalence and conflict about their cultural identity; and especially as the rewards within the society become more fairly distributed among cultural groups, they are likely to become less ethnocentric and culturally encapsulated.

Stage 3: Cultural Identity Clarification

At this stage the individual is able to clarify personal attitudes and cultural identity, to reduce intrapsychic conflict, and to develop clarified positive attitudes toward his or her cultural group. The individual learns self-acceptance, thus developing the characteristics needed to accept and respond more positively to outside cultural groups. Self-acceptance is a requisite to accepting and responding positively to outside individuals and groups. During this stage, the individual is able to accept and understand both the positive and negative attributes of his or her cultural group. The individual's pride in his or her cultural group is not based on the hate or fear of outside groups. Cultural pride is genuine rather than contrived. Individuals are more likely to experience this stage when they have attained a certain level of economic and psychological security and have been able to have positive experiences with members of other cultural groups.

Stage 4: Biculturalism

The individual within this stage has a healthy sense of cultural identity and the psychological characteristics and skills needed to participate successfully in his or her own cultural community as well as in another cultural community (Banks, 1984). The individual also has *a strong desire to function effectively in two cultures.* We can describe such an individual as bicultural. Levels of biculturalism vary greatly. Many Latinos, in order to attain social and economic mobility, learn to function effectively in Anglo-American culture during the formal working day. The private lives of these individuals, however, may be highly Latino and monocultural.

People of color in the United States are forced to become bicultural to some extent in order to experience social and economic mobility. However, members of mainstream groups such as Anglo-Americans can and often do live almost exclusive monocultural lives.

Stage 5: Multiculturalism and Reflective Nationalism

The Stage 5 individual has clarified, reflective, and positive personal, cultural, and national identities; has positive attitudes toward other cultural, ethnic and racial groups; and is self-actualized. The individual is able to function, at least beyond superficial levels, within several cultures within his or her nation and to understand, appreciate, and share the values, symbols, and institutions of several cultures within the nation. Such multicultural perspectives and feelings, I hypothesize, help the individual live a more enriched and fulfilling life and formulate creative and novel solutions to personal and public problems.

Individuals within this stage have a commitment to their cultural group, an empathy and concern for other cultural groups, and a strong but *reflective* commitment and allegiance to the nation-state and its idealized values, such as human dignity and justice. Thus, such individuals have reflective and clarified cultural and national identities and are effective citizens in a democratic pluralistic nation. Stage 5 individuals realistically view the United States as the multicultural and multilingual nation that it is. They have cross-cultural competency within their own nation and commitment to the national ideals, creeds, and values of the nation-state.

The socialization that most individuals experience does not help them attain the attitudes, skills, and perspectives needed to function effectively within a variety of cultures and communities. Although many people participate in several cultures at superficial levels, such as eating ethnic foods and listening to ethnic music (called Level 1 in Chapter 3), few probably participate at more meaningful levels and learn to understand the values, symbols, and traditions of several cultures and are able to function within other cultures at meaningful levels (Level 2 through 3, see Chapter 3).

Stage 6: Globalism and Global Competency

The individual within Stage 6 has clarified, reflective, and positive cultural, national, and global identities and the knowledge, skills, attitudes, and abilities needed to function within cultures within his or her own nation as well as within cultures outside his or her nation in other parts of the world. The Stage 6 individual has the ideal delicate balance of cultural, national, and global identities, commitments, literacy, and behaviors. This individual has internalized the universalistic ethical values and principles of humankind and has the skills, competencies, and commitment needed to take action within the world to actualize personal values and commitments.

Characteristics of the Cultural Identity Typology

This typology is an ideal-type construct (see Figure 7.1) and should be viewed as dynamic and multidimensional rather than as static and linear. The characteristics within the stages exist on a continuum. Thus, within Stage 1, individuals are more or less psychologically captive; some individuals are more psychologically captive than are others.

The division between the stages is blurred rather than sharp. Thus, a continuum also exists between as well as within the stages. The culturally encapsulated individual (Stage 2) does not suddenly attain clarification and acceptance of his or her cultural identity (Stage 3). This is a gradual and developmental process. Also, the stages should not be viewed as strictly sequential and linear.

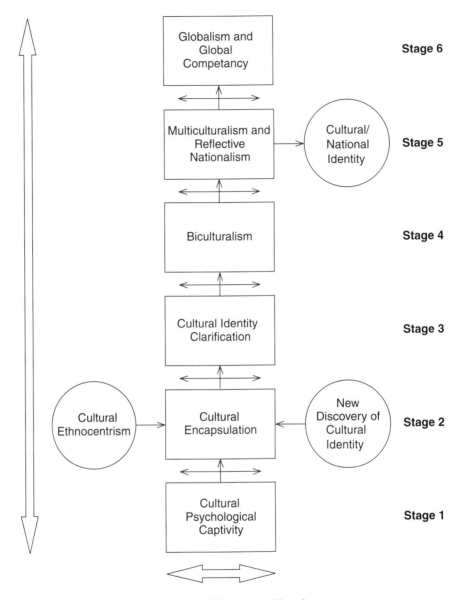

FIGURE 7.1   The Stages of Cultural Identity: A Typology

I am hypothesizing that some individuals may never experience a particular stage. However, I hypothesize that once an individual experiences a particular stage, he or she is likely to experience the stages above it sequentially and developmentally. I also hypothesize that individuals may experience the stages upward, downward, or in a zigzag pattern. Under certain conditions, for example, the bicultural (Stage 4) individual may become multicultural (Stage 5); under new conditions the same individual may become again bicultural (Stage 4), culturally identified (Stage 3), and culturally encapsulated (Stage 2). Jewish Americans, who tend to express more positive attitudes toward groups of color than do other White ethnic groups in the United States, became increasingly in-group-oriented as Israel became more threatened and as the expressions of anti-Semitism escalated in the 1970s and 1980s (Forster & Epstein, 1974). Northern White ethnic groups became increasingly more culturally and ethnically encapsulated as busing for school desegregation gained momentum in northern cities in the 1970s (Glazer, 1983).

Figure 7.1 illustrates the dynamic and multidimensional characteristics of the development of cultural identity among individuals. Note especially the arrowed lines that indicate that continua exist both horizontally and vertically.

Preliminary Curricular Implications of the Stages of Cultural Identity Typology

The discussion that follows on the curricular implications of the stages of cultural identity typology should be viewed as a set of tentative hypotheses that merit testing by educators and researchers interested in cultural diversity and education. *The reader should keep foremost in mind the tentative and exploratory nature of the following discussion.*

Curricular Implications of Cultural Identity: Stage 1

Students within this stage of cultural identity can best benefit from monocultural content and experiences that will help them to develop cultural awareness and a heightened sense of cultural consciousness. Such monocultural experiences should be designed to help students come to grips with their personal cultural identities. They should learn how their cultural group has helped to liberate as well as to victimize other cultural, racial, and ethnic groups. It is important for White students to learn not only about how Whites have oppressed African Americans and Native Americans, but also how Whites have helped these groups to attain more justice and rights within our society. White students, as well as African American students, need to study about slaveowners as well as about White abolitionists and Whites who participated in the civil rights movement.

It is very important for White students to learn about White leaders who took antiracist actions because they need role models to imitate (Howard, 1999). Consequently, students should study about Whites who played important roles in the past such as Helen Hunt Jackson, John Brown, and Lillian Smith (1978), author of *Killers of the Dream*. They should also learn about Whites today who are doing visible antiracist work, such as Morris Deees (in social action) and Gary Orfield (in scholarship on desegregation and affirmative action).

Students who are members of cultural and ethnic groups that have been victimized and marginalized need to learn how their cultural groups have been victimized by the larger society and by institutions, such as the media and the schools, which reinforce and perpetuate dominant societal myths and ideologies. Cultural studies courses and units, conceptualized in *interdisciplinary* and *humanistic* ways, and other monocultural experiences, can help individuals within this stage to raise their levels of cultural consciousness. Strategies that facilitate moral development and decision-making skills should be an integral part of the curriculum for the culturally psychologically captive individual (Banks & Banks, with Clegg, 1999).

Curricular Implications of Cultural Identity:
Stage 2

Individuals within this stage can best benefit from curricular experiences that give them an opportunity to examine and understand their hostile feelings toward outside cultural groups. Teachers can help students in this stage to develop more positive feelings toward themselves and others only when negative feelings toward other groups are uncovered and expressed in a safe and democratic classroom. A strong affective curricular component that helps students clarify their negative feelings toward outside groups should be a major part of the curriculum. The students should be helped to deal with their hostile feelings toward outside groups in constructive ways. The teacher should help the individual begin the process of attaining cultural identity clarification during the later phases of this stage.

Curricular Implications of Cultural Identity:
Stage 3

Curricular experiences within this stage should be designed to reinforce the student's emerging cultural identity and clarification. The student should be helped to attain a balanced perspective on his or her cultural group. A true acceptance of one's cultural group involves accepting its glories as well as its shortcomings. The individual in this stage of cultural identity can accept an objective view and analysis of his or her cultural group, whereas an objective analysis is often very difficult for Stage 1 and Stage 2 individuals to accept. Value clarification and moral development techniques should be used to enhance the individual's emerging cultural identity clarification.

Curricular Implications of Cultural Identity:
Stage 4

Curricular experiences should be designed to help the student master concepts and generalizations related to a cultural group other than his or her own and to help the student view events and situations from the perspective of another cultural group. The student should be helped to compare and contrast his or her own cultural group with another cultural group. Strategies should also be used to enhance the individual's moral development and ability to relate positively to his or her own cultural group and to another cultural group.

Curricular Implications of Cultural Identity: Stage 5

The curriculum at this stage of cultural identity should be designed to help the student develop a global sense of cultural literacy and to master concepts and generalizations about a wide range of cultural groups. The student should also be helped to view events and situations from the perspectives of different cultural, ethnic, and racial groups within the United States as well as within other nations. The student should explore the problems and promises of living within a multicultural society and discuss ways in which a multicultural society may be nurtured and improved. Strategies such as moral dilemmas and case studies should be used to enable the individual to explore moral and value alternatives and to embrace values, such as human dignity and justice, that are needed to live in a multicultural community and global world society.

Curricular Implications of Cultural Identity: Stage 6

At this stage, the student has acquired three levels of identities that are balanced: a cultural, national, and global identity and related cross-cultural competencies. Because the typology presented in this chapter constitutes a continuum, the process of acquiring an effective balance of cultural, national, and global identities and related cross-cultural competencies is a continuous and ongoing process. Thus, the individual never totally attains the ideal cultural, national, and global identities and related cross-cultural skills for functioning within his or her cultural group, nation, and world. Consequently, a major goal of the curriculum for the Stage 6 individual is to help the student function at Stage 6 more effectively.

Knowledge, skills, attitudes, and abilities that students need to function more effectively within their cultural group, nation, and world should be emphasized when teaching students at Stage 6. This knowledge includes information about the individual's own cultural group, other cultural groups, the national culture, and information about other nations in the world. Valuing strategies, such as moral dilemmas and case studies that relate to the individual's cultural group, nation, and world, should also be effectively used at this stage to enhance the student's developing sense of cultural, national, and global identifications. A major goal of teaching students within this stage is to help them understand how to determine which particular allegiance—whether cultural, national, or global—is most appropriate within a particular situation. Cultural, national, and global attachments should be given different priorities within different situations and events. The student within Stage 6 should learn how to determine which identity is most appropriate for particular situations, settings, and events.

Summary

When planning multicultural experiences for students and teachers, we need to consider the cultural characteristics of individuals. In designing curricula related to cultural identity, we often assume that cultural groups are monolithic and have rather homogeneous needs and characteristics. However, students differ greatly in their cultural identities and characteristics just as they differ in their general cognitive and affective development (Greeno, 1996; Petty & Wegener, 1998). Consequently, some attempt should be made to individualize experiences for students within the multicultural curriculum.

The description of a typology that attempts to outline the basic stages of the development of cultural identity among individual members of groups is presented in this chapter. This typology is a preliminary ideal-type construct in the Weberian sense and constitutes a set of hypotheses based on the existing and emerging theory and research and the author's observations of cultural behavior. The six stages within the typology are:

Stage 1: Cultural Psychological Captivity
Stage 2: Cultural Encapsulation
Stage 3: Cultural Identity Clarification
Stage 4: Biculturalism
Stage 5: Multiculturalism and Reflective Nationalism
Stage 6: Globalism and Competency.

It is hypothesized that individuals within these different stages should be exposed to curricular experiences consistent with their levels of cultural identity. The curricular implications of each of the stages of cultural identity are discussed.

R E F E R E N C E S

Banks, J. A. (1976). The Emerging Stages of Ethnicity: Implications for Staff Development. *Educational Leadership, 34*(3), 190–193.

Banks, J. A. (1984). Black Youths in Predominantly White Suburbs: An Exploratory Study of Their Attitudes and Self-Concepts. *Journal of Negro Education, 53*(1), 3–17.

Banks, J. A. (1997). *Teaching Strategies for Ethnic Studies* (6th ed.). Boston: Allyn and Bacon.

Banks, J. A., & Banks, C. A. M., with Clegg, A. A., Jr. (1999). *Teaching Strategies for the Social Studies: Decision-Making and Citizen Action* (5th ed.). New York: Longman.

Bean, T. W., Readence, J. E., & Mallette, M. H. (1996). Selecting Young Adult Novels: Identity Criteria for use with Banks' Typology.

In D. J. Leu, C. K. Kinzer, & K. A. Hinchman (Eds.), *Literacies for the 21st Century: Research and Practice.* Forty-Fifth Yearbook of the National Reading Conference (pp. 296–305). Chicago: National Reading Conference.

Belenky, M. F., Clinchy, B. M., Goldberger, N. R., & Tarule, J. M. (1986). *Women Ways of Knowing: The Development of Self, Voice, and Mind.* New York: Basic Books.

Bly, R. (1990). *Iron John: A Book about Men.* Reading, MA: Addison-Wesley.

Clark, K. B. (1963). *Prejudice and Your Children.* Boston: Beacon Press.

Code, L. (1991). *What Can She Know? Feminist Theory and the Construction of Knowledge.* Ithaca, NY: Cornell University Press.

Collins, P. H. (1990). *Black Feminist Thought: Knowledge, Consciousness, and the Politics of Empowerment.* New York: Routledge.

Cross, W. E., Jr. (1991). *Shades of Black: Diversity in African-American Identity.* Philadelphia: Temple University Press.

Erting, C. J., et al. (Eds.). (1994). *The Deaf Way: Perspectives from the International Conference on Deaf Culture.* Washington, DC: Gallaudet University Press.

Flexner, S. B., & Hauck, L. C. (Eds.). (1987). *The Random House Dictionary of the English Language* (2nd. Ed.). New York: Random House.

Ford, M. (1979). The Development of an Instrument for Assessing Levels of Ethnicity in Public School Teachers, Ed.D. diss., University of Houston.

Forster, A., & Epstein, B. R. (1974). *The New Anti-Semitism.* New York: McGraw-Hill.

Gibbs, J. T. (Ed.). (1988). *Young, Black, and Male in America: An Endangered Species.* Dover, MA: Auburn House.

Giles, H. (Ed.) (1987). *Language, Ethnicity, and Intergroup Relations.* New York: Academic Press.

Gilligan, C. (1982). *In a Different Voice: Psychological Theory and Women's Development.* Cambridge, MA: Harvard University Press.

Glazer, N. (1983). *Ethnic Dilemmas 1964–1982.* Cambridge, MA: Harvard University Press.

Goldberger, N., Tarule, J., Clincy, B., & Belenky, M. (Eds.). (1996). *Knowledge, Difference, and Power.* New York: Basic Books.

Greeno, J. G. (1996). Cognition and Learning. In D. C. Berliner & R. C. Calfee (Eds.). *Handbook of Educational Psychology* (pp. 15–46). New York: Macmillan.

Gurian, M. (1996). *The Wonder of Boys.* New York: Putnam.

Gurian, M. (1999). *The Good Son: Shaping the Moral Development of Our Boys and Young Men.* New York: Putnam.

Harding, S. (1991). *Whose Knowledge, Whose Science? Thinking from Women's Lives.* Ithaca, NY: Cornell University Press.

Harrington, M. (1962). *The Other America.* New York: Macmillan.

Harvard Educational Review (1996). Lesbian, Gay, Bisexual, and Transgender People and Education (Special Issue), *66*(2), 173–435.

Helms, J. E. (Ed.). (1990). *Black and White Racial Identity: Theory, Research, and Practice.* New York: Greenwood Press.

Helms, J. E., & Cook, D. A. (1999). *Using Race and Culture in Counseling and Psychotherapy: Theory and Process.* Boston: Allyn and Bacon.

Herdt, G. (Ed.). (1992). *Gay Culture in America: Essays from the Field.* Boston: Beacon Press.

Howard, G. (1999). *We Can't Teach What We Don't Know: White Teachers, Multiracial Schools.* New York: Teachers College Press.

Isaacs, H. R. (1992). Language as a Factor in Inter-Group Conflict. In J. Crawford (Ed.), *Language Loyalties: A Source Book on the Official English Controversy* (pp. 466–478). Chicago: The University of Chicago Press.

Jencks, C., & Peterson, P. E. (Eds.). (1991). *The Urban Underclass.* Washington, DC: Brookings Institution.

Kardiner, A., & Ovesey, L. (1951). *The Mark of Oppression: A Psychosocial Study of the American Negro.* New York: Norton.

Karon, B. P. (1958). *The Negro Personality.* New York: Springer Publishing Co.

Kunjufu, J. (1986). *Countering the Conspiracy to Destroy Black Boys* (Vol. 2). Chicago: African American Images.

Kuper, A. (1999). *Culture: The Anthropologists' Account.* Cambridge, MA: Harvard University Press.

Lewis, O. (1965). *La Vida: A Puerto Rican Family in the Culture of Poverty.* New York: Vintage Books.

Maher, F. A., & Tetreault, M. K. T. (1994). *The Feminist Classroom.* New York: Basic Books.

Mallette, M. H., Bean, T. W., & Readence, J. E. (1998). Using Banks' Typology in the Discussions of Young Adult, Multiethnic Literature: A Multicase Study. *Journal of Research and Development in Education, 31*(4), pp. 193–204.

McIntosh, P. (1997). White Privilege: Unpacking the Invisible Knapsack. In V. Cyrus (Ed.), *Experiencing Race, Class, and Gender in the United States* (2nd ed.) (pp. 194–198). Mountain View, CA: Mayfield.

Miel, A., with Kiester, E., Jr. (1967). *The Shortchanged Children of Suburbia.* New York: Institute of Human Relations Press, The American Jewish Committee.

Padden, C., & Humphries, T. (Eds.). (1988). *Deaf in America: Voices from a Culture.* Cambridge, MA: Harvard University Press.

Petty, R. E., & Wegener, D. T. (1998). Attitude Change: Multiple Roles for Persuasion Variables. In D. Gilbert, S. T. Fiske, & G. Lindzey (Eds.). *The Handbook of Social Psychology* (Vol. 1) (pp. 323–390). New York: McGraw-Hill.

Phinney, J. S., & Rotheram, M. J. (Eds.). (1987). *Children's Ethnic Socialization.* Newbury Park, CA: Sage.

Pollack, W. (1998). *Real Boys: Rescuing Our Sons form the Myths of Boyhood.* New York: Henry Holt.

Ramírez, M. III, & Castañeda, A. (1974). *Cultural Democracy, Bicognitive Development, and Education.* New York: Academic Press.

Reber, A. S. (1985). *The Penguin Dictionary of Psychology.* New York: Penguin.

Rhoads, R. A. (1994). *Coming out in College: The Struggle for a Queer Identity.* Westport, CT: Bergin & Garvey.

Riis, J. A. (1957). *How the Other Half Lives.* New York: Hill and Wang. (original work published 1890)

Rodriguez, C. E. (1995). Puerto Ricans in Historical and Social Science Research. In J. A. Banks & C. A. M. Banks (Eds.), *Handbook of Research on Multicultural Education* (pp. 223–244). New York: Macmillan.

Rothbart, M., & John O. P. (1993). Intergroup Relations and Stereotype Change: A Social-Cognitive Analysis and Some Longitudinal Findings. In P. M. Sniderman, P. E. Telock, & E. G. Carmines (Eds.), *Prejudice, Politics, and the American Dilemma* (pp. 32–59). Stanford, CA: Stanford University Press.

Shepherd, S., & Wallis, M. (Eds.). (1989). *Coming on Strong: Gay Politics and Culture.* Boston: Unwin Hyman.

Smelser, N. J., & Alexander, J. C. (Eds.). (1999). *Diversity and Its Discontents: Cultural Conflict and Common Ground in Contemporary American Society.* Princeton, NJ: Princeton University Press.

Smith, E. R., & Mackie, D. M. (1995). *Social Psychology.* New York: Worth Publishers.

Smith, L. (1978). *Killers of the Dream.* New York: Norton. (originally published in 1949)

Spencer, M. B. (1982). Personal and Group Identity among Black Children: An Alternative Synthesis. *Genetic Psychology Monographs, 106,* 59–84.

Spencer, M. B. (1984). Black Children's Race Awareness, Racial Attitudes, and Self-Concept: A Reinterpretation. *Journal of Child Psychology and Psychiatry, 25,* 433–441.

Spencer, M. B. (1985). Cultural Cognition and Social Cognition as Identity Correlates of Black Children's Personal-Social Development. In M. B. Spencer, G. K. Brookins, & W. R. Allen (Eds.), *Beginnings: The Social and Affective Development of Black Children.* (pp. 215–230). Hillsdale, NJ: Lawrence Erlbaum.

Tannen, D. (1990). *You Just Don't Understand: Women and Men in Conversation.* New York: William Morrow.

Tomlinson, L. M. (1995). *The Effects of Instructional Interaction Guided by a Typology of Ethnic Identity Development: Phase One.* Athens: National Reading Center, University of Georgia.

Tomlinson, L. M. (1996). *Teachers' Application of Banks' Typology of Ethnic Identity Development and Curriculum Goals to Story Content and Classroom Discussion: Phase Two.* Athens: National Reading Research Center, University of Georgia.

Valentine, C. A. (1968). *Culture and Poverty: Critique and Counter-Proposals.* Chicago: The University of Chicago Press.

Wilson, W. J. (1996). *When Work Disappears: The World of the New Urban Poor.* New York: Knopf.

PART THREE

Knowledge Construction and School Reform

Chapter 8
Race, Disability, Giftedness, and School Reform

Chapter 9
The Lives and Values of Transformative Scholars
and Citizenship Education

The culture and organization of the school, including curriculum and pedagogy, are undergirded by a set of assumptions, conceptions, and ideologies that are based on knowledge. The knowledge that underlies school practices and pedagogy is rarely examined by teachers and other practitioners. Much of the knowledge on which current school practices is based justifies educational inequality for low-income students and students of color. Consequently, an uncovering and transformation of the knowledge, assumptions, and ideologies that underlie school practices are essential to the implementation of school reform.

The two chapters in Part Three describe knowledge systems and paradigms that underlie school practices and pedagogy and the ways in which existing knowledge systems can be transformed. They also describe the ways in which new concepts and paradigms that support equity and liberation for marginalized groups have been created and institutionalized.

Chapter 8 describes how race, mental retardation, and giftedness are socially constructed categories that have been used to reinforce the privileged positions of powerful groups as well as established practices and institutions. This chapter also describes how marginalized groups have contested these concepts and have created oppositional knowledge, the aim of which is to increase educational opportunities and possibilities.

The ways in which the lives and values of researchers influence the knowledge they construct is described in Chapter 9. This chapter also presents a typology of cross-cultural researchers and describes the lives and work of a select group of social scientists who exemplify the categories in the typology. It also describes the implications of knowledge construction for citizenship education.

8 Race, Disability, Giftedness, and School Reform

Je est un autre (I am an other)
—Arthur Rimbaud (French poet, 1854–1891, cited in Todorov, 1987, p. 3)

Historical, political, and social developments within the last half century were a watershed in the quest for educational equality in the United States. Racial segregation within the nation's educational institutions and within the larger society received a major blow in 1954, when the Supreme Court, in *Brown v. the Board of Education of Topeka,* declared separate but equal schools unconstitutional. The Brown decision paved the way for the civil rights movement of the 1960s and 1970s, which changed the nation in fundamental ways.

Many educational developments whose goal was to increase educational equality emerged out of the civil rights movement, including school desegregation, affirmative action, bilingual education, and multicultural education. Each of these developments has been contested and has stimulated acid debates, but each has changed the nation and its educational institutions in ways that will have profound consequences in the new century. Because of these developments, equality will be an essential component of educational discourse in the twenty-first century.

School desegregation, bilingual education, multicultural education, and affirmative action have brought the nation closer to the democratic values stated in its founding documents, (i.e, the Declaration of Independence, the Constitution, and the Bill of Rights). However, movement toward these ideals during the last half century has been cyclic and uneven, rather than linear and straightforward.

Note: I am grateful to the following colleagues for their perceptive and helpful comments on an earlier draft of this chapter: Cherry A. McGee Banks, Ron Brandt, Eugene B. Edgar, Sonia Nieto, and Christine E. Sleeter.

Movement toward democratic ideals will continue during the new century, but will also be cyclic and uneven. Periods of progress toward equality will be followed by periods of retrogression. However, during times of retrogression some of the progress attained in previous periods will be maintained. Also, regression and progress will often occur at the same time. Today, for example, bilingual education is being strongly contested in some communities, while multicultural content is becoming institutionalized in school textbooks and also in college and university courses throughout the nation.

Each of the developments that brought the nation closer to educational equality during the last 30 years has revealed the inconsistency between America's democratic ideals and its educational practices. Myrdal (1944) called the gap between the nation's democratic ideals and its practices the "American dilemma." The uncovering of the American dilemma is an essential step in the march toward change and educational equality. One of the most hopeful developments within the last 30 years was the uncovering of issues related to educational equality, the discussion of these issues in public forums, and the implementation of programs and practices designed to create greater educational equality for groups on the margins of society.

Aims of This Chapter

The quest for educational equality that began as a consequence of the civil rights movement resulted in greater participation of women, people of color, language minority groups, and people with disabilities in the shaping of educational research, policy, and practice. One consequence of the greater participation of these groups in educational research and decision-making is that they uncovered—as well as contested—the established paradigms, canons, categories, and concepts that they believed justified their marginalized status, defined them as the Other, and played an important role in denying them equal educational opportunities.

The battle over whose knowledge should be institutionalized in the schools, colleges, and universities was one of the most important consequences of the quest for educational equality in the closing decades of the twentieth century (Schlesinger, 1991; Sleeter, 1995). *The struggle over knowledge and who controls it will continue in the twenty-first century.* The groups that have the most power largely determine what knowledge is produced and becomes institutionalized in the popular culture and in the nation's schools, colleges, and universities. Consequently, the struggle over knowledge production will continue until groups on the margins become equal-status participants in mainstream U.S. society. This chapter describes a case study of the contest that ensued over three major concepts. The issues related to these concepts will continue to be manifested in significant ways in the new century.

This chapter, which is grounded in the sociology of knowledge (Berger & Luckmann, 1966; Mannheim, 1985) examines *race, mental retardation,* and *giftedness.* I describe how these concepts are socially constructed categories that have been used to reinforce the privileged positions of powerful groups as well as established practices and institutions. I also describe how marginalized groups have contested these concepts and created oppositional knowledge whose aim is to increase their educational opportunities and possibilities.

In examining the ways in which race, mental retardation, and giftedness are socially constructed categories, I do not intend to obscure their distinct histories, purposes, and aims. I realize that most special and gifted educators believe that their concepts and programs help to actualize educational equality by providing essential resources and support for targeted groups of students. However, some educational programs with humanitarian goals have latent functions that contradict those goals and promote inequality (Tomlinson, 1982). For example, classes for mentally retarded students—the public aim of which is to provide special instruction for students who need it—are overpopulated by males, low-income students, and students of color. The sociological analysis in this chapter focuses on the *latent* rather than the *manifest* function of knowledge and the institutions it supports (Merton, 1968).

As Berger and Luckmann (1966) point out, any body of knowledge can be socially established as reality. Varenne and McDermott (1998) call socially constructed knowledge "cultural facts." The "cultural facts" about race, mental retardation, and giftedness have often been used to justify and legitimize educational practices that have limited the academic achievement of students of color, language minority students, students with disabilities, and students from lower socioeconomic groups.

I encourage readers to consider these questions as they read this chapter:

Who has the power to define groups and to institutionalize their conceptions within the schools, colleges, and universities?

What is the relationship between knowledge and power?

Who benefits from the ways in which race, mental retardation, and giftedness are defined and conceptualized in the larger society and within educational institutions? Who loses?

How can race, mental retardation, and giftedness be reconstructed in ways that will empower marginalized groups and create greater educational equality?

To provide a historical context for discussing the construction of categories and the quest for educational equality, this chapter first describes the state of race relations as we enter the new century.

Race Relations at the Dawn of a New Century

Race relations and the quest for equality in the United States are at a turning point. The nation made notable progress toward eliminating racial, ethnic, and gender discrimination from the 1960s to the early 1980s. Significant advances in racial equality continued from the *Brown* decision (1954) to the Reagan presidential years (1981 to 1989), when progress toward equality was slowed. Even during the Reagan and Bush years, however, people of color and women made substantial progress toward educational equality and inroads toward full inclusion into mainstream society. Because they were already a part of mainstream society and had substantial educational, financial, and cultural capital, middle- and upper-class White women made considerably more progress than ethnic groups of color within the last 25 years. However, they still face intractable glass ceilings in some of the most coveted jobs and in the world of business and finance.

Although racial and ethnic groups and women made considerable progress in the decades between 1960 and 1980, the gap between the rich and poor widened considerably within the last several decades (Wilson, 1996). After declining for 40 years, the share of the nation's wealth held by the wealthiest households (0.5 percent) rose sharply in the 1980s. In 1976, this segment of the population held 14 percent of the nation's wealth. In 1983 it held 26.9 percent (Phillips, 1990). In 1992 the top 20 percent of U.S. households received 11 times as much income as the bottom 2 percent. In 1997, 35.6 percent of people in the United States were living in poverty; this number included a high concentration of African Americans and Hispanics (U.S. Bureau of the Census, 1988a). In 1997, the poverty rate for non-Hispanic Whites was 8.6 percent, compared to 25.5 percent and 27.1 percent for African Americans and Hispanics, respectively.

Although groups of color, such as African Americans, Puerto Ricans in the United States, and Mexican Americans, have disproportionately high poverty rates, many individuals of color joined the middle class. Class divisions increased within both ethnic minority and majority groups during the last three decades.

The nation's student population reflects the widening social-class gap. In 1990, about one in five students lived below the official government poverty line (U.S. Bureau of the Census, 1998a). The class division between teachers and students, and between middle-class and low-income students, will be a major factor influencing the quest for educational equality in the twenty-first century.

As the new century dawns, the nation seems exhausted by the quest for equality. Some conservative opinion leaders and scholars argue that the playing field is now even and that people of color must join the race for progress without governmental intervention or help (Steele, 1998; Thernstrom & Thernstrom, 1997). These individuals appear to ignore the long history of institutionalized discrimination in the United States; they have not acknowledged that we cannot correct problems in several decades that have been in the making for nearly four centuries (Franklin, 1993; Lawrence & Matsuda, 1997).

We begin the new century with the problems of institutional discrimination still with us and with a nationally organized and effective conservative backlash. This backlash is not only stemming the tide of governmental intervention to create a more just society but is also eroding some of the gains that ethnic minorities have made within the last three decades. The actions of conservative groups and institutions, which include the actions by federal courts, have been both ominous and effective. They include the decision in the *Hopwood* v. *State of Texas* case, which ended affirmative action at the University of Texas Law School, and initiatives 209 in California and 200 in Washington state, which prohibit affirmative action in government employment and university admissions (Orfield & Miller, 1998).

That affirmative action is being dismantled at the same time that the first data-based study reveals its success is ironic: Affirmative action has enabled more African Americans to gain admission to college and graduate school, enter main-stream society, and contribute substantially to their communities and society (Bowen & Bok, 1998). Institutions of higher education in California and Washington state must now find new ways to achieve student and faculty diversity now that most established practices are illegal. Success in California and Washington will most likely encourage affirmative action opponents to take their campaign to other states. Affirmative action policies within several schools have also been challenged, a trend that is likely to continue into the foreseeable future.

The Challenge of Fostering Diversity

Two somewhat contradictory developments make it imperative for U.S. educators to set a high priority on diversity and equity. One development is the challenge from individuals and groups opposed to affirmative action and other diversity in-itiatives. The other is the growth of ethnic, cultural, and language diversity in the nation. Educators need to be a counterforce and to help students acquire a strong commitment to democratic values and become reflective citizens. Students should also be helped to understand that a gap between ideals and realities always exists in a democratic society and that their roles as citizens is to take actions to help close that gap (Banks, 1997a).

I call the significant changes in the racial, ethnic, and language groups that make up the nation's population the *demographic imperative* (Banks, 1997a). The United States is currently experiencing its largest influx of immigrants since the beginning of the twentieth century. Immigrants are changing the face and ethnic texture of the nation. Between 1980 and 1990, 80 percent of the documented immi-grants to the United States came from nations in Latin America and Asia (U.S. Bureau of the Census, 1994). Only 9 percent came from Europe. The U.S. Census projects that people of color will make up 47.5 percent of the nation's population by 2050.

The students in the nation's schools are becoming increasingly ethnically, ra-cially, and linguistically diverse. It is projected that students of color will make up about 48 percent of the nation's school-age youths by 2020 (Pallas, Natriello, & McDill, 1989). The U.S. Census (1994) indicates that in 1990 14 percent of school-age youths spoke a first language at home other than English. States the *Standards* published by the Teachers of English to Speakers of Other Languages (1997), "Current projections estimate that by the year 2000 the majority of the school-age population in 50 or more major U.S. cities will be from language minority back-grounds" (p. 1). A research synthesis published by the National Research Council highlights the nation's growing language minority population and describes its instructional needs as an important priority for the nation's schools (August & Hakuta, 1997).

The increasing diversification of the nation's school population has significant implications for educators. Many of these groups have serious academic and social problems that need urgent and thoughtful attention in the schools. Despite the achievement gains they have made within the last decade, African American and Latino youths are still substantially behind Anglo mainstream youths on many indices of academic achievement; they also have lower high school graduation rates and higher retention, suspension, and dropout rates (Gay, 1997).

The increasing diversification of the nation's schools requires that the curriculum and the school be reformed in significant ways so that students from diverse racial, ethnic, and language groups will learn how to live together in civic, moral, and just communities that respect and value the rights and cultural characteristics of all students. This is a serious challenge because an increasing percentage of students of color attend racially segregated schools (Orfield, Eaton, & The Harvard Project on School Desegregation, 1996). Segregation often exists within racially and ethnically mixed schools because of tracking and special programs.

A Focus on Difference

Increasing diversity, the widening gap between the rich and the poor, and renewed efforts by marginalized groups to gain recognition and legitimacy have focused attention on issues related to difference within the last three decades. Because such issues are unresolved (for example, backlashes against affirmative action and bilingual education), this focus is likely to increase and intensify in the new century.

An antibilingual movement has emerged in response to the significant increase in the percentage of students who speak a first language other than English. U.S. English, a group formed in the 1980s, lobbies to make English the nation's official language and the only language used in public places. By 1998, 25 states had made English their official language, either by amending their state constitutions or by enacting new legislation (U.S. English, 1999). Arizona's law, which was enacted in 1988, was declared unconstitutional by the Arizona Supreme Court in 1998. Another indication of antibilingual sentiment in the nation is the large number of California residents who voted for Proposition 227 (also known as the Unz Amendment, after the millionaire Ron Unz, who led the campaign for it). Proposition 227, which essentially eliminates bilingual education, was approved overwhelmingly at the polls. This is ironic because research indicates that the best way for students to learn a second language, such as English, is to strengthen—not to eradicate—their first language (August & Hakuta, 1997).

A major problem facing the nation-state is how to recognize and legitimize difference and yet construct an overarching national identity that incorporates the voices, experiences, and hopes of the diverse groups that make up the nation-state. The groups that will participate in constructing a new national identity and the factors that can be used to motivate powerful groups to share power with marginalized groups are also issues that have to be addressed. Power sharing is an essential characteristic of a nation-state that reflects the cultures of its diverse population.

New Conceptions of Difference

Traditional categories used to differentiate and define human population groups will become more contested as marginalized racial, ethnic, and language groups grow in size, power, and legitimacy. Uncovering and deconstructing these institutionalized conceptions that deny human population groups equal educational opportunities, and replacing them with liberatory concepts, paradigms, and theories, are important agenda items for the new century. These new conceptions should view human potential as unlimited and should describe ways in which group boundaries are flexible and interactive, rather than limited and distinct. Schools, colleges, and universities should integrate these ideas into programs to educate teachers and educational leaders.

The Social Construction of Race

Race is one of the main categories used to construct differences in the United States and in other societies (Montagu, 1997). Racialization is a characteristic of both past and present societies (Hannaford, 1996). Groups holding social, political, and economic power construct racial categories to give their groups privilege and to marginalize outside groups. Jacobson (1998) calls races "invented categories" (p. 4). Omi and Winant (1994) state that the "determination of racial categories is…an intensely political process" (p. 3). Their theory of *racial formation* "emphasizes the social nature of race, the absence of any essential racial characteristics, the historical flexibility of racial meanings and categories…and the irreducible political aspect of racial dynamics" (p. 4).

Racial categories have shifted over time, established categories have been deconstructed, and new ones have been formed. The large influx of immigrants from Ireland in the 1840s and from Eastern, Southern, and Central Europe in the late 1800s challenged the category of Whiteness. White ethnic groups that were already established in the United States and that had social, economic, and political power defined the "huddled masses" of new immigrants as peoples from different races. Writes Jacobson (1998), "upon the arrival of the massive waves of Irish immigrants in the 1840s, whiteness itself would become newly problematic, and in some quarters, would begin to lose its monolithic character" (pp. 37–38).

Jacobson (1998) describes these developments as "the fracturing of whiteness" (p. 38). Various groups of Whites became distinct races that were ranked, such as the Celtic, Slav, Hebrew, Iberic, Mediterranean, and Anglo Saxon. Anglo Saxon was classified as the superior race. One writer stated that because of their "Celtic blood," the Irish threatened the American republic (Jacobson, 1998, p. 49). A newspaper described the Irish as a "savage mob," "a pack of savages," and "incarnate devils"

(Jacobson, 1998, p. 55). The Irish became defined as the Other and consequently were denied opportunities that the Anglo Saxons enjoyed.

Italians and Jews also were defined as the Other near the turn of the century and experienced racial discrimination and hostility. Italians were often called disparaging terms, such as "dagos" and "White niggers." In some parts of the South, Italians were forced to attend all-Black schools (Waters, 1990). In 1891, during the height of American nativism, eleven Italians were lynched after being accused of murdering the police chief of New Orleans.

Leo Frank, a Jewish northerner, became a victim of anti-Semitism and racial hostility when he was accused of murdering a White girl who worked in a pencil factory he co-owned. In 1915, he was found guilty in an unfair trail. When the governor of Georgia commuted his sentence, a White mob forcibly removed him from jail and lynched him.

Multiple categories that had described the races among White ethnic groups in the mid-nineteenth century become one racial category in the twentieth century (Alba, 1990; Ignatiev, 1995; Jacobson, 1998). A single White racial category formed when various White ethnic groups assimilated culturally, racially identified as one group, and defined themselves in opposition to African Americans (Morrison, 1992).

Lessons from the Past

The past has taught us that racial categories and their meanings will keep changing, that groups with power will construct race to benefit themselves and to disadvantage powerless groups, and that race is a powerful variable in the American conscience and society. Politicians are keenly aware of the power of race. This savviness became evident when George Bush, who was lagging in the presidential polls in 1988, used a commercial that featured a Black escaped criminal (Willie Horton) to solicit support from White voters.

History also has taught us that once groups attain power, they will challenge existing conceptions of race if necessary and push for redefining the meaning of racial categories. Such opposition will most likely come from biracial individuals and from Latino groups, which are expected to outnumber African Americans by 2020 if their current birthrates and immigration rates into the United States continue.

In 1990, biracial individuals challenged the racial categories that the U.S. Census Bureau used. After reviewing the results of tests and hearings, the Office of Management and Budget changed the 2000 Census question related to race so that an individual may check one or more categories (U.S. Bureau of the Census, 1998b). The Bureau expects this change to affect its results only slightly because "fewer than 2 percent of respondents in recent tests used this option" (U.S. Bureau of the Census, 1998b).

Many biracial individuals who have one African American and one White parent do not believe that they should be forced to belong to one racial category, but should be able to indicate that they are both African American and White. Ironically, the push by biracial individuals to create new racial categories reifies the concept of race itself, which many scholars think is a bogus and unscientific concept (Montagu, 1997).

Biracial births and marriages in the United States have increased significantly within the last several decades and are likely to continue to increase in the new century. Interracial births more than doubled between 1978 and 1992, while total births increased 22 percent (Kalish, 1995). Between 1970 and 1992, the number of African American–White couples quadrupled to 246,000 (Kalish, 1995). Interracial marriages are also increasing in the United States.

The biracial and multiracial student population is increasing, creating a greater need for educators to help students realize that interracial relationships and biracial children from these unions have a long history in the United States. That history is evidenced by the relationship between Sally Hemings and Thomas Jefferson (Gordon-Reed, 1997; Murray & Duffy, 1998), the often silenced and denied Black heritages within White families (Ball, 1998), and the mixed racial heritage of many eminent African Americans. Both Booker T. Washington and Frederick Douglass had White fathers and mothers who were enslaved.

Whites and African Americans, Indians and Whites, and Indians and African Americans have produced offspring with mixed heritages since these groups first interacted in the Americas (Nash, 1982). The dominant racial and ethnic group in Mexico and throughout most of Latin America is racially mixed. The Mexicans people were created when the Spaniards colonized Mexico and produced offspring with Indian women, who are called *mestizos*. The Africans who were brought to Mexico added to its ethnic mix. Consequently, Mexican Americans are a racially mixed people. The legitimization of interracial mixtures in the United States is a rather recent phenomenon. However, interracial mixture itself is historic. This is an important distinction that teachers and students need to understand.

Existing racial categories are also challenged by how some students perceive their racial and ethnic identification. In their research in inner-city communities, Heath and McLaughlin (1993) found that many youth of color refused to identify with a particular ethnic group. Many of them said that they were simply "ethnic." Writes Heath (1995), "Contrary to general perceptions, within the daily lives of young people in many (not all) inner cities, racial or ethnic identities are always situated and multiple" (p. 48). As Nieto (1998) insightfully points out, ethnic identities are not fixed but are constantly changing, in part because of the interactions among groups within a society characterized by racial, ethnic, language, and religious diversity. Both mainstream White students and students of color are changed in these interaction processes.

The complex and changing status of ethnic groups within U.S. society, which will continue at accelerated rates in the new century, poses serious challenges to such concepts as ethnic learning styles, lists that give static characteristics of particular ethnic groups, and to the idea that educators can accurately identify the racial or ethnic group membership of individuals by their physical characteristics or behaviors. Another serious challenge to existing conceptions of particular ethnic groups is the significant number of African American and Latino students who have entered and will continue to enter the middle and upper classes. Class and ethnicity interact in complex ways that defy defining ethnic group characteristics in static and essentialized ways.

The Continuing Significance of Race

The salience of race in U.S. society problematizes the findings by Heath and McLaughlin (1993) about the youth of color in their study who refused to identify with a particular ethnic group. In a society such as the United States, in which racism is embedded within the structures of institutions, how individuals identify themselves racially might be quite at odds with how they are viewed by outside groups and responded to by institutions. Many biracial students who have an African American parent and a biracial identification are viewed and responded to by the school as African American. The fact that individuals who classify themselves as biracial but who are considered African American by the schools and other individuals and groups indicates that self-identification of race is an insufficient factor for establishing one's racial identification within a racially stratified society.

The Continuing Significance of Culture

Cultural issues are likely to continue to be important in educating students from diverse groups into the foreseeable future because culture and social class interact in complex ways and because of the large number of students of color who are socialized in low-income, predominantly minority communities. In these communities students learn cultural behaviors, communication styles, and values that are often at odds with the mainstream culture of the schools (Anyon, 1997; Wilson, 1996).

A number of researchers have described the cultures of various ethnic groups, argued that cultural conflicts exist between the schools and the cultures of ethnic minority students, and described ways in which teachers can adapt their teaching to make it culturally congruent with the cultures of diverse students. Philip's (1983) study of the participation structures used by Native American students, Au's (1980) study of participation structures used by Native Hawaiian students, Heath's (1983) study of language socialization patterns in an African American and a White community, and Lee's (1993) study of African American language usage are among the most significant of these studies. In an influential and informative study, Ladson-Billings (1994) profiles eight teachers who implement culturally congruent teaching in their classrooms.

The work on the cultural differences of students from diverse groups is important and informative. However, it must be conceptualized, viewed, and used by practitioners within the context of the complex and changing ethnic identities and cultural characteristics of students.

Expansion of Equality for Students with Disabilities

An important consequence of the civil rights movement of the 1960s and 1970s was the renewed quests by people with disabilities to secure more rights and equal educational opportunities. Prior to the civil rights movement, many students with disabilities were isolated in special schools and classes, stigmatized, viewed as the Other, and sometimes denied the opportunity to attend their local public schools. Parents of children with disabilities were encouraged by the opportunities that African Americans attained as a result of their leadership and work in the civil rights movement.

The Supreme Court's decision in the *Brown* case established the principle that segregated schooling on the basis of race was inherently unequal and denied students equal educational opportunities. Advocates for students with disabilities reasoned that if it were unconstitutional to segregate students on the basis of race, then segregating students with disabilities could also be challenged. They contested the segregation of students with disabilities within schools and classrooms and experienced a major victory in 1975, when Congress enacted Public Law 94–142, the Education for All Handicapped Children Act.

Intellectual Hierarchies

Because of the strong and historic influence of psychology on educational theory, research, and practice, the bell curve and its assumptions are entrenched within the schools. The bell curve assumes that only small percentages of the population will have high or low levels of intellectual ability. It does not focus on ways in which intellectual ability can be created and nurtured. The hierarchical notion of mental ability institutionalized within schools is reflected in practices such as academic tracking, in which students are given differential access to high-status knowledge and skills (Darling-Hammond, 1995; Oakes, 1985).

Hierarchical conceptions of intellectual ability have also led to a focus on the *individual* characteristics of students rather than on the ways in which *social systems* structure academic norms and expectations (Brookover, Beady, Flood, Schweitzer, & Wisenbaker, 1979). The ways in which intellectual ability can be created by changing norms and expectations within social systems have received insufficient attention in schools (Levine & Lezotte, 1995). The institutionalized acceptance of hierarchical beliefs about intellectual ability is manifested in programs for mentally retarded students and for gifted students.

Disability and Race

One of the most contested aspects of special education programs is the disproportionate percentage of African American and Latino students who are categorized as mildly mentally retarded and as having emotional/behavior disorders (Artiles & Trent, 1994). Special education programs designed for students with speech and language problems tend to have a disproportionate percentage of Latino students enrolled (Artiles & Trent, 1994).

The disproportionate percentage of students of color enrolled in special education programs has been legally challenged by parents and other student advocates.

Several courts have ruled in favor of the plaintiffs, including verdicts in the *Diana* v. *California State Board of Education* (1970) and *Larry P.* v. *Wilson Riles* (1986) cases. In the *Diana* case, the plaintiffs alleged that the California State Board of Education used biased tests in the procedures that assigned Mexican American and Chinese American students to special education classes. The state of California agreed to develop tests that reflect its diverse cultures. In the *Larry P.* case, the U.S. District Court for the Northern District of California prohibited the use of IQ tests for the placement of African Americans in special education programs (Mercer, 1989).

The Social Construction of Mental Retardation

In her pioneering work, Mercer (1973) conceptualizes mental retardation as a social construction and describes it from both a *clinical* and *social system* perspective. Mental retardation is viewed as a handicapping condition within the clinical perspective. It results because the attributes of individuals prevent them from functioning effectively within mainstream society. This condition within the individual "can be diagnosed by clinically trained professionals using properly standardized assessment techniques" (p. 2). Mercer states that the clinical perspective uses a pathological or medical model that classifies individuals as mentally retarded when they deviate from the mean or norm of the mainstream population.

Mercer (1973) describes how the clinical perspective is problematic within a diverse society in which many individuals are socialized within socioeconomic and ethnic cultures that differ in some substantial ways from the dominant mainstream culture. Many individuals within these microcultures have cultural characteristics that are normative within their cultural communities but are considered deviant within the mainstream society. Behaviors that are functional and sanctioned within certain ethnic and socioeconomic communities may be devalued within the mainstream society and considered deviant. *Consequently, students who are judged competent in their ethnic subsocieties may be labeled mentally retarded in the mainstream society and in the schools.* Mercer states that the core mainstream society consists primarily of cultural patterns of middle- and upper-class Anglo-Protestant Americans.

Normal behavior is determined within the social system perspective by examining how the individual functions within his or her cultural community. The point of reference is the cultural community, not the mainstream society (Mercer, 1973). Behavior is judged deviant when it varies greatly from behavior expected by the cultural or ethnic community. When the social system perspective is used to determine mental retardation, the same individuals who are considered normal in their families or neighborhoods might be considered mentally retarded in a setting such as the school. Mercer found that Mexican American youths who were considered normal in their families and communities and who functioned effectively in those settings were labeled mentally retarded in school. She writes, "Mental retardation is not a characteristic of individuals, nor a meaning inherent in behavior, but a *socially determined status,* which he [or she] may occupy in some social systems and not in others, depending on their norms" (p. 31) (emphasis added).

The Social Construction of Giftedness

The socioeconomic groups and groups of color that are overrepresented in programs and classes for mentally retarded students and for students with emotional/behavior disorders are underrepresented in classes and programs for gifted and talented students. Whites made up 71 percent of the student population in 1984, but were 81.4 percent of the students enrolled in programs for gifted and talented students (Fisher et al., 1998). Latinos and African Americans were 9.1 percent and 16.2 percent of the student population, but made up 4.7 percent and 8.4 percent respectively of students enrolled in programs for gifted and talented students.

Giftedness is a socially constructed concept because it is contextual and situational. The individuals and groups who are defined as gifted vary with the times, the state and school district guidelines and procedures, the assessment measures used to identify gifted students, and the opportunities to learn that have been available to the students being considered for gifted programs. Write Oakes and Lipton (1994), "The particular criteria are constantly changing and vary from place to place. What all programs share is their attempt to identify children they think are especially deserving of extra opportunities" (p. xi).

Political factors also influence which students become categorized as gifted. A number of school districts in large cities have lost many middle-class White students to suburban school districts and to private schools within the last two decades. Special programs, magnet schools, and gifted programs are sometimes used in these districts—which have declining enrollments and an eroding tax base—to lure White middle-class parents back to city schools. Middle-class White parents also have more political and cultural capital than most lower socioeconomic parents and parents of color. They consequently use their cultural know-how and political clout to pressure school districts to admit their children to programs for gifted and talented students. Parents compete to get their children admitted to programs for talented and gifted students because they view the benefits of these programs as a limited resource.

Programs for gifted and talented students tend to have better qualified teachers, lower teacher-pupil ratios, and more intellectually engaging teaching than classes for lower-track students (Oakes, 1985). Classes for lower-track students tend to be characterized by low-level instruction, drill exercises, and the lack of higher-level content. Most of the students in classes for gifted and talented students are White and middle class. This is true even in many racially desegregated schools. Schools that are racially desegregated are often characterized by within-school segregation because of gifted, special education, and bilingual programs and classes.

The factors that result in higher levels of enrollments of African Americans and Latinos in classes for mentally retarded students are probably the same ones that account for their low enrollment in classes for gifted and talented students. These factors include their lower scores on standardized tests that are often used to determine placement in both special education classes and classes for gifted and talented students. Other factors are their cultural and language characteristics that are inconsistent with those valued by the schools and test makers, and fewer opportunities to learn the content and skills that are measured on tests and other assessments that are used to determine placement in both special education and gifted classes.

Knowledge, Power, and the Construction of Categories

People and groups who have power exercise authority over others and influence their perceptions, beliefs, and behaviors. Shafritz (1988) states that *expert power* "is based on the perception that the leader possesses some special knowledge or expertise" (p. 427). He also states that leaders exercise *legitimate power* when followers believe that they have "the legitimate right or authority to exercise influence" (p. 427). Bourdieu (cited in Swartz, 1997) argues that power cannot be exercised unless it is legitimate.

One way in which powerful groups legitimize their power is through the construction of knowledge, which includes concepts and propositions that justify their privilege position and explain why marginalized groups deserve their low status in society. An important way in which groups exercise power in through the construction and naming of concepts. When Columbus arrived in the Caribbean, he knew that the Indians called the islands *Guanahani,* yet he renamed them in the process of making his claim of ownership (Todorov, 1987). Writes Todorov, "Columbus knows perfectly well that these islands already have names…however, he seeks to rename places in terms of the rank they occupy in his discovery, to give them the right names; moreover nomination [naming] is equivalent to taking possession" (p. 27).

In the process of establishing categories related to *race, mental retardation,* and *giftedness,* individuals and groups who have the power construct categories and characteristics that benefit the established hierarchies and the distribution of rewards and privileges within society (Sapon-Shevin, 1994; Sleeter, 1986). Writes Ford (1996), "No group has a monopoly on giftedness…. It is illogical and statistically impossible for giftedness to be the prerogative of one racial, gender, or socioeocnomic group. Nonetheless, gifted programs represent the most segregated programs in public schools; they are disproportionately White and middle class" (pp. ix–x). Sapon-Shevin (1994) describes giftedness "as a social construct, a way of thinking and describing that exists in the eyes of the definers" (p. 16).

However, just as groups with power and hegemony construct knowledge and categories that benefit established institutions, individuals and groups on the margins of society create *oppositional knowledge* that contests and challenges established knowledge, ideologies, practices, behaviors, and institutions (Banks, 1996). These groups also demand that hegemonic knowledge structures be dismantled and that more democratic forms of knowledge be created and implemented in institutions, including schools, colleges, and universities. Chapter 9 describes case studies of the lives of researchers and the ways in which their community cultures, biographical journeys, and status within the social structure influence the knowledge they construct. The chapter also describes how mainstream researchers construct concepts and paradigms that reinforce their privilege positions, and how researchers on the margins of society contest knowledge systems and canons that privilege established groups and contribute to the victimization of marginalized groups.

To create democratic and just schools, colleges, and universities, the established concepts and knowledge systems must not privilege any particular racial, ethnic, social-class, or gender group, but must reflect the experiences of the diverse groups that make up the nation-state. Consequently, the cultures of the nation's schools, as well as the curriculum, must be reformed in ways that institutionalize and legitimize the knowledge systems, perspectives, ideologies, and behaviors of diverse ethnic, racial, cultural, social-class, and language groups. This requires that more liberatory and multicultural paradigms and canons be constructed and institutionalized within the nation's educational institutions. The significant work that has been done in ethnic studies (Banks, 1997b), women's studies (Schmitz, Butler, Rosenfelt, & Guy-Sheftall, 1995), and in multicultural education (Banks & Banks, 1995) within the last two decades is an important foundation for the development and implementation of multicultural paradigms and canons within the nation's schools, colleges, and universities. Much of this work is reviewed and discussed in the *Handbook of Research on Multicultural Education* (Banks & Banks, 1995).

Reforming Schools

In the twenty-first century, schools, colleges, and universities can play an important role in helping teachers and students to uncover old conceptions of difference and in constructing and institutionalizing new conceptions of marginalized groups and of the United States. Teachers and students need to rethink, re-imagine, and reconstruct their images and representations of groups of color and of U.S. exceptionalism as it is presented in textbooks and in the popular culture (Appleby, 1992; Banks, 1996).

Students bring to the school community a set of values, commitments, ideologies, assumptions, and knowledge that influence their interactions with teachers, with other students, and with the knowledge in the school curriculum. The kinds of knowledge students bring to the classroom is becoming increasingly varied as student diversity increases within the nation's schools, colleges, and universities. Student diversity will continue to increase in the new century. Teachers should help students to critically examine their cultural and community knowledge, to understand how it relates to institutionalized knowledge systems, and to construct new paradigms and conceptions about human diversity.

Teacher education needs to be reformed in ways that will provide opportunities for teachers to critically examine their personal knowledge and values. Teachers also need to uncover and examine the knowledge and values that underlie, justify, and legitimize practices in schools, such as the classification of racial and ethnic groups, special education programs, and programs for gifted and talented students.

Teachers educators need to help teachers to construct new ways to view human groups and the human experience. Like students, teachers bring knowledge to the classroom that is situated within a set of deeply held values that result from their personal and professional experiences. However, often the values that teachers hold, and their knowledge related to those values, are unexamined. Teachers need to carefully and critically examine the value assumptions that underlie their personal knowledge, the knowledge taught in the curriculum, and the values that underlie institutionalized structures and practices in their schools.

Concepts such as *race, mental retardation,* and *giftedness* are undergirded by strong normative claims and assumptions. The concept of race assumes that human groups can be divided on the basis of their biological and physical characteristics, a highly contested claim (Omi & Winant, 1994; Montagu, 1997). The concept of mental retardation focuses on the characteristics of individuals rather than on the social systems in which they are required to function (Mehan, Hertweck, & Meihls, 1986; Mercer, 1973; Tomlinson, 1982; Varenne & McDermott, 1998). The concept of giftedness is rarely defined in a way that indicates that all individuals have gifts as well as disabilities (Sapon-Shevin, 1994).

Other concepts in the school curriculum and in teacher education that are often used without deep reflection and the uncovering of their implicit meanings carry strong value claims and assumptions. Such concepts include the *Westward movement, at-risk students*, and *busing*. The concept of the Westward movement implies that a group foreign to a land can name as well as claim it. The term also suggests that the West was a wilderness before it was settled by European *pioneers,* another value-loaded concept. The concept of at-risk students suggests that some groups of students are at-risk and that others are not; and that the at-risk students can be identified (Cuban, 1989). Missing from this concept is the idea that every student and individual, including every educator, is at-risk on some variable. The concept of busing is not used to describe the transportation of students from their homes in predominantly White neighborhoods to predominantly White schools. Rather, busing is a term that contains specific value judgments about race and racial mixing in schools.

Teacher education should help teachers to uncover the assumptions and cultural values that underlie their personal knowledge, the knowledge taught in the school curriculum, their professional knowledge, and the knowledge related to institutionalized beliefs in the schools, such as knowledge about skill grouping (Mosteller, Light, & Sachs, 1996), about the characteristics of Black English or Ebonics (Baugh, 1983), and about the effects of loss of first language on learning English as a second language (August & Hakuta, 1997).

The Road Ahead

The new century poses serious challenges, but it also offers opportunities in the continuing quest for equality and justice in education. Challenges include the widening gap between the rich and the poor, the growing isolation of low-income inner-city students within our nation's aging cities, and the conservative backlashes against affirmative action and bilingual education.

The growing percentages of racial, ethnic, and language groups within the society and the schools pose serious challenges to established institutions but are a potential source of hope and renewal for our nation. As Okihiro (1994) points out in his thoughtful and empowering book, *Margins and Mainstreams*, the groups on the margins of U.S. society have forced it to live up to its democratic ideals when they were most severely tested and challenged. A salient example was the civil rights movement of the 1960s and 1970s, which forced the United States to eradicate the institutionalized apartheid that betrayed its democratic ideals and embarrassed it throughout the world. As groups in the twenty-first century that are victimized by established concepts and practices challenge and reconstruct them—and therefore acquire more freedom and liberation—all of us will become more humanized and free because all Americans are "caught in an inescapable network of mutuality" and "tied in a single garment of destiny" (King, 1994, p. 3). We are the other; and the other is us.

REFERENCES

Alba, R. D. (1990). *Ethnic Identity: The Transformation of White America.* New Haven, CT: Yale University Press.

Anyon, J. (1997). *Ghetto Schooling: A Political Economy of Urban Educational Reform.* New York: Teachers College Press.

Appleby, J. (1992). Recovering America's Historic Diversity: Beyond Exceptionalism. *The Journal of American History, 79*(2), 413–431.

Artiles, A. J., & Trent, S. C. (1994). Overrepresentation of Minority Students in Special Education: A Continuing Debate. *The Journal of Special Education, 27* (4), 410–437.

Au, K. (1980). Participation Structures in a Reading Lesson with Hawaiian Children. *Anthropology and Education Quarterly, 11*(2), 91–115.

August, D., & Hakuta, K. (1997). *Improving Schooling for Language-Minority children: A Research Agenda.* Washington, DC: National Academy Press.

Ball, E. (1998). *Slaves in the Family.* New York: Farrar, Strauss & Giroux.

Banks, J. A. (Ed.). (1996). *Multicultural Education, Transformative Knowledge, and Action: Historical and Contemporary Perspectives.* New York: Teachers College Press.

Banks, J. A. (1997a). *Educating Citizens in a Multicultural Society.* New York: Teachers College Press.

Banks, J. A. (1997b). *Teaching Strategies for Ethnic Studies* (6th ed.). Boston: Allyn and Bacon.

Banks, J. A., & Banks, C. A. M. (Eds.). (1995). *Handbook of Research on Multicultural Education.* New York: Macmillan.

Baugh, J. (1983). *Black Street Speech: Its History, Structure, and Survival.* Austin: University of Texas Press.

Berger, P. L., & Luckmann, T. (1966). *The Social Construction of Reality: A Treatise in the Sociology of Knowledge.* New York: Anchor.

Bowen, W. G., & Bok, D. (1998). *The Shape of the River: Long-Term Consequences of Considering Race in College and University Admissions.* Princeton, NJ: Princeton University Press.

Brookover, W. B., Beady, C., Flood, P., Schweitzer, J., & Wisenbaker, J. (1979). *Schools Social Systems and Student Achievement: Schools Can Make a Difference.* New York: Praeger.

Cuban, L. (1989). The "At Risk" Label and the Problem of Urban School Reform. *Phi Delta Kappan, 70,* 780–801.

Darling-Hammond, L. (1995). Inequality and Access to Knowledge. In J. A. Banks & C. A. M. Banks (Eds.), *Handbook of Research on Multicultural Education* (pp. 465–497). New York: Macmillan.

Fisher, M. (with S. M. Perez, B. Gonzalez, J. Njus, & C. Kamasaki). (1998). *Latino Education: Status and Prospects: State of Hispanic America 1998.* Washington, DC: National Council of La Raza.

Ford, D. Y. (1996). *Reversing Underachievement among Gifted Black Students: Promising Practices and Programs.* New York: Teachers College Press.

Franklin, J. H. (1993). *The Color Line: Legacy for the Twenty-First Century.* Columbia: University of Missouri Press.

Gay, G. (1997). Educational Equality for Students of Color. In J. A. Banks & C. A. M. Banks (Eds.), *Multicultural Education: Issues and Perspectives* (3rd ed.) (pp. 195–228). Boston: Allyn and Bacon.

Gordon-Reed, A. (1997). *Thomas Jefferson and Sally Hemings: An American Controversy.* Charlottesville: University Press of Virginia.

Hannaford, I. (1996). *Race: The History of an Idea in the West.* Baltimore: The Johns Hopkins University Press.

Heath, S. B. (1983). *Ways with Words: Language, Life and Work in Communities and Classrooms.* New York: Cambridge University Press.

Heath, S. B. (1995). Race, Ethnicity, and the Defiance of Categories. In W. D. Hawley & A. W. Jackson (Eds.), *Toward a Common Destiny: Improving Race and Ethnic relations in America* (pp. 39–70). San Francisco: Jossey-Bass.

Heath, S. B., & McLaughlin, M. W. (Eds.). (1993). *Identity and Inner-City Youth: Beyond Ethnicity and Gender.* New York: Teachers College Press.

Ignatiev, N. (1995). *How the Irish Became White.* New York: Routledge.

Jacobson, M. F. (1998). *Whiteness of a Different Color: European Immigrants and the Alchemy of Race.* Cambridge, MA: Harvard University Press.

Kalish, S. (1995). Multiracial Birth Increases as U.S. Ponders Racial Definitions. *Population Today, 23*(4), 1–2.

King, M. L. (1994). *Letter from the Birmingham Jail.* New York: HarperCollins.

Ladson-Billings, G. (1994). *The Dreamkeepers: Successful Teachers of African American Children.* San Francisco: Jossey-Bass.

Lawrence, C. R. III, & Matsuda, M. J. (1997). *We Won't Go Back: Making the Case for Affirmative Action.* Boston: Houghton Mifflin.

Lee, C. E. (1993). *Signifying as a Scaffold for Literary Interpretation: The Pedagogical Implications of an African American Discourse.* Urbana, IL: National Council of Teachers of English.

Levine, D. U., & Lezotte, L. W. (1995). Effective Schools Research. In J. A. Banks &. C. A. M. Banks (Eds.), *Handbook of Research on Multicultural Education* (pp. 525–547). New York: Macmillan.

Mannheim, K. (1985). *Ideology and Utopia: An Introduction to the Sociology of Knowledge.* San Diego, CA: Harcourt Brace (original work published 1936)

Mehan, H., Hertweck, A., & Meihls, J. L. (1986). *Handicapping the Handicapped: Decision Making in Students' Educational Careers.* Stanford, CA: Stanford University Press.

Mercer, J. R. (1973). *Labeling the Mentally Retarded.* Berkeley: University of California Press.

Mercer, J. R. (1989). Alternative Paradigms for Assessment in Pluralistic Society. In J. A. Banks & C. A. M. Banks (Eds.), *Multicultural Education: Issues and Perspectives* (1st ed.) (pp. 289–304). Boston: Allyn and Bacon.

Merton, R. K. (1968). Manifest and Latent Functions. In R. K. Merton, *Social Theory and Social Structure* (enlarged ed.) (pp. 73–138). New York: The Free Press.

Montagu, A. (1997). *Man's Most Dangerous Myth: The Fallacy of Race.* Walnut Creek, CA: AltaMira Press.

Morrison, T. (1992). *Playing in the Dark: Whiteness and the Literary Imagination.* Cambridge, MA: Harvard University Press.

Mosteller, F., Light, R. J., & Sachs, J. A. (1996). Sustained Inquiry in Education: Lessons from Skill Grouping and Class Size. *Harvard Educational Review, 66,* 797–828.

Murray, B., & Duffy, B. (1998, November 9). Did the Author of the Declaration of Independence take a Slave for His Mistress? DNA Tests Say Yes. *US. News & World Report, 125*(18), 59–63.

Myrdal, G. (with the assistance of R. Sterner & A. Rose). (1944). *An American Dilemma: The Negro Problem and Modern Democracy.* New York: Harper.

Nash, G. B. (1982). *Red, White, and Black: The Peoples of Early America* (2nd ed.). Englewood Cliffs, NJ: Prentice-Hall.

Nieto, S. (1998). On Becoming American: An Exploratory Essay. In W. Ayers & J. L. Miller (Eds.), *A Light in Dark Times: Maxine Greene and the Unfinished Conversation* (pp. 45–57). New York: Teachers College Press.

Oakes, J. (1985). *Keeping Track: How Schools Structure Inequality.* New Haven, CT: Yale University Press.

Oakes, J., & Lipton, M. (1994). Foreword. In M. Sapon-Shevin, *Playing Favorites: Gifted Education and the Disruption of Community* (pp. ix–xvi). Albany: State University of New York Press.

Okihiro, G. Y. (1994). *Margins and Mainstreams: Asians in American History and Culture.* Seattle: University of Washington Press.

Omi, M., & Winant, H. (1994). *Racial Formation in the United States: From the 1960s to the 1990s* (2nd ed.). New York: Routledge.

Orfield, G., Eaton, S. E., & The Harvard Project on School Desegregation. (1996). *Dismantling Desegregation: The Quiet Reversal of Brown v. Board of Education.* New York: The New Press.

Orfield, G., & Miller, E. (1998). *Chilling Admissions: The Affirmative Action Crisis and the Search for Alternatives.* Cambridge, MA: Harvard Education Publishing Group.

Pallas, A. M., Natriello, G., & McDill, E. L. (1989). The Changing Nature of the Disadvantaged Population: Current Dimensions and Future Trends. *Educational Researcher, 18*(5), 16–22.

Philips, S. (1983). *The Invisible Culture: Communication in Classroom and Community on the Warm Springs Indian Reservation.* New York: Longman.

Phillips, K. (1990). *The Politics of Rich and Poor: Wealth and the American Electorate in the Reagan Aftermath.* New York: Random House.

Sapon-Shevin, M. (1994). *Playing Favorites: Gifted Education and the Disruption of Community.* Albany: State University of New York Press.

Schlesinger, A. M. (1991). *The Disuniting of America: Reflections on a Multicultural Society.* Knoxville, TN: Whittle Direct Books.

Schmitz, B., Butler, J. E., Rosenfelt, D., & Guy-Sheftall, B. (1995). Women's Studies and Curriculum Transformation. In J. A. Banks & C. A. M. Banks (Eds.), *Handbook of Research on Multicultural Education* (pp. 708–728). New York: Macmillan.

Shafritz, J. M. (1988). *The Dorsey Dictionary of American Government and Politics.* Chicago: The Dorsey Press.

Sleeter, C. E. (1986). Learning Disabilities: The Social Construction of a Special Education Category. *Exceptional Children, 53*(1), 46–54.

Sleeter, C. E. (1995). An Analysis of the Critiques of Multicultural Education. In J. A. Banks & C. A. M. Banks (Eds.), *Handbook of Research on Multicultural Education* (pp. 81–96). New York: Macmillan.

Steele, S. (1998). *A Dream Deferred: The Second Betrayal of Black Freedom in America.* New York: HarperCollins.

Swartz, D. (1997). *Culture and Power: The Sociology of Pierre Bourdieu.* Chicago: The University of Chicago Press.

Teachers of English to Speakers of Other Languages, Inc. (1997). *ESL Standards for Pre-K–12 Students.* Alexandria, VA: Author.

Thernstrom, S., & Thernstrom, A. (1997). *America in Black and White: One Nation, Indivisible.* New York: Simon & Schuster.

Todorov, T. (1987). *The Conquest of America: The Question of the Other.* New York: HarperCollins.

Tomlinson, S. (1982). *A Sociology of Special Education.* London: Routledge & Kegan Paul.

U.S. Bureau of the Census. (1998a). *Statistical Abstract of the United States* (118th ed.). Washington, DC: U.S. Government Printing Office.

U.S. Bureau of the Census. (1998b). Questions and Answers about Census 2000 [On-line]. Available: [http://www.census.gov/dmd/www/advisory.htm]

U.S. Bureau of the Census. (1994). *Statistical Abstract of the United States* (114th ed.). Washington, DC: U.S. Government Printing Office.

U.S. English. (1999). States with Official English Laws [On-line]. Available: [http://.us.english-org]

Varenne, H., & McDermott, R. (1998). *Successful Failure: The School America Builds.* Boulder, CO: Westview Press.

Waters, M. C. (1990). *Ethnic Options: Choosing Identities in America.* Berkeley: University of California Press.

Wilson, W. J. (1996). *When Work Disappears: The World of the New Urban Poor.* New York: Knopf.

9 The Lives and Values of Transformative Scholars and Citizenship Education

I was an elementary school student in the Arkansas delta in the 1950s. One of my most powerful memories is the image of the happy and loyal slaves in my social studies textbooks. I also remember that there were three other Blacks in my textbooks: Booker T. Washington, the educator; George Washington Carver, the scientist; and Marian Anderson, the contralto. I had several persistent questions throughout my school days: Why were the slaves pictured as happy? Were there other Blacks in history beside the two Washingtons and Anderson? Who created this image of slaves? Why? The image of the happy slaves was inconsistent with everything I knew about the African American descendants of enslaved people in my segregated community. We had to drink water from fountains labeled "colored," and we could not use the city's public library. But we were not happy about either of these legal requirements. In fact, we resisted these laws in powerful but subtle ways each day. As children, we savored the taste of "White water" when the authorities were preoccupied with more serious infractions against the racial caste system.

An Epistemological Journey

Throughout my schooling, these questions remained cogent as I tried to reconcile the representations of African Americans in textbooks with the people I knew in my family and community. I wanted to know why these images were highly divergent. My undergraduate curriculum did not help answer my questions. I read one essay by a person of color during my four years in college: "Stranger in the Village" by James Baldwin (1953/1985). In this powerful essay, Baldwin describes how he was treated as the "Other" in a Swiss village. He was hurt and disappointed—not happy—about his treatment.

When I entered graduate school at Michigan State University in 1966, I studied with professors who understood my nagging questions about the institution-

Note: I am grateful to the following colleagues for helpful comments on an earlier draft of this chapter that enabled me to strengthen it: Cherry A. McGee Banks, Carlos E. Cortés, Christine E. Sleeter, and Walter G. Stephan.

alized representations of African Americans in American culture and facilitated my quest for answers. The anthropologist Charles C. Hughes taught me about the relationship between culture and knowledge production. The sociologist James B. McKee introduced me to the sociology of knowledge. Under his tutelage, I read *Ideology and Utopia: An Introduction to the Sociology of Knowledge* by Karl Mannheim (1936/1985) and Thomas F. Kuhn's (1962/1970) *The Structure of Scientific Revolutions.* I read John Hope Franklin's (1967) *From Slavery to Freedom: A History of Negro Americans* in an independent reading with the educational psychologist Robert L. Green. There were no courses in African American history at Michigan State in the mid-1960s.

My epistemological quest to find out why the slaves were represented as happy became a lifelong journey that continues, and the closer I think I am to the answer, the more difficult and complex both my question and the answers become. This question—Why were the slaves represented as happy?—has taken different forms in various periods of my life. Most recently, it has taken the form of a series of questions: Why are African Americans described as intellectually inferior in a book, published in 1994, that became a bestseller (Herrnstein & Murray, 1994)? Why are questions still being raised about the intelligence of African Americans as we enter a new century? Whose questions are these? Whom do they benefit? Whose values and beliefs do they reflect?

I have lived with these questions all of my professional life. I will describe my most recent thinking about them. *I now believe that the biographical journeys of researchers greatly influence their values, their research questions, and the knowledge they construct.* The knowledge they construct mirrors their life experiences and their values. The happy slaves in my school textbooks were invented by the Southern historian Ulrich B. Phillips (1918/1966). The images of enslaved people he constructed reflected his belief in the inherent inferiority of African Americans and his socialization in Georgia near the turn of the century (Smith & Inscoe, 1993).

The Values of Researchers

Social scientists are human beings who have both minds and hearts. However, their minds and the products of their minds have dominated research discourse in the United States and throughout the Western world. The hearts of social scientists exercise a cogent influence on research questions, findings, concepts, generalizations, and theories. I am using *heart* as a metaphor for values, which are the beliefs, commitments, and generalized principles to which social scientists have strong attachments and commitments. The value dimensions of social science research was largely muted and silenced in the academic community and within the popular culture until the neutrality of the social sciences was severely challenged by the postmodern, women's studies, and ethnic studies movements of the 1960s and 1970s (King, 1995; Ladner, 1973; Rosenau, 1992).

Social science research has supported historically and still supports educational policies that affect the life chances and educational opportunities of students. The educational policies supported by mainstream social science and educational researchers have often harmed low-income students and students of color. Yet, as this chapter documents, the values of social scientists are complex within a diverse society such as the United States. Social science and educational research in the United States, over time and often within the same era, have both reinforced inequality and supported liberation and human betterment.

Aims of This Chapter

First, this chapter describes why it is necessary to uncover the values that underlie social science research and argues that objectivity should be an important aim of social science research even though it has a significant value dimension. Next, the text presents a typology of cross-cultural researchers. The chapter then describes the lives and work of a select group of social scientists who exemplify the categories in the typology. The discussion focuses on the lives of social scientists who created knowledge that helps to empower marginalized communities and who embraced democratic values. Focusing on researchers who did anti-egalitarian research would be just as instructive. However, I have selected individuals I admire and whose work has influenced my values, my work, and my journey as a scholar and teacher/educator. I discuss the implications of my analysis for educating citizens in a democratic society in the last part of this chapter.

The aim of the discussion and analysis is to provide evidence for these five claims:

1. The cultural communities in which individuals are socialized are also epistemological communities that have shared beliefs, perspectives, and knowledge (Nelson, 1993).
2. Social science and historical research are influenced in complex ways by the life experiences, values, and personal biographies of researchers.
3. It is not their experiences per se that cause individuals to acquire specific values and knowledge during their socialization within their ethnic or cultural communities; rather, it is their *interpretations* of their experiences.
4. How individuals interpret their cultural experiences is mediated by the interaction of a complex set of status variables, such as gender, social class, age, political affiliation, religion, and region.
5. An individual scholar's ideological commitments and knowledge claims cannot be predicted by his or her ethnic socialization because of the complex factors that influence knowledge production. Individuals socialized within cultural communities may endorse or oppose knowledge within their indigenous communities for a number of complex reasons.

Educational Research, Policy, and Practice

There are important reasons we need to uncover and to better understand the values that influence social science and educational research. Historically, in the

United States, many of the localized values and cultural perspectives of mainstream researchers were considered neutral, objective, and universal. Many of these value-laden perspectives, paradigms, and knowledge systems became institutionalized within the mainstream popular culture, the schools, and the nation's colleges and universities, in part, because they reinforced institutionalized beliefs and practices and were regarded as objective, universal, and neutral. A claim of neutrality enables a researcher to support the status quo without publicly acknowledging that support (Hubbard, cited in Burt & Code, 1995). The neutrality claim also enables the researcher to avoid what Code (1987) calls "epistemic responsibility" to the studied community.

Institutionalized concepts, theories, and paradigms considered neutral often privilege mainstream students and disadvantage low-income students, students of color, and female students. These knowledge systems and paradigms are often used to justify the educational neglect of desperate and needy students, to privilege groups who are advantaged, and to legitimize and justify discriminatory educational policies and practices.

A litany of mainstream paradigms and perspectives that harm and justify the disempowerment of low-income groups and groups of color could be cited. However, I cite only several. They include Ulrich B. Phillips's (1966) construction of the happy and contented slave in his classic and influential book published in 1918, *American Negro Slavery;* Frederick Jackson Turner's influential essay, "The Significance of the Frontier in American History," delivered in 1893 at a meeting of the American Historical Association in Chicago (1894/1989); and *Losing Ground: American Social Policy, 1950–1980* by Charles Murray (1984). Murray is the coauthor of another book in this genre, published 10 years later, *The Bell Curve* (Herrnstein & Murray, 1994). Murray's two books are part of the post-1970 political, social, and scholarly movement that sociologist Herbert J. Gans (1995) calls "the war against the poor." Although the works by Phillips and Turner were published near the turn of the century, they established research paradigms that still echo in the popular culture and in the school curriculum. Mainstream paradigms that disempower marginalized groups are characterized by historical consistency. *The Bell Curve* is one of the most recent manifestations of this historical continuity, which includes the work by Arthur R. Jensen (1969) on the intellectual abilities of African Americans and Whites.

In each case cited above, the researchers were outsiders in relation to the communities they studied. They described cultures and peoples with whom they had little insider knowledge, respect, or compassion. Phillips (1918/1966) identified with slave owners rather than with the people who were enslaved. Turner (1894/1989) perceived the West as a wilderness, although it was populated by Native American and Mexican American groups with rich cultures and languages. Murray (1984) views welfare mothers as burdens on the nation rather than as human beings who live desperate lives in a land of plenty.

In contrast to research that disempowers low-income groups and groups of color, there is also social science research that supports educational equality for marginalized communities. This research is created by researchers with life experiences and values that differ in significant ways from those of the researchers described above. This research includes the anti-racist paradigm constructed during the 1930s and 1940s by Franz Boas and the anthropologists he trained at Columbia University; the research summarized in the brief filed by a group of social scientists to support the plaintiffs in the *Brown* v. *Board of Education* Supreme Court decision of 1954 that declared de jure racial segregation in schools unconstitutional (Kluger, 1975); and the reconstruction of historical knowledge about African Americans, Asian Americans, Latinos, and women by historians such as Gerda Lerner (1973), John Hope Franklin (1989), Ramón A. Gutiérrez (1991), Ronald Takaki (1993), and Darlene Clark Hine (1994).

Values and the Quest for Objectivity

We also need to better understand and to make explicit the biographical journeys and values of researchers so that we can more closely approach the aim of objectivity in social science research. Even though values are embedded in social science and educational research, objectivity should remain an important goal in the human sciences. It is an ideal toward which we should continue to strive, although it will always remain elusive (Code, 1991). Making the values of researchers explicit will contribute to the attainment of what the philosopher Sandra Harding (1993) calls "strong objectivity."

In his insightful book *The Nature of Social Science,* George C. Homans (1967) states, "What makes a science are its aims not its results" (p. 4). Even in this postmodern age, social science and educational researchers should have as an important goal making their disciplines sciences. An important aim of a science is to strive for objectivity. Objectivity must be an aim in the human sciences because there is no other reasonable way to construct public knowledge that will be considered legitimate and valid by researchers and policymakers in diverse communities. However, we need to rethink and to reconceptualize objectivity so that it will have legitimacy for diverse groups of researchers and will incorporate their perspectives, experiences, and insights. Sociologist Patricia Hill Collins (1995) states that the most objective truths result when diverse groups participate in validating ideas. Harding (1993) argues that broad participation is needed to attain strong objectivity.

Researchers should strive for objectivity even though it is an unattainable, idealized goal. Knowledge has both subjective and objective components (Code, 1991). Traditionally, these two components of knowledge have been conceptualized as discrete and dichotomous. Objective research was defined as research in which subjective or personal components did not influence the research process and products (Hempel, 1965).

One important epistemological contribution of feminist scholarship to social science within the last two decades has been its reconceptualization of the relationship between the subjective and objective components of knowledge. Feminist scholars state that the objective/subjective dichotomy is a false one and describe ways in which these two components of knowledge are interconnected and interrelated (Code, 1991; Collins, 1990). Dewey also viewed the knower as connected to what he or she studied. He defended "objective truth" but emphasized the active role of the researcher in knowledge production and argued that knowledge construction is a process in which the subject and object interact (cited in Fox & Koppenberg, 1995). Dewey also believed that truth claims had to be revisited in different contexts and situations.

Social science and educational researchers should strive for objectivity, but they should also acknowledge how the subjective and objective components of knowledge are interconnected and interactive. Acknowledging the subjective components of knowledge does not mean that we abandon the quest for objectivity. Making the value premises of research explicit can help social scientists become more objective. Myrdal (1969) argues that if value premises—or what he calls *valuations*—remain "implicit and vague," the door is left open for biases to creep in without the researcher's knowledge (p. 55). He writes, "The only way in which we can strive for 'objectivity' in theoretical analysis is to expose the valuations to full light, make them conscious, specific, and explicit, and permit them to determine the theoretical research" (pp. 55–56). Myrdal also argues that "No social science can ever be 'neutral' or simply 'factual,' indeed not 'objective' in the traditional meaning of these terms. *Research is always and by logical necessity based on moral and political valuations, and the researcher should be obliged to account for them explicitly*" (p. 74) (emphasis added).

The Quest for Authentic Voices

A major goal of the civil rights movement of the 1960s and 1970s was to eliminate institutionalized discrimination in the nation's schools, colleges, and universities. Epistemological battles ensued when schools and colleges became populated with students from diverse racial, ethnic, and social-class groups. Students within the margins of these institutions, usually students of color and low-income students, felt that the knowledge embedded within the curriculum privileged mainstream cultures and groups and marginalized their voices and experiences (Hu-DeHart, 1995). Many scholars of color challenged traditional interpretations of their histories and cultures that had been written by mainstream scholars and researchers (Ladner, 1973). It was during this period that what Edmund W. Gordon (1997) calls an "epistemological crisis" began.

The epistemological crisis during the 1960s and 1970s was characterized by heated discussions and debates of questions such as: Who should speak for whom? Whose voice is legitimate? Who speaks with moral authority and legitimacy? Can the outsider ever understand the cultures and experiences of insiders or speak with moral authority about them? Sociologist Robert K. Merton (1972) published an important and influential article on the epistemological crisis, "Insiders and Outsiders: A Chapter in the Sociology of Knowledge." Insiders claim that only a member of their ethnic or cultural group can really understand and accurately describe the group's culture because socialization within it gives them unique insights into it. The outsider claims that outsiders can more accurately describe a culture because group loyalties prevent individuals from viewing their culture objectively.

Merton (1972) explicates and assesses the claims by both insiders and outsiders and rejects the extreme arguments of both. He writes, "*Either* the Insider *or* the Outsider has access to the sociological truth" (p. 40) (italics in original). Merton concludes that both insider and outsider perspectives are needed in the "process of truth seeking." He states, "We no longer ask whether it is the Insider or the Outsider who has monopolistic or privileged access to social truth; instead, we begin to consider their distinctive and interactive roles in the process of truth seeking" (p. 36).

Merton (1972) problematizes the relationship between knowledge construction and group affiliations. He points out that individuals have not one but multiple social statuses and group affiliations that interact to influence their behavior and perspectives. The social categories to which individuals belong include race, ethnicity, gender, age, class, region, and occupation. The social context or situation determines which social status affiliation assumes primacy. Merton (1972) describes how insiders exaggerate the uniformity of perspectives within a group because they fail to recognize

> the structural analysis which maintains that there is a *tendency for, not a full determination of*, socially patterned differences in the perspectives, preferences, and behavior of people variously located in the social structure. The theoretical emphasis on tendency, as distinct from total uniformity, is basic, not casual or niggling. It provides for a range of variability in perspectives and behavior among members of the same groups or occupants of the same status. (p. 27) (italics in original)

Race and Gender

Although many social status affiliations interact to influence the knower's perception of reality and knowledge production, Merton underestimates the power of race in cross-cultural interactions in U.S. society. In a society highly stratified by race, such as the United States, race often assumes primacy in cross-ethnic and cross-cultural interactions because of its salience and persuasiveness (Pettigrew, 1980). A *People* magazine reporter asked the tennis star Arthur Ashe, who had just announced that he had AIDS, "Mr. Ashe, I guess this must be the heaviest burden you have ever had to bear, isn't it?" Ashe replied, "It's a burden, all right. But AIDS isn't the heaviest burden I have had to bear.... Being black is the greatest burden I've had to bear" (quoted in Ashe & Rampersad, 1993, p. 139).

Race and gender also interact in complex ways to influence knowledge production. Collins (1990) discusses ways in which gender interacts with race to provide African American women with a unique standpoint, which she calls the "outsider-within" perspective. Collins (1995) argues that African American women "as a group, experience a different world than those who are not black and female. Second, these experiences simulate a distinctive black feminist consciousness concerning that material reality" (p. 33). She states that marginalized groups not only experience a different reality but also interpret that reality differently. This important question, however, is not resolved by Collins's important analysis: Under what conditions do individual African American women fail to incorporate a Black feminist standpoint? In other words, how do we explain the standpoint of the highly politically conservative Black woman?

A Typology of Cross-Cultural Researchers

Merton's *insider-outsider* and Collins's *outsider-within* conceptualizations help to clarify and add needed complexity to the ideological debates and discussions about whose knowledge is authentic, who can know what, and who speaks for whom. Another important dimension of these questions is the relationship between knowledge and power. For example: What factors determine the knowledge systems and canons that become institutionalized or marginalized in mainstream institutions?

Although the Merton and Collins conceptualizations are important and helpful, additional concepts and finer distinctions are needed to better describe the epistemological complexity related to knowledge construction, race, ethnicity, and culture. Building on the work of Merton and Collins, I describe a *typology of cross-cultural researchers* that further problematizes the types of knowers within a pluralistic democratic society. Like the conceptualizations by Merton and Collins, this typology is a Weberian ideal-type conceptualization that approximates reality but does not describe it in its total complexity. An ideal-type typology "is not designed to correspond exactly to any single empirical observation," but to facilitate descriptions, comparisons, and hypothesis testing (Theodorson & Theodorson, 1969, p. 193).

This typology is based on the assumption that in a diverse pluralistic society such as the United States, individuals are socialized within ethnic, racial, and cultural communities in which they internalize localized values, perspectives, ways of knowing, behaviors, beliefs, and knowledge that can differ in significant ways from those of individuals socialized within other microcultures. Individuals endorse the institutionalized beliefs and knowledge within their microcultures at greatly varying levels. A number of other status characteristics of individuals, such as age, social class, gender, and occupation, influence the extent to which people manifest the beliefs and knowledge of their cultural communities. However, individuals within a particular ethnic or cultural community are more likely to exemplify the institutionalized beliefs and knowledge of that community than are individuals outside it.

Depending on the situations and contexts, we are all both insiders and outsiders (Merton, 1972). Also, a researcher's insider-outsider status may change over the course of a lifetime, either because the institutionalized knowledge and paradigms within the studied community change or because the researcher's value commitments are significantly modified. This typology is not necessarily a general description of a researcher over the course of his or her career. In *The Vulnerable Observer: Anthropology That Breaks Your Heart,* Ruth Behar (1996) describes how she was a somewhat dispassionate outsider when she observed the death of farmers in a Spanish village but became an emotionally involved insider when she observed her own grandfather's death in Miami Beach.

Although this chapter focuses on insiders and outsiders as they relate to race and ethnicity, this typology can also be applied to other status groups such as gender, social class, and religion. Men studying women, middle-class researchers studying low-income students, and Protestant researchers studying Muslims are outsiders.

The *typology of cross-cultural researchers* has four types of knowers or researchers: the *indigenous-insider,* the *indigenous-outsider,* the *external-insider,* and the *external-outsider* (see Table 9.1).

The *indigenous-insider* endorses the unique values, perspectives, behaviors, beliefs, and knowledge of his or her primordial community and culture. He or she is also perceived by significant others and opinion leaders within the community as a legitimate member of the community who has a perspective and the knowl-

TABLE 9.1 A Typology of Cross-Cultural Researchers

Type of Researcher	Description
The Indigenous-Insider	This researcher endorses the unique values, perspectives, behaviors, beliefs, and knowledge of his or her indigenous community and culture and is perceived by people within the community as a legitimate community member who can speak with authority about it.
The Indigenous-Outsider	This researcher was socialized within his or her indigenous community but has experienced high levels of cultural assimilation into an outside or oppositional culture. The values, beliefs, perspectives, and knowledge of this individual are identical to those of the outside community. The indigenous-outsider is perceived by indigenous people in the community as an outsider.
The External-Insider	This researcher was socialized within another culture and acquires its beliefs, values, behaviors, attitudes, and knowledge. However, because of his or her unique experiences, the individual questions many of the values, beliefs, and knowledge claims within his or her indigenous community and endorses those of the studied community. The external-insider is viewed by the new community as an "adopted" insider.
The External-Outsider	The external-outsider is socialized within a community different from the one in which he or she is doing research. The external-outsider has a partial understanding of and little appreciation for the values, perspectives, and knowledge of the community he or she is studying and consequently often misunderstands and misinterprets the behaviors within the studied community.

edge that will promote the well-being of the community, enhance its power, and enable it to maintain cultural integrity and survive.

The *indigenous-outsider* was socialized within the cultural community but has experienced high levels of desocialization and cultural assimilation into an outside or oppositional culture or community. The values, beliefs, perspectives, and knowledge of this individual are indistinguishable from those of an outside culture or community. This individual is not only regarded as an outsider by indigenous members of the cultural community but is also viewed with contempt because he or she is considered to have betrayed the indigenous community and "sold out" to the outside community. The indigenous-outsider is often chosen by leaders of the mainstream community as their spokesperson for public and visible issues related to his or her ethnic group, is often highly praised and rewarded by the mainstream community, and is viewed as legitimate by the mainstream but not by the indigenous community.

The *external-insider* was socialized within another culture and acquires its beliefs, values, behaviors, attitudes, and knowledge. However, because of unique experiences, such as personal experiences within an outside culture or community or marginalization within the culture into which he or she was socialized, the individual questions many of the values, beliefs, and knowledge claims within the community in which he or she was socialized. The external-insider may also become publicly oppositional to many of the cultural assumptions and beliefs of his or her cultural community. This individual internalizes and acts on the institutionalized beliefs and knowledge claims of his or her second or adopted community. The external-insider individual is viewed by the new community as an adopted member and is often negatively perceived and sanctioned by his or her first community.

The *external-outsider* was socialized within a community different from the one in which he or she is doing research. He or she has a partial understanding of and little appreciation for the values, perspectives, and knowledge of the community he or she is studying. Because of a lack of understanding of and empathy for the culture or community that is being studied, the external-outsider often misunderstands and misinterprets the behaviors within the community, distorts when comparing them with outsider behaviors and values, and describes the studied community as pathological or deviant. The external-outsider views the studied community as the Other. The external-outsider believes that he or she is the best and most legitimate researcher to study the subject community because he or she has a more objective view of the community than researchers who live within it. The external-outsider is criticized by members of the studied community but is often praised and highly rewarded by the outside community, which is often more powerful and influential than the studied community.

The external-outsider may violate the integrity of the communities he or she studies. His or her work may contribute to the disempowerment and oppression of these communities, and policymakers may use it to justify the marginalized positions of the indigenous people in the studied community. The external-outsider's research and the policy derived from it often raise serious ethical problems about the responsibility of researchers to the communities they study.

Case Studies of the Lives of Researchers

The case studies that follow examine the lives and values of a select group of researchers who have done race relations research that has important implications for education. I describe critical incidents in their biographical journeys that are related to their values, to race relations research, and to educational policy. The lives of these individuals exemplify and support the observations and conceptual distinctions made in the theoretical discussion and in the typology described above.

African American culture is used as the basis for classifying the scholars and researchers. I first describe the lives and works of the psychologist Kenneth B. Clark and historian John Hope Franklin, individuals who may be considered indigenous-insiders within the African American community for most of their careers. I then discuss the lives and works of a group of social scientists who were external to the African American community but who did work that was empowering and liberating for African Americans. These researchers were, to varying extents, external-insiders in reference to the African American community. They are Franz Boas and two of his students, Ruth Benedict and Otto Kleinberg, and social psychologist Thomas F. Pettigrew, who did pioneering research on race relations and school desegregation.

Kenneth B. Clark and Research on Race

The research, scholarship, and actions of psychologist Kenneth B. Clark (b. 1914) illustrate the ways in which personal experiences, perspectives, and values influence scholarship and how scholarship influences action. Clark's work also epitomizes the role of the socially responsible scholar in a democratic, pluralistic society. Throughout his career, Clark consistently opposed institutionalized structures that promoted racism and inequality and constructed scholarship that challenged existing knowledge systems and paradigms (see Photo 9.1).

The values and perspectives that underlie Clark's scholarship, research, and action were developed early in his life. His mother taught him, by her examples, to strongly oppose racial discrimination. She and her two children emigrated from the Panama Canal Zone to New York City when Clark was five years old. She took a job as a seamstress in a sweatshop, helped organize a union in the shop, and became a steward for the International Ladies Garment Workers Union (Moritz, 1964).

Clark's early experiences with racial discrimination and his mother's decisive action against it strongly influenced his perception of race in the United States; the research questions, issues, and people he studied; and his commitment to act both as a scholar and a citizen to help create a more just society. Clark and his mother were refused service at Childs Restaurant when he was six years old. His mother reacted with "verbal hostility" and "threw a dish on the floor" (Clark, 1993, p. 3). When he was in the ninth grade, Clark again witnessed his mother's strong reaction to discrimination when his White guidance counselor told him that he should attend a vocational high school. Writes Clark, "I again saw the anger on my mother's face that I had seen at Childs Restaurant. She said, 'You will not go to a vocational high school. You are going to an academic high school'" (p. 5).

Photo 9.1 Mamie Phipps Clark and Kenneth B. Clark (Library of Congress, Washington, D.C.)

The lessons that Clark's mother taught him were reinforced by his personal experiences and by his professors at Howard University, the historically Black university where he earned his bachelor's and master's degrees. Clark's professors at Howard included philosopher Alain Locke and political scientist Ralph Bunche. When Clark was a senior at Howard, he and a group of students demonstrated inside the U.S. Capitol because African Americans were not served in the Capitol's restaurant. When the president of Howard and the disciplinary committee wanted to suspend or expel the students for "threatening the security of the university" (Clark, 1993, p. 8), Ralph Bunche strongly defended the students and threatened to resign if the students were disciplined.

Bunche and the students won the day; the students were not punished. This incident taught Clark important lessons about contradictions in U.S. society. He writes:

> Howard University was the beginning of the persistent preoccupation I have had with American racial injustice.... At this stage in my personal development, I became engrossed in the contradictions which exist: the eloquence of American

"democracy" and academic hypocrisy. These members of the Howard faculty I respected all became my mentors against American racism. *My life became dominated by an ongoing struggle against racial injustice....* These outstanding professors made it very clear to me that under no circumstances should I ever accept racial injustice. (Clark, 1993, p. 7) (emphasis added)

Clark's research on racial attitudes and their effects on the personality development of African American children, for which he became widely known, was an extension of work originally done by Mamie Phipps Clark for her master's thesis at Howard University. The Clarks, who met at Howard, were married in 1938. From 1939 to the 1950s, they conducted a series of important and influential studies on the racial awareness, preference, and racial self-identification of African American children (Clark & Clark, 1939, 1940, 1947, 1950).

John Hope Franklin's Experiences with Race

Historian John Hope Franklin (b. 1915), a specialist in Southern history, grew up in the South at a time when it was highly segregated by race. Franklin's view of history, of the United States, and of the efforts it will take to create a just society in the United States have been strongly influenced by his early socialization in his native Oklahoma. "Two factors," writes Franklin, "plagued my world of learning for all my developing years. One was race, the other was financial distress; and each had a profound influence on every stage of my development" (1991, p. 352) (see Photo 9.2).

Franklin was born in Rentiesville, Oklahoma, the all-Black town to which his parents moved after his father, a lawyer, was expelled from court by a White judge because he was Black. Franklin's parents strongly believed that they should not accept any form of racial segregation. They moved to an all-Black town to escape racial discrimination. The move made a lasting impression on their son, the future historian. The family later moved to Tulsa to seek better work, educational, and recreational opportunities. While living in Tulsa, Franklin's parents refused to attend any events that were racially segregated, including the concerts at Convention Hall that greatly appealed to their son. However, they allowed their son to attend the concerts.

As a college student at Fisk University in Nashville (a historically Black university), Franklin had a number of powerful and memorable personal experiences with racial discrimination that left their marks. When he bought a streetcar ticket with the only money he had—a $20 bill—the clerk screamed racial epithets and gave him $19.75 change in dimes and quarters. The 16-year-old Franklin was shocked and stunned by the incident. Three years later, a young Black man, Cordie Cheek, was taken by a gang of Whites from a Fisk-owned house and lynched on the edge of campus.

Franklin did not acquire a monolithic view of Whites during his coming of age in the South. Approximately half of the Fisk faculty was White. Franklin admired and respected most of his Fisk professors. He changed his lifelong ambition to follow his father's footsteps and become a lawyer because of the exciting lec-

Photo 9.2 John Hope Franklin (Jennifer Warburg, Durham, NC)

tures given by his White history professor, Theodore S. Currier. Currier became Franklin's mentor when he decided to become a historian. He borrowed $500 and gave it to Franklin so that he could attend Harvard University.

Franklin and the Reconstruction of American History. Franklin's important work to reconstruct and reinterpret American history with African Americans in visible and significant roles draws on and extends the research of African American historians who were his predecessors, such as Carter G. Woodson, Charles H. Wesley, W. E. B. Du Bois, and Luther B. Jackson. Franklin published the first edition of *From Slavery to Freedom: A History of Negro Americans* in 1947. This influential book is now in its seventh edition (Franklin & Moss, 1994). When the first edition of the book was published, African Americans were largely invisible in most mainstream school and college textbooks. When they did appear, they were often stereotyped as happy slaves who were loyal to their masters. Ulrich B. Phillips's (1966) view of slavery dominated textbooks as well as mainstream intellectual discourse about slavery. Although Franklin's textbook received a warm reception in predominantly Black colleges and universities when it was first published, not until the civil rights movement of the 1960s and 1970s did his work begin to significantly permeate mainstream textbooks and scholarship. Prior to the 1960s, scholars such as Woodson, Du Bois, and Franklin worked primarily in the margins of their disciplines to construct the history of African Americans and to reconstruct mainstream American history.

Franklin has written a score of scholarly books, monographs, and articles that reinterpret Southern history and the role of African Americans in the development of the United States. In some of his most insightful writings, Franklin (1989) describes how the Founding Fathers and the Constitution played a significant role in racializing the United States.

Throughout his long and impressive career, Franklin has been viewed by most members of the African American community as an indigenous-insider. He is also highly respected by the mainstream scholarly and public communities. He is a former president of each of the major national historical professional associations. He was appointed by President Bill Clinton to chair the Advisory Board for the President's Initiative on Race and Reconciliation in 1997.

The Antiracism Project of Anthropologists

The rise and spread of Nazism in Europe and racial conflicts and riots in the United States stimulated a rich period of race relations research and writings during World War II and the postwar period. A number of the books published during this period became classics, including *An America Dilemma: The Negro Problem and Modern Democracy* by Gunnar Myrdal (1944), the Swedish economist; *Man's Most Dangerous Myth: The Fallacy of Race* by Ashley Montagu (1942); *The Authoritarian Personality* by Theodore W. Adorno et al. (Adorno, Frenkel-Brunswik, Levinson, Sanford, & Nevitt, 1950); and *The Nature of Prejudice* by Gordon Allport (1954). Much of the work published during the 1940s and 1950s was born out of the hope of stemming the tide of Nazism and anti-Semitism.

Franz Boas (1858–1942) (see Photo 9.3) of Columbia University and the anthropologists he trained initiated a major project to discredit scientific racism, which was widespread and institutionalized when Boas arrived in the United States in 1887 (Stocking, 1974). Boas immigrated to the United States from Germany because of the limited opportunities for Jewish scholars in his homeland (Barkan, 1992). The antiracist work done by Boas and his former students was very important in countering racist scholarship and knowledge. Boas and other anthropologists became involved in an anti-racist project for a number of reasons. Some of Boas's Jewish students, such as Otto Klineberg and Melville Herskovits, realized that a racist ideology not only victimized African Americans but other groups as well, including Jewish Americans.

The antiracism project initiated by Boas and his colleagues benefited African Americans as well as other racial, ethnic, and cultural groups. Much of their research and writing opposed and deconstructed racist ideologies that argued that

Photo 9.3 Franz Boas (American Philosophical Society, Philadelphia, PA)

African Americans were genetically inferior to Whites (Klineberg, 1935). The work of Boas and his anthropology colleagues indicates that outsiders may identify with and promote equality for a studied community in part because they view the interests of the studied community and their own personal and community interests as interconnected. By opposing racist theories directed against African Americans, Boas and Klineberg were pursuing the interests of their own cultural communities while promoting the public good.

Otto Klineberg (1899–1992), a former Boas student who did significant and influential work that challenges and undercuts scientific racism, was of Canadian Jewish descent. He believed that his professional training with Boas and a chance visit to an American Indian community were the major factors that motivated his work on racial and ethnic issues. He minimized the role that his personal ethnic experiences played in his desire to study race and to oppose scientific racism.

While visiting an Indian community in Washington state, Klineberg (1973) conducted a study and found that the Indian students took longer to complete an intelligence test but made fewer errors than did the White students. He concluded that the conception and use of time in Indian and White cultures, rather than differences in intelligence, explained variations in performance on the test. He felt that the results of this study "entirely vindicated" Boas's views on the influence of culture and learning on intelligence test performance (Klineberg, 1973, p. 41).

Boas's experience with anti-Semitism and Klineberg's work with Boas and research experience in an American Indian community are important factors that help to explain their race-related work and the values exemplified in their research. Other researchers who become involved in race relations research and who become antiracists are mainstream Americans who pursue research and exemplify values that are often oppositional to those institutionalized within their cultural communities. In his study of scholars who specialized in race relations research during the 1950s and 1960s, Stanfield (1993) found that White men of Southern and/or Jewish origin were among the most prominent of these scholars. Ruth Benedict and Thomas F. Pettigrew are two mainstream scholars who did influential race relations work.

Ruth Benedict and Antiracism Work

Ruth Benedict (1887–1948) (see Photo 9.4) was a former Boas student who later became his colleague at Columbia University. The focus of her work was the study of culture, not race. She became involved in race relations work reluctantly, in part because she realized she was not an expert in the field. In 1940, she published *Race: Science and Politics.* In popular language, Benedict described both the scientific facts and the myths about race. She (1940/1947) wrote, "Racism is an ism to which everyone in the world is exposed; for or against, we must take sides. And the history of the future will differ according to the decision which we make" (p. 5). In 1943, Benedict published (with Gene Weltfish) the *Races of Mankind* for a popular audience (1940/1947). Both *Race: Science and Politics* and *The Races of Mankind* were widely disseminated and influential. Benedict and a high school teacher in 1941 wrote a teaching unit, *Race and Cultural Relations: America's Answer to the Myth of the Master Race.*

Benedict became involved in Boas's antiracism project for several reasons. First, antiracism work was an extension of her earlier research on the characteristics of culture. A key assumption of Benedict's (1934) cultural project was the need for people to view outside cultures as similar to their own. Benedict's family experiences are another factor that compelled her interest and participation in the antiracist project. These experiences caused her to be interested in other cultures, to reach beyond her own cultural world, and to study cultural and racial differences.

According to her biographers, Benedict felt alienated and marginalized within the Anglo-American culture into which she was socialized (Caffrey, 1989; Mead, 1974; Modell, 1984). Writes Mead (1974), "She often spoke of how she had come to feel, very early, that there was little in common between the beliefs of her family and neighbors and her own passionate wondering about life, which she learned to keep to herself" (p. 6). Fleming (1971) also describes Benedict's alienation and sense of marginalization within her family and community culture. He writes, "She had been estranged from what she took to be the inevitable nature of

*Photo 9.4 Ruth Benedict (Special Collections, Vassar College Librar-
ies, Poughkeepsie, New York)*

life; she now asked if she might have been more at home in another time and culture, say in ancient Egypt" (p. 130).

Benedict also became involved in Boas's antiracism project because of her
high personal regard for him. She greatly admired and respected her influential
mentor, friend, and colleague. Becoming involved in his race relations project was
an expression of loyalty to Boas, which he appreciated and expected from his
former students.

Thomas F. Pettigrew and School
Desegregation Research

Thomas F. Pettigrew (b. 1931), of Scottish-American descent, grew up in Richmond,
Virginia, in the 1930s and 1940s. He witnessed racial discrimination and often

challenged it when he was a youth. Pettigrew (1993) attributes the development of his progressive racial attitudes and his interest in race relations research to his family and to Mildred Adams, his family's African American housekeeper (see Photo 9.5).

Pettigrew was expelled from school several times for calling his seventh-grade teacher a bigot because she praised Hitler's anti-Semitism and used derogatory names when referring to African Americans. His mother and grandmother went to the principal's office and defended his actions each time he was expelled. Pettigrew (1993) was deeply influenced by the harsh racial discrimination that Mildred Adams had experienced, which she shared with him. He writes:

> Once a "white" movie theater refused us admission, although she had taken care to dress in an all-white uniform. By the time I was 10 years old, the many psychological defenses that blind most white Americans to the racial injustice that surrounds them were no longer available to me. (p. 160)

Photo 9.5 Thomas F. Pettigrew (Courtesy of Thomas F. Pettigrew)

Other factors influenced Pettigrew's decision to become a social psychologist and specialize in race-relations research. These included a social psychology class he took at the University of Virginia, his professor's suggestion that he do graduate work at Harvard and study with Gordon Allport, and Allport's (1954) work in race relations. Allport (1954) was writing *The Nature of Prejudice*, which became a classic, when Pettigrew was doing graduate work with him.

Pettigrew has made major contributions to race relations research. He has summarized research on the intellectual abilities of African Americans that refutes theories of Black inferiority (Pettigrew, 1964), and he has been a major researcher and activist scholar supporting school desegregation. Pettigrew was the chief investigator of the massive study of race and education sponsored by the U.S. Commission on Civil Rights in response to a request made by President Lyndon B. Johnson in 1965. The report, *Racial Isolation in the Public Schools* (U.S. Commission on Civil Rights, 1967), concluded that racial isolation in the public schools was extensive and that it harmed the nation's students.

Intellectual Leadership and Action

The researchers discussed in this chapter were transformative scholars and intellectual leaders (Banks, 1993, 1995); they were researchers who also had value aims, which they pursued through action to influence public and educational policies (Burns, 1978). Klineberg, Clark, and Franklin supported, in various ways, the plaintiffs in the *Brown* v. *Board of Education* Supreme Court case. Pettigrew was an outspoken advocate of school desegregation during the 1960s and 1970s. He challenged Coleman's "White flight" thesis, which stated that large school districts risked losing White students and parents when desegregation took place under certain conditions (Pettigrew & Green, 1976). Benedict was a minor participant in the intergroup education movement (Caffrey, 1989).

Scholars who become intellectual leaders have many opportunities to make a difference in their communities and in the nation. However, they also experience conflicts, dilemmas, and problems. Scholars, especially those who work within marginalized communities and who promote policies and practices that conflict with those institutionalized within the mainstream academic community, take a number of academic risks when they become intellectual leaders. They are open to charges by mainstream researchers that they are political, partisan, and subjective. Mainstream scholars who promote policies consistent with those institutionalized within the mainstream academic community are less subject to these risks; their normative-oriented work is more likely to be viewed as objective and neutral.

Intellectual leaders within marginalized communities are keenly aware of these risks. Historically, most African American scholars have considered themselves objective scholars. They believed that objective scholarship would help to correct the distorted representations of African Americans in mainstream scholarship. Many African American scholars became involved in civil rights work and activities. However, they viewed their roles as *scholar* and as *citizen* as separate.

Historian Carter G. Woodson considered himself an objective historian and did not become involved in any direct civil rights activities. Woodson's actions were limited primarily to professional tasks such as promoting Negro history week (now African American history month) and to soliciting funds for the Association for the Study of Negro Life and History.

John Hope Franklin considers himself an objective historian. Although he has promoted civil rights, he considers his action as part of his role as a citizen, not as a historian. Franklin helped prepare the brief for the *Brown v. Board of Education* Supreme Court case. He participated in the Selma, Alabama, civil rights march in 1965 to protest legalized segregation. Franklin presented a statement to the judiciary committee opposing the nomination of Robert H. Bork for the Supreme Court.

Kenneth B. Clark views his action as an essential extension of his scholarship. Throughout his career, Clark (1963) has consistently used his research and scholarship to influence public policy and to guide action to improve race relations. In his books and articles, he describes the ways in which racial prejudice and discrimination damage both White and African American children. Much of Clark's scholarship and activism have focused on efforts to desegregate the nation's schools. He played an important role in the 1954 *Brown* decision. Clark coordinated the expert witnesses for the case and submitted to the Supreme Court, with a group of other social scientists, the *Social Science Index to the Legal Brief.* This research is cited in footnote 11 of the *Brown* decision. In 1946, Kenneth and Mamie Clark established the Northside Center for Child Development to improve the life chances and possibilities for Harlem youth (Markowitz & Rosner, 1996). He organized Harlem Youth Opportunities Unlimited (HARYOU) in 1962 to reduce the number of school dropouts, juvenile delinquents, and unemployed youth in Harlem.

Social Action for Scholars: Benefits and Risks

Transformative scholars who become involved in action are not only subject to criticism from their academic colleagues; they are also subject to the vagaries, whims, and contradictions of political struggle in the real world. When the HARYOU project was joined with Associated Community Teams (ACT) in 1964, Clark became involved in a bitter controversy over control of the project with Congressman Adam Clayton Powell that resulted in Clark resigning from the HARYOU-ACT board.

Although Clark had spent most of his career actively working for school desegregation, he was harshly criticized by many African American nationalists during the late 1960s and 1970s, when the utopian hopes for desegregation were fading and cries for Black power echoed throughout the nation. Clark's beliefs about the possibilities of desegregation hardened as some scholars began to criticize his position. Clark's biography documents how a scholar who had been viewed as an indigenous-insider began to be perceived by many people within his community as an indigenous-outsider when the beliefs and ideologies of many vocal members of the African American community began to change. Clark remained consistent in his beliefs, but the beliefs and ideologies of many leaders and scholars in his community changed.

Social scientists increase their possibilities for direct influence when they become involved in social and community action. However, they also increase their possibilities for risks and disappointments. Clark's biography exemplifies the high risks taken when scholars become involved in social and political action. As Clark was witnessing the nation's retreat from desegregation, affirmative action, and other equity issues late in his life, he expressed a sense of despair. This is ironic because Clark had strongly influenced the lives of many scholars—including mine—and had been a highly influential intellectual and policy activist for several decades. At age 76, he described his disappointment with his career (Clark, 1993):

> Reluctantly, I am forced to face the likely possibility that the United States will never rid itself of racism and reach true integration. I look back and I shudder at how naïve we all were in our belief in the steady progress racial minorities would make through programs of litigation and education, and while I very much hope for the emergence of a revived civil rights movement with innovative programs and dedicated leaders, I am forced to recognize that my life has, in fact, been a series of glorious defeats. (p. 19)

The risks of social action became painfully evident to Franklin after the Bork Supreme Court hearings. Franklin, who testified against Bork, was deeply disappointed when President Ronald Reagan said that the people who opposed Bork's nomination were a "lynch mob" (quoted in Franklin, 1991, p. 364). Writes Franklin: "One must be prepared for any eventuality when he makes any effort to promote legislation or to shape the direction of public policy or to affect the choice of those in public service" (pp. 363–364).

Implications for Citizenship Education in a Multicultural Society

Implications for Students and Teachers

A significant challenge facing educators in the twenty-first century is how to respect and acknowledge the community cultures and knowledge of students while helping to construct a democratic public community with an overarching set of values to which all students will have a commitment and with which all will identify (Banks, 1997). In other words, our challenge is to create an education that will help foster a just and inclusive pluralistic national society that all students and groups will perceive as legitimate. This is a tremendous challenge but an essential task in a pluralistic democratic society. An important aim of the school curriculum should be to educate students so that they will have the knowledge, attitudes, and skills needed to help construct and to live in a public community in which all groups can and will participate.

Teachers should help students to examine and uncover the community and culture knowledge they bring to school and to understand how it is similar to and different from school knowledge and the cultural knowledge of other students. Students should also be helped to understand the ways in which their values undergird their personal and community knowledge and how they view and interpret school knowledge.

Teachers, like students, also bring to the classroom personal and cultural knowledge that is situated within a set of deeply held values that result from their personal and professional experiences. However, the values that teachers hold, and their knowledge related to those values, are often unexamined. Teachers need to critically examine the value assumptions that underlie their personal knowledge, the knowledge taught in the curriculum, and the values that support the institutionalized structures and practices in the schools. Because of the increasing social-class, racial, ethnic, and gender gap between teachers and students, teachers can also be classified using the typology described in this chapter. Teachers are also indigenous-insiders, indigenous-outsiders, external-insiders, and external-outsiders. An important goal of teacher education should be to identify teacher education candidates who are able to acquire the knowledge, skills, and perspectives needed to become insiders within the communities in which they teach.

To educate citizens for the twenty-first century, it is also important to revise the school curriculum in substantial ways so that it reflects the nation's new, emerging national identity and describes the process of becoming an American. Students from diverse groups will be able to identify with a curriculum that fosters an overarching American identity only to the extent that it mirrors their perspectives, struggles, hopes, and possibilities. A curriculum that incorporates only the knowledge, values, experiences, and perspectives of mainstream powerful groups marginalizes the experiences of students of color and low-income students. Such a curriculum will not foster an overarching American identity because students will view it as one that has been created and constructed by outsiders, people who do not know or understand their experiences. Educators should try to create a curriculum that all students will perceive as being in the broad public interest.

Implications for Researchers

Researchers can play a significant role in educating students for citizenship in a diverse society. Their most important responsibility is to conduct research that empowers marginalized communities, that describes the complex characteristics of ethnic communities, and that incorporates the views, concepts, and visions of the communities they study. Each social science and educational researcher is, depending on the context and situation, likely to function at some point as an indigenous-insider, an indigenous-outsider, an external-insider, and an external-outsider. This typology describes individual researchers within particular contexts, times, and situations.

As noted earlier in this chapter, Kenneth B. Clark's status as indigenous-insider was seriously challenged when he continued to conduct research on racial desegregation and to advocate school desegregation when many African American intellectuals and leaders began to endorse Black nationalism and to search for alternatives to school desegregation. Researchers should not avoid studying a community because they are external to it or because they are criticized for the way in which the community has been studied by previous external researchers. Wilson (1996), for example, points out that many social science researchers abandoned research on poverty after Moynihan (1965) and other mainstream researchers were harshly criticized for their research on low-income communities and communities of color in the 1960s and 1970s.

Outsider researchers should continue to study marginalized communities but should change some of the ways in which they are now studied. External researchers need to be keenly sensitive to their own research status within the studied community and to work with people indigenous to the community who can provide them with an accurate knowledge of the perspectives, values, and beliefs within the community and who can help them to acquire insider status. One way to do this is to involve indigenous community members in the study as researchers. Myrdal (1944), the Swedish economist, involved a number of African American researchers in his study, *An American Dilemma*, published in 1944. Myrdal did not escape criticism; he was criticized by mainstream policymakers because they considered his findings too challenging to the status quo. Some African American scholars criticized him because of his interpretations of African American culture—which he minimized—and because of what they considered their marginalized role in the study (Southern, 1987).

Despite the criticisms of his work, Myrdal created a classic study of U.S. race relations. The reception of Myrdal's study indicates another consequence of conducting research cross-culturally: Cross-cultural researchers will be criticized no matter how culturally sensitive they are or how well they do their jobs. Such criticism is an essential part of the discourse within an academic community. It is one consequence of researchers doing their work, especially in cross-cultural settings.

Researchers indigenous to a marginalized community also face important challenges. When they become professionally trained at research universities, they are likely to experience at least two important risks: They may become distanced from their communities during their professional training and thus become indigenous-outsiders, or they may be perceived by many members of their indigenous communities as having sold out to the mainstream community and thus can no longer speak for the community or have an authentic voice. In an informative article called "The Colonizer/Colonized Chicano Ethnographer," Sofia Villenas (1996) describes her struggle to remain an insider within a Latino community she was studying. She was identified and treated by the mainstream community as an insider, one of them. The Anglo community viewed the Latino community she was studying as the Other. She found maintaining legitimacy in both worlds difficult and frustrating.

The Need for Committed and Caring Researchers

As Jonothan Kozol (1991) points out, there are many "savage inequalities" within U.S. society and within the schools. We are living in a time that Stephen Jay Gould

(1994) calls "a historical moment of unprecedented ungenerosity, when a mood for slashing social programs can be powerfully abetted by an argument that beneficiaries cannot be helped, owing to inborn cognitive limits expressed as low IQ scores" (p. 139). Social science and educational researchers cannot be neutral in these troubled homes. As Martin Luther King (1994) stated in his *Letter From the Birmingham Jail,* "Injustice anywhere is a threat to justice everywhere" (pp. 2–3).

Because education is a moral endeavor, educational researchers should be scientists as well as citizens who are committed to promoting democratic ideals. In other words, they should be intellectuals. Political scientist James McGregor Burns (1978) defines intellectuals as researchers who pursue normative ends. He writes, "The person who deals with analytical ideas and data alone is a theorist; the one who works only with normative ideas is a moralist; the person who deals with both and unites them through disciplined imagination is an intellectual" (p. 141). Intellectuals should be knowledgeable about the values that are exemplified in their research and be committed to supporting educational policies that foster democracy and educational equality. Kenneth B. Clark (1974) argues that the intellectual must seek the truth, but that this quest must be guided by values. Clark believes that "The quest for truth and justice [is] meaningless without some guiding framework of accepted and acceptable values. These terms—*truth* and *justice*—have no meaning independent of a value system" (p. 21). Clark (1965) incorporates a value commitment into his beliefs as a social scientist:

> An important part of my creed as a social scientist is that on the grounds of absolute objectivity or on a posture of scientific detachment and indifference, a truly relevant and serious social science cannot be taken seriously by a society desperately in need of moral and empirical guidance in human affairs. (p. xxi)

Social scientists cannot be "neutral on a moving train" (Zinn, 1994) because the fate of researchers are highly connected to the fate of all of the nation's citizens. James Baldwin (1971), in an open letter to Angela Davis, wrote, "If we know, then we must fight for your life as though it were our own—which it is—and render impassable with our bodies the corridors to the gas chamber. For if they come for you in the morning, they will be coming for us that night" (p. 23).

R E F E R E N C E S

Adorno, T. W., Frenkel-Brunswik, E., Levinson, D. J., Sanford, R., & Nevitt, R. N. (1950). *The Authoritarian Personality.* New York: Norton.

Allport, G. (1954). *The Nature of Prejudice.* Reading, MA: Addison-Wesley.

Ashe, A., & Rampersad, A. (1993). *Days of Grace: A Memoir.* New York: Ballantine Books.

Baldwin, J. (1971). An Open Letter to My Sister, Angela Y. Davis. In A. Y. Davis and Other Political Prisoners (Eds.), *If They Come in the Morning* (pp. 19–23). New York: Signet.

Baldwin, J. (1985). Stranger in the Village. In J. Baldwin, *The Price of the Ticket: Collected Nonfiction 1948–1985* (pp. 79–90). New York: St. Martin's. (original work published 1953)

Banks, J. A. (1993). The Canon Debate, Knowledge Construction, and Multicultural Education. *Educational Researcher, 22*(5), 4–14.

Banks, J. A. (1995). The Historical Reconstruction of Knowledge about Race: Implications for Transformative Teaching. *Educational Researcher, 24*(2), 15–25.

Banks, J. A. (1997). *Educating Citizens in a Multicultural Society.* New York: Teachers College Press.

Barkan, E. (1992). *The Retreat of Scientific Racism: Changing Concepts of Race in Britain and the United States between the World Wars.* New York: Cambridge University Press.

Behar, R. (1996). *The Vulnerable Observer: Anthropology That Breaks Your Heart.* Boston: Beacon Press.

Benedict, R. (1934). *Patterns of Culture.* Boston: Houghton Mifflin.

Benedict, R. (1947). *Race: Science and Politics* (rev. ed., with *The Races of Mankind* by R. Benedict & G. Weltfish). New York: Viking. (original work published 1940)

Burns, J. M. (1978). *Leadership.* New York: Harper & Row.

Burt, S., & Code, L. (Eds.). (1995). *Changing Methods: Feminists Transforming Practice.* Orchard Park, NY: Broadview Press.

Caffrey, R. (1989). *Ruth Benedict: Stranger in This Land.* Austin: University of Texas Press.

Clark, K. B. (1963). *Prejudice and Your Child* (2nd ed., enlarged). Boston: Beacon Press.

Clark, K. B. (1965). *Dark Ghetto: Dilemmas of Social Power.* New York: Harper.

Clark, K. B. (1974). *Pathos of Power.* New York: Harper & Row.

Clark, K. B. (1993). Racial Progress and Retreat: A Personal Memoir. In H. Hill & J. E. Jones Jr. (Eds.), *Race in America: The Struggle for Equality* (pp. 3–18). Madison: The University of Wisconsin Press.

Clark, K. B., & Clark, M. P. (1939). The Development of Consciousness of Self and the Emergence of Racial Identification in Negro Preschool Children. *Journal of Social Psychology, 10,* 591–599.

Clark, K. B., & Clark; M. P. (1940). Skin Color as a Factor in Racial Identification and Preference in Negro Children. *Journal of Negro Education, 19,* 341–358.

Clark, K. B., & Clark, M. P. (1947). Racial Identification and Preference in Negro Children. In T. M. Newcomb & E. L. Hartley (Eds.), *Readings in Social Psychology* (pp. 169–178). New York: Holt, Rinehart Winston.

Clark, K. B., & Clark, M. P. (1950). Emotional Factors in Racial Identification and Preference in Negro Children. *Journal of Negro Education, 19,* 341–350.

Code, L. (1987). *Epistemic Responsibility.* Hanover, NH: University Press of New England.

Code, L. (1991). *What Can She Know? Feminist Theory and the Construction of Knowledge.* Ithaca, NY: Cornell University Press.

Collins, P. H. (1990). *Black Feminist Thought: Knowledge, Consciousness, and the Politics of Empowerment.* New York: Routledge.

Collins, P. H. (1995). The Social Construction of Black Feminist Thought. In B. Guy-Sheftall (Ed.), *Words Affire: An Anthology of African-American Feminist Thought* (pp. 338–357). New York: The New Press.

Fleming, D. (1971). Benedict, Ruth Fulton. In E. T. James, J. W. James, & P. S. Boyer (Eds.), *Notable American Women: A Biographical Dictionary* (Vol. 1, pp. 128–131). Cambridge, MA: Harvard University Press.

Fox, R. W., & Koppenberg, J. T. (Eds.). (1995). *A Companion to American Thought.* Cambridge, MA: Blackwell.

Franklin, J. H. (1967). *From Slavery to Freedom: A History of Negro Americans* (3rd. ed.). New York: Knopf.

Franklin, J. H. (1989). *Race and History: Selected Essays 1938–1988.* Baton Rouge: Louisiana State University Press.

Franklin, J. H. (1991). A Life of Learning. In H. L. Gates Jr. (Ed.), *Bearing Witness: Selections from African-American Autobiography in the Twentieth Century* (pp. 351–368). New York: Pantheon Books.

Franklin, J. H., & Moss, A. A., Jr. (1994). *From Slavery to Freedom: A History of Negro Americans* (7th ed.). New York: McGraw-Hill.

Gans, H. J. (1995). *The War against the Poor.* New York: Basic Books.

Gordon, E. W. (1997). Task Force on the Role and Future of Minorities, American Educational Research Association. *Educational Researcher, 26*(3), 44–52.

Gould, S. J. (1994). Curveball. *The New Yorker, 70*(38), 139–149.

Gutiérrez, R. A. (1991). *When Jesus Came, the Corn Mothers Went Away: Marriage, Sexuality and Power in New Mexico, 1500–1846.* Stanford, CA: Stanford University Press.

Harding, S. (1993). Rethinking Standpoint Epistemology: "What Is Strong Objectivity?" In L. Alcoff & E. Potter (Eds.), *Feminist Epistemologies* (pp. 49–82). New York: Routledge.

Hempel, C. G. (1965). *Aspects of Scientific Explanation and Other Essays in the Philosophy of Science.* New York: The Free Press.

Herrnstein, R. J., & Murray, C. (1994). *The Bell Curve.* New York: The Free Press.

Hine, D. C. (1994). *Hine Sight: Black Women and the Re-construction of American History.* Bloomington: Indiana University Press.

Homans, G. C. (1967). *The Nature of Social Science.* New York: Harcourt.

Hu-DeHart, E. (1995). Ethnic Studies in U.S. Higher Education: History, Development, and Goals. In J. A. Banks & C. A. M. Banks (Eds.), *Handbook of Research on Multicultural Education* (pp. 696–707). New York: Macmillan.

Jensen, A. R. (1969). How Much Can We Boost IQ and Scholastic Achievement? *Harvard Educational Review, 39,* 1–123.

King, J. L. (1995). Culture-Centered Knowledge: Black Studies, Curriculum Transformation, and Social Action. In J. A. Banks & C. A. M. Banks (Eds.), *Handbook of Research on Multicultural Education* (pp. 265–290). New York: Macmillan.

King, M. L. (1994). *Letter from the Birmingham Jail.* San Francisco: Harper.

Klineberg, O. (1935). *Race Differences.* New York: Harper & Brothers.

Klineberg, O. (1973). Reflections of an International Psychologist of Canadian Origin. *International Social Science Journal, 25,* 39–54.

Kluger, R. (1975). *Simple Justice: A History of Brown v. Board of Education and Black America's Struggle for Equality.* New York: Vintage.

Kozol, J. (1991). *Savage Inequalities: Children in America's Schools.* New York: Crown.

Kuhn, T. S. (1970). *The Structure of Scientific Revolutions* (2nd ed., rev.). Chicago: The University of Chicago Press. (original work published 1962)

Ladner, J. A. (Ed.). (1973). *The Death of White Sociology.* New York: Vintage.

Lerner, G. (Ed.). (1973). *Black Women in White America: A Documentary History.* New York: Vintage.

Mannheim, K. (1985). *Ideology and Utopia: An Introduction to the Sociology of Knowledge.* San Diego, CA: Harcourt Brace. (original work published 1936)

Markowitz, G., & Rosner, D. (1996). *Children, Race, and Power: Kenneth and Mamie Clark's Northside Center.* Charlottesville: University Press of Virginia.

Mead, M. (1974). *Ruth Benedict.* New York: Columbia University Press.

Merton, R. K. (1972). Insiders and Outsiders: A Chapter in the Sociology of Knowledge. *The American Journal of Sociology, 78*(1), 9–47.

Modell, J. (1984). *Ruth Benedict: Patterns of a Life.* London: Hogarth Press.

Montagu, M. F. A. (1942). *Man's Most Dangerous Myth: The Fallacy of Race.* New York: Harper.

Moritz, C. (Ed.). (1964). Clark, Kenneth Bancroft. *Current Biography* (pp. 80–83). New York: H. W. Wilson Company.

Moynihan, D. P. (1965). *The Negro Family: The Case for National Action.* Washington, DC: U.S. Government Printing Office.

Murray, C. (1984). *Losing Ground: American Social Policy, 1950–1980.* New York: Basic Books.

Myrdal, G. (1944). *An American Dilemma: The Negro Problem and Modern Democracy.* New York: Harper & Row.

Myrdal, G. (1969). *Objectivity in Social Research.* New York: Pantheon Books.

Nelson, L. H. (1993). Epistemological Communities. In L. Alcoff & E. Potter (Eds.), *Feminist Epistemologies* (pp. 121–159). New York: Routledge.

Pettigrew, T. F. (1964). *A Profile of the Negro American.* Princeton, NJ: Van Nostrand.

Pettigrew, T. F. (1980). The Changing—Not Declining—Significance of Race: Essay Review of W. Wilson's *The Declining Significance of Race. Contemporary Sociology, 9,* 19–21.

Pettigrew, T. F. (1993). How Events Shape Theoretical Frames: A Personal Statement. In J. H. Stanfield (Ed.), *A History of Race Relations Research: First-generation Recollections* (pp. 159–178). Newbury Park, CA: Sage Publications.

Pettigrew, T. F., & Green, R. L. (1976). School Desegregation in Large Cities: A Critique of the Coleman "White flight" Thesis. *Harvard Educational Review, 46*(1), 1–53.

Phillips, U. B. (1966). *American Negro Slavery.* Baton Rouge: Louisiana State University Press. (original work published 1918)

Rosenau, P. M. (1992). *Post-Modernism and the Social Sciences.* Princeton, NJ: Princeton University Press.

Smith, J. D., & Inscoe, J. C. (Eds.). (1993). *Ulrich Bonnell Phillips: A Southern Historian and His Critics.* Athens: The University of Georgia Press.

Southern, D. W. (1987). *Gunnar Mydral and Black-White Relations: The Use and Abuse of An American Dilemma, 1944–1969.* Baton Rouge: Louisiana State University Press.

Stanfield, J. H. (Ed.). (1993). *A History of Race Relations Research: First-Generation Recollections.* Newbury Park, CA: Sage Publications.

Stocking, G. W., Jr. (1974). *A Franz Boas Reader: The Shaping of American Anthropology, 1883–1911.* Chicago: The University of Chicago Press.

Takaki, R. (1993). *A Different Mirror: A History of Multicultural America.* Boston: Little Brown.

Theodorson, G. A., & Theodorson, A. G. (1969). *A Modern Dictionary of Sociology.* New York: Barnes & Noble.

Turner, F. J. (1989). The Significance of the Frontier in American History. In C. A. Milner II (Ed.), *Major Problems in the History of the American West* (pp. I-34). Lexington, MA: D. C. Heath. (original work published 1894)

U.S. Commission on Civil Rights. (1967). *Racial Isolation in the Public Schools* (2 Vols.). Washington, DC: U.S. Government Printing Office.

Villenas, S. (1996). The Colonizer/Colonized Chicana Ethnographer: Identity, Marginalization, and Co-Option in the Field. *Harvard Educational Review, 66,* 711–731.

Wilson, W. J. (1996). *When Work Disappears: The World of the New Urban Poor.* New York: Knopf.

Zinn, H. (1994). *You Can't be Neutral on a Moving Train: A Personal History of Our Times.* Boston: Beacon Press.

Curriculum and Teaching Strategies for Decision-Making and Action

To implement multicultural education successfully, teaching strategies must be implemented that help students acquire knowledge from the perspectives of diverse cultural and ethnic groups, clarify and analyze their values, identify courses of action, and act in ways consistent with democratic and humane values. An important goal of multicultural teaching is to help students understand the nature of knowledge, how it is constructed, and how knowledge reflects the values, perspectives, and experiences of its creators.

The three chapters in Part Four describe teaching strategies that can be used to help students to better understand how knowledge is constructed, to become knowledge builders themselves, to learn to care, and to take effective personal, social, and civic action. Chapter 10 describes the nature of knowledge and a unit that a junior high school teacher uses to help his students understand the nature of knowledge and to learn decision-making and social action skills. Chapter 11 illustrates how teachers can plan and implement units on social issues that have decision-making and social action components. This chapter describes a sample unit that focuses on the following question: Should institutions establish public policies that acknowledge and support racial, ethnic, and cultural diversity? Chapter 12 describes the extent to which curriculum reform has occurred, how diverse cultural and ethnic perspectives enrich the curriculum, and how the teacher can become a cultural mediator and change agent.

10 A Curriculum for Empowerment, Action, and Change

When students are empowered, they have the ability to influence their personal, social, political, and economic worlds. Students need specific knowledge, skills, and attitudes in order to have the ability to influence the worlds in which they live. They need knowledge of their social, political, and economic worlds, the skills to influence their environments, and humane values that will motivate them to participate in social change to help create a more just society and world.

This chapter describes the nature of knowledge and the dominant canons, paradigms, and perspectives that are institutionalized within the school, college, and university curriculum. Much of the knowledge institutionalized within the schools and the larger society neither enables students to become reflective and critical citizens nor helps them to participate effectively in their society in ways that will make it more democratic and just. This chapter proposes and describes a curriculum designed to help students to understand knowledge as a social construction and to acquire the data, skills, and values needed to participate in civic action and social change.

Types of Knowledge

This chapter defines knowledge as "familiarity, awareness, or understandings gained through experience or study. The sum or range of what has been perceived, discovered or inferred" (*American Heritage Dictionary*, 1983, p. 384). Bruner's (1996) definition is also useful. He defines knowledge as "justified belief" (p. 59). My conceptualization of knowledge is broad and is used the way in which it is usually used in the sociology of knowledge literature to include ideas, values, and interpretations (Berger & Luckman, 1966; Farganis, 1986).

This chapter identifies and describes five types of knowledge (Banks, 1996): (1) *personal/cultural*; (2) *popular*; (3) *mainstream academic*; (4) *transformative academic*; and (5) *school* (see Table 10.1). Personal/cultural knowledge consists of the concepts, explanations, and interpretations that students derive from their personal experiences in their homes, families, and community cultures. The facts, concepts, explanations, and interpretations that are institutionalized within the mass media

TABLE 10.1   Types of Knowledge

Knowledge Type	Definition	Examples
Personal/Cultural	The concepts, explanations, and interpretations that students derive from personal experiences in their homes, families, and community cultures.	Understandings by many African Americans and Latino students that highly individualistic behavior will be negatively sanctioned by many adults and peers in their cultural communities.
Popular	The facts, concepts, explanations, and interpretations that are institutionalized within the mass media and other institutions that are part of the popular culture.	Movies such as *Birth of a Nation, How the West Was Won,* and *Dances with Wolves.*
Mainstream Academic	The concepts, paradigms, theories and explanations that constitute traditional Western-centric knowledge in history and the behavioral and social sciences.	Ulrich B. Phillips, *American Negro Slavery;* Frederick Jackson Turner's Frontier theory; Arthur R. Jensen's theory about Black and White intelligence.
Transformative Academic	The facts, concepts, paradigms, themes, and explanations that challenge mainstream academic knowledge and expand and substantially revise established canons, paradigms, theories, explanations, and research methods. When transformative academic paradigms replace mainstream ones, a scientific revolution has occurred. What is more normal is that transformative academic paradigms coexist with established ones.	George Washington Williams, *History of the Negro Race in America;* W. E. B. Du Bois, *Black Reconstruction;* Carter G. Woodson, *The Mis-Education of the Negro;* Gerda Lerner, *The Majority Finds Its Past;* Rodolfo Acuña, *Occupied America: A History of Chicanos;* Herbert Gutman, *The Black Family in Slavery and Freedom 1750–1925.*
School	The facts, concepts, generalizations, and interpretations that are presented in textbooks, teachers' guides, other media forms, and lectures by teachers.	Lewis Paul Todd and Merle Curti, *Rise of the American Nation;* Richard C. Brown, Wilhelmena S. Robinson, & John Cunningham, *Let Freedom Ring: A United States History.*

and in other institutions that are part of the popular culture constitute popular knowledge.

Mainstream academic knowledge consists of the concepts, paradigms, theories, and explanations that constitute traditional Western-centric knowledge in history and in the behavioral and social sciences. Social and behavioral scientists on the margins of the academic establishment create transformative academic knowledge that challenges established paradigms, concepts, and findings in the social, behavioral, natural, and physical sciences (Collins, 1998; Gould, 1996). Transformative academic knowledge consists of the facts, concepts, paradigms, themes, and explanations that challenge mainstream academic knowledge and expand and substantially revise established canons, paradigms, theories, explanations, and research methods. When transformative academic paradigms replace mainstream ones, a scientific revolution has occurred (Kuhn, 1970). What is more normal in the social sciences and history is that transformative paradigms coexist with established ones.

School Knowledge

The facts, concepts, generalizations, and interpretations that are presented in textbooks, teachers' guides, other media forms, and lectures by teachers constitute school knowledge. Students are usually taught school knowledge as a set of facts and concepts to be memorized and later recalled (Loewen, 1995; Nash, Crabtree, & Dunn, 1997). They are rarely encouraged to examine the assumptions, values, and the nature of the knowledge they are required to memorize or to examine the ways in which knowledge is constructed. Knowledge in the school curriculum is usually viewed as objective, neutral, and not subject to critical analysis and reconstruction.

Popular writers such as Hirsch (1996) and Ravitch and Finn (1987) have contributed to the school conception of knowledge as a body of facts not to be questioned, critically analyzed, and reconstructed. Hirsch (1996) writes as if knowledge is neutral and static. He developed *The Dictionary of Cultural Literacy* with his colleagues (Hirsch, Kett, & Trefil, 1988). This work contains a list of important facts that students should master in order to become culturally literate. Ravitch and Finn (1987) identify and lament the factual knowledge that U.S. high school students do not know. Neither Hirsch nor Ravitch and Finn discuss the limitations of factual knowledge or point out that knowledge is dynamic, changing, and constructed within a social context rather than neutral and static.

I agree with Hirsch and Ravitch and Finn that all people in the United States need to master a common core of shared knowledge. However, the important question is: *Who will participate in the formulation of that knowledge and whose interests will it serve?* We need a broad level of participation in the identification, construction, and formulation of the knowledge that we expect all students to master. Such knowledge should reflect cultural democracy and should serve the interests of all of the people within the nation. It should contribute to the public good. The knowledge institutionalized within the schools, colleges, and universities, and within the popular culture should reflect the interests, experiences, and goals of all of the people in the nation. It should empower all people to participate effectively in a democratic society.

Knowledge and Empowerment

To empower students to participate effectively in their civic community, the ways in which they acquire, view, and evaluate knowledge must be changed. We must engage students in a process of attaining knowledge in which they are required to critically analyze conflicting paradigms and explanations and the values and assumptions of different knowledge systems, forms, and categories. Students must also be given opportunities to construct knowledge themselves so that they can develop a deep understanding of the nature and limitations of knowledge. Students also need to understand the extent to which knowledge is a social construction that reflects the social, political, and cultural context in which it is formulated.

Participating in processes in which they formulate and construct various knowledge forms will also enable students to understand how various groups within a society often formulate, shape, and disseminate knowledge that supports their interests and legitimizes their power. Groups with little power and influence often challenge the dominant paradigms, knowledge systems, and perspectives that are institutionalized within society. Knowledge and paradigms consistent with the interests, goals, and assumptions of powerful groups are institutionalized within the schools, colleges, and universities as well as within the popular culture. A latent function of such knowledge is to legitimize the dominant political, economic, and cultural arrangements.

The Attempt to Reformulate the Canon

The ethnic studies and women studies movements, which emerged from the civil rights movement of the 1960s and 1970s, have as a major goal a reformulation of the canon that is used to select and evaluate knowledge for inclusion into the school and university curriculum. The demand for a reformulation of the curriculum canon has evoked a concerted and angry reaction from a few mainstream scholars (D'Souza, 1995; Schlesinger, 1991). They have described the push by ethnic and feminist scholars for a reformulation of the canon as an attempt to politicize the curriculum and to promote special interests. Two national organizations established by mainstream scholars resist efforts by ethnic and feminist scholars to reformulate and transform the canon. They are the Madison Center and the National Association of Scholars (Heller, 1989).

Transformative scholars want to transform the school, college, and university curriculum so that it will more accurately reflect the experiences, visions, and goals of people of color and of women. The National Association of Multicultural Education supports the implementation of a diverse curriculum in the schools and in teacher education. The Modern Language Association, the National Council of Teachers of English, and the National Council for the Social Studies—as well as a number of other professional and discipline-based associations—support ethnic and cultural diversity through sessions at their annual conventions and in their publications.

The mainstream scholars who have labeled the curricular goals of women and of people of color *special interests* view their own interests as universal and in the public good; they view claims that challenge their own interests as *special interests.* Powerful groups within a society not only view their own interests as identical to the public interest but also are usually able to get other groups, including marginalized groups, to internalize this belief. The school, college and university curriculum helps students acquire the belief that the interests, goals, and values of powerful groups are identical to those of the civic community.

School Knowledge and the Dominant Canon

To develop a sense of the need for social change, a commitment to social participation, and the skills to participate effectively in social action, the knowledge that students acquire must have certain characteristics. It must describe events, concepts, and situations from the perspectives of the diverse cultural, racial, gender, and social-class groups within a society, including those that are politically and culturally dominant as well as those that are structurally excluded from full societal participation. Much of school knowledge as well as knowledge in the popular culture presents events and situations from the perspectives of the victors rather than the vanquished and from the perspectives of those who dominate the social, economic, and political institutions in society rather than from the points of view of those who are victimized and marginalized.

School and societal knowledge that presents issues, events, and concepts primarily from the perspectives of powerful groups tends to justify the status quo, rationalize racial and gender inequality, and make students content with the status quo. Two important latent functions of such knowledge are to convince students that the current social, political, and economic institutions are just and to persuade them that substantial change within society is neither justified nor required.

The ways in which the current structures are justified in the school, college, and university curricula are usually subtle rather than blatant. These justifications are consequently more effective because they are infrequently suspected, recognized, questioned, or criticized. These dominant perspectives emanate from the canon that is used to define, select, and evaluate knowledge in the school, college, and university curriculum in the United States and in other Western nations. This canon has traditionally been European-centric and male-dominated. It is rarely explicitly defined or discussed. It is taken for granted, unquestioned, and internalized by writers, researchers, teachers, professors, and students.

The Western-centric and male-centric canon often marginalizes the experiences of people of color, Third World nations and cultures, and the perspectives and histories of women. It results in the Americas being called the "New World," in the notion that Columbus "discovered" America (Bigelow & Peterson, 1998; Stannard, 1992), in the Anglo immigrants to the West being called "settlers" rather than "immigrants," and in the description of the Anglo immigrants' rush to the West as the "Westward Movement" (Grossman, 1994).

Calling the Americas "The New World" subtly denies the nearly 40,000 years that Native Americans have lived in the Americas. The implication is that history did not begin in the Americas until the Europeans arrived. From the perspectives of the Lakota Sioux, the Anglo settlers in the West were invaders and conquerors. The Westward Movement is a highly Eurocentric concept. The Lakota Sioux did not consider their homeland the West but the center of the universe. And, of course, it was the Anglo immigrants who were moving West and not the Sioux. From the perspective of the Lakota Sioux, it was not a Westward Movement but the Great Invasion.

Concepts such as The New World, The Westward Movement, hostile Indians, and lazy welfare mothers (Gans, 1995) not only justify the status quo and current social and economic realities, but they also fail to help students understand why there is a need to substantially change current social, political, and economic realities or to help them develop a commitment to social change and political action. These Anglocentric and Eurocentric notions also fail to help students of color and female students develop a sense of empowerment and efficacy over their lives and their destinies.

Both the research by Coleman et al. (1966) and the research on locus of control (Lefcourt, 1976) indicate that people need a sense of control over their destiny in order to become empowered to achieve or to act. Many students of color and female students are victimized and marginalized by the knowledge that results from the Eurocentric canon because they are made to believe that problems such as racism and sexism either do not exist in any substantial way or result from their own actions or shortcomings.

The Dominant Canon and the Popular Culture

The popular culture frequently reinforces and extends the dominant canon and paradigms taught in the school and university curriculum. An example is the popular Disney film, *Pocahontas.* In the Disney version of this legend, institutionalized ideas about Native Americans and Whites are reinforced. Captain John Smith is depicted as heroic and bigger than life. Pocahontas, who was a child of about twelve or thirteen when she convinced her father to save Smith's life (Barbour, 1971), is portrayed as a mature adult and a sex icon who falls in love with Smith. The filmmaker changes what we know about historical reality to depict Whites and Indians in ways that reinforce their status in society today.

Ward Churchill (1992), the Native American scholar, calls images of Indians and Whites like those presented in *Pocahonto*s "fantasies of the master race." He states that the depiction of Native Americans by filmmakers is "an unbridled justification and glorification of the conquest and subordination of Native America. As such, it is a vitally necessary ingredient in the maintenance and perfection of the Euroempire which began when the Pilgrims landed in 1620" (p. 240).

A Transformative Curriculum for Empowerment

The previous section of this chapter describes the nature and goals of the dominant Eurocentric curriculum in the nation's schools and colleges. This curriculum reinforces the status quo, makes students passive and content, and encourages them to accept the dominant ideologies, political and economic arrangements, and the prevailing myths and paradigms used to rationalize and justify the current social and political structure.

A transformative curriculum designed to empower students, especially those from victimized and marginalized groups, must help students develop the knowledge and skills needed to critically examine the current political and economic structure and the myths and ideologies used to justify it. Such a curriculum must teach students critical thinking skills, the ways in which knowledge is constructed, the basic assumptions and values that undergird knowledge systems, and how to construct knowledge themselves.

A transformative curriculum cannot be constructed merely by adding content about cultural groups and women to the existing Eurocentric curriculum or by integrating or infusing cultural content or content about women into the mainstream curriculum. When the curriculum is revised using either an additive or an infusion approach, the basic assumptions, perspectives, paradigms, and values of the dominant curriculum remain unchallenged and substantially unchanged, despite the addition of cultural content or of content about women. In such a revised curriculum, the experiences of women and of people of color are viewed from the perspectives and values of mainstream males with power.

When the meeting of the Lakota Sioux and the Anglos from the East is conceptualized as the Westward Movement, adding content about the Lakota and about women neither changes nor challenges the basic assumptions of the curriculum or the canon used to select content for inclusion into it. The Lakota and women heroes selected for study are selected using the Western-centric, male-dominated paradigm. When the dominant paradigm and canon are used to select ethnic and women heroes for inclusion into the curriculum, the heroes selected for study are those who are valued by dominant groups and not necessarily those considered heroes by nonmainstream groups. Ethnic heroes selected for study and veneration are usually those who helped Whites conquer or oppress powerless people rather than those who challenged the existing social, economic, and political order. Consequently, Pocahontas and Booker T. Washington are more likely to be selected for inclusion into the mainstream curriculum than are Geronimo and Nat Turner.

Critical Thinking and Multiple Voices

A curriculum designed to empower students must be transformative in nature and must help students develop the knowledge, skills, and values needed to become social critics who can make reflective decisions and can implement their decisions in effective personal, social, and civic action (Lewis, 1991). In other words, reflective decision-making and personal and civic action must be the primary goals of a transformative and empowering curriculum.

The transformative curriculum must help students reconceptualize and rethink the experiences of people in both the United States and the world, to view the human experience from the perspectives of a range of cultural, ethnic, and social-class groups, and to construct their own versions of the past, present, and future. In the transformative curriculum multiple voices are heard and legitimized: the voices of textbooks, the voices of literary and historical writers, the voices of teachers, and the voices of other students. Students can construct their own versions of the past, present, and future after listening to and reflecting on the multiple and diverse voices in the transformative classroom. Literacy in the transformative curriculum is reconceptualized to include diverse voices and perspectives and is not limited to literacy in the Hirsch (1996) sense, that is, to the mastering of a list of facts constructed by authorities. Writes Starrs (1988),

> In the new definition literacy should be seen as a struggle for voice. As such the presence of different voices is an opportunity and a challenge. All students will deal with the fact that their voices differ from one another's, from their teachers,' from their authors.' All learners will somehow cope with the issue of translating their many voices, and in the process they will join in creating culture—not simply receiving it. (p. 8)

The transformative curriculum teaches students to think and reflect critically on the materials they read and the voices they hear. Baldwin (1985), in a classic essay, "A Talk to Teachers," states that the main goal of education is to teach students to think: "The purpose of education…is to create in a person the ability to look at the world for himself, to make his own decisions, to say to himself this is black or this is white, to decide for himself whether there is a God in heaven or not. To ask questions of the universe, and then to live with those questions, is the way he achieves his identity" (p. 326). Although Baldwin believed that thinking was the real purpose of education, he also believed that no society was serious about teaching its citizens to think. He writes further: "But no society is really anxious to have that kind of person around. What society really, ideally, wants is a citizenry which will simply obey the rules of society. If a society succeeds in this, that society is about to perish" (p. 326).

The transformative curriculum can teach students to think by encouraging them, when they are reading or listening to resources, to consider the author's purposes for writing or speaking, his or her basic assumptions, and how the author's perspective or point of view compares with that of other authors and resources. Students can develop the skills to critically analyze historical and contemporary resources by being given several accounts of the same event or situation that present different perspectives and points of view.

A Lesson with Different Voices

In a junior high school lesson I developed (Banks with Sebesta, 1982, Vol. 1), "Christopher Columbus and the Taino (Arawak) Indians," the teacher reads to the students selections from *The Tainos: Rise and Decline of the People Who Greeted Columbus* by Irving Rouse (1992). The students are presented with an excerpt from Columbus's diary that describes his arrival in a Taino Caribbean community in 1492. These are among the things that Columbus (Jane, 1930) writes about the Tainos:

> They took all and gave all, such as they had, with good will, but it seemed to me that they were a people very lacking in everything. They all go naked as their mothers bore them, and the women also, although I saw only one very young girl.... They should be good servants and quick to learn, since I see that they very soon say all that is said to them, and I believe that they would easily be made Christians, for it appeared to me that they had no religious beliefs. Our Lord willing, at the time of my departure, I will bring back six of them to Your Highnesses, that they may learn to talk. I saw no beast of any kind in this island, except parrots. (pp. 23–24)

The students are then encouraged to view Columbus's voice from the perspective of the Tainos. The Tainos had an aural culture and consequently left no written documents. However, archaeologist Fred Olsen studied Taino artifacts and used what he learned from them to construct a day in the life of the Tainos, which he describes in his book, *On the Trail of the Arawaks* (Olsen, 1974). The students are asked to read an excerpt from Olsen's account of a day in the life of the Tainos and to respond to these questions (Banks, with Sebasta, Vol. 1):

> Columbus wrote in his diary that he thought the Arawaks had no religious beliefs. You read about Arawak life in the report by Fred Olsen. Do you think Columbus was correct? Why? Accounts written by people who took part in or witnessed (saw) an historical event are called primary sources. Can historians believe everything they read in a primary source? Explain. (p. 43)

After reading the expert from Olsen's book, the teacher reads *Morning Girl* by Michael Dorris (1992) to the students. This is the story of a twelve-year-old Taino girl who reveals life on a Bahamian island in 1492.

Key Concepts and Issues

In addition to helping students view events and situations from diverse ethnic, gender, and social-class perspectives, a transformative curriculum should be organized around powerful concepts and social issues (Banks, 1997). The conceptual-issue-oriented curriculum facilitates the teaching of decision-making and social action skills in several important ways. First, a conceptual curriculum helps students understand the ways in which knowledge is constructed. It also enables them to formulate concepts themselves and to understand the ways in which the concepts formulated reflect the values, purposes, and assumptions of the conceptualizers. In an inquiry-oriented conceptual curriculum, students are not passive consumers of previously constructed knowledge, but are encouraged to formulate new ways to organize, conceptualize, and think about data and information.

The conceptual approach also allows the teacher to rethink the ways that topics, periods, and literary movements are structured and labeled. Periodization in history, literature, and art tend to reflect a Eurocentric perspective, such as the

Middle Ages, the Renaissance, and the Westward Movement. When content is organized around key interdisciplinary concepts, such as culture, communication, and values, the teacher can structure lessons and units that facilitate the inclusion of content from diverse cultures as well as content that will help students develop the knowledge, values, commitments, and skills needed to participate in effective personal and civic action.

In the U.S. junior high school textbook I authored (Banks with Sebesta, 1982), a key concept, *revolution,* is used to organize a unit rather than to focus the unit exclusively on the revolution in the English colonies in 1776. By organizing the unit around the concept of revolution rather than a particular revolution, the students were able to examine three American revolutions, to study each in depth, and to derive generalizations about revolutions in general. They were also able to identify ways in which these three revolutions were alike and different. They also used the definition and generalizations they derived about revolutions from this unit to determine whether events such as the civil rights movement of the 1960s and 1970s and the women rights movement of the 1970s could accurately be called "revolutions." The three American revolutions they studied were the (1) The Pueblo Revolt of 1680, in which Pope led a resistance against the conquering Spaniards; (2) The Revolution in the British Colonies, in 1776; and (3) The Mexican Revolution of 1810, the aim of which was to acquire Mexico's independence from Spain.

The Moral Component of Action

After students have mastered interdisciplinary knowledge related to a concept or issue, such as racial discrimination or gender discrimination, they should participate in value or moral inquiry exercises. The goal of such exercises should be to help students develop a set of consistent, clarified values that can guide purposeful and reflective personal or civic action related to the issue examined. This goal can best be attained by teaching students a method or process for deriving their values within a democratic classroom atmosphere. In this kind of democratic classroom, students must be free to express their value choices, determine how those choices conflict, examine alternative values, consider the consequences of different value choices, make value choices, and defend their moral choices within the context of human dignity and other American creed values. Students must be given an opportunity to derive their own values reflectively in order to develop a commitment to human dignity, equality, and to other democratic values. They must be encouraged to reflect on values choices within a democratic atmosphere in order to internalize them (Banks & Banks, with Clegg, 1999).

Teachers can use the Banks value inquiry model to help students identify and clarify their values and make reflective moral choices. The model consists of these nine steps (Banks & Banks, with Clegg, 1999, p. 444):

1. Defining and recognizing value problems
2. Describing value-relevant behavior
3. Naming values exemplified by the behavior

4. Determining conflicting values in behavior described
5. Hypothesizing about the possible consequence of the values analyzed
6. Naming alternative values to those described by behavior observed
7. Hypothesizing about the possible consequences of values analyzed
8. Declaring value preferences; choosing
9. Stating reasons, sources, and possible consequences of value choice; justifying, hypothesizing, predicting

This section illustrates how Mr. Carson, a junior high school social studies teacher, used this model while teaching a unit on the civil rights movement. Mr. Carson wanted his students to acquire an understanding of the historical development of the civil rights movement, to analyze and clarify their values related to integration and segregation, and also to conceptualize and perhaps take some kinds of actions related to racism and desegregation in their personal lives, the school, or the local community. Mr. Carson is a social studies teacher in a predominantly White suburban school district near a city in the Northwest that has a population of about 2 million. The metropolitan area in which Mr. Carson's school is located has a population of about 3 million.

The Long Shadow of Little Rock

Mr. Carson used the Banks value inquiry model to help his students analyze the value issues revealed in Chapter 8 of *The Long Shadow of Little Rock* by Daisy Bates (1987). In this excellently written and moving chapter, Mrs. Bates describes the moral dilemma she faced when serving as head of the National Association for the Advancement of Colored People (NAACP) in Little Rock, Arkansas, when Central High School was desegregated by nine African American high school students. The desegregation of Central High school began during the 1957–1958 school year.

Mrs. Bates was the leading supporter and organizer for the nine students. Her husband, L. C. Bates, was a journalist. They owned a newspaper, *The States Press*. In Chapter 8 of *The Long Shadow of Little Rock,* Mrs. Bates describes how a middle-aged White woman came to her home at 3:00 one afternoon and told her to call a press conference and announce that she was withdrawing her support for the nine students and advising them to withdraw from Central High School and return to the Black schools. The woman said she represented a group of "Southern Christian women." Mrs. Bates asked the woman what would happen if she didn't do what she told her to do. She looked at Mrs. Bates straight in the eye and said, "You'll be destroyed—you, your newspaper, your reputation…. Everything."

During her long, anguished night, Mrs. Bates wondered whether she had the right to destroy sixteen years of her husband's work—the newspaper. Yet she felt that she could not abandon a cause to which she and many other African Americans were deeply committed. By morning Mrs. Bates had made her difficult and painful decision. She called her visitor and said, "No." Later, she told her husband, L. C., what she had done. He said, "Daisy, you did the right thing." Mrs. Bates's visitor kept her promise. *The State Press* was closed because advertising from it was withdrawn by all of the major stores and businesses in Little Rock. The Bates family suffered financial and personal turmoil because of the closing of *The State Press* and because of threats and attempts on Mrs. Bates's life.

Using the Banks value inquiry model, these are some of the questions Mr. Carson asked his students:

Defining and Recognizing Value Problems

1. What value problem did Mrs. Bates face after she was visited by the woman?

Naming Values Exemplified by Behavior Described

2. What did the visitor value or think was important? What did Mrs. Bates value? What did Mr. Bates value?

Hypothesizing about the Sources of Values Analyzed

3. How do you think Mrs. Bates's visitor developed the values she had? How do you think Mr. and Mrs. Bates developed the values they showed in this selection?

Declaring Value Preferences: Choosing

4. Try to put yourself in Mrs. Daisy Bates's place on October 29, 1959. What decision would you have made?

Stating Reasons, Sources, and Possible Consequences of Value Choice

5. Why should Mrs. Bates have made the decision you stated above? What were the possible consequences of her saying "no" and saying "yes" to her visitor?

Give as many reasons as you can about why Mrs. Bates should have made the decision you stated above.

Keep in mind that Mrs. Bates knew that if she said yes to her visitor she would probably have been able to keep her property but that the nine students would have probably had to return to Black schools and that segregation would have been maintained in Little Rock. On the other hand, by saying no, she risked losing all of her property and her husband's property, including his newspaper. Also, consider the fact that she did not involve him in making her decision.

Mr. Carson wanted the students to view the school desegregation events in Little Rock from the perspective of one of the nine African American students who worked with Mrs. Bates and who personally endured the pain of the events. He read to them excerpts from a book by one of these students, *Warriors Don't Cry* by Melba Pattillo Beals (1994). Beals has also written a more recent book about experiences at Central High and about her life afterwards, *White Is a State of Mind: A Memoir* (Beals, 1999).

Decision-Making and Citizen Action

After Mr. Carson's students had derived knowledge about the civil rights movement of the 1950s and 1960s and had clarified their values regarding these issues, he asked them to list all of the possible actions they could take to increase desegregation in their personal lives as well as in the life of the school and the community. Mr. Carson was careful to explain to the students that action should be broadly conceptualized. He defined action in a way that might include a personal commitment to do something, such as making an effort to have more friends from different racial and ethnic groups or making a commitment to see a recent film about African Americans or to read a book by an African American author such as Toni Morrison or Alice Walker. Among the possible actions the students listed that they could take were these:

1. Making a personal commitment to refuse to laugh at racist jokes and to tell the individuals telling them how we feel.

2. Making a commitment to challenge our own racial and ethnic stereotypes either before or after we verbalize them.

3. Compiling an annotated list of books about ethnic groups that we will ask the librarian to order for our school library.

4. Asking the principal to order sets of photographs that show African Americans and other people of color who have jobs that represent a variety of careers. Asking the principal to encourage our teachers to display these photographs on their classroom walls.

5. Observing television programs to determine the extent to which people of color, such as African Americans and Asian Americans, are represented in such jobs as news anchors and hosts of programs. Writing to local and national television stations to express our concern if we discover that people of color are not represented in powerful and visible roles in news or other kinds of television programs.

6. Contacting a school in the inner city to determine if there are joint activities and projects in which we and they might participate.

7. Asking the principal or the board of education in our school district to require our teachers to attend workshops that will help them learn ways in which to integrate content about ethnic and racial groups into our courses.

8. Sharing and discussing with our parents some of the facts that we have learned in this unit, such as that by the year 2050, people of color will make up 47 percent and Non-Hispanic Whites will make up 53 percent of the nation's population (U.S. Bureau of the Census, 1998).

9. Making a personal commitment to have a friend from another racial, ethnic, or religious group by the end of the year.

10. Making a personal commitment to read at least one book a year that deals with a racial, cultural, or ethnic group other than my own.

11. Do nothing; take no actions.

The Decision-Making Process

After the students had made a list of possible actions they could take regarding the issues studied in the unit (including no actions), Mr. Carson asked them to consider the possible consequences of each of the actions identified, such as:

If I Take No Actions

Then I will be doing nothing to improve race relations in my personal life, in my school, my community, or nation.

But I will not risk trying to do something that could fail. I will also be indicating to others, by my behavior, that I am not concerned about improving race relations in my personal life, my family, school, or community.

If I Make a Personal Commitment to Tell No More Racist Jokes

Then I will be improving my personal behavior that relates to other racial, ethnic, and cultural groups. I will also demonstrate to others that I am concerned about improving race relations in my personal life.

But I will be doing little directly to improve the behaviors of other people in my family, school, and community.

After the students had worked in groups of five to identify and state the possible consequences of various courses of actions, Mr. Carson asked them to continue working in their groups and to select one or two personal or group actions they would like to take related to the problems they had studied in the unit. Mr. Carson also asked the students to be prepared to defend and/or explain the course of action or actions they chose, to tell whether it was feasible for them to carry out the action or actions, and to provide a time-line for its initiation and completion (if possible). These are among the actions the students chose:

■ Kathy and Susan decided to read the play *A Raisin in the Sun* by Lorraine Hansberry to try to get a better understanding of the experience of African Americans in the United States during the 1950s.

■ Clay's group, which included Clay, Pete, Tessie, Rosie, and Maria, decided that it would prepare a list of books on ethnic cultures and ask the school librarian to order them for the school library. Clay's group planned to ask Mr. Carson to help them find resources for the preparation of the annotated list of books.

■ Roselyn decided that she wanted to improve her understanding of ethnic cultures by reading. She decided to read these books during the year: *Let the Circle Be Unbroken* by Mildred D. Taylor, *A Jar of Dreams* by Yoshiko Uchida, and *America Is in the Heart* by Carlos Bulosan.

■ Aralean's group, which included Juan, James, Angela, and Patricia, decided that it wanted to develop a proposal that would require teachers in the district to attend multicultural education workshops. They will develop their plan with Mr. Carson and present it to the principal and then to the Board of Education for possible adoption.

The Role of the Teacher in an Empowerment and Transformative Curriculum

An effective transformative and empowerment curriculum must be implemented by teachers who have the knowledge, skills, and attitudes needed to help students understand the ways in which knowledge is constructed and used to support power group relationships in society. Teachers are human beings who bring their cultural perspectives, values, hopes, and dreams to the classroom. They also bring their prejudices, stereotypes, and misconceptions to the classroom. The teacher's values and perspectives mediate and interact with what they teach and influence the way that messages are communicated to and perceived by their students. A teacher who believes that Christopher Columbus discovered America and one who believes that Columbus came to America when it was peopled by groups with rich and diverse cultures will send different messages to their students when the European exploration of America is studied.

Because the teacher mediates the messages and symbols communicated to the students through the curriculum, it is important for teachers to come to grips with their own personal and cultural values and identities in order for them to help students from diverse racial, ethnic, and cultural groups to develop clarified cultural identities and to relate positively to each other. I am hypothesizing that self-clarification is a prerequisite to dealing effectively with and relating positively to outside ethnic and cultural groups. An Anglo-American teacher who is confused about his or her cultural identity and who has a nonreflective conception of the ways that Anglo-American culture relates to other groups in the United States will have a difficult time relating positively to outside ethnic groups such as African Americans and Mexican Americans.

Effective teacher education programs should help pre- and in-service teachers explore and clarify their own ethnic and cultural identities and develop more positive attitudes toward other racial, ethnic, and cultural groups. To do this, such programs must recognize and reflect the complex ethnic and cultural identities and characteristics of the individuals within teacher education programs. Teachers should also learn how to facilitate the identity quest among students and help them become effective and able participants in the common civic culture.

Effective teachers in the transformative curriculum must not only have clarified personal and cultural identifications, but they must also be keenly aware of the various paradigms, canons, and knowledge systems on which the dominant curriculum is based and those that it eschews. Because teacher-education students attain most of their knowledge without analyzing its assumptions and values or without engaging in the process of constructing knowledge themselves, they often leave teacher-education programs with many misconceptions about culturally and racially different groups and with conceptions about their national history and culture that are incomplete, misleading, and ethnocentric. Consequently, the knowledge that many teachers bring to the classroom contributes to the mystification rather than to the clarification of social, historical, and political realities. This knowledge also perpetuates inequality rather than contributing to justice, liberation, and empowerment.

In order to educate teachers so that they will convey images, perspectives, and points of view in the curriculum that will demystify social realities and promote cultural freedom and empowerment, we must radically change the ways in which they acquire knowledge. We must engage them in a process of attaining knowledge in which they are required to analyze the values and assumptions of different paradigms and theories. Teachers must also be given the opportunity to construct concepts, generalizations, and theories so that they can develop an understanding of the nature and limitations of knowledge and comprehend the extent to which knowledge reflects the social and cultural context in which it is formulated.

Participating in processes in which they formulate and construct knowledge forms will also help teachers to understand how various groups in society who formulate, shape, and disseminate knowledge often structure and disseminate knowledge that supports their interests and legitimizes their power. This knowledge often legitimizes dominant institutions and helps to make marginalized groups politically passive and content with their marginalized status. Teachers must not only understand how the dominant paradigms and canon help keep victimized groups powerless but also must be committed to social change and action if they are to become agents of liberation and empowerment.

REFERENCES

American Heritage Dictionary. (1983). New York: Dell Publishing.

Baldwin, J. (1985). *The Price of the Ticket: Collected Nonfiction, 1948–1985.* New York: St. Martin's Press.

Banks, J. A. (Ed.). (1996). *Multicultural Education, Transformative Knowledge, and Action: Historical and Contemporary Perspectives.* New York: Teachers College Press.

Banks, J. A. (1997). *Teaching Strategies for Ethnic Studies* (6th ed.). Boston: Allyn and Bacon.

Banks, J. A., with Sebesta, S. (1982). *We Americans: Our History and People,* Vols. 1 & 2. Boston: Allyn and Bacon.

Banks, J. A., & Banks, C. A. M., with Clegg, A. A., Jr.. (1999). *Teaching Strategies for the Social Studies: Decision-Making and Citizen Action* (5th ed.). White Plains, NY: Longman.

Barbour, P. L. (1971). Pocahontas. In E. T. James, J. W. James, & P. S. Boyer (Eds.), *Notable American Women,* Vol. 3, (pp. 78–81). Cambridge, MA: Harvard University Press.

Bates, D. (1987). *The Long Shadow of Little Rock.* Fayetteville: The University of Arkansas Press.

Beals, M. P. (1994). *Warriors Don't Cry.* New York: Pocket Books.

Beals, M. P. (1999). *White Is a State of Mind: A Memoir.* New York: Putnam's Sons.

Berger, P., & Luckman, T. (1966). *The Social Construction of Reality.* New York: Doubleday.

Bigelow, B., & Peterson, B. (1998*). Rethinking Columbus: The Next 500 Years.* Milwaukee: Rethinking Schools.

Bruner, J. (1996). *The Culture of Education.* Cambridge, MA: Harvard University Press.

Churchill, W. (1992). (Edited by M. A. Jaimes). *Fantasies of the Master Race: Literature, Cinema and the Colonization of American Indians.* Monroe, ME: Common Courage Press.

Coleman, J. S., et al. (1966). *Equality of Educational Opportunity.* Washington, DC: U.S. Government Printing Office.

Collins, P. H. (1998). *Fighting Words: Black Women and the Search for Justice.* Minneapolis: University of Minnesota Press.

Dorris, M. (1992). *Morning Girl.* New York: Hyperion Books.

D'Souza, D. (1995). *The End of Racism.* New York: The Free Press.

Farganis, S. (1986). *The Social Construction of the Feminine Character.* Totowa, NJ: Russell & Russell.

Fleming, J. (1985). *Blacks in College: A Comparative Study of Students' Success in Black and White Institutions.* San Francisco: Jossey-Bass Publishers.

Gans, H. (1995). *The War against the Poor: The Underclass and Antipoverty Policy.* New York: Basic Books.

Gould, S. J. (1996). *The Mismeasure of* Man (rev. ed.). New York: Norton.

Grossman, J. R. (1994). *The Frontier in American Culture: Essays by Richard White and Patricia Nelson Limerick.* Berkeley: University of California Press.

Heller, S. (1989). Press for Campus Diversity Leading to More Closed Minds, Say Critics. *The Chronicle of Higher Education, 35,* pp. A13, ff A22.

Hirsch, E. D., Jr. (1996). *The Schools We Need and Why We Don't Have Them.* New York: Doubleday.

Hirsch, E. D, Jr., Kett, J. F, & Trefil, J. (1988*). Dictionary of Cultural Literacy: What Every American Needs to Know.* Boston: Houghton Mifflin.

Jane, L. C. (1930). *The Voyages of Christopher Columbus.* London: The Argonaut Press.

Kuhn, T. S. (1970). *The Structure of Scientific Revolutions* (2nd ed.). Chicago: The University of Chicago Press.

Lefcourt, H. M. (1976). *Locus of Control: Current Trends in Theory and Research.* New York: John Wiley.

Lewis, B. A. (1991). (Edited by P. Espeland*). The Kid's Guide to Social Action.* Minneapolis: Free Spirit Publishing.

Loewen, J. W. (1995). *Lies My Teacher Taught Me.* New York: The New Press.

Nash, G. B., Crabtree, C., & Dunn, R. E. (1997). *History on Trial: Culture Wars and the Teaching of the Past.* New York: Knopf.

Olsen, F. (1974). *On the Trail of the Arawaks.* Norman: University of Oklahoma Press.

Ravitch, D., & Finn, C. E., Jr. (1987). *What Do Our 17-Year-Olds Know? A Report on the First National Assessment of History and Literature.* New York: Harper and Row.

Rouse, I. (1992). *The Tainos: Rise and Decline of the People Who Greeted Columbus.* New Haven: Yale University Press.

Schlesinger, A. M. (1991). *The Disuniting of America: Reflections on a Multicultural Society.* Knoxville, TN: Whittle Direct Books.

Stannard, D. E. (1992). *American Holocaust: Columbus and the Conquest of the New World.* New York: Oxford University Press.

Starrs, J. (1988). Cultural Literacy and Black Education. Paper submitted to James A. Banks as a partial requirement for the course EDC&I 469, University of Washington, Seattle.

U.S. Bureau of the Census (1998*). Statistical Abstract of the United States: 1998* (118th ed.). Washington, DC.: U.S. Government Printing Office.

11 Teaching Decision-Making and Social Action Skills

The multicultural curriculum should help students develop the ability to make reflective decisions so they can resolve personal problems and, through social action, influence public policy and develop a sense of political efficacy (Banks & Banks, with Clegg, 1999; Lewis, 1991). Many ethnic studies units and lessons emphasize the memorization and testing of isolated historical facts about shadowy ethnic heroes of questionable historical significance. In these types of curricula, ethnic content is merely an extension of the traditional curriculum.

The multicultural curriculum should have goals that are consistent with the needs of a diverse and complex society. We live in a world society that is beset with serious social and human problems. Effective solutions to these problems can be found only by an active and informed citizenry capable of making sound public decisions. The school should play an important role in educating citizens capable of making reflective decisions on social issues and taking effective actions to help solve them.

Elements of Reflective Decision-Making

Decision-making consists of several components, including the derivation of knowledge, prediction, value analysis and clarification, the synthesis of knowledge and values and the affirmation of a course of action (see Figure 11.1). All decisions consist of knowledge, valuing, and prediction components, but reflective decisions must also satisfy other requirements. To make a reflective decision, the decision-maker must use the scientific method to attain knowledge. The knowledge must not only be *scientific*, it must also be *interdisciplinary* and must cut across disciplinary lines. Knowledge from any one discipline is insufficient to help us make reflective decisions. To make reflective decisions about social issues, such as about ways to reduce racial segregation, citizens must view problems from the perspectives of such disciplines as sociology, economics, political science, and anthropology. The perspectives of any one discipline are too limited to guide reflective decision-making and action. Racial segregation, which is increasing within

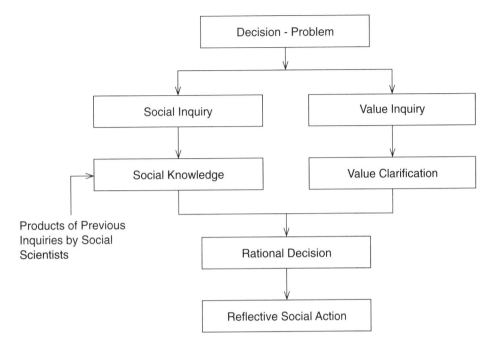

FIGURE 11.1   The Decision-Making Process

(*Source:* Adapted from *Teaching Strategies for the Social Studies: Decision-Making and Citizen Action,* 5th ed. by James A. Banks & Cherry A. McGee Banks with Ambrose A. Clegg, Jr. © 1999, New York: Longman. Reprinted by permission of Addison Wesley Educational Publishers, Inc.)

the nation and its schools (Orfield, Easton, & The Harvard Project, 1996), is a problem that deserves citizen action.

This chapter consists of a teaching unit based on the decision-making model described in Figure 11.1. The key question in this sample unit is: *Should institutions establish public policies that acknowledge and support racial, ethnic, and cultural diversity?*

Some Subissues Related to the Major Problem

There is a wide range of questions related to racial, ethnic, and cultural diversity in a pluralistic society that students can state and research. Housing discrimination, Afrocentrism (Asante, 1987), interracial marriage, and affirmative action (Edley, 1996) are some of the key issues and problems the class can explore when studying about ethnicity and race. Specific problems related to the major question in this unit include:

■ Should students of color be judged by different criteria than Whites when applying for employment and admission to colleges and universities?

- Should institutions practice affirmative action for the hiring and admission of women and people of color?
- Should persons of color be permitted to establish separate facilities and organizations in publicly supported institutions?
- Should busing be used to desegregate public schools?
- Should interracial and interethnic marriage be encouraged and socially accepted?
- Should all-male African American academies be supported with public funds?

Stages in Considering This Issue

Gathering Scientific Data

To make a reflective decision on a social issue such as *whether institutions should establish public policies that acknowledge and support racial, ethnic, and cultural diversity,* students need to acquire knowledge. However, decisions can be no better than the knowledge on which they are based. To make reflective decisions, students must study high-level concepts and generalizations. Generalizations can be taught in a variety of ways. However, it is necessary for students to use the scientific method to derive generalizations needed for decision-making. When planning lessons to help students gain knowledge, the teacher should identify social science and related generalizations that will help them make reflective decisions. Concepts should be selected from several disciplines, such as sociology, anthropology, history, and geography. *Discrimination, assimilation, ethnic group, culture, powerlessness,* and *separatism* are key concepts related to racial, ethnic, and cultural diversity. After key concepts are identified, organizing (or key) generalizations related to the concepts are identified, and subideas related to the organizing generalizations and to the content chosen for study are stated. (A detailed example of this type of curriculum planning is discussed at considerable length in two other publications—Banks, 1997; Banks & Banks with Clegg, 1999.)

Value Inquiry

After the students have had an opportunity to derive social science generalizations related to a social issue, they should undertake lessons that will enable them to *identify, analyze,* and *clarify* their values related to these generalizations. Value lessons should be conducted in an open classroom atmosphere so the students will be willing to express their beliefs freely and to examine them openly. If the teacher is authoritarian, the students will not express their feelings and attitudes. Beliefs that are unexpressed cannot be examined openly. Because of the way in which most students view teachers, it is a good idea for teachers to withhold their own views on controversial issues until the students have had an opportunity to express their beliefs.

When teachers reveal their position on a social issue, many students make statements they believe teachers want them to make rather than say things they actually believe. The teacher who opens a discussion on interracial marriage or housing discrimination by saying that everybody should have the right to marry whomever they please or that laws that prohibit housing discrimination violate a seller's constitutional rights cannot expect the students to state opposing beliefs. Some students will openly disagree with the teacher, but most will be reluctant to disagree openly. I am not suggesting that teachers should not state their positions on issues. However, experience suggests that when teachers openly express their views early in class discussions, the dialogue usually becomes stifled or slanted in one direction.

Decision-Making and Social Action

After students have derived social science generalizations and have clarified their values regarding the social issue, the teacher should ask them to list possible actions they could take regarding racial, ethnic, and cultural diversity in their school and community and to predict the possible consequences of each alternative. The alternatives and consequences that the students identify should be realistic and based on the knowledge they have mastered during the scientific phase of the unit. Alternatives and consequences should be thoughtful, predictive statements and not ignorant guesses or wishful thinking. After the students have discussed and weighed alternative courses of action, they should decide on courses of action most consistent with their own values and implement them within their school or community. For example, the students, or some of them, may decide that racial, ethnic, and cultural diversity should be important public policy goals in a pluralistic society but that such diversity does not exist within their school. They might design and implement a plan to increase ethnic and racial harmony and interactions in their school. Figure 11.2 summarizes the major steps discussed for studying a social issue.

The Origin of the Issue

The teacher can begin a study of the key issues discussed in this chapter by asking the students to search the Internet and find web sites that deal with such issues as housing discrimination, affirmative action, job discrimination, and the experiences of students of color on predominantly White school and university campuses. The students can also find items, news stories, and features dealing with these issues in newspapers and magazines.

The Definition of Key Concepts

When studying problems related to racial, ethnic, and cultural diversity, the class should clarify the definitions of key terms and reach general agreement about

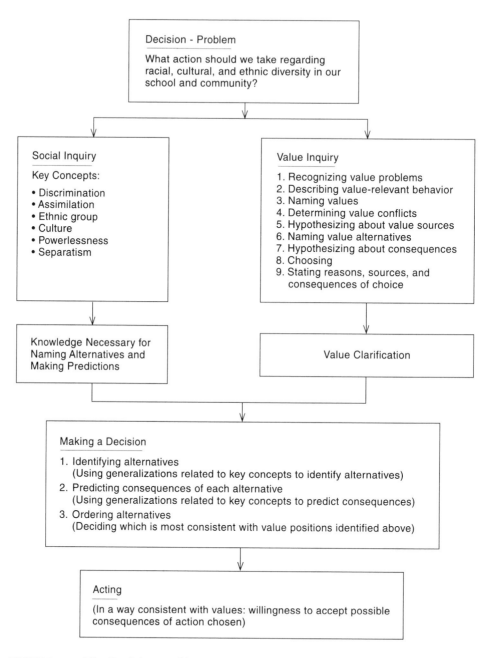

FIGURE 11.2   The Decision-Making Process

(*Source:* Adapted from *Teaching Strategies for the Social Studies: Decision-Making and Citizen Action,* 5th ed. by James A. Banks & Cherry A. McGee Banks with Ambrose A. Clegg, Jr. © 1999, New York: Longman. Reprinted by permission of Addison Wesley Publishers, Inc.)

what these terms mean. Terms such as *integration, race, desegregation, separatism, racism, discrimination,* and *cultural pluralism* are examples of key concepts that should be defined when policies related to racial, ethnic, and cultural diversity are studied. Several of these terms are discussed below.

Some writers make a distinction between *integration* and *desegregation.* They define *desegregation* as the mere physical mixing of different racial and ethnic groups. *Integration,* for these writers, means much more. It occurs only when mutual respect and acceptance develop between different racial and ethnic groups that are members of the same institutions.

Separatism is sometimes said to exist when ethnic groups that are excluded from the mainstream society establish ethnic organizations and institutions to meet their exclusive needs. Students can find and discuss other definitions of separatism and identify instances of it within their communities. When discussing separatism, the class should try to distinguish *separatism* and *segregation*. These terms are highly related and are often confused. Separatist institutions are designed to help an ethnic group attain self-determination and political power and to enhance its ethnic culture. Segregated institutions in *minority communities* are usually created by the dominant society in order to keep minorities marginalized. These types of institutions are designed and controlled by the powerful groups in a society and not by the ethnic minority community. Thus, *separatist* and *segregated* institutions in minority communities are fundamentally different in structure and function.

Students will also need to define a *culturally pluralistic society.* We can define a culturally pluralistic society as an open society in which individuals are able to take full advantage of the social, economic, and educational advantages of a society and yet are able to maintain their unique ethnic identities and allegiances. Individuals would not necessarily have to become assimilated into the dominant culture in order to satisfy their survival needs.

The examples cited above merely suggest the kinds of working definitions students can formulate for some of the key concepts in this unit. Many other examples and definitions could be given. It is extremely important for students to know how the concepts they are using are defined by themselves and other people. Without a clear understanding of the key terms they are using, their most diligent research efforts will be frustrated.

Hypotheses

Students can formulate many hypotheses related to racial, ethnic, and cultural diversity when studying public policies related to these concepts. What follows is a list of possible hypotheses.

If persons of color are required to meet the same qualifications as Whites, then most institutions and firms will remain predominantly White and segregated. This hypothesis is based on the assumption that most persons of color, perhaps for a variety of reasons, will be unable to compete successfully with Whites for jobs and in educational institutions if present criteria and methods are used to screen and select employees and students. An opposing hypothesis might state that if persons of color are required to have the same qualifications as Whites, they would eventually be able to satisfy them because persons of color could and would obtain the experiences and knowledge needed to do so.

If institutions and firms establish quotas for persons of color, some qualified minorities and Whites will be discriminated against. This hypothesis assumes that there are more qualified persons of color for positions and slots than quotas would provide for, that some nonqualified persons of color may be hired in preference to qualified ones, and that if a White and a person of color are equally qualified, firms with quotas would hire the individuals of color until their quotas had been attained. It also assumes that qualified persons of color would not be hired once such quotas were reached. A different hypothesis might suggest that firms and schools will recruit and hire persons of color only if they are required to fulfill quotas.

If open laws against housing discrimination are enacted and enforced, then Whites will be forced to sell their homes at a tremendous loss. This hypothesis assumes that property values are greatly reduced when individuals of color move into predominantly White neighborhoods. A related hypothesis might state that if laws against housing discrimination are not enacted and enforced, housing segregation will increase.

If creative ways are not used to desegregate the public schools, then school segregation will continue to increase in the nation. This hypothesis assumes that because ethnic and racial groups tend to live in segregated communities, school segregation will continue to increase in the nation unless thoughtful ways are found to increase the number of schools that are racially and ethnically mixed. Another hypothesis might state that the best way to promote racial and ethnic mixing in the schools is to increase social class mobility among ethnic groups of color.

Testing the Hypotheses

The students will need to gather data to test the hypotheses they have formulated. Like any other problems related to human behavior, problems in race relations are exceedingly complex. If is difficult to say "If A then B" when studying human behavior. The effects of affirmative action, for example, will vary greatly depending on the way in which it is implemented, the commitment that the leaders of the organization have to making it work, and the attitudes that existed in the institutions among the different racial and ethnic groups before it was implemented (Bowen & Bok, 1998; Lawrence & Matsuda, 1997).

When students are gathering data to test hypotheses related to diversity, they should be helped to see how difficult it is to establish relationships with a high degree of reliability. Another caveat is in order. Much information and data related to ethnic and racial problems reflect the positionality or perspective of the writer. This tendency is exemplifed by the literature on affirmative action. D'Souza (1995) strongly opposes affirmative action. Authors who have written books describing the benefits of affirmative action include Edley (1996), Ezorsky (1991), and Lawrence and Matsuda (1997). Bowen and Bok (1998) provide the first data-based study on the effects of affirmative action. Their data show that affirmative action for African Americans in higher education has been quite positive and successful.

Some Tentative Conclusions

The students *might* reach the following four tentative conclusions after they have studied issues and policies related to racial, ethnic, and cultural diversity and examined their values regarding race relations.

1. Persons of color should be required to have the same qualifications for jobs and to enter college as any other persons. However, the ways in which these qualifications are determined should be modified so they reflect ethnic diversity and so that individuals of color will not be victimized by discriminatory tests and other selective devices based exclusively on the dominant culture. Institutions and firms should aggressively recruit workers of color to increase the pool from which they can select. This type of policy will, in the long run, result in the hiring of individuals of color who are as qualified as their White counterparts. In the short run, however, it might mean that businesses and universities will not be able to increase the numbers of individuals of color in their populations at a very rapid rate.

2. Institutions should not establish quotas for persons of color, but they should implement affirmative action programs that will enable them to recruit people of color aggressively and give preference to them if persons of color and Whites are equally qualified. The goal should be to have an integrated staff or student body that includes people who represent diverse ethnic and racial groups, and not to get a specific number from each ethnic or racial group. This policy will result in the employment of workers of color but will not restrict their number or encourage the hiring of individuals of color who are less qualified than White employees, or the admission of students of color who cannot succeed in college.

3. Laws against housing discrimination should be enacted in all communities to ensure that every person has the opportunity to buy the house he or she wants and can afford regardless of race or ethnic group. If effectively enforced, laws that prohibit housing discrimination are not likely to result in many interracial communities because Whites usually move out of neighborhoods when numbers of people of color move into them. No legal actions should be taken to prevent freedom of movement by Whites. However, planned interracial communities should be established because people who grow up in interracial communities have more positive racial attitudes and are more likely to live in interracial neighborhoods and to send their children to interracial schools (Schofield, 1995).

4. The establishment of interracial schools should be a major societal goal. Any reasonable plans, including those requiring transportation, should be implemented if they are needed to establish and maintain desegregated schools. Parents opposed to interracial schools and/or busing should have the right to take their children out of the public schools. However, they should not be allowed to dictate or unduly influence school policy. Major societal goals and democratic values (such as equality and justice) should take precedence over the wishes of special interest and pressure groups. If a school district takes a strong position vis-à-vis interracial schools and busing, hostile pressure groups, which are usually small but

vocal minorities, will eventually accept the school's policy and lose both community support and wide public forums for their views.

Suggested Methods for Teaching about Racial, Ethnic, and Cultural Diversity and Public Policies

Initiating the Unit

The teacher can begin a study of racial, ethnic, and cultural diversity and public policies by reading the class a current case study taken from the Internet or a newspaper that deals with a controversial policy and/or issue related to racial, ethnic, or cultural diversity. An example of such a case study taken from the Internet is Proposition 200 in Washington state. This proposition, which was modeled after California's Proposition 209, was approved by Washington's voters in November 1998. Here is an excerpt from the Internet that describes Proposition 209:

> Opponents of affirmative action have apparently gathered enough signatures to make Washington state the next battleground in the war over racial preferences, Reuters reports.
>
> Supporters of Initiative 200, which would ban race and gender preferences in government hiring, contracting and university admissions, delivered petitions with more than 284,000 voter signatures to the state capitol—well over the 180,000 needed.
>
> Commenting on the Reuter report, Kathleen Taylor, Executive Director of the ACLU of Washington, said that "affirmative action programs are important tools to overcome the effects of discrimination." (*Source:* American Civil Liberties Union News)

Questions

1. Why did Reuters use the term *racial preferences?* Is this an accurate or unbiased way to refer to affirmative action? Why or why not?

2. What effect will banning affirmative action have on the enrollment of African Americans and Latinos in colleges and universities in Washington state?

3. Proposition 200 was passed by a wide margin in Washington state. Why do you think it passed by such a wide margin?

Social Science Inquiry

When the teacher has initiated a study of racial, ethnic, and cultural diversity with a case study such as the one above, the students should study historical information that will enable them to understand the forces that have shaped public policy regarding racial, ethnic, and cultural diversity. Attention should be given to the legalization of segregation that took place in the decades after the Civil War in the

United States. Ask individual students to prepare and present reports on the following topics:

- the Black codes
- the poll tax
- the grandfather clause
- the Dred Scott Decision
- *Plessy* v. *Ferguson*
- Proposition 209 in California (which ended affirmative action in California's public institutions)
- *Hopwood* v. *State of Texas* (a district court case that ended affirmative action at the University of Texas Law School)

When these reports are presented to the class, the students should discuss these questions: Why did segregation become widespread in the post–Civil War period? Why was it legalized? How did these laws affect African Americans? White Americans? Latinos? Asian Americans?

1. Ask the students to pretend they are in the Supreme Court in 1896 and are hearing the case of Homer Plessy, a mulatto who complains that he has to sit in separate cars on trains passing through his native state of Louisiana. Plessy argues that this type of segregation violates protection guaranteed to him by the Fourteenth Amendment to the Constitution. Ask individual students to role play the Supreme Court justices, Homer Plessy, and the prosecuting and defense attorneys. After the arguments on both sides have been presented to the Court, the justices should deliberate and then rule on the case. After the role-play situation, the class should discuss these ideas:

   a. Ways in which their simulated court was similar to and different from the actual Supreme Court in 1896.
   b. Whether the role players were successfully able to assume the attitudes and viewpoints of people who lived in 1896.
   c. What the "separate but equal" doctrine meant in 1896 and and how it relates to the quest for affirmative action today.

2. At the turn of the previous century, two major civil rights organizations were formed to fight for the rights of African Americans: the National Association for the Advancement of Colored People (NAACP) and the National Urban League. Also during this period two major civil rights leaders became nationally eminent, Booker T. Washington and W. E. B. Du Bois. Washington and Du Bois became strong opponents because they held opposing views about racial equality and the ways in which African Americans should be educated. Ask the class to read Washington's autobiography, *Up from Slavery,* and selections from W. E. B. Du Bois's *The Souls of Black Folks.* The class should discuss the views of these two men and determine which of their ideas were valid and which were not. After the class has discussed the views of Washington and Du Bois, ask two students to role play a debate between the two men regarding steps African Americans should take to achieve racial equality.

3. Most national civil rights organizations in the early 1900s were interracial. Ask the students to do required readings on the history and development of the NAACP and the National Urban League. When they have completed the readings, they should compare and contrast these two organizations with the Niagara Movement and earlier Black protest movements, such as the Negro Convention Movement and the African Civilization Society. Particular attention should be paid to (1) reasons the organizations emerged, (2) who made policy and held key positions within them, (3) types of problems that arose within the organizations, (4) the major goals of the organizations, and (5) ways in which the organizations succeeded or failed and why.

4. Black separatist movements developed early in U.S. history. Some of the earliest were led by such African Americans as Martin R. Delaney and Paul Cuffee. Ask the students to research the lives of these men and to present dramatizations that show ways in which they were advocates of Black nationalism. Marcus Garvey, another Black separatist, attained eminence in the 1930s. Ask the class to read his biography, *Black Moses,* by E. D. Cronon, and to list ways in which Garvey was similar to and different from earlier Black nationalist leaders.

5. In the 1930s, 1940s, 1950s, and 1960s racial segregation received a number of severe blows that culminated in the *Brown* decision of 1954 and the Civil Rights Act of 1964. Ask the students to develop a chronology that lists the major civil rights legislation enacted between 1930 and 1964. After the chronology is developed, the students should discuss these two questions:

    a. What were the major social and political factors that led to the passage of each of these bills?

    b. Why has racial segregation actually increased in U.S. society since the 1960s even though so many civil rights bills have been enacted?

6. The major goal of the civil rights movement in the 1950s was to desegregate public accommodation facilities and other institutions. Action tactics and court battles achieved much desegregation. However, by 1965, many African Americans, especially young African American activists, were disillusioned with the attainments of the movement and realized that integration alone would not eliminate the African Americans' major social, economic, and political problems. These young activists felt that both the goals and tactics of the movement should be changed (Halberstam, 1998). They issued a call for "Black Power!" The students can gain an understanding of the concept of Black power by reading *Black Power: The Politics of Liberation in America* by Stokely Carmichael and Charles V. Hamilton. Many Black integrationists rejected the views of Black power advocates. Ask the class to research the views of the men and women listed below and to simulate a national convention of African American civil rights leaders in which they discuss the problem, "What should be the future course of African Americans: Integration or Separatism?"

(a) Martin Luther King, Jr.
(b) Roy Wilkins
(c) Roy Innis
(d) Angela Davis
(e) Stokely Carmichael
(f) H. Rap Brown
(g) Vernon Jordan
(h) Rev. Jesse Jackson
(i) Shirley Chisholm
(j) Bobby Seale
(k) Huey Newton
(l) Imamu Amiri Baraka
(m) Richard G. Hatcher
(n) Julian Bond
(o) Ronald V. Dellums
(p) Barbara Jordan

Individual students should be asked to research and play the roles of each leader in the convention. After the major question has been discussed, the convention participants should develop an action agenda for African Americans in the 2000s that they all can endorse.

Value Inquiry

After the students have had an opportunity to gather factual data related to racial, ethnic, and cultural diversity, they should examine their own values, attitudes, and beliefs. A wide variety of strategies and materials can be used to help students examine and clarify their values. Some valuing exercises appropriate for studying racial, ethnic, and cultural diversity are given below. These strategies are adapted from techniques developed by Simon, Howe, and Kirschenbaum (1978).

Spread of Opinion. The teacher should divide the class into several small groups and give each group a piece of paper with one of these issues written on it:

- busing to achieve desegregated schools
- interracial marriage
- laws against housing discrimination
- affirmative action
- separatism
- interracial adoptions
- interracial dating
- segregated fraternities and sororities
- African American all-male academies and schools

Each group should identify a number of positions that can be taken on its issue. Each group member should write a statement defending one position, whether in agreement or not. When the statements have been completed, the students should discuss each issue and state their own positions on it.

Unfinished Sentences.   The teacher should duplicate the following list of statements and give a copy to each student. The students should be asked to complete the statements with the words and phrases they first think of when they read each statement. After the students have completed the statements, the teacher should divide the class into small groups and ask the students to discuss, "What I learned about myself from this exercise."

1. If I were African American (or White, Mexican American, etc.) I would…
2. Most African Americans are…
3. If an African American (or a Mexican American, etc.) family moved into my neighborhood, I would…
4. If I were forced to ride a bus to a desegregated school each day, I would…
5. If my sister married an African American (or a White, Latino, etc.), I would…
6. People of other races make me feel…
7. A racist is a person who…
8. If I were called a racist, I would…
9. Most Whites are…
10. Special programs created for people of color are…
11. Persons of color who participate in special programs are…
12. People who are opposed to interracial marriage are…
13. People of color who score poorly on IQ tests are…

Strongly Agree/Strongly Disagree.   The teacher should duplicate the following list of statements and give a copy to each student. Ask the students to indicate the extent to which they agree or disagree with the statements by writing one of the following letter combinations in front of each statement:

- SA = Strongly agree
- AS = Agree somewhat
- DS = Disagree somewhat
- SD = Strongly disagree

After the students have responded to each statement, divide the class into small groups and ask the students to discuss the responses in their groups.

_____ 1. I am prejudiced toward some racial and ethnic groups.
_____ 2. I would not live in a predominantly African American (or White, Latino, etc.) neighborhood.
_____ 3. Most Latinos are poor because they are lazy.
_____ 4. Most Whites are racists.
_____ 5. I would encourage my sister to marry an African American (or a White, Latino, etc.) if she wanted to.
_____ 6. Persons of color should meet the same college admission requirements as Whites.
_____ 7. IQ tests are unfair to persons of color and should be abandoned.

_____ **8.** Students should not be required to be bused to desegregated schools.
_____ **9.** Universities and firms should establish quotas for persons of color.
_____ **10.** White fraternities and sororities should be required to admit African Americans, Latinos, Asian Americans, and other persons of color.

Values Grid.   An effective summary valuing activity for this unit is the valuing grid in Table 11.1. Make copies for each student.

Ask the students to make brief notes about how they feel about each of the eleven issues listed in the table. Each issue will have been discussed during earlier parts of the unit. The following seven questions are taken from the valuing strategy developed by Simon et al. (1978). List the following questions on the board and explain each one to the students.

1. Are you proud of (do you prize or cherish) your position?
2. Have you *publicly affirmed* your position?
3. Have you chosen your position from *alternatives?*
4. Have you chosen your position after *thoughtful consideration* of the pros and cons and consequences?
5. Have you chosen your position *freely?*
6. Have you *acted* on or done anything about your beliefs?
7. Have you acted with *repetition,* pattern, or consistency on this issue?

TABLE 11.1   Race Relations Values Grid

Issue	1	2	3	4	5	6	7
1. Forced busing							
2. Interracial housing							
3. Interracial marriage							
4. Interracial dating							
5. Racial quotas							
6. Segregated schools							
7. Afrocentrism							
8. White racism							
9. Affirmative-action programs							
10. Black English							

(*Source:* Copyright © 2001 by Allyn and Bacon, Inc. Reproduction of this material is restricted to use with *Cultural Diversity and Education: Foundations, Curriculum and Teaching,* 4th ed., by James A. Banks.)

Ask the students to write *Yes* or *No* in each square in the chart to indicate their responses to each of the seven questions for each issue. When the students have individually completed the grid, they should break up into groups of threes and discuss as many of their responses as they would like to discuss.

Decision-Making and Social Action

When the students have gathered scientific data and clarified their values, they should identify *alternative courses of actions* they can take regarding racial, ethnic, and cultural diversity in a diverse society, and the *possible consequences* of each course of action. Individual and/or groups should then formulate plans to implement courses of action that are most consistent with their values. Below are possible action projects that some students may decide to implement.

Action Projects

1. Conducting a survey to determine the kinds of jobs most persons of color have in local hotels, restaurants, and firms, and, if necessary, urging local businesses to hire more individuals of color in top-level positions. Conducting boycotts of local businesses that refuse to hire persons of color in top-level positions.

2. Conducting a survey to determine the treatment of ethnic groups in courses and textbooks in the school and recommending ways in which the school curriculum can become more integrated; suggesting that a permanent review board be established to examine teaching materials and determine how they present ethnic groups. Presenting these recommendations to appropriate school officials and pressuring them to act on the recommendations.

3. Conducting a survey to determine the local ethnic organizations and leaders within the community. Inviting some of them to participate in school programs and projects, such as assemblies and classes.

4. Conducting a survey to determine whether the school and public libraries have adequate collections of books and materials about ethnic groups. If necessary, recommending books and materials to be purchased and pressuring the libraries to buy them.

5. Conducting a survey to determine what local laws exist (and how they are enforced) regarding housing discrimination and discrimination in public accommodations, and, if necessary, developing recommendations regarding changes to be made in the laws or in how they should be implemented. Presenting these recommendations to appropriate public officials and pressuring them to act on the recommendations.

6. If the school is racially segregated: Developing plans for exchange activities and programs with a school whose population is predominantly of another race, ethnic, or religious group.

7. Conducting a survey to determine the racial and ethnic composition of the school staff (including secretaries, teachers, janitors, etc.) and, if necessary, recommending appropriate action to take to make the school more racially integrated. Presenting these recommendations to appropriate school officials and pressuring them to act on the recommendations.

8. Conducting a survey to determine whether the posters, bulletin boards, photographs, and school holidays reflect the ethnic diversity within society and, if necessary, implementing a plan to make the total school environment more integrated and multicultural.

9. If the school is interracial: Conducting a survey to determine if there are examples of racial conflict and tension within the school. For example, do African American, White, and Latino kids tend to sit with their own ethnic groups in the school cafeteria (Tatum, 1997). If they do, why? If there are ethnic and racial tensions within the school, formulating and implementing plans to alleviate them.

Summary

This chapter illustrates how teachers can help students develop decision-making and social action skills by studying the possible consequences of public policies related to racial, ethnic, and cultural diversity. The decision-making model illustrated in this chapter consists of social science inquiry, value inquiry, the synthesis of knowledge and values, and reflective decision-making and social action. The sample unit illustrates how each component of the decision-making model can be implemented. Possible actions the students might take related to racial, ethnic, and cultural diversity in their school and community are also described.

REFERENCES

Asante, M. K. (1987). *The Afrocentric Idea.* Philadelphia: Temple University Press.

Banks, J. A. (1997). *Teaching Strategies for Ethnic Studies* (6th ed.). Boston: Allyn and Bacon.

Banks, J. A., & Banks, C. A. M., with Clegg, A. A., Jr. (1999). *Teaching Strategies for the Social Studies: Decision-Making and Citizen Action.* New York: Longman.

Bowen, W. G., & Bok, D. (1998). *The Shape of the River: Long-Term Consequences of Considering Race in College and University Admissions.* Princeton, NJ: Princeton University Press.

D'Souza, D. (1995). *The End of Racism: Principles for a Multiracial Society.* New York: The Free Press.

Edley, C., Jr. (1996). *Not All Black and White: Affirmative Action and American Values.* New York: Hill and Wang.

Ezorsky, G. (1991). *Racism and Justice: The Case for Affirmative Action.* Ithaca, NY: Cornell University Press.

Halberstam, D. (1998). *The Children.* New York: Random House.

Lawrence, C. R. III, & Matsuda, M. J. (1997). *We Won't Go Back: Making the Case for Affirmative Action.* Boston: Houghton Mifflin.

Lewis, B. A. (1991). (Edited by P. Espeland). *The Kid's Guide to Social Action.* Minneapolis: Free Spirit Publishing.

Orfield, G., Eaton, S. E., & The Harvard Project on School Desegregation. (1996). *Dismantling Desegregation: The Quiet Reversal of Brown v. Board of Education.* New York: The New Press.

Schofield, J. W. (1995). Review of Research on School Desegregation's Impact on Elementary and Secondary School Students. In J. A. Banks & C. A. M. Banks (Eds.), *Handbook of Research on Multicultural Education* (pp. 597–616). New York: Macmillan.

Simon, S. B., Howe, L. W., & Kirschenbaum, H. (1978). *Values Clarification. A Handbook of Practical Strategies for Teachers and Students.* New York: Hart Publishing. (Reprinted with permission of A & W Publishers, Inc. Copyright 1972; copyright 1978 by Hart Publishing Co., Inc., pp. 35–37, 241–257, 252–254.)

Tatum, B. D. (1997). *"Why Are All the Black Kids Sitting Together in the Cafeteria?" And Other Conversations about Race.* New York: Basic Books.

12 The Curriculum, Cross-Cultural Teaching, and Social Change

This chapter describes the visions and goals that transformative scholars had for multicultural studies during the civil rights movement and the extent to which these goals have been realized. The chapter also identifies the factors that have limited curriculum reform. Finally, the text proposes a reform strategy that views the teacher as a change agent and cultural mediator. The cross-cultural teacher interprets diverse cultures for all students and helps them understand why social change is essential if we are to close the gap between our nation's democratic ideals and its realities.

Life-Style versus Life-Chance Approaches

During the early phases of cultural revitalization movements, leaders insist that their heroes and cultures become a part of the school, college, and university curriculum. Educators often respond to these demands quickly and without careful planning and sufficient staff development. As a result, cultural heroes such as Booker T. Washington and Eleanor Roosevelt are inserted into the curriculum along with bits and pieces of content about the history and traditions of groups.

This *additive approach* to the study of cultural content arises from several assumptions that prevent curriculum transformation, perpetuate stereotypes and misconceptions of cultures, and prevent teachers from dealing in-depth with such concepts as racial and gender discrimination, class stratification, and the reforms needed to empower marginalized groups. Figure 12.1 conceptualizes the additive approach as Model B. The curriculum is *transformative* when it exemplifies Models C and D; at these phases students view concepts and issues from diverse perspectives within the United States (Model C) and the world (Model D). Model A is the mainstream curriculum, in which concepts and issues are viewed only from mainstream perspectives.

When educators add cultural heroes and bits and pieces of cultural content to the curriculum, the assumption is made that such heroes and content are not integral parts of mainstream U.S. history and society. Consequently, it is also assumed

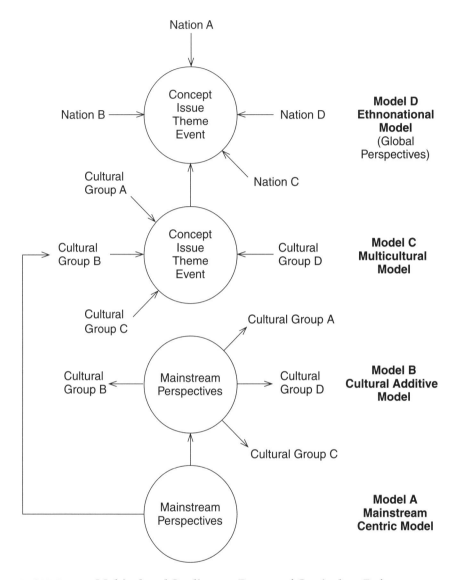

FIGURE 12.1   Multicultural Studies as a Process of Curriculum Reform
Multicultural studies is conceptualized as a process of curriculum reform that can lead from a total mainstream perspective on a society's history and culture (Model A), to multicultural perspectives as additives to the major curriculum focus (Model B), to a completely multicultural curriculum in which every event, concept, and issue is viewed from the perspectives of different cultural and ethnic groups (Model C). In Model D, the ultimate goal of curriculum reform, students view events, concepts, and issues from the perspectives and points of view of various groups within different nations.

that it is sufficient to add special units and festivals in order to teach about cultural groups and their experiences. Particularly in the elementary grades, cultural content is often taught with special lessons and pageants on holidays and birthdays. African Americans often dominate lessons during Afro-American History Month and women during Women's History Month. These groups are often largely invisible in the curriculum during the rest of the year. Even though groups of color and women are now a more integral part of textbooks than they were 20 years ago, their presence is neither comprehensive nor sufficiently integrated into the total curriculum (Sleeter & Grant, 1991).

The infusion of bits and pieces of cultural content into the curriculum not only reinforces the idea that some cultural groups are not integral parts of U.S. society, but it also results in the trivialization of their histories and cultures. The study of the foods eaten by Mexican Americans or of Indian teepees will not help students develop a sophisticated understanding of Mexican American culture (Gonzales, 1999) and of the tremendous cultural diversity among Native Americans (Champagne, 1994). This kind of teaching about groups often perpetuates misconceptions and stereotypes about them and leads well-meaning but misinformed teachers to believe they have integrated their curricula with cultural content and helped their students better understand diverse groups.

Superficial teaching about cultural groups and their histories may do more harm than good. Excluding a study of certain groups in the curriculum might be preferable to the trivialization and marginalization of their cultures and life-styles. The distortion of cultural and ethnic groups that has taken place in the schools has led some critics of the way multicultural education is often practiced to argue that teaching about cultural groups in the schools should focus on their *life-chances* rather than on their *life-styles* (Lee, 1998; Moodley, 1995; Nieto, 1999).

A curriculum that focuses on life-chances describes the ways structurally excluded cultural groups are victimized by social, economic, and political variables such as institutionalized racism, sexism, class stratification, and political powerlessness. Critics of multicultural education who make this argument are concerned that a focus on cultures and life-styles not only trivializes the cultures of groups, but also diverts attention from the real causes of their structural exclusion. They believe that a focus on life-styles might cause majority groups to blame the victims for their victimization and thus help entrench institutionalized stereotypes. This approach to multicultural education has been described as the "museum approach" that reinforces an "us and them" feeling.

Teachers do not need to decide whether they will approach the teaching of cultural content from a life-style or life-chance perspective. Both cultural knowledge and knowledge about why many cultural groups are victimized by institutionalized discrimination and class stratification are needed in a transformative curriculum that accurately reflects the experience of diverse groups. Both perspectives are needed to help students gain a comprehensive and in-depth understanding of the experiences of different cultural groups in the United States and in other nations.

Teaching accurately and sensitively about the experiences of different cultural groups is a complex and difficult task. It involves not just adding cultural and ethnic content to the curriculum and viewing it from mainstream perspectives and points of view. It also involves changing the curriculum in ways that enable students to see concepts and events from the perspectives of different groups (Models C and D in Figure 12.1). To teach about diverse cultures accurately, teachers must help students understand that cultural groups, especially within a modernized society such as the United States, are dynamic, holistic, and changing processes (Berger, 1995).

Students also need to understand that a culture consists of many aspects or variables, such as symbols, language, and behavior, and that an individual member of a culture may exemplify the characteristics of a group completely or hardly at all (see Chapter 4). Consequently, knowing what have been described as the cultural characteristics of boys (Gurian, 1996; Pollack, 1998), of women (Gilligan, 1982; Goldberger et al., 1996), gays (Herdt, 1992), or the deaf (Padden & Humphries, 1988) may give teachers few clues about the behavior and values of an individual student. Individual students are members of several groups at the same time.

The Search for New Perspectives

Major goals of the cultural revival movements of the 1960s and 1970s were not only to include more information about the cultures and history of marginalized groups in the curriculum, but also to infuse the curriculum with new perspectives, frames of reference, and values. However, in textbooks and in teaching, even though cultural events and heroes are often added to the curriculum, the interpretations and perspectives on these events and heroes often remain those of mainstream historians and scholars (Banks, 1996). When concepts, events, and situations in the curriculum are viewed only or primarily from the perspectives of mainstream scholars and historians, students obtain a limited view of social reality and an incomplete understanding of the human experience. As James Baldwin (1985) perceptively points out in several incisive essays, White Americans cannot fully understand their history unless they study African American history from myriad perspectives because the histories of African Americans and Whites are intricately interwoven.

As discussed in Chapter 9, social and historical knowledge reflects the values, experiences, times, and social structure in which scholars are socialized and work. In a culturally, ethnically, and racially stratified society such as the United States (Conley, 1999), insiders within marginalized communities also influence the formulation of knowledge. Social scientists and historians who are insiders in the African American community and those who are outsiders are likely to agree on many observations about African American life and behavior; they also are likely to formulate some findings and interpretations that differ in significant ways. Many mainstream social scientists conducted studies of African Americans before the civil rights movements of the 1960s that were strongly attacked by African American social scientists in the 1970s (Ladner, 1973). Much of this controversy focused on historical interpretations of such topics as slavery and the Civil War, sociological interpretations of the African American family, and descriptions and interpretations of Black English and African American culture. Mainstream social scientists frequently described African American culture and life as disorganized, pathological, and deviant (Ladner, 1973). African American students were often labeled *culturally deprived* (Riessman, 1962). Traditional research assumptions, methods, and conclusions of mainstream social scientists often differed sharply from those of African American transformative scholars during this period (Banks, 1996; Ladner, 1973).

Even though culture, ethnicity, and race often influence the knowledge claims, research, and perspectives of social scientists and historians, these influences are complex and difficult to describe precisely. Individual women, gay people, or scholars of color may be influenced more by their class interests, commitment to scholarly objectivity, or other values than they are by culture, ethnicity, or race (Chavez, 1991; Steele, 1990). The revisionist and sensitive studies of African Americans by White social scientists such as Baratz (1970), Gutman (1964), and Genovese (1974) are cases in point, as are the more conservative analyses of the African American experience written by African American scholars such as Sowell (1984), Steele (1990), and Carter (1991).

Although the influences of culture, ethnicity, and class on social knowledge are complex and difficult to describe precisely, they are nonetheless significant and far-reaching. Insider perspectives on such important social and historical events as the Holocaust (Dawidowicz, 1981), the internment of Japanese Americans (Uchida, 1982), and the civil rights movements of the 1960s (Hampton & Fayer, 1990) provide students with insights, perspectives, and feelings about these events that cannot be gained from reading source materials or accounts by individuals who have experienced these events only from a distance. Scholars who are socialized within the communities in which these events are important parts of the social and cultural history are also likely to have perspectives on them that differ from those of mainstream scholars.

It is important for students to experience a curriculum that presents the histories of groups in accurate and sensitive ways, and from the perspectives of different groups. Such a curriculum is needed to help students understand the complexity of the human experience and how a nation's various groups have strongly influenced each other culturally and interacted within the social structure. Table 12.1 summarizes the dominant and desirable characteristics of multicultural studies.

The Extent of Institutionalization of Multicultural Education

Multicultural curriculum reforms are becoming institutionalized in the nation's schools, colleges, and universities. However, the reform has been cyclic and inconsistent rather than continuous. Periods of significant reform have been followed

TABLE 12.1   Dominant and Desirable Characteristics of Multicultural Studies

Dominant Characteristics	Desirable Characteristics
Focuses on isolated aspects of the histories and cultures of groups.	Describes the history and cultures of groups holistically.
Trivializes the histories and cultures of groups.	Describes the cultures of groups as dynamic wholes and processes of change.
Presents events, issues, and concepts primarily from mainstream perspectives and points of view.	Presents events, issues, and concepts from diverse cultural and ethnic perspectives.
Is Eurocentric: shows the development of America primarily as an extension of Europe into the Americas.	Is multidimensional and geocultural: shows how peoples and cultures came to America from many different parts of the world, including Asia and Africa, and the important role they played in developing U.S. society.
Content about cultural groups is an appendage to the regular or core curriculum.	Content about cultural groups is an integral part of the regular or core curriculum.
Marginalized cultures are described as deprived or pathological.	Marginalized cultures are described as different from mainstream Anglo culture but as normal and functional.
Concepts such as institutionalized racism, sexism, and class stratification are given little attention.	An important focus in on such concepts as institutionalized racism, sexism, and class stratification.
The curriculum is dominated by the assimilationist ideology. Pluralist and radical ideologies are either ignored or marginalized.	The curriculum reflects a multicultural ideology, with some attention given to radical ideas and concepts.
Focuses on lower-level factual knowledge, cultural heroes, and the recall of factual information.	Focuses on higher-level knowledge, such as concepts, generalizations, and theories.
Emphasizes the mastery of knowledge and cognitive outcomes.	Emphasizes decision-making and citizen action. Knowledge, decision-making, and action are important learning outcomes.
Encourages the acceptance of existing cultural, ethnic, and class stratification.	Focuses on social criticism, civic action, and change.

by periods of retrenchment (Banks & Banks, 1995). Most examples of blatant racism, sexism, and stereotypes of cultural groups have been deleted from textbooks and teaching materials (Sleeter & Grant, 1991). However, content about racial and cultural groups is not yet thoroughly integrated into the structure of the curriculum and into teaching. Teaching about cultural, ethnic, and racial groups is relegated in some schools to special units and holidays and are appendages to the main story of the development of U.S. society.

Most content about African Americans is studied when topics such as slavery, Reconstruction, and the civil rights movement of the 1960s are covered (Sleeter & Grant, 1991). A unilinear, Eurocentric approach is used most frequently to teach about the development of U.S. history and society. The story of the development of the United States is often told by describing the sojourn of the Europeans across the Atlantic to the Americas and then from the Atlantic to the Pacific oceans. The focus of the story is on European settlers, on the way they shaped America in their image, created a nation that promised freedom for all people, and made the United States a world power (Appleby, 1992). Groups of color, such as African Americans, Mexican Americans, and Native Americans, are discussed primarily at points at which they interacted with the Europeans in North America.

The Root of the Problem: Ideological Resistance

Educators offer many reasons they do not teach more about cultural, ethnic, and racial groups, including the following:

1. Our students are unaware of racial differences; we will merely create problems that don't exist if we teach ethnic content. All of our students, whether African American or White, are happy and like one another. They don't see colors or ethnic differences (Schofield, 1997).

2. We don't have any racial problems in our school and consequently don't need to teach about ethnic groups.

3. We don't teach about ethnic groups because we have so few of them attending our school.

4. Ethnic studies will negatively affect societal unity and the common national culture. It is divisive and will Balkanize the nation.

5. We don't have time to add more content to what we are already teaching. We can't finish the books and units we already have. Ethnic content will overload our curriculum.

6. We don't teach much about ethnic groups because we don't have the necessary materials. Our textbooks are inadequate.

7. We can't teach ethnic studies in our schools and colleges because most of our teachers are inadequately educated in this area of study. Many of them also have negative attitudes toward different racial, ethnic, and cultural groups. They would probably do more harm than good if they tried to teach about ethnic and racial groups.

8. The local community will strongly object if we teach about race and ethnicity in our schools.

9. We don't teach much about ethnic groups in our schools because ethnic studies scholarship is so political and polemical.

Some of these explanations, *but not most of them,* have a degree of validity and partially explain why multicultural content has not become completely institutionalized within the nation's schools, colleges, and universities. However, most of these explanations do not reveal the root of the problem. *Ideological and philosophical conflicts between pluralistic and mainstream educators (who are basically assimilationists) are the major reasons that educational reforms related to cultural and ethnic diversity have not become totally institutionalized within the nation's schools, colleges and universities.* In other words, the resistance to multicultural education is basically *ideological and political.* Many mainstream scholars and researchers, who have the most power, view multicultural education as threatening to their power positions. These scholars claim that multicultural education will Balkanize the nation-state (Schlesinger, 1991).

An *ideology* is a system of ideas, beliefs, traditions, principles, and myths held by a social group or society that reflects, rationalizes, and defends its particular social, political, and economic interests (Bullivant, 1986). Dominant cultural and ethnic groups develop ideologies to defend and rationalize their attitudes, goals, and social structure. Writes Bullivant (p. 103):

> In an analysis of ethnoculturally pluralistic societies the term *ideology* can be used to refer to the system of beliefs and values employed by a dominant ethnocultural group to legitimize its control over the life chances of subordinate ethnocultural groups.

Bullivant calls this situation a form of *cultural hegemony.*

The dominant ideology related to diversity in the United States has been described with several different concepts, including the *melting pot, Anglo-conformity,* and *cultural assimilation* (Gordon, 1964). This ideology—called cultural assimilation in Chapter 6—states that the diverse cultural and racial groups within the United States not only should but also eventually will abandon their unique cultural and ethnic characteristics and acquire those of Anglo or mainstream Americans. Robert E. Park (Coser, 1977), the eminent U.S. sociologist who played a key role in the development of the Chicago School of Sociology (Bulmer, 1984), believed that race and cultural relations were characterized by four inevitable phases: *contact, conflict, accommodation,* and *assimilation.*

Park's notion about inevitable cultural assimilation dominated U.S. social science until the ethnic revival movements emerged in the 1960s (Glazer & Moynihan, 1975). As pointed out in Chapter 6, the assimilationist conception is not so much wrong as it is flawed and incomplete (Apter, 1977). In the late 1960s most groups of color had become disillusioned with assimilation as a societal goal and with the assimilationist ideology. They began to seriously question not only its desirability but also its latent function. Many leaders and scholars of color began to view it as a tool of dominant cultural groups used to rationalize and maintain their power and to keep marginalized cultural groups content with the status quo and yet striving to attain impossible goals (Sizemore, 1973).

Teaching for Social Change

A major goal of education has traditionally been to socialize students so they would accept without question the existing ideologies, institutions, and practices within their society and nation-state (Kanpol & McLaren, 1995). Political education within the United States has traditionally fostered political passivity rather than action. Although several experimental political studies courses designed to foster political action were developed for students during the flurry of social studies curricular activity during the 1970s (Hahn, 1998), these projects did not change political education in U.S. schools. Students are taught to vote and to participate in the political systems in ways that will not significantly reform U.S. society. Writes Newmann (1968):

> By teaching that the constitutional system of the U.S. guarantees a benevolent government serving the needs of all, the schools have fostered massive public apathy. Whereas the Protestant ethic calls for engagement (to survive economically one must earn a living), the political creed breeds passivity. One need not struggle for political rights, but only maintain a vague level of vigilance, obey the laws, make careful choices in elections, perform a few duties (taxes, military service), and his [or her] political welfare is assured. (p. 536)

Even though the schools teach students the expressed ideals about justice and equality that are dominant within U.S. society, rarely do we deliberately educate students for social change and help them acquire the knowledge, attitudes, and skills needed to help close the gap between our democratic ideals and societal realities. A major goal of the curriculum should be to help students acquire the knowledge, values, and skills they need to participate in social change so that structurally excluded groups can become full participants in their societies. To participate effectively in social change, students must be taught social criticism and helped to understand the inconsistency between our ideals and realities, the work that must be done to close this gap, and how they can, as individuals and groups, become empowered to influence the social and civic life of their societies.

When conceptualizing a curriculum designed to promote civic action and change, educators need to ponder seriously the arguments by radical scholars and critical multiculturalists (Kanpol & McLaren, 1995). They argue that it is difficult for schools to teach students to be change agents because among their major roles are to reproduce the social structure and to socialize students so they will passively accept their position in our class and racially stratified society. The radical critics of the schools, especially those in the United Kingdom, have been keenly critical of multi-cultural education as a strategy to promote social change (Modgil, Verma, Mallick, & Modgil, 1986). They argue that multicultural education is a palliative to keep ex-cluded and oppressed groups from rebelling against a system that promotes struc-tural inequality and institutionalized racism. The radical scholars also claim that multicultural education avoids any serious analysis of class, racism, power, capital-ism, and other systems that keep excluded cultural groups powerless (McCarthy, 1988). Multicultural education, they argue, diverts attention from the real problems and issues. Instead, it focuses on the victim as the problem.

It is difficult to reject completely the argument that one of the school's major roles is to socialize students so they will fit into the existing social order. However, radical scholars overstate the case when they argue that the schools merely social-ize students into the existing social order. The school itself is contradictory, be-cause it often professes democratic values while at the same time contradicting them. The school does socialize students into the existing social structure. How-ever, it also enables some students to acquire the knowledge, attitudes, and skills needed to participate effectively in social action and change. Radical critics have not always recognized fully that both students and teachers have agency. They are not complete victims of social, political and economic structures.

The Teacher as Cultural Mediator and Change Agent

Whether they are deliberate goals of the school or not, many students learn com-passion and democratic ideals and develop a commitment to participate in social change from powerful and influential classroom teachers. These teachers are also cultural mediators who interpret the mainstream and marginalized cultures to students from diverse groups and help students understand the desirability of and possibility for social change. Many such teachers participated in social action in the 1960s and 1970s to promote social justice and human rights. Today, many teachers are deeply concerned about violence in the schools, about racist groups such as the Skinheads, and about the widening gap between the rich and the poor in the United States.

The school—primarily through the influence of teachers who have clarified and reflective commitments to democratic values, knowledge, and pedagogical skills and who have the charisma to inspire other people—can play a significant role in teaching social criticism and in motivating students to become involved in social change (see Figure 12.2). Some teachers have a significant influence on the values, hopes, and dreams of their students. The classroom should be a forum of open inquiry, where diverse points of view and perspectives are shared and ana-lyzed reflectively. Teachers who are committed to human freedom should feel free to express their views in the classroom, provided that students have first had an opportunity to express freely and to defend their own beliefs and that teachers defend their beliefs reflectively and in ways consistent with democratic values. In

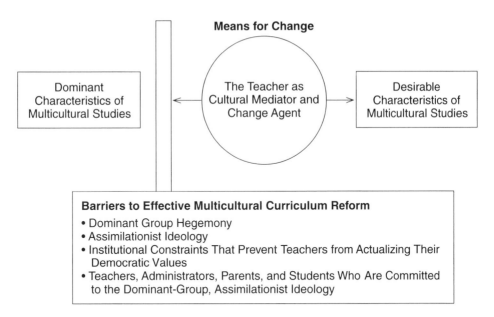

FIGURE 12.2 **The Teacher as Cultural Mediator and Social Change Agent**

the democratic classroom, both students and teachers should have the freedom to express their values and beliefs but should be required to defend them and to point out ways in which their moral choices are related to overarching democratic ideals, such as human dignity, justice, and equality (Evans & Saxe, 1996).

In a democratic society, students and teachers should freely express morally and intellectually defensible values and beliefs about human freedom. Teaching, like social science inquiry, is not a value-neutral activity (Harding, 1991). This is especially the case in multicultural studies, where teachers and students must deal with human problems, conflicts, and dilemmas toward which it is impossible to remain neutral. Both teachers and social scientists have often been told to strive for objectivity in their work. Teachers should not use the classroom as a forum to promote partisan political beliefs, but they should, like caring social scientists, become *involved observers,* to use Kenneth B. Clark's (1965) apt phrase. They should support and defend moral and ethical positions that are consistent with democratic values and ideals.

Teachers who support human freedom, justice, and equality can motivate students to engage in social action to improve the human condition (Lewis, 1991). It is individual teachers—and not schools per se—who often help students develop the ideals, knowledge, and skills needed to become citizens who make a difference. They do this by showing a commitment to democratic values in the content they select, in their interpretations of social and historical events, and in their words and deeds. Teachers, while respecting the beliefs and diversity of their students and helping them develop social science inquiry skills, can support democracy, equality, and the empowerment of marginalized cultural, ethnic, and racial groups (Cummins, 1986).

A Typology of Cross-Cultural Teachers

Chapter 9 presents a *Typology of Cross-Cultural Researchers* (see Table 9.1, p. 174). Teachers can also be classified using a modified version of this typology. Readers should refer to the typology in Chapter 9 for a discussion of the limitations and complexity of this type of typology.

Teachers, like researchers, are socialized within ethnic, racial, and cultural communities in which they internalize localized values (Geertz, 1983), perspectives, ways of knowing, beliefs, and knowledge that can differ in significant ways from those of individuals socialized within other cultural communities. Teachers endorse the institutionalized beliefs and knowledge within their cultural communities at greatly varying levels. I have adapted this typology for use with teachers with the hope that it will facilitate discussions, observations, and research about the types of teachers needed for diverse classrooms and schools.

This typology can be applied to a range of cultural groups, such as ethnicity, race, gender, social class, and religion. Men teaching women, middle-class teachers teaching low-income students, and Protestant teaching Muslims are outsiders.

The Typology of Cross-Cultural Teachers has four types of teachers: the *indigenous-insider,* the *indigenous-outsider,* the *external-insider,* and the *external-outsider* (see Table 12.2).

The Indigenous-Insider

This teacher endorses the unique values, perspectives, behaviors, beliefs, and knowledge of his or her indigenous community and culture. Parents and students perceive this teacher as a legitimate community member who can teach with authority and legitimacy within it.

The Indigenous-Outsider

This teacher was socialized within his or her indigenous community but has experienced high levels of cultural assimilation into an outsider or oppositional culture. The values, beliefs, perspectives, and knowledge of this individual are identical to those of the outside community. The indigenous-outsider is perceived by parents and students as an outsider.

The External-Insider

This teacher was socialized within another culture and has acquired its beliefs, values, behaviors, attitudes, and knowledge. However, because of his or her unique experiences, the teacher seriously questions or rejects many of the values, beliefs,

TABLE 12.2 A Typology of Cross-Cultural Teachers

Type of Teacher	Description
The Indigenous-Insider	This teacher endorses the unique values, perspectives, behaviors, beliefs, and knowledge of his or her indigenous community and culture and is perceived by people within the community as a legitimate community member who can speak with authority about it.
The Indigenous-Outsider	This teacher was socialized within his or her indigenous community but has experienced high levels of cultural assimilation into an outside or oppositional culture. The values, beliefs, perspectives, and knowledge of this teacher are identical to those of the outside community. The indigenous-outsider is perceived by indigenous people in the community as an outsider.
The External-Insider	This teacher was socialized within another culture and acquires its beliefs, values, behaviors, attitudes, and knowledge. However, because of his or her unique experiences, the teacher questions many of the values, beliefs, and knowledge claims within his or her indigenous community and endorses those of the community in which he or she teaches. The external-insider is viewed by the new community as an "adopted" insider.
The External-Outsider	The external-outsider is socialized within a community different from the one in which he or she is teaching. The external-outsider has a partial understanding of and little appreciation for the values, perspectives, and knowledge of the community in which he or she is teaching and consequently often misunderstands and misinterprets the behaviors of students, parents, and others within the community.

and knowledge claims within his or her indigenous community and endorses those of the community in which he or she teaches. The external-insider is viewed by the new community and by the parents and students as an adopted insider.

The External-Outsider

The external-outsider is socialized within a community different from the one in which he or she is teaching. The external-outsider has a partial understanding of and little appreciation for the values, perspectives, and knowledge of the community in which he or she is teaching and consequently often misunderstands and misinterprets the behaviors of students, parents, and others within the community.

The external-outsider is criticized by members of the community in which he or she teachers but is often praised and highly rewarded by the outside community, which is often more powerful and influential than the community in which the teacher works. The external-outsider may violate the integrity of the students he or she teaches and may contribute to their disempowerment and marginalization.

The Effective Multicultural Teacher

The *internal-insider* and the *external-insider* will be most effective in serving as cultural mediators and in helping students to become effective civic participants in their societies and nation-states. If teachers are to be the primary agents for change in schools, then when we select and educate individuals for teaching we must give high priority to their ability to function as insiders within the cultural communities in which they teach (Haberman, 1995; 1996). A major goal of our selection and professional education process must be to place in the classroom teachers who have strong and clarified democratic values and the knowledge and skills to implement a curriculum that will enable students to acquire the knowledge and skills needed to participate in democratic social and political change.

Teacher education programs that are designed to help teachers become effective cultural mediators and change agents must help them to acquire (a) social science knowledge, derived using a process in which the goals, assumptions, and values of knowledge are learned; (b) clarified cultural identifications; (c) positive intergroup and racial attitudes; and (d) pedagogical skills (see Figure 12.3). To select and educate teachers successfully is probably the most challenging and difficult task that lies ahead for those of us who would like to see the schools—and the multicultural curriculum in particular—become a vehicle for social change and human betterment.

Summary

A major goal of the ethnic and cultural movements of the 1960s and 1970s was to change the school, college, and university curriculum so that the images of marginalized cultural groups and the roles people of color had played in the development of their nation-states and societies would be accurately and comprehensively represented.

This chapter describes the curricular visions and goals of the cultural revival movements, the extent to which these goals have been realized, and the factors that have prevented complete institutionalization of multicultural reforms. This chapter proposes a reform strategy that conceptualizes the teacher as a cultural mediator, cross-cultural insider, and a change agent who promotes social criticism and action to improve the human condition.

R E F E R E N C E S

Appleby, J. (1992). Recovering America's Historic Diversity: Beyond Exceptionalism. *The Journal of American History,* 79(2), 419–431.

Apter, D. E. (1977). Political Life and Cultural Pluralism. In M. M. Tumin and W. Plotch (Eds.), *Pluralism in a Democratic Society* (pp. 59–91). New York: Praeger.

Baldwin, J. (1985). *The Price of the Ticket: Collected Nonfiction 1984–1985.* New York: St. Martin's.

Banks, J. A. (Ed.). (1996). *Multicultural Education, Transformative Knowledge and Action: Historical and Contemporary Perspectives.* New York: Teachers College Press.

Banks, J. A., & Banks, C. A. M. (Eds.). (1995). *Handbook of Research on Multicultural Education.* New York: Macmillan.

Baratz, J. C. (1970). Teaching Reading in an Urban Negro School System. In F. Williams (Ed.),

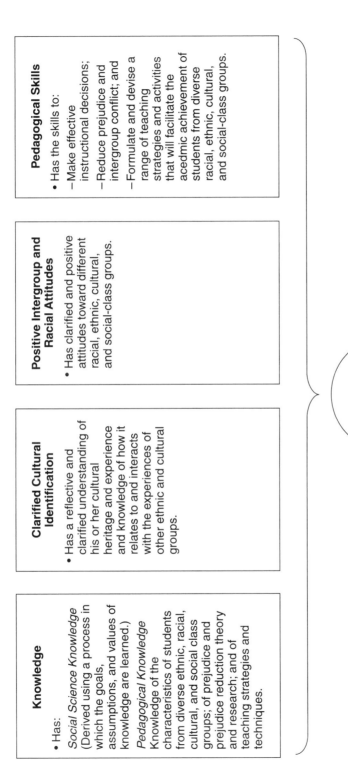

Knowledge

• Has:

Social Science Knowledge
(Derived using a process in which the goals, assumptions, and values of knowledge are learned.)

Pedagogical Knowledge
Knowledge of the characteristics of students from diverse ethnic, racial, cultural, and social class groups; of prejudice and prejudice reduction theory and research; and of teaching strategies and techniques.

Clarified Cultural Identification

• Has a reflective and clarified understanding of his or her cultural heritage and experience and knowledge of how it relates to and interacts with the experiences of other ethnic and cultural groups.

Positive Intergroup and Racial Attitudes

• Has clarified and positive attitudes toward different racial, ethnic, cultural, and social-class groups.

Pedagogical Skills

• Has the skills to:

–Make effective instructional decisions;

–Reduce prejudice and intergroup conflict; and

–Formulate and devise a range of teaching strategies and activities that will facilitate the acedmic achievement of students from diverse racial, ethnic, cultural, and social-class groups.

The Effective Multicultural Teacher

FIGURE 12.3   Characteristics of the Effective Teacher in a Multicultural Society

Language and Poverty: Perspectives on a Theme (pp. 11–24). Chicago: Markham Publishing Co.

Berger, B. M. (1995). *An Essay on Culture.* Berkeley: University of California Press.

Bullivant, B. (1986). Multicultural Education in Australia: An Unresolved Debate. In J. A. Banks & J. Lynch (Eds.), *Multicultural Education in Western Societies* (pp. 98–124). New York: Praeger.

Bulmer, M. (1984). *The Chicago School of Sociology: Institutionalization, Diversity, and the Rise of Sociological Research.* Chicago: The University of Chicago Press.

Carter, S. L. (1991). *Reflections of an Affirmative Action Baby.* New York: Basic Books.

Champagne, D. (1994). *Native America: Portrait of the Peoples.* Detroit: Visible Ink.

Chavez, L. (1991). *Out of the Barrio.* New York: Basic Books.

Clark, K. B. (1965). *Dark Ghetto: Dilemmas of Social Power.* New York: Harper Torchbooks.

Conley, D. (1999). *Being Black, Living in the Red: Race, Wealth, and Social Policy in America.* Berkeley: University of California Press.

Coser, L. A. (1977). *Masters of Sociological Thought: Ideas in Historical and Social Context* (2nd ed.). New York: Harcourt.

Cummins, J. (1986). Empowering Minority Students: A Framework for Intervention. *Harvard Educational Review, 56,* 18–36.

Dawidowicz, L. S. (1981). *The Holocaust and the Historians.* Cambridge, MA: Harvard University Press.

Evans, R. W., & Saxe, D. W. (Eds.). (1996). *Handbook on Teaching Social Issues* (NCSS Bulletin 93). Washington, DC: National Council for the Social Studies.

Geertz, C. (1983). *Local Knowledge: Further Essays in Interpretive Anthropology.* New York: Basic Books.

Genovese, E. D. (1974). *Roll, Jordan Roll: The World the Slaves Made.* New York: Pantheon.

Gilligan, C. (1982). *In a Different Voice.* Cambridge, MA: Harvard University Press.

Glazer, N., & Moynihan, D. P. (Eds.). (1975). *Ethnicity: Theory and Experience.* Cambridge, MA.: Harvard University Press.

Goldberger, N., Tarule, J., Clinchy, B., & Belenky, M. (Eds.). (1996). *Knowledge, Difference, and Power.* New York: Basic Books.

Gonzales, M. G. (1999). *Mexicanos: A History of Mexicans in the United States.* Bloomington: Indiana University Press.

Gordon, M. M. (1964). *Assimilation in American Life.* New York: Oxford University Press.

Gurian, M. (1996). *The Wonder of Boys.* New York: Putnam.

Gutman, H. G. (1964). *The Black Family in Slavery and Freedom, 1750–1925.* New York: Oxford University Press.

Haberman, H. (1995). *Star Teachers of Children in Poverty.* West Lafayette, IN: Kappa Delta Pi.

Haberman, M. (1996). Selecting and Preparing Culturally Competent Teachers for Urban Schools. In J. Sikula, T. J. Buttery, & E. Guyton (Eds.), *Handbook of Research on Teacher Education* (2nd ed.) (pp. 747–760). New York: Macmillan.

Hahn, C. (1998). *Becoming Political: Comparative Perspectives on Citizenship Education.* Albany: State University of New York Press.

Hampton, H., & Fayer, S. (Eds.). (1990). *Voices of Freedom: An Oral History of the Civil Rights Movement from the 1950s through the 1980s.* New York: Bantam.

Harding, S. (1991). *Whose Knowledge? Whose Science? Thinking from Women's Lives.* Ithaca, NY: Cornell University Press.

Herdt, G. (Ed.). (1992). *Gay Culture in America: Essays from the Field.* Boston: Beacon Press.

Kanpol, B., & McLaren, P. (Eds.). (1995). *Critical Multiculturalism: Uncommon Voices in a Common Struggle.* Westport, CT: Bergin & Garvey.

Ladner, J. A. (Ed.). (1973). *The Death of White Sociology.* New York: Vintage Books.

Lee, E. (1998). Anti-Racist Education: Pulling Together to Close the Gaps. In E. Lee, D. Menkart, & M. Okazawa-Rey (Eds.), *Beyond Heroes and Holidays* (pp. 26–34). Washington, DC: Network of Educators on the Americas.

Lewis, B. A. (1991). *The Kids' Guide to Social Action.* (Edited by P. Espeland). Minneapolis: Free Spirit Publishing.

McCarthy, C. (1988). Rethinking Liberal and Radical Perspectives on Racial Inequality in Schooling: Making the Case for Nonsynchrony. *Harvard Educational Review, 58,* 265–279.

Modgil, S., Verma, G. K., Mallick, K., & Modgil, C. (Eds.). (1986). *Multicultural Education: The Interminable Debate.* London: The Falmer Press.

Moodley, K. A. (1995). Multicultural Education in Canada: Historical Development and Current Status. In J. A. Banks & C. A. M. Banks (Eds.), *Handbook of Research on Multicultural Education* (pp. 801–820). New York: Macmillan.

Newmann, F. M. (1968). Discussion: Political Socialization in the Schools. *Harvard Educational Review, 38,* 536–545.

Nieto, S. (1999). *The Light in Their Eyes: Creating Multicultural Learning Communities.* New York: Teachers College Press.

Padden, C., & Humphries, T. (1988). *Deaf in America: Voices from a Culture.* Cambridge, MA: Harvard University Press.

Pollack, W. (1998). *Real Boys.* New York: Henry Holt & Co.

Riessman, F. (1962). *The Culturally Deprived Child.* New York: Harper and Row.

Schlesinger, A. M., Jr. (1991). *The Dismantling of America: Reflections on a Multicultural Society.* Knoxville, TN: Whittle Direct Books.

Schofield, J. W. (1997). Causes and Consequences of the Colorblind Perspective. In J. A. Banks & C. A. M. Banks (Eds.), *Multicultural Education: Issues and Perspectives* (3rd ed.) (pp. 251–271). Boston: Allyn and Bacon.

Sizemore, B. A. (1973). Shattering the Melting Pot Myth. In J. A. Banks (Ed.), *Teaching Ethnic Studies: Concepts and Strategies* (pp. 73–101). Washington, DC: National Council for the Social Studies.

Sleeter, C. E., & Grant, C. A. (1991). Race, Class, Gender, and Disability in Current Textbooks. In M. W. Apple & L. K. Christian-Smith (Eds.), *The Politics of the Textbook* (pp. 78–110). New York: Routledge.

Sowell, T. (1984). *Civil Rights: Rhetoric or Reality?* New York: William Morrow.

Steele, S. (1990). *The Content of Our Character.* New York: St. Martin's.

Uchida, Y. (1982). *Desert Exile: The Uprooting of a Japanese-American Family.* Seattle: University of Washington Press.

PART FIVE

Gender, Language, Intergroup Relations, and Guidelines

The chapters in Part Five focus on four significant and continuing issues that must receive serious attention in educational institutions that implement effective multicultural education: (1) the ways in which gender influences educational equity; (2) issues related to language and culture; (3) helping students to develop democratic racial attitudes and values; and (4) guidelines for establishing effective multicultural classrooms and schools.

Race, class, culture, and gender interact in complex ways to influence educational outcomes. Chapter 13 examines the ways in which gender influences students' attitudes, conceptions, and school experiences. A key goal of multicultural education is to help students attain democratic racial attitudes, conceptions, and behaviors. The research, theory, and strategies related to reducing student prejudice are described in Chapter 15. The characteristics of the effective multicultural teacher are also described in this chapter.

Many students in the multicultural classroom speak languages and dialects that differ from those fostered by the school and the mainstream society. Chapter 14 presents information and insights about language diversity that teachers will find useful when working with students from diverse cultural and language groups. The final chapter, Chapter 16, describes guidelines that teachers and other practicing educators can use to create multicultural curricula and learning environments. This chapter also summarizes some of the major issues, problems, and recommendations discussed in this book.

13 Gender and Educational Equity

This chapter describes issues related to gender equity in schools. The first part provides an overview of the issues. The second describes research on the effects of materials and other curricular experiences, such as courses and units, on the gender perceptions, attitudes, and beliefs of students. The final part describes gaps that still exist in the educational experiences of males and females. It is reprinted from *Gender Gaps: Where Schools Still Fail Our Children,* a report issued by the American Association of University Women Educational Foundation.

The Educational Status of Females

One consequence of the civil rights movement of the 1960s and 1970s was a renewed quest for the rights of women and female students. The National Organization for Women (NOW) was founded in 1966 to support "full equality for women in America in a truly equal partnership with men" (Chernow & Vallasi, 1993, p. 1887). The women studies movement stimulated a rich and diverse scholarship on women (Schmitz et al., 1995). A number of publications described the academic and social problems that females experience in the schools and in the wider society. One of the most important of these publications was *How Schools Shortchange Girls: A Study of Major Findings on Girls and Education,* published in 1992 by the American Association of University Women (AAUW). Among the problems noted in this report were the small number of women represented in textbooks, the ways in which teachers favored boys in classroom interactions, the poor self-esteem of girls, and the low achievement of girls in science and math when compared to boys.

Women and girls have made significant gains in educational attainment within the last three decades. They have also made significant gains in entering the professions and in obtaining doctoral degrees. Women made up 55 percent of college students in the United States in 1995. They now earn the majority of both bachelor and master's degrees granted (Kleinfeld, 1999). They received 40 percent of all professional degrees and about 40 percent of all doctoral degrees in 1994 (Kleinfeld, 1999). Women receive more doctorates than men in some fields, such as health, psychology, English, and education. Despite the educational progress they have made within the last four decades, males still outperform females on standardized tests of basic skills while women outperform men on tests of writing ability and reading achievement (Kleinfeld, 1999).

Concerns about Males

Within the last decade a number of popular writers and educators have written about the problems that males experience in the schools and in the wider society. The attention to the problems of males intensified after the rash of killings by males that occurred in places such as Columbine High School in Colorado and in a Jewish early childhood center in Los Angeles. Advocates for boys point out that boys make up the majority of students referred to special education, are only 45 percent of the nation's college students, have higher dropout rates than girls, are more often disciplined by teachers, and have a much higher rate of participation in crime than girls. Some males suffer from body-image disorders because of the emphasis that society places on the physical looks for men and boys (Hall, 1999). Several books by male advocates have become best-sellers, including *Real Boys: Rescuing Our Sons from the Myths of Boyhood* by William Pollack (1998) and *The Wonder of Boys* by Michael Gurian (1996). Gurian (1996) writes passionately about the problems of boys:

> The majority of schizophrenics are boys. The majority of retarded children are boys; emotionally disturbed boys outnumber girls 4 to 1. Learning-disabled boys outnumber girls 2 to 1; boys are twice as likely as girls to be the victims of physical abuse at the hands of parents and caregivers.... Today an African-American boy in an urban area is more likely to die of a gunshot wound than was an African-American male who served in the Vietnam war. (pp. xvii–xviii)

Broude (1999) strongly criticizes what she describes as the "boy advocates." She argues that the proportion of boys suffering serious problems is small and that many of the problems that boys experience in society and in the schools do not result from the ways in which they were socialized in families and in schools. They result from the biological characteristics of males and females. She points out, for example, that males are more aggressive than females in all cultures, times, and species. She writes:

> Each of the problems described by the boy advocates is exhibited by some boys. But so do girls display these behaviors, and often in equal or greater numbers. And girls have troubles on their own, as reflected in higher rates of eating disorders that rarely turn up in boys, higher rates of depression and attempted suicide, lagging performance in math and science in school, and greater willingness to give up in the face of failure. The moral: Boys and girls face somewhat different life challenges. (p. 8)

Kleinfeld (1999) believes that the widespread attention given to females and girls since the 1960s has resulted in a neglect of the serious problems of boys—especially certain groups of boys, such as African American boys—who experience many problems in schools and in society. She writes, "Policy makers should be as concerned about the educational progress of boys as girls. For it is boys, not girls, who lag behind in verbal skills, who are falling behind in college attendance, and who believe that schools are hostile to them" (p. 4).

Implications of the Gender Debate for Schools

Some writers and groups, such as the American Association of University Women, focus of the problems of females. Other writers, such as Gurian (1996) and Pollack (1998), focus on the problems of boys. Both groups of advocates make important observations that have implications for achieving gender equity in schools. Teachers must be knowledgeable about and sensitive to the special problems of both girls and boys in order to help all students experience academic and social success. Both girls and boys face unique challenges within school and the larger society. It is more productive and educationally sound to identify the unique problems of each group and ways to help them overcome their problems than to try to determine whether girls or boys have more serious problems.

Educators should also give special attention to specific groups of boys and girls that have unique problems, such as African American boys. In 1995, African American males made up only 38 percent of Blacks in college; they received 43 percent of the professional degrees awarded to African Americans in 1994 (Kleinfeld, 1999). Kunjufu (1984) and Gibbs (1988) are among the writers and researchers who have studied and brought the special problems of African American males to the attention of educators and policy makers.

The Role of Multicultural Content in the Curriculum

A multicultural curriculum that includes information that helps students to examine and clarify their gender stereotypes and misconceptions will help both girls and boys to attain educational equity. This part of Chapter 13 describes the effects of multicultural content on students' perceptions, beliefs, and attitudes toward females and males. However, it is important for readers to realize that the justification for the inclusion of multicultural content in the school curriculum is not grounded in the empirical demonstration of the effects of such materials on student behavior and attitudes, but rather on two other important factors: (1) the need for historical accuracy and (2) the national commitment to a democratic society.

A study of the American Revolution is included in the social studies curriculum primarily because educators believe that it is necessary to give students an accurate depiction of the development of U.S. society and culture. Content about people of color, women, and persons with disabilities should be included in the curriculum for the same reason: to give students an accurate view of U.S. society and culture. Multicultural content should also be included in the school curriculum because of the nation's commitment to fostering a democratic society (Myrdal, with Sterner & Rose, 1944). A pluralistic democratic society functions best when its diverse groups believe they are an integral part of its institutions and social structure.

When groups within a democratic society feel excluded and experience anomie and alienation, polarization develops (Patterson, 1977). Thus, schools in a pluralistic democratic society, in order to promote the structural inclusion of diverse groups and help them to develop a commitment to the national ethos and ideology, should structure a curriculum that reflects the perspectives and experiences of the diverse groups that constitute the nation-state.

Even though there are important historical and philosophical reasons for including multicultural content in the school curriculum, it is also important to determine the effects of such content on students' attitudes, perceptions, and beliefs. This knowledge can help us to design curricular interventions that will, in turn, help students to develop attitudes and beliefs consistent with a democratic ideology. It can also contribute to the developing theory in multicultural education and intergroup relations.

Gender and Teaching Materials

Research indicates that sex role attitudes and gender associations develop early and that teaching materials, the mass media, and society at large often reinforce sex role stereotyping (Guttentag & Bray, 1976; Katz, 1986; Klein, 1985; Maccoby, 1998; McGhee & Frueh; 1980; Weitzman, 1972). A number of researchers have investigated the ways in which small-scale curriculum interventions, such as stories, vocational information, and television, influence sex role attitudes. However, there are few studies that examine the effects of curriculum units and courses on children's sex role attitudes and gender associations.

The research on the effects of curricular interventions on students' sex role attitudes and gender associations shares many of the problems with the research on racial attitudes and curricular interventions. The studies tend to be short-term interventions and to have measurement problems. They rarely examine the relationships between attitudes and behavior. The role of the teacher and the effects of teacher training on the teacher's ability to help students to develop less stereotyped gender role conceptions are rarely examined in research studies.

In-Service Education and Materials

Tetreault (1979) examined the effects of teacher training and curriculum materials on students' gender attitudes. She compared the gender attitudes of students following participation in three experimental conditions: (1) having a teacher who completed a 26-hour course on the inclusion of women in U.S. history and who used a classroom set of materials on women's history; (2) having a teacher who had only the in-service training; and (3) having a teacher who only used the materials on women's history. The teachers of control group classes neither participated in the in-service training nor used the curriculum materials on women's history.

Students in the experimental classes taught by teachers who participated in the in-service course and used the curriculum materials developed less stereotyped attitudes about males and females. However, the sex role attitudes of the teachers who participated in the in-service program and used the curriculum materials were no different from the attitudes of the teachers in the other two experimental groups and in the control group. Most of the teachers who participated in the in-service training program, however, used three times more women's history materials than did teachers who received the materials but were not trained.

This study is important for several reasons. It is one of the few studies on gender attitudes in which an intervention that lasted for an entire academic year was examined. The study also had a large sample: 1,074 students in 55 classrooms. By defining in-service training and materials as separate variables, the investigator was able to determine their separate and combined effects. The two variables were effective when combined and less effective when each was used alone. The results of this study underscore the need for curriculum interventions designed to change sex role attitudes to have a teacher in-service component.

No data were reported on the attitudes of students who were members of different racial and ethnic groups. Likewise, few studies of racial attitudes analyze data by gender. Future studies will contribute more to knowledge development if data are analyzed for the main effects of both race and gender (Grant & Sleeter, 1986) as well as for their interactions with the treatment. The results of the Tetreault (1979) intervention, for example, may have been different for African American and White students.

Teachers who participated in several workshops that gave them access to curriculum materials designed to promote gender equity made little use of these materials in an intervention by Woolever (1976). However, there was a statistically significant positive correlation between the amount of teacher intervention and pupil attitude changes for grades kindergarten through two. This finding, however, did not hold for grades three through six.

The Effects of Reading Materials

A number of researchers have examined the effects of fiction and factual readings on the gender-role attitudes and perceptions of students in various grades. These interventions are usually short term and their long-term effects are rarely determined.

The effects of egalitarian books and stories on the sex-type attitudes of three-, four-, and five-year-old White students enrolled in a kindergarten were examined by Flerx, Fidler, and Rogers (1976). Two experiments were reported. In the first experiment, the students in the experimental group were read egalitarian stories and shown pictures illustrating the stories in which males and females pursued careers and shared household duties. Another group heard stories that described men and women in traditional stereotyped roles and occupations. In the second experiment, a third treatment was added, a film condition in which egalitarian acts were modeled by males and females in the film. The students who participated in the egalitarian book and film groups developed more egalitarian and less stereotyping sex-role attitudes.

There was some evidence that the boys were not as strongly affected by the treatment as were the girls and that the film had a more enduring influence than the picture books. The results of this study are encouraging because of the short duration of the treatment—2.5 hours for Experiment 1, and 2 hours for Experiment 2.

Other researchers have also found that stories can influence gender-role attitudes and sex-role choices. Three hundred preschool boys and girls participated in a study by Lutes-Dunckley (1978). One group heard a story that depicted traditional sex-role behavior; another group heard a story in which all sex roles were reversed. A control group heard no story at all. The children who heard the story in which all sex roles were reversed made more nontraditional choices when asked to indicate which of two things they would rather do or which they liked better. There were no differences in the choices made by students who heard the traditional story and those who heard no story.

Berg-Cross and Berg-Cross (1978) found that listening to four books had a positive effect on students' social attitudes, including their attitudes toward boys who play with dolls, as assessed by responses to open-ended questions. Evidence of the reliability and validity of the assessment was not presented; consequently, its results should be interpreted with caution. However, the results of this study are consistent with the findings of other studies reviewed in this chapter.

The effects on children's sex-role perceptions and story evaluations of stories that portrayed a female main character in a traditionally male role were examined by Scott and Feldman-Summers (1979). Male characters were replaced with female main characters in several stories. The third- and fourth-grade students read two stories a week for four weeks. The three experimental conditions were the combination of male and female main characters in the stories: (1) female-majority, (2) male-majority, and (3) equal proportions. Students who read stories with females in nontraditional roles increased their perceptions of the number of girls who can engage in these same activities. However, their perceptions of sex-role activities not presented in the stories were not affected.

In a study with 4th- , 7th- , and 11th-grade students, Scott (1986) confirmed the results of the Scott and Feldman-Summers (1979) investigation. She found that students who read narratives that showed females and males in nontraditional roles were more likely to think that both males and females should and could do the activity of the main character than were students who read traditional narratives. Scott also found that neither comprehension nor interest was diminished by the use of sex-fair materials. However, Kropp and Halverson (1983) found that preschool children tended to prefer stories whose main characters were of the same sex as they were and who engaged in stereotypic activities. Jennings (1975) had obtained similar results with preschool students, but they had better recall of stories in which the character's sex role was atypical.

The reading of a picture book to preschool children can influence the kinds of toys they choose (Ashton, 1983). The children were observed playing with toys for two minutes. They were then read a picture book that presented a character of the same sex playing with a stereotypic or nonstereotypic toy. Next, the children were given an opportunity to play with experimental toys for two more minutes. The children who heard a nonstereotypic story more often chose a nonstereotypic toy after the intervention. The reverse was the case for the children who heard a stereotypic story.

Vocational Choices and Expectations

A number of investigators have examined the effects of curriculum interventions on male and female students' vocational choices and expectations. In general, these interventions have had statistically significant effects. Barclay (1974) examined the effects on the gender-role attitudes of suburban and inner-city kindergarten children of reading books about women working and general career information without reference to sex. The three treatments were (1) reading and discussing three books dealing with working women, (2) reading and discussing a career information pamphlet, and (3) viewing a flannelboard demonstration of the story of the Gingerbread Man, with later discussion (a nonrelated control treatment). The treatment in each group lasted 15 minutes for 3 days. The boys and girls exposed to the books dealing with working women increased the number of jobs they considered appropriate for females. The general career information enabled girls, but not boys, to see women in a greater number of vocational roles.

The choices made by high school juniors on the basis of sex stereotypes or lack of knowledge of probability of success in a given occupation can be influenced by vocational information that describes new opportunities for women (Hurwitz & White, 1977). The attitudes of ninth graders toward sex-typed careers can also be changed by career information that describes nontraditional role models. After reading such materials, the students in a study by Greene, Sullivan, and Beyard-Tyler (1982) thought that more of the jobs they had read about were appropriate for both females and males. The females in the study had less sex-typed attitudes about sex appropriateness of careers then did males. Both males and females thought that it was more appropriate for females than males to enter nontraditional sex-typed occupations. These latter two findings are consistent with those of most other investigators who have investigated the gender-role attitudes of females and males—females tend to have more flexible gender-role attitudes and perceptions than do males.

The effects of an innovative economics curriculum project, Mini-Society, on students' perceptions of entrepreneurship and occupational sex stereotyping were investigated by Kourilsky and Campbell (1984). Among the strengths of the study were its large sample (938 children in grades three through six), its geographic scope (students from three cities in different states), and its ethnic mix. The duration of the intervention is also noteworthy; it lasted 10 weeks, longer than most of the interventions reviewed in this chapter. Like the Tetreault (1979) study, this intervention had a teacher in-service education component, a 24-hour workshop that took place over a 4-week period. Another strength of the study is that it was an investigation of an actual school curriculum, rather than of merely reading a story or viewing a film, as was the case in most studies of gender attitudes reported in this chapter.

The most serious limitation of the study was the lack of a control group; a pre-experimental, single-group, pretest-posttest design (Campbell & Stanley, 1963) was used. Consequently, causal inferences about the intervention are difficult. On the pretest, the students viewed entrepreneurial roles as primarily a male domain. After participation in the Mini-Society curriculum, both boys and girls placed more females in entrepreneurial positions on the posttest. However, the change for boys was not statistically significant; the boys still saw entrepreneurship as predominantly a male domain. The interaction effects of race and gender were also examined. Most of the girls, except for the African American girls, did not initially attempt entrepreneurship in the early phase of the Mini-Society curriculum.

The Effects of Television and Films

Some investigators have studied the effects of television and films on children's gender-role attitudes and perceptions. DiLeo, Moely, and Sulzer (1979) investigated the effects on the sex-typed behavior of toy choices and game preferences of nursery school, kindergarten, and first-grade children of a film showing a model choosing non-sex-typed toys. Before the intervention, the children evidenced high levels of sex typing in their choice of toys. After viewing the film, the students in the experimental groups made fewer sex-typed toy choices. On both the pre- and posttests, males and older children made more highly sex-typed choices than did females and younger children.

The effects of television cartoons on the sex-role stereotypes of kindergarten girls was investigated by Davidson, Yasuna, and Tower (1979). The girls viewed one of three television network cartoons: high stereotype, low stereotype, or neutral. After the intervention, they were tested for sex-role stereotyping. The children who viewed the low-stereotyped television cartoon scored significantly lower on the sex-role stereotype measure than did the girls who viewed the high-stereotyped or neutral cartoons. The scores of the girls who reviewed the high-stereotyped and neutral cartoons did not differ.

The findings by DiLeo, Moely, and Sulzer (1979) and by Davidson, Yasuna, and Tower (1979) were not confirmed by Drabman et al. (1981). They found that preschool, first-, and fourth-grade students maintained their sex-role stereotypes after viewing a videotape that depicted a male nurse working with a female physician. After viewing the videotape, the students were asked to identify photographs or names of the physician and the nurse. The students in preschool, first, and fourth grade selected male names or pictures for the physician and female names or pictures for the nurse. The seventh-grade students correctly identified the names of the nurse and the physician.

The investigators conducted three different experiments in order to strengthen various aspects of the study. The findings were essentially the same in the first experiment and in the two replications. The investigators concluded that the responses of the students in preschool, first, and fourth grades were influenced more strongly by their stereotypes than by the film they viewed. The nature of the experiment, the visual presentation, the social setting, and the region might be among the reasons that the findings of this study failed to confirm the two previous ones.

Curriculum Interventions and Gender-Role Attitudes

Although the findings are not totally consistent, the studies reviewed above indicate that different kinds of curriculum interventions can help students to develop less stereotypic gender-role attitudes. The inconsistent results may have resulted from varied interventions, pupil ages, duration of interventions, social settings, and teacher attitudes and behavior. The research reviewed also indicates that students' conceptions of gender-appropriate occupations can be modified with curriculum interventions. While the studies are, on the whole, encouraging to educators, they do share several problems. Only a few have examined the relationship between attitudes and behavior, the duration of treatment as a variable, or have been designed to modify the attitudes and behavior of teachers. The next section of this chapter describes gender gaps that exist in educational achievement and school reform efforts that can address them.

Gender Gaps: Where Schools Still Fail Our Children[1]

New Approaches to Gender and Education Research

Educational equity implies quality education and equal opportunities for all students. Valerie Lee (1998) describes equity as "a concern for unequal educational outcomes by social background"—variables such as sex, class, socioeconomic status, race and ethnicity (p. 41). Equity differs from equality, which sets up a comparison, generally between two groups. If our concern were *equality*, the critical question would be whether students receive the *same* education.

Equity poses a different question: Do students receive the right education to achieve a shared standard of excellence? Although "equity" implies that students' educational performance and outcomes will be the same across groups of students, it does not imply that students need the same things to *achieve* those outcomes. Equity is a difficult and complex concept, particularly in U.S. culture, which thinks more of equality—sameness—than equity (Scott, 1988). As Ellen Wahl (1997) writes, "The idea that same might not be equal is not a well-accepted

[1]This section is reprinted from *Gender Gaps: Where Schools Still Fail Our Children*. New York: Marlowe & Co. 1998, pp. 4–8, 121–124, 128–129. Used with permission of the American Association of University Women Educational Foundation, the copyright holder.

concept in this society. Eric Jolly often uses the example of two children, one starving and the other overweight. He asks, 'Do you feed them the same diet?'"

Rejecting the Deficit Model

Equitable education, ideally, addresses the needs of both girls and boys, rather than questioning whether each receives the same thing. In practice, though, definitions of equity often have implied an opposition—that is, boys have advantages, and girls do not. This logic views boys as the norm against which girls are measured: Boys are "top performers." Girls need to "catch up." Girls tend to be compared to boys in a limited number of subject areas—those in which they are outperformed by boys. Rather than challenge the unequal distribution of resources in education as an institutional problem, this version of equity proposes that girls must overcome their deficits in comparison to boys.

The "deficit model" of equity sets other limits. The model tends to focus nearly exclusively on what is wrong with girls rather than what is right. This approach leaves little room for the recognition and leveraging of strengths, abundant though they are for girls of all racial and socioeconomic groups. Programs based on the deficit model typically focus on "fixing girls" who fall short of boys, and dispelling myths that "girls can't do science/math/technology." Adherents typically fail to see that boys, having outperformed girls on some subjects, could stand to learn from girls on others—that they might in fact benefit from cultivating some of girls' strengths. To be sure, some deficit model programs have produced positive outcomes for girls, but crucially, these outcomes focus less on institutions—and institutional changes in how we think about learning or gender relations—and more on changing individual girls (Berube, 1996; Blank et al., 1997).

Probing Intragender Differences

Racial, class, and ethnic differences have further complicated the equity question in education research since 1992. Girls are not a uniform group, nor are their needs singular. Over the past five years, research on girls has moved from an assumption of homogeneity to a focus on "intragender" differences—differences among girls (Sandler et al., 1996). An exploration of differences not only between the undifferentiated populations of "boys and girls" but also among the population of girls by race, ethnicity, or class makes research more complex, but produces a more finely detailed, accurate portrait of students' school identities.

When other social variables are introduced into gender equity research, studies begin to challenge who, precisely, is meant by the term "girls." For example, Carol Gilligan's (1982) pathbreaking work on female adolescence in the 1980s noted that girls suffer a drop in self-esteem during their teenage years, slowly losing their voice and becoming less intellectually and socially confident. Yet 1991 research by the American Association of University Women discovered that Black girls of the same age do not, in fact, experience the drop in self-esteem that Gilligan observed in the population she studied—predominantly white, upper-class girls attending an elite private school. The observation that adolescent girls lose self-esteem, unless it is modified by race, buries the experiences of African American girls under the general category of "girls."

Research on differences among girls also challenges the idea that Caucasian students always have advantages, and African American and Hispanic students always have secondary deficits because of race. Researchers today increasingly recognize that Caucasians should no more be the model against which African Americans and Hispanics are measured than boys should be the model against which girls are compared. Undoubtedly, a nonwhite girl in American schools often does face both gender and race discrimination. Yet research has documented that African American girls as a population have higher self-esteem, healthier body image, and greater social assertiveness than their white female counterparts, and stronger academic performance by many indicators than their Black male counterparts.

Clearly assumptions about who "girls" are and how schools ideally should operate help us redefine our notions of educational equity. Instead of comparing girls only to boys, we also compare boys to girls, and compare girls against their own prior performance. Instead of limiting comparisons to areas that emphasize traditional male strengths, we extend the analysis to include girls' strengths. Differences in educational outcome by gender—whether these differences favor boys or girls—belong in the equity research agenda. And instead of presenting girls as a uniform group, we recognize the diversity of girls. It is important to note that, in 1998, researchers are just beginning to collect and examine data by both race and gender, and the scale of such efforts is still quite limited.

Acknowledging Individual Differences

We also recognize that girls and boys as *individuals* are diverse. Clearly, not all girls suffer from fear of math, or conform to stereotypes of feminine behavior, and not all boys judge literacy a female domain. Individual experiences quite often defy statistical norms, as parents, teachers, and students will readily confirm. Furthermore, girls and boys are far more alike in their skills, competencies, and educational outcomes than they are different.

Research on equity and education examines differences in the *aggregate,* between *populations* of girls and *populations* of boys, rather than between individual boys and girls. It asks, in David Tyack's (1990) words, "How do schools look when viewed through the lens of gender?" Equity researchers are interested in differences between populations that cannot be explained by chance or by varying individual preferences. These kinds of differences—ones that exist between populations—are the much-discussed "gaps," or uneven outcomes, to which gender equity refers.

The deficits and strengths we identify, in our view, do not *innately* belong to girls or boys. Differences between girls and boys, or between and among racial groups or socioeconomic categories, cannot and should not be attributed to biological differences. Girls are not *inherently* more talented in writing, languages, or music. Opportunities and expectations are shaped by social phenomena, notably the idea that there are two genders, with oppositional characteristics. The idea is conveyed as a social expectation, both inside and outside of school, and influences the ways that girls view themselves, as well as how adults view them. Social forces shape the strengths that girls and boys develop, which are then displayed and sometimes reinforced in schools. Regardless of the sources of gender gaps—whether "nature" or "nurture"—schools have a mission to educate all students to levels of competency and to broaden individual opportunities rather than reinforce group stereotypes about student skills and options.

Rethinking the Role of Schools

Advancing the goal of equity requires institutional and systematic change, rather than an emphasis on changing girls or boys to conform better to the educational status quo. School personnel—teachers, coaches, counselors, and administrators—are powerfully situated to challenge stereotypes about what girls and boys can and cannot do. The surest way to reinforce these limiting stereotypes is by failing to act. Limitations on student behavior appear in the uneven interests of girls and boys (evidenced by course taking, for example) and uneven pursuit of career options. When we speak of equity for girls, we refer to several aspects of equity, including: equity in access, equity in resources, and equity in outcomes (Kahle, 1996; Cambell & Steinbrueck, 1996). Equity, from this perspective, is dependent in many cases on institutional and systematic change in education.

We contend there is an inherent and crucial link, rather than a conflict, between the achievement of equity goals and the achievement of high academic standards for all students. In many respects, the two movements seek the same objective: educational outcomes that don't vary by gender, race, class, or ethnicity. Standards propose that all students can succeed, no matter how disadvantaged or challenged they are. Similarly, the equity agenda proposes that educational outcomes need not be determined by social background. Indeed, by definition, an inequitable education (one that produces uneven achievement for some groups—for example, girls in science or math) falls short of the standards movement goals of comparable—and high—levels of achievement for all students.

However, the link between equity and rigorous, uniform educational standards has been missed in much of the implementation of education reform. Setting high standards for all students is both a compelling and dangerous goal: In many cases, the goal obscures the needs of historically disadvantaged groups. Hence, the crucial goal of seeing students in public schools achieve to "the same" high standards is not linked to equity concerns—the recognition that particular groups may need different things from their education to achieve the same standards. We consider the potential standards—*when paired with the equity agenda*—to achieve in reality what it supports in rhetoric: meeting the needs of *all students.*

Demographic Changes: Differences among Girls

We have documented progress for girls as a whole, yet have also noted to the extent possible, some differences among girls according to race, ethnicity, and class. Given projections about demographic changes in the twenty-first century, these differences in performance among groups of girls—often masked under general data that compares "girls" to "boys"—threaten to become more extreme and profound in consequence.

The Growth of the Hispanic Population

The Hispanic population, projected to reach 59 million by 2030, will become the largest racial/ethnic group in the United States. It is crucial that girls in this population receive an education that doesn't limit them to unskilled, subsistence, and seasonal or contingent jobs. Public education in the United States historically has supported the ideas of mobility and aspiration for minority and immigrant groups. Yet K–12 education to date apparently has not served the Hispanic population well. The Hispanic dropout rate hovers around 30 percent, prompting a 1998 Department of Education report, *No More Excuses* (U.S. Department of Education, 1998), to recommend $100 million in dropout prevention programs targeted to Hispanics. Soberingly, the dropout rate is worse among second-generation students than those newly arrived, suggesting that the problem becomes more rather than less pronounced the longer families have been in the [United States], and is not exclusively a function of non-English-speaking status.

Hispanic girls face unique struggles and risks, both in relation to white and African American girls and in relation to their male peers. The dropout rate for Hispanic females age 16 to 24 reached 30 percent in 1995, and the Hispanic teen pregnancy and birth rates have not followed the decline of white and African American rates. Furthermore, as Hispanic educators note, "the Latino culture values education…but values family above all. And when it comes to choosing between going to school and helping the family, the family will win." Another Hispanic professor notes that the "greatest discrepancy between Hispanic and non-Hispanic white seniors has to do with the compatibility of students' home life with schooling." This incompatibility has especially powerful effects on some academically ambitious Hispanic girls who, according to scholar Rosa Maria Gil, when "faced with an American culture that promotes independence, self-fulfillment, and assertiveness," can "easily become overwhelmed by stress, conflict, and guilt." By the same token, however, high-achieving Hispanic females in academia routinely cite the resources of "family, language, and culture," and "family support" as critical to their success (Cooke, 1998; Gil, 1996; McGlynn, 1998; Mellander, 1998).

Immigration and the Education of New American Girls

Immigration, especially from Asia and Mexico, will contribute substantially to the public school enrollment "boomlet" in the next decades. A few reports from 1998 support the argument that the children of immigrants do better in school than other American children. Yet schools are ill-prepared to cultivate the strengths and potential of this growing student population.

Although some districts in Florida, Texas, and California already have sizable immigrant populations (leading to the phenomenon of "majority-minority" schools), it is too early to tell what unique challenges and opportunities this public school influx will create for gender equity goals. Clearly, gender expectations and cultural norms among a white, middle-class American population differ in some respects from those upheld in other cultures. For example, a high-achieving female student in a 1998 study of immigration in San Diego's schools observed, "Hmong girls are expected to marry young and so are discouraged from pursuing education much beyond high school." Although this is not an expectation currently relevant to most native-born American girls, policymakers and researchers will have to confront a more complex array of gender values and cultures as the century progresses.

The National Center for Immigrant Students describes that in school, "immigrant girls…encounter U.S. stereotypes of females…. In their families, they also cope with powerful stereotypes" from their birth culture. A rise in female teen suicides, female gangs, and illicit drug commerce in immigrant communities attests to the cultural strains placed on this population of girls, in particular. The center notes further that terms such as "self-esteem" and "leadership" development, staples of American gender equity conversations may have radically different meanings or contexts for immigrant girls (Lee & Sing, 1993; Viadero, 1998; Woo, 1997).

Regional Differences among Girls

Control over education and the allocation of education dollars has been shifting steadily toward the states and away from the federal government. Consequently, differences in outcome among girls by region may become more acute in the [twenty-first century]. For example, the Southern Regional Education Board (SREB) reported in 1998 a substantial gender gap on 1996 NAEP math scores in Southern states. Girls in rural Southern regions perform at a lower level in mathematics and science than other girls across the country, and consistently below Southern region boys. The largest female achievement gap occurs between girls who live in rural areas of the Southern region states and rural girls elsewhere in the country. The gap is not seen in comparable rural, low-income sectors of other regions. While the SREB could not explain the gender gap, the gap's existence suggests that regional differences between girls may increase, despite an overall leveling off of gender differences in test performance nationwide (Cooney, 1998).

What to Watch. *As girls as a whole move toward parity with boys in enrollment, performance, and educational opportunities, it will be critical to monitor subgroups of girls for significant discrepancies in their opportunities and performance. Gaps among girls based on racial, ethnic, economic, and regional differences may become pronounced, even as the gaps between boys and girls in the aggregate diminish. These differences in educational outcomes must be monitored closely, particularly as demographic trends reconfigure the public school population.*

School Reform

Gender largely has been overlooked in the equity discussion surrounding charter schools, vouchers, home schooling, and other structural reforms in public education. Equity research has focused instead on the school reform's potential to minimize class disparities in outcome. If these reform trends continue to gain popularity, it will be crucial to assess what effects, if any, they are having on the gender equity agenda. Reforms deemed successful for *all* students in the abstract may not benefit specific groups of students within the schools to the same extent that they benefit other groups.

The possibility that some education reforms may benefit some groups of students more than others underscores the imperative that high standards movement incorporate equity concerns.

Several reform movements, including charter and home schooling, for example, champion local and parental control over education, and decry "interventions" by the federal government. Their positions invite some questions: Does a standards-driven charter school, whose contract renewal hinges on its students' satisfactory test performance, facilitate or impede the remediation of gender gaps in performance? Do charter schools foster more or less equitable learning environments and pedagogical approaches? How does home schooling, currently practiced for one million students and growing at a 20 percent rate per year, affect the intellectual and social development of girls, especially given that many parents opt for home schooling to inculcate traditional, conservative ideologies and to shelter their children from the culture that they reject in the public schools?

From another perspective, some parents opt for home schooling arrangements because they fear that traditional gender stereotypes and harassment in the public schools will hinder their girls' intellectual growth. Equity issues, one researcher concludes, "will almost certainly remain a central focus of future research" on experimental schools and home schooling. The research focus on equity, however, should not be confined to class and race, but extended to consider gender *as well* (Goldhaber, 1997; Jacobson, 1996; Wohlstetter, et al., 1997).

Summary

This chapter describes some of the major issues, problems, and possible actions related to creating educational equity for both females and males. The first part describes some major problems that boys and girls experience in the schools and within the larger society. The second part reviews research on the effects of materials and other curriculum interventions on the gender perceptions, attitudes, and beliefs of students. The final part describes gender gaps that still exist between males and females and school reform efforts that are needed to address these gaps.

REFERENCES

American Association of University Women. (1992). *How Schools Shortchange Girls.* Washington, DC: Author.

Ashton, E. (1983). Measures of Play Behavior: The Influence of Sex-Role Stereotyped Children's Books. *Sex Roles, 9,* 43–47.

Barclay, L. K. (1974). The Emergence of Vocational Expectations in Preschool Children. *Journal of Vocational Behavior, 4,* 1–14.

Berg-Cross, L., & Berg-Cross, G. (1978). Listening to Stories May Change Children's Social Attitudes. *The Reading Teacher, 31,* 659–663.

Berube, M. R. (1996). The Politics of National Standards. *The Clearing House, 69*(3), 151–153.

Blank, R. K., et al. (1997). *Mathematics and Science Content Standards and Curriculum Frameworks: State Progress on Development and Implementation.* Washington, DC: Council of Chief State School Officers.

Broude, G. J. (1999). Boys Will Be Boys. *The Public Interest, 136* (Summer), 3–17.

Campbell, D. T., & Stanley, J. C. (1963). *Experimental and Quasi-Experimental Designs for Research.* Chicago: Rand McNally.

Cambell, P. B., & Steinbrueck, K. (1996). *Striving for Gender Equity: National Programs to Increase Student Engagement with Math and Science.* Washington, DC: Collaboration for Equity, Fairness in Science and Mathematics Education.

Chernow, B. A., & Vallasi, G. A. (1993). *The Columbia Encyclopedia* (5th ed.). New York: Columbia University Press.

Cooke, S. (1998). Why Hispanic-American Women Succeed in Higher Education. *Women in Higher Education, 7*(2), 8.

Cooney, S. (1998). *Education's Weak Link: Student Performance in the Middle Grades.* Southern Regional Education Board. Atlanta.

Davidson, E. S., Yasuna, A., & Tower, A. (1979). The Effects of Television Cartoons on Sex-Role Stereotyping in Young Girls. *Child Development, 50,* 597–600.

Gibbs, J. T. (Ed.). (1988). *Young, Black, and Male in America: An Endangered Species.* Dover, MA: Auburn House Publishing Company.

Gil, R. M. (1996). *The Maria Paradox: How Latins Can Merge Old World Traditions with New World Self-Esteem.* New York: G. P. Putnam's Sons.

DiLeo, J. C., Moely, B. E., & Sulzer, J. L. (1979). Frequency and Modifiability of Children's Preferences for Sex-Typed Toys, Games, and Occupations. *Child Study Journal, 9,* 141–159.

Drabman, R. S., Robinson, S. J., Patterson, J. N., Jarvie, G. J., Hammer, D., & Cordua, G. (1981). Children's Perception of Media-Portrayed Sex Roles. *Sex Roles, 7,* 379–389.

Flerx, V. C., Fidler, D. S., & Rogers, R. W. (1976). Sex Role Stereotypes: Developmental Aspects and Early Intervention. *Child Development, 47,* 998–1007.

Gilligan, C. (1982). *In a Different Voice: Psychological Theory and Women's Development.* Cambridge, MA: Harvard University Press.

Goldhaber, D. (1997). School Choice as Education Reform. *Phi Delta Kappan, 79*(2), 143.

Grant, C. A., & Sleeter, C. E. (1986). Race, Class, and Gender in Education Research: An Argument for Integrative Analysis. *Review of Educational Research, 56,* 195–211

Greene, L. A., Sullivan, H. J., & Beyard-Tyler, K. (1982). Attitudinal Effects of the Use of Role Models in Information About Sex-Typed Careers. *Journal of Educational Psychology, 74,* 393–398.

Gurian, M. (1996). *The Wonder of Boys: What Parents, Mentors and Educators Can Do to Shape Boys into Exceptional Men.* New York: Putnam.

Guttentag, M., & Bray, H. (1976). *Undoing Sex Stereotypes: Research and Resources for Educators.* New York: McGraw-Hill.

Hall, S. S. (1999). The Bully in the Mirror. *The New York Times Magazine* (August, 22), Section 6, 30–35, ff. 58, 62, 64–65.

Hurwitz, R. E., & White, M. A. (1977). Effect of Sex-Linked Vocational Information on Reported Occupational Choices of High School Juniors. *Psychology of Women Quarterly, 2,* 149–154.

Jacobson, L. (1996, Nov. 6). Under the Microscope: Charter Schools. *Education Week, 16*(10), 21–23.

Jennings, S. A. (1975). Effects of Sex Typing in Children's Stories on Preference and Recall. *Child Development, 46,* 22–223.

Kahle, J. B. (1996). Opportunities and Obstacles: Science Education in the Schools. In *The Equity Education: Fostering the Advancement of Women in the Sciences.* San Francisco: Jossey-Bass.

Katz, P. A. (1986). Modification of Children's Gender-Stereotyped Behavior: General Issues and Research Considerations. *Sex Roles, 14,* 591–602.

Klein, S. S. (Ed.). (1985). *Handbook for Achieving Sex Equity through Education.* Baltimore: The Johns Hopkins University Press.

Kleinfeld, J. (1999). Student Performance: Males versus Females. *The Public Interest, 134* (Winter), 3–20.

Kourilsky, M., & Campbell, M. (1984). Sex Differences in a Simulated Classroom Economy: Children's Beliefs about Entrepreneurship. *Sex Roles, 10,* 53–65.

Kropp, J. J., & Halverson, C. F. (1983). Preschool Children's Preferences and Recall for Stereotyped Versus Nonstereotyped Stories. *Sex Roles, 8,* 261–272.

Kunjufu, J. (1984). *Developing Positive Self-Images and Discipline in Black Children.* Chicago: African-American Images.

Lee, V. E. (1998). Is Singled-Sex Secondary Schooling a Solution to the Problem of Gender Inequity? In *Separated by Sex: A Critical Look at Single-Sex Education for Girls.* Washington, DC: American Association of University Women.

Lee, V., & Sing, R. (1993). Gender Equity in Schools for Immigrant Girls. *New Voices, Newsletter From the National Center for Immigrant Students, 3*(2), 1.

Lutes-Dunckley, C. J. (1978). Sex-Role Stereotypes as a Function of Sex of Storyteller and Story Content. *The Journal of Psychology, 100,* 151–158.

Maccoby, E. E. (1998). *The Two Sexes: Growing Up Apart, Coming Together.* Cambridge, MA: Harvard University Press.

McGhee, P. E., & Frueh, T. (1980). Television Viewing and the Learning of Sex-Role Stereotypes. *Sex Roles, 6,* 179–188.

McGlynn, A. (1998). Hispanic Women, Academia and Retention. *Hispanic Outlook in Education, 8*(12).

Mellander, G. A. (1998). College-Bound Hispanics: Making the Path. *Hispanic Outlook in Higher Education, 8*(12), 4.

Myrdal, G., with Sterner, R., & Rose, A. (1944). *An American Dilemma: The Negro Problem and Modern Democracy* (Vols. 1 and 2). New York: Harper & Brothers.

Patterson, O. (1977). *Ethnic Chauvinism: The Reactionary Impulse.* New York: Stein & Day.

Pollack, W. (1998). *Real Boys: Rescuing Our Sons from the Myths of Boyhood.* New York: Henry Holt and Company.

Sandler, B. R., et al. (1996). *The Chilly Classroom: A Guide to Improve the Education of Women.* Washington, DC: National Association for Women in Education.

Schmitz, B., Butler, J. E., Rosenfelt, D., & Guy-Sheftall, (1995). Women's Studies and Curriculum Transformation. In J. A. Banks & C. A. M. Banks (Eds.), *Handbook of Research on Multicultural Education* (pp. 708–728). New York: Macmillan.

Scott, J. (1988). Deconstructing Equality v. Difference, or the Uses of Poststructuralist Theory for Feminism. *Feminist Studies, 14,* 33–50.

Scott, K. P. (1986). Effects of Sex-Fair Reading Materials on Pupils' Attitudes, Comprehension, and Interest. *American Educational Research Journal, 28,* 105–116.

Scott, K. P., & Feldman-Summers, S. (1979). Children's Reactions to Textbook Stories in Which Females Are Portrayed in Traditionally Male Roles. *Journal of Educational Psychology, 71,* 396–402.

Tetreault, M. K. T. (1979). *The Inclusion of Women in the United States History Curriculum and Adolescent Attitudes toward Sex-Appropriate Behavior.* Unpublished Doctoral Dissertation, Boston University School of Education, Boston.

Tyack, D. (1990). *Learning Together: A History of Coeducation in American Public Schools.* New Haven, CT: Yale University Press.

U.S. Department of Education, Office of Bilingual Education and Minority Affairs. (1998). *No More Excuses: The Final Report of the Hispanic Dropout Project.* Washington, DC: Author.

Viadero, D. (1998, April 1). Immigrant Children Succeed Despite Barriers. *Education Week, 7*(29), 14.

Wahl, E. (1997). *The Case for Equity and Excellence in Math and Science Education.* Washington, DC: Collaboration for Equity, The American Association for the Advancement of Science.

Weitzman, L. J. (1972). Sex-Role Socialization in Picture Books for Preschool Children. *American Journal of Sociology, 77,* 1125–1150.

Wohlstetter, P., et al. (1997). First Lessons: Charter Schools as Learning Communities. *CPRE Policy Briefs,* 1.

Woo, E. (1997, June 16). School Success of Immigrants' Children Tracked. *Los Angeles Times,* Section A.

Woolever, R. (1976). *Expanding Elementary Pupils' Occupational and Social Role Perceptions: An Examination of Teacher Attitudes and Behavior and Pupil Attitude Change.* Unpublished Doctoral Dissertation, University of Washington, Seattle.

14 Language, Culture, and Education

RICARDO L. GARCÍA

All teachers teach language and communication. In the United States, teachers teach the full range of school-English language arts on a daily basis. Yet, most teachers rarely think of themselves as language or communication teachers. They go about their daily classroom activities encouraging students to listen, follow directions, take good notes, and think before acting, speaking, or writing. Communicating, knowing, and thinking are universal instructional aims taught through the medium of the English language. This is as it should be—the better students use the English language, the better they know, think, and communicate. And, if all students were fully literate in school English, there would be little need for most of this chapter. The reality, however, is that we live in a multilingual society within the context of a global village in which many languages are spoken and heard.

Many students enter school speaking a non-English language or a dialect of American English. These students are variously described as English language learners, linguistically different, linguistic minorities, bilingual, bidialectal, or as LEP, the federal government's acronym for students who are limited-English proficient. Being linguistically different involves more than merely speaking a foreign language or a different English dialect. Speaking a language or dialect links one to particular ethnic and cultural groups that hold values and attitudes, which may or may not conform to with the prevailing values and attitudes held by teachers and other people in a school's community.

Some linguistic differences are innocuous. No one is too concerned if a student speaks with a Hoosier twang. Or, if a student from Boston says "Cuba" as though it were pronounced "Cuber," no one seems to worry about the mispronunciation. But if an African American student prefers to say "I be sick" rather than "I am sick," or if a Latino student pronounces "sit" as though it were "seat," concern emerges about the student's purported language deficiencies.

Yet, some linguistic differences are not innocuous, especially if they cause communication breakdowns between teachers and students. Problems for both

Ricardo L. García is Professor of Education at Teachers College, The University of Nebraska–Lincoln.

teachers and students arise when the classroom communication system—couched in the culture reflected by speakers of school English—conflicts with the student's communication system. Subtle but potent instances of miscommunication can lead to larger problems of student alienation, discontent, and academic failure. In effect, students who experience communicative conflict may retreat or withdraw from the school's society.

The Relationship between Language and National Policy

Does linguistic diversity impede national cohesion? Is it possible to have a nation in which everyone speaks a different language, as in the Old Testament's Tower of Babel? Nationalism and ethnicity are similar group phenomena. Both involve group identity, a sense of peoplehood, and an interdependence of fates, requiring allegiance to some group. At times, the two phenomena conflict. Countries throughout the world have had to deal with the issue of how to build national unity while allowing ethnic group diversity. If ethnic groups are given too much autonomy, national unity is threatened; if ethnic groups are suppressed too much, ethnic group dissent emerges—again threatening national cohesion.

Central to a nation's development of nationalism is the designation of an official language. An official language serves the functions of political and psychological integration on a national scope. A nation's official language(s) embodies, carries, and conveys the nation's symbols. National anthems, slogans, and oaths of allegiance in the national language(s) meld a nation's spirit. The national language(s) act as the political unification agent and communication medium among the nation's citizens.

Some nations have one or more languages stipulated as their official language(s). Some nations, such as France, have an official language regulated by a language academy. Other nations have an official bilingual policy, such as Canada, allowing for English and French to coexist as official languages. Some nations (India and Russia, for example) have one official language that is used nationally and allow regional languages and dialects to be used and taught within their respective regions. Due to the centrality of language to nationalism, the selection as to which language or languages to use in a nation's school as the medium(s) of instruction is a critical national decision.

Language Policy in the United States

The United States government has no official language policy; it has an informal national standard, American English. Social customs and usage, rather than governmental agencies, tend to regulate languages in the United States. Non-English languages are allowed in public documents and institutions; their use is limited by varying state laws. To a great extent the United States is still an English-centric language nation. Non-English languages are considered foreign languages—even the languages of Native Americans, languages indigenous to the United States—are viewed as foreign by some people in the United States.

Within the United States, some ethnic groups developed dual or multiple dialects of English. Almost everyone in U.S. society is somewhat bidialectal in the sense that everyone speaks his or her individual idiolect as well as a group dialect. However, here the term *bidialectalism* is used to mean the ability to speak two distinctively different American English regional or cultural group dialects. For example, as a group, African Americans speak the Black English dialect as well as standard English. However, not all African Americans speak Black English, or what is currently called Ebonics.

Some groups have developed bilingual abilities. *Bilingualism* is used here to mean the ability to speak with two distinctively different language systems, such as Spanish and English, or German and English. At one time, German Americans were the most literate bilinguals in the United States. Bilingual German schools, newspapers, periodicals, radio programs, and books attested to a high level of German-English bilingualism (Fishman, 1966). However, the anti-Germanic feelings sparked by World War I, and inflamed by World War II with Germany, substantially doused German-English bilingualism. Currently, as a group, Puerto Ricans speak Spanish and English. In Puerto Rico, Spanish is considered the native language, but a speaking knowledge of U.S. English is required for high school graduation.

Again, as with bidialectalism, not all members of a group need to be bilingual for the group to be considered bilingual. In the above illustration, Puerto Ricans as a group are Spanish-English bilingual, but not all Puerto Ricans are bilingual. The level of bilingualism varies within different bilingual groups. Some groups, such as many Native American tribes, are attempting to restore their native languages. Other groups (e.g., Greek Americans) are working diligently to teach their youth the native language. Other groups use two languages for daily transactions (e.g., Chinese Americans and Cuban Americans).

More than 25 European languages are spoken in the United States. Some of these languages are Czech, Spanish, Italian, German, Polish, French, Yiddish, Russian, Swedish, Hungarian, and Norwegian. There are many others. Add these languages to the Asian and Middle Eastern languages now spoken as well as the historically spoken Native American languages, and it is obvious that the United States is multilingual.

The most recent additions are the languages of the Hmong, Vietnamese, Laotian, Cambodian, and ethnic Chinese people. Referred to as Indochinese, these people come from an area of the world that is culturally diverse. In Laos, Cambodia, and Vietnam at least 20 languages are spoken. It is important that Indochinese peoples be recognized as culturally diverse. They should not be lumped together as a single group. What they have in common is that they are refugees in an industrialized Western nation and have relocated from Asia to the United States. Beyond these shared characteristics, the people from each group speak their unique language or dialect and practice their own distinct culture.

The languages cited here are evidence of linguistic pluralism, a legacy that permeates the development of language policy in the United States (Crawford, 2000; Ferguson & Heath, 1981; Fishman, 1966; Ovando & Collier, 1998). Through social, economic, and political forces, American English was established as the nation's common language. Yet, the Constitution provided religious freedom, which fostered religious pluralism and the notion that the United States was a diversified nation. As immigrants settled in urban and rural parts of the United States, they often adhered to their native religions, cultures, and languages. Neighborhoods in cities thus became ethnic enclaves, providing individuals a buffer zone that eased assimilation into the new culture. Often rural settlements evolved into villages and towns peopled by one or several ethnic groups that could be identified by the national denomination of their churches. In urban enclaves and rural settlements, native, non-English languages were used in business affairs, schools, and religious institutions.

Government interference in language planning was minimal during the nation's beginning stages. Thomas Jefferson believed the mark of an educated person was bilingualism. He taught himself Spanish and spoke French. While Benjamin Franklin was not opposed to bilingualism, he decried the use of German by so many Pennsylvania residents. He feared that German might supplant English as the nation's language. Yet, he assisted the development of Pennsylvania's German language schools. His concern presaged the current dilemma in the United States—how to foster pluralism (including multilingualism) while building a common, national culture based on one language.

John Adams proposed the establishment of English as the nation's official language with a national academy to regulate and standardize English. The proposal was rejected by Congress as antidemocratic. Noah Webster's dictionaries and spellers attempted to regulate and standardize American English. His efforts, along with the efforts of other lexicographers, did much to standardize American English spelling but did not result in making English the nation's official language. However, in his attempt to break away from British English and to demonstrate that American English was distinctively different from British English, Webster included many Spanish, German, French, and Native American words as "American English." This led to the creation of an American English vocabulary that is culturally diverse at its base.

By the middle 1800s a bilingual tradition existed in schools. As the public school movement spread, so did the idea that local communities could conduct school in their native languages, especially since the antecedent schools—the religious schools—had taught native religions, cultures, and languages. Also, to encourage immigrant parents to place their children in school rather than the workplace, some public schools ensured that the home language and culture would be taught in the public schools. School districts in Milwaukee, New York, St. Louis, and Cleveland provided native language and, sometimes, bilingual instruction in elementary grades as recruitment inducements. Through the Civil War a governmental noninterference attitude prevailed, accommodating linguistic pluralism and often encouraging public school attendance. After the Civil War era and into the era of the Industrial Revolution, the need for a common language emerged to conduct business and governmental affairs. English language ethnocentrism began to percolate.

English-Language Ethnocentrism

English-language ethnocentrism started as a matter of practicality. Participation in civic affairs necessitated English literacy. Most state laws, government documents, and government affairs were conducted in English. This fact required a speaking and reading knowledge of English. Also, in business and industry, non-English speakers were seriously in danger at the workplace. Unable to read the safety procedures written in English, or unable to understand warnings shouted in English, the non-English-speaking workers were often injured on the job. Consequently, knowing how to speak, read, and write in English became necessary for civic participation, upward mobility, and economic success. Events between 1890 and 1920 added a new dimension to the importance of English literacy.

English-language ethnocentrism evolved from practicality to political power and control. The exclusive use of English—and the suppression of other languages and nonstandard dialects—evolved as an instrument to maintain political and economic power. By 1900, the national origins of European immigrants to the United States had changed substantially. Before 1812 most European immigrants to the United States came from Northern and Western Europe, primarily from Britain, Germany, France, Sweden, Norway, the Netherlands, and Switzerland. Between 1890 and 1920 the overwhelming majority came from Southern and Eastern Europe, primarily from the Balkan countries, Italy, Russia, and Poland. These immigrants were viewed with distrust by many earlier immigrant citizens. The new immigrants were predominantly Jewish or Catholic; they represented diverse political traditions—monarchies, dictatorships, and democracies. The reaction to the demographic shift was xenophobia. The fear arose that these new immigrants would not meld into the melting pot and would not be loyal to the traditional ways of the earlier immigrants.

The xenophobia was reflected in the labor unrest during this time when the United States was industrializing. Labor leaders were often portrayed as agitators or anarchists bent on the overthrow of democratic traditions and the free enterprise system. The xenophobia was exacerbated by racist perceptions about the new immigrants. Europeans from Southern and Eastern Europe were considered genetically and culturally inferior to the older immigrants. The xenophobic flame was later fueled as war with Germany seemed imminent and relations with Japan and China worsened. Xenophobia reached its peak immediately following World War I, when German-American language and cultural activities (including parochial schools, magazines, and lodge meetings) and Chinese and Japanese immigration were curtailed.

Attempts to quell the xenophobia culminated in bills requiring immigrants to learn English as a condition for citizenship. At this time, American English became the country's unofficial national language. The Nationality Act of 1906 required immigrants to speak English as a prerequisite for naturalization. The English requirement remained in force in the Nationality Act of 1940. In the Internal Security Act of 1950 the law was extended to include English reading and writing.

The public schools of the middle 1800s tolerated, at times even nurtured, the immigrant student's native language and culture. In states such as Wisconsin, many communities conducted all instruction in students' native languages, especially in private schools. As xenophobia increased the desire to forge a national identity based on the English language and Anglo-Saxon culture, the public schools shifted toward the Americanization and assimilation of non-English-speaking immigrants. The transformation started with state laws stipulating that certain school subjects be taught in English.

English-Only Laws

The Bennett Law, passed in 1889 in Wisconsin, stipulated an English-only requirement in certain subjects. The law's major intents were to control child labor and to provide compulsory school attendance. But, the law's English-only requirement meant that the German parochial schools would have to change their medium of instruction from German to English. Also, the local public school officials resented the loss of local control; they would be under greater scrutiny by the state. The Bennett Act was summarily repealed in 1891 due to the strong reactions against it. Nonetheless, the stage was set for the English-only laws.

The original intent of the English-only laws was to ensure English literacy for the multilingual, immigrant populations as part of the Americanization process. Often the laws were applied to the private and parochial schools. Primarily, the English-only laws were directed toward the German-American schools, which consisted of a wide network of bilingual (elementary) and second language (secondary) programs in parochial, private, and public schools. For example, in 1914, at least one-third of the elementary students in the Milwaukee, Cincinnati, Cleveland, and Dayton public school districts were in bilingual (German/English) classrooms. Between 1917 and 1919, however, when the United States was at war with Germany, the German/English bilingual programs, along with many of the secondary-level German programs, were drastically reduced; practically speaking, the bilingual programs were eliminated. The English-only laws also stopped bilingual instruction in other languages, including Swedish, Norwegian, Danish, Dutch, Polish, French, Czech, and Spanish (Ovando & Collier, 1998).

The laws often prohibited the teaching of a foreign language. The anti-foreign-language part of Nebraska's English-only law was challenged at the state level—where the law was left intact—and then at the U.S. Supreme Court in *Meyer* v. *Nebraska.*. The Meyer decision ruled that the Nebraska statutory prohibition against teaching a foreign language in grades lower than ninth grade in religious schools limited the student's right to learn and the parents' right to control what their children would study. The intent of the statute was to use the schools as agents for Americanization and assimilation. The Meyer decision left intact former court rulings that the state could require English-only instruction in publicly funded schools.

The English-only laws remained in effect until the civil rights movement of the late 1960s. Before the civil rights movement, the English-only laws were enforced to promote the assimilation of linguistic minorities in the Southwestern states, where large populations of linguistic minorities resided, as well as in Indian boarding schools operated by the Bureau of Indian Affairs. In fact, the Indian boarding schools (most have been closed) severely punished Native American children who attempted to speak their native languages.

Although the anti-foreign-language laws of the 1920s were deemed unconstitutional, the laws precipitated a tradition of excluding foreign languages from the elementary public school curriculum. During the middle 1950s foreign language programs were included in the elementary grades. These programs relied heavily on federal funds provided by the National Defense Education Act (NDEA). When federal funding ended, some public schools tried to continue the foreign language programs. Primarily for financial reasons the programs did not maintain their initial thrusts, and by slow degrees they were discontinued. Few, if any, existed in the 1970s.

Equal Educational Opportunities and Language Education

During the late 1960s and the 1970s, the federal government formulated an equal educational policy that focused on language education programs. Particularly the Bilingual Education Act and the U.S. District Court decisions, *Lau* v. *Nichols* and *School Children* v. *Ann Arbor School Board,* established policies that impacted public school language instruction.

In 1968, Public Law 90-247, The Bilingual Education Act, was enacted. The Bilingual Education Act, the seventh amendment to the Elementary and Secondary Education Act of 1965 (Title VII), declared that it was (Geffert et al., 1975)

> to be the Policy of the United States to provide financial assistance to local education agencies to develop and carry out new and imaginative elementary and secondary school programs designed to meet the special education needs [of] children who come from environments where the dominant language is other than English. (pp. 121–123)

The act stipulated that it would be U.S. government policy to assist financially in the development and implementation of bilingual education programs in U.S. public schools and trust territories.

In 1973, the act was changed to the Comprehensive Bilingual Education Amendment Act of 1973. The act was extended for training bilingual teachers and bilingual teacher trainers. The act's policy recognized that (1) large numbers of children have limited English-speaking ability, (2) many of these children have a cultural heritage that differs from that of English-speaking people, and (3) a primary means by which a child learns is through using language and cultural heritage. The act provided financial assistance for extending and improving existing bilingual-bicultural programs in public schools, for improving resource and dissemination centers, and for developing and publishing bilingual-bicultural curriculum materials. Assistance was also provided for stipends and fellowships so that teachers and teacher educators could be trained in bilingual-bicultural methodology.

A major catalyst for bilingual instruction was the Supreme Court ruling of *Lau* v. *Nichols* that provisions for the same teachers, programs, and textbooks in the same language for all students in the San Francisco school district did not provide equal educational opportunity when the native language of a sizable number of the student body was not English. In part, the ruling held (*Lau* v. *Nichols*, 1974):

> There is no equality of treatment merely by providing students with the same facilities, textbooks, teachers, and curriculum; for students who do not understand English are effectively foreclosed from any meaningful education.... Where inability to speak and understand the English language excludes national origin-minority group children from effective participation in the education program offered by a school district, the district must take affirmative steps to rectify the language deficiency in order to open its instructional program to these students. (p. 563)

The ruling did not mandate bilingual instruction for non-English-speaking students, but it did stipulate that special language programs were necessary—if schools were to provide equal educational opportunity for such students.

Equal educational opportunity policy regarding speakers of Ebonics (also called Black English) has been formulated. The policy was precipitated by the District Court ruling in *Martin Luther King Jr. Elementary School* v. *Ann Arbor School District* in 1979. A case was made for students who spoke Ebonics as a home and community language. The plaintiffs argued that language differences impeded the equal participation of the African American students in the school's instructional program because the instructional program was conducted entirely in the standard school-English dialect. Using linguistic and educational research evidence, the lawyers for the students established (Martin Luther King, Jr., 1979)

> that unless those instructing in reading recognize (1) the existence of a home language used by the children in their own community for much of their nonschool communications, and (2) that this home language may be a cause of the superficial difficulties in speaking standard English, great harm will be done. The child may withdraw or may act out frustrations and may not learn to read. A language barrier develops when teachers, in helping the child to switch from the home (Ebonics) language to standard English, refuse to admit the existence of a language that is the acceptable way of talking in his local community. (p. 71861)

Therefore, the court required the defendant board to take steps to help its teachers recognize the home language of the students and to use that knowledge in their attempts to teach reading skills in standard English. *Students who use Ebonics should be taught standard English.* Yet, teachers of students who speak Ebonics should be aware of the linguistic and semantic variations of the English dialects spoken by African Americans so they can better teach standard English to Ebonics speakers.

During the 1980s, in response to the geopolitical climate and the recognized need to teach students the languages and cultures of other countries, foreign language education programs emerged in some elementary schools. Primarily, these programs emerged in large city school districts, such as Seattle, Los Angeles, Boston, New York, Miami, and Chicago, whose communities are engaged in global communications and commerce.

Political Interest Groups

During the 1980s two language political interest groups formed, U.S. English and English Plus. U.S. English group advocates English as the nation's official language based on a philosophy that English is the nation's common language and should be the primary language of government. The group lobbies for federal and state laws that will eliminate the use of any languages other than English in all public and private sectors. The Arizona law it promoted, for example, would have prohibited the use of any language other than English by government workers at all times, even during their lunch hours. The law was declared unconstitutional by a federal court as a violation of First Amendment rights.

However, in the late 1990s, the English-only political interest groups made strong headway in California. In June 1999, these groups managed to successfully campaign to get Proposition 227, also called the Unz Amendment, voted into law. The law requires California children with limited English-speaking ability to be taught "overwhelmingly" in English for one year before being moved into regular English-only classrooms; that is, the law prevents the use of bilingual instruction in California schools, with few minor exceptions:

> All children in California public schools shall be taught English by being taught in English. In particular, this shall require that all children be placed in English language classrooms. (California Education Code, 1999)

This section of the California Code quoted above, Section 305, actually defines "bilingual instruction" incorrectly as "a language acquisition process for pupils in which much or all instruction, textbooks, and teaching materials are in the child's native language (California Education Code, 1999). Curiously, the English-only law defines "bilingual instruction" (which means instruction in two languages) as "monolingual instruction," which means instruction in one language. Clearly, the law was passed to eliminate true bilingual instruction in California public schools. The underlying intent of the new law was political rather than educational.

The English-only interests in California also managed to quell the use of Ebonics in California schools late in the 1990s. In March 1996, the Oakland School

Board recognized Ebonics as a valid linguistic system and issued a resolution that Ebonics could be used in Oakland schools to put the school district in compliance with the U.S. Supreme Court ruling in *Martin Luther King Jr.* v. *Ann Arbor School District, 1979,* described above. The intent of the resolution was to allow teachers to use Ebonics to teach African American students about their ethnic heritage as well as to teach them Standard English—both educationally valid strategies. The resolution's intent *was not* to suggest the teaching of Ebonics in place of Standard English.

English-only proponents managed to get national media attention by implying that the Oakland School's resolution intended to teach African American students in Ebonics only. Even though the implication was inaccurate and incorrect, a perception was created that African American students were not going to be taught Standard American English. Understandably, fears within African American communities were raised—that African American students in Oakland would be linguistically ghettoized—if they were taught Ebonics-only instead of Standard English. And worse, if the Oakland Resolution were truly an Ebonics-only strategy, the fear was that the resolution would set a bad precedent for other communities in the United States.

A furious debate arose over the use of Ebonics in the classroom, culminating in a special hearing before the U.S. Senate's Committee on Appropriations (Committee on Appropriations, 1997). The Committee listened and recorded the testimony of linguists, educators, pastors, national civil rights leaders, teachers, students, parents, and other concerned citizens and scholars. Overall, the drift of the testimony affirmed the use of Ebonics as a valid instrument for teaching African American students their ethnic heritage as well as for teaching them Standard English—the actual intent of the Oakland School District's Resolution on Ebonics as well as the intent of the *Martin Luther King, Jr.* v. *Ann Arbor* court ruling. The Congressional hearing also affirmed that school curriculum and teachers should show respect for the language spoken by African American children. Further, the hearing affirmed that African American children must be taught Standard English.

As time passed, and tempers cooled, the Ebonics debate simmered down. However, the acrimonious nature of the debate left many school boards leery of criticism. To avoid criticism, school boards now may back away from discussions about appropriate strategies for teaching African American students their ethnic heritage and Standard English. The Oakland Schools Ebonics debate was a case of democracy going awry. The politics of fear was injected into the dialogue, causing the Oakland School Board to recoil from otherwise normal activities—keeping the school district in compliance with civil rights requirements as well as providing leadership for legitimate educational goals.

By August 1999, the English-only thrust had made headway in 24 states that had either amended their constitutions or enacted statutes making English their official language. Georgia enacted an English-only resolution that has the effect of law. Hawaii's law makes Native Hawaiian coequal to English as its official languages. Table 14.1 lists the states for which English was the official language in 1999 (U.S. English, Inc. www.us-english.org/states.htm, Wednesday, August 4, 1999).

TABLE 14.1   States in Which English Is the Official Language

State	Year of Enactment
Alabama	1990
Alaska	1998
Arkansas	1987
California	1986
Colorado	1988
Florida	1988
Georgia	1986
Hawaii	1978
Illinois	1969
Indiana	1984
Kentucky	1984
Massachusetts	1975
Mississippi	1987
Missouri	1998
Montana	1995
Nebraska	1923
New Hampshire	1997
N. Carolina	1987
N. Dakota	1987
S. Carolina	1987
S. Dakota	1995
Tennessee	1984
Virginia	1981
Wyoming	1996

Source: Based on information in *U.S. English,* "States with Official English Laws." At http://www.us-english.org/states.htm Reprinted with permission of *U.S. English.*

The English Plus group (National Council for Languages and International Studies, 1992) advocates linguistic pluralism:

> We hold that all persons in our culturally rich and linguistically diverse nation should be provided the opportunity and be encouraged to become proficient in more than one language. (p. 1)

The group advocates the enactment of laws to foster educational programs that offer opportunities to learn a second language and develop cultural sensitivity. The Joint National Committee for Languages (JNCL) provides the group a forum for discussion and cooperation with language professionals. JNCL consists of 36 language associations that encompass most areas of the language profession, including the major and less commonly taught languages as well as English, English-as-a-Second-Language, bilingual education, and the classics. JNCL's political arm, the National Council for Languages and International Studies, lobbies Congress and state legislatures to facilitate the passage of laws that will provide funds for second-language education programs.

English Plus posits that bilingualism, especially when used in educational programs, emergency services, and ballots, greatly helps non-English speakers make the transition from their native language to English. Further, the group posits that bilingualism is necessary in educational and other social service agencies to assist with the assimilation of non-English speakers; otherwise, non-English-speaking citizens and residents will be alienated from participation in public affairs, thereby posing a threat to national solidarity (Shumway, 1986).

Attitudes toward Learning Standard English as a Second Language

Attitudes toward learning Standard English as a second language vary. A large body of research (Good, 1981) shows that many teachers judge their students' intellectual abilities by the way they speak English in the early grades (i.e., teachers label non-standard-English-speaking youngsters as being less intelligent than students who speak standard English) and then expect less of the non-standard-English-speaking student. Once the students are labeled less intelligent than their standard-English-speaking peers, the label sticks and a self-fulfilling prophecy sets in—the youngsters "live down" to the lowered expectations of their teachers and achieve less compared to their standard-English-speaking peers.

Other studies report that low-income students resist learning standard English, as did Willis (1977) in England, and Anyon (1980) and Ogbu (1988) in the United States. In these studies, the low-income students who were studied perceived the language and curriculum of the school as their "enemy." They were concerned that the school's curriculum and its language—standard British English or Standard American English—would cause them to lose their cultural identities. Therefore, they resisted learning the language and curriculum of the school, which they perceived as ethnocentric at the core.

While the attitude studies cited above pertaining to standard-English acquisition are somewhat dated, notions of standard-English ethnocentrism still cling to the minds of some educators. A recent study of Mexican American students in a Midwestern middle school by Nielsen (1998) supports the notion that some educators still use the students' language or dialect as a "marker" to label their intellectual abilities. In a study by Garcia and Diaz (1992), Spanish-English Latino bilinguals were asked which language they valued the most—they selected English over Spanish. While they supported the notion of Spanish-English bilingualism, they reported that they considered English the language of opportunity and access in the United States. They reported valuing English above Spanish and did not resist learning standard English. In fact, they embraced a mastery of standard English.

Our language policies and practices are now at a crossroads. The two advocacy groups, U.S. English and English Plus, exemplify the second-language ambivalence held by people in the United States as the legacies of linguistic pluralism and English language ethnocentrism battle for political support of their causes.

Educators should focus on the instructional intent of language education strategies, always asking this question: Which strategies are in the best long-range interest of their students? Knowing one's ethnic heritage, and knowing Standard English, it seems to me, are in the long-range interest of all students, as affirmed by the study of the Committee on the Prevention of Reading Difficulties in Young Children, a committee of the National Research Council of the National Academy of Sciences (Burns & Snow, 1999). The debate over which language—or dialect—is appropriate in the classroom is volatile because it is a debate about culture, ethnicity, power, and identity (Perry & Delpit, 1998). Those who desire to maintain a Eurocentric American culture and identity through the schools advocate an English-only policy to the detriment of students who differ in language, dialect, or culture. Those who desire to foster a pluralistic American culture and identity through the schools advocate an English-plus policy to the betterment of all students.

Research and Theory on Language and Dialect

As children grow they develop a dialect spoken by their parents and immediate family. A dialect is a variation of an idealized language model; that is, a dialect is a valid communication medium that contains its own rules of logic and grammar. In the United States, most people speak a dialect of standard American English, which is the idealized version of the English language within the United States. (Of course, for some people in the United States, English is not the first dialect.) Standard American English is construed as the language's grammatical rules taught in the U.S. public schools and the usage of journalists, television newscasters, and the educated populace. However, even though teachers, journalists, and the educated populace write in standard American English, they nonetheless speak in a dialect of English. No one is immune from speaking dialect.

Dialects of American English

Language and dialect are not the same. A language is an idealized model for communication; it is an abstraction and exists in the minds of grammarians, linguists, and others who study language. A dialect is a real speech and grammatical system a group uses for communication. A dialect exists in the empirical world, and it exists whenever people communicate. Swiss linguist Ferdinand Saussure (1983) provided a distinction between the two: he called a language *langue* and a dialect *parole.*

The *langue* of U.S. society is so-called standard English; its *parole* consists of at least four distinctive dialects: Ebonics, Eastern English, General American, and

Southern English. The dialects are mutually intelligible, but they do differ in intonations and vocabulary. Also, the dialects are diverse; Eastern English can be divided into three subdialects, as can the Southern dialect; the General American dialect is a conglomeration of all remaining United States English dialects spoken in the Midwest, Southwest, Far West, and Northwest. The three regional dialects differ primarily in vocabulary, intonation, and idioms; they are mutually intelligible, and their grammatical systems do not differ significantly.

The dialects spoken by African Americans, when compared to the other American English dialects, do differ grammatically. Robert L. Williams (1975), professor emeritus at Washington University, combined two terms to define the term *Ebonics*: the term *ebony,* meaning *black,* and *phonics,* meaning the *science of speech sounds.* In Williams's book, *Ebonics: The True Language of Black Folks* (1975), *Ebonics* is defined as

> the linguistic and paralinguistic features which, on a concentric continuum, represent the communication competence of the West African, Caribbean, and U.S. slave descendents of African origin. It includes the grammar, various idioms, patois, argots, idiolects, and social dialects of black people. (p. iv)

The scholarship on Ebonics is rich in linguistic, sociolinguistic, grammatical, and cultural descriptions. Also, there is a rich body of African American prose and poetry written in the various Ebonic *patois.* Here are two excellent references: Holloway (1990) and Smitherman (2000). One practical way to become familiar with the Ebonics used by students is for teachers to listen to Ebonics-speaking students. Teachers should seek permission from their students (and parents) to tape record the students' speech patterns in both formal and informal settings. The tapes should be transcribed and analyzed by a competent linguist who can identify the grammatical and semantic variations of the recorded dialect. Awareness of the variations can better help educators as they make decisions about teaching standard English to speakers of Ebonics. An in-depth knowledge of the local dialect is crucial—if the teachers desire to make data-based decisions about how best to teach standard English to their Ebonics-speaking students. Also, keep in mind, not all African Americans use Ebonics when speaking.

Occasionally, criticism is heard from language purists claiming that American English is being adulterated by its many dialects and by the many foreign languages spoken in the United States. The notion that American English was once pure and now faces adulteration by other languages and dialects flies in the face of the fact that American English is very diverse. From its inception, the language has proved to be a sponge that borrows words from other languages and cultures (Simpson, 1986). Table 14.2 shows some commonly used American English words borrowed from various cultures.

These are common words taken from five different cultural groups. There are many others words taken from other languages. The words, which are not exotic or exceptional, are drawn from different U.S. groups and reflect the pluralism in the United States.

TABLE 14.2   English Words Borrowed from Other Languages

Dutch	French	German	Native American	Spanish
boss	depot	dunk	hickory	coyote
cookie	cab	noodle	pecan	corral
waffle	gopher	ouch	moose	ranch

Linking Culture, Ethnicity, and Language

The fundamental role of a language or a dialect is group communication. Even though people are not restricted to language for communication, language is of overarching importance because it is the fundamental medium through which ethnicity is transmitted and cultural identity is formed. A language system in general, and a dialect in particular, serve as tools to categorize, interpret, and share experiences. Ethnicity and language thus intertwine, language being the medium and ethnicity the message.

Youngsters learn the content of their ethnicity—and their cultures and identities—through the medium of their parents' dialect. The dialect is used to convey cultural meaning to the youngsters; later, as the youngsters master the dialect, they use it to convey cultural content. The dialect serves the youngsters in the formation of their perceptions, attitudes, and values about their physical and social environments, which is fundamental to cultural development. An individual's dialect reflects his or her views and perceptions of reality. For example, in American English there exist only several conceptions of snow (e.g., powder snow or wet snow). Within the Alaskan native languages, however, there exist many conceptions of snow. The reason for the difference is that snow is of greater economic and social importance to the Native Alaskans than it is to most English-speaking peoples. The vocabulary of a group's language reflects distinctions and categories important to the group. Conversely, relatively unimportant categories are reflected minimally, or the category may be nonexistent within the group's vocabulary.

The grammatical system of a group's language reflects the group's attitude toward its physical environment. For example, the Navajo language emphasizes the reporting of events in motion. When describing a large mountain in the Navajo language, a Navajo may say "the mountain is busy being big and blue." The Navajo describes the physical environment as fluid. In U.S. English, however, the mountain's description, "the mountain is big and blue," is a description of a static physical environment. The Navajo and English descriptions reflect differing cultural interpretations of the same natural environment (Hoijer, 1951).

These comments should not be interpreted to mean that language determines ethnicity or cultural orientations. Rather, language serves as a mirror of ethnicity and culture, reflecting a person's values, beliefs, and attitudes. Note the subtle differences of attitudes in the two following examples of what is being said in Spanish and then in English:

> *El avión se fué.* Literal translation: *"The plane left me."* In idiomatic English, one would say: *"I missed my plane."*
>
> *El plato sé cayó.* Literal translation: *"The plate dropped from my hand."* In idiomatic English, one would say: *"I dropped the plate."*

The differences in meanings between the two languages are subtle, but they reveal contrasting attitudes about locus of responsibility. In the first Spanish example, one attributes the fault of missing an airplane to the airplane itself, as in *"the airplane left me."* In idiomatic English, one attributes the fault of missing the airplane to oneself, as in *"I missed my plane."* In the second Spanish example, one attributes the falling of a plate to the plate itself, as in *"The plate dropped from my hand."* In idiomatic English, one attributes the falling of the plate to oneself, as in *"I dropped the plate."*

Culture impacts language, in particular its vocabulary items, in significant ways. Consequently, culture—as a broadly based emotion and sense of group identity—is reflected in a group's dialect and vocabulary. Because a cultural group uses a dialect to embody and transmit its cultural content, knowledge about the cultural group presupposes knowledge of its dialect. To better understand the people from a particular culture, one should study that people's dialect.

Language Acquisition of Native Bilinguals

Much confusion persists regarding bilingual persons. The ideal bilingual person can speak, read, write, and think in two languages with nativelike control of both languages. Few persons ever reach the ideal. Rather, many bilinguals tend to favor one language over the other. Native bilinguals have used two languages since their preschool and primary years in school. Some have acquired both languages in their natural social settings by using them within the speech community of each language where the language is used for practical, communicative functions. Others have acquired their first language in a natural setting—the home and community—but have learned their second language in the formal setting of school, where language is used both to communicate and conduct abstract thinking, which is decontextualized or removed from the practical, day-to-day affairs of most people.

Most people follow the same pattern when they acquire their first language. People have the innate ability to learn the sounds, rules, and patterns of any language. Through interaction with other people, infants experiment with speech and attempt to communicate. Their babble may be serious attempts to communicate, but until they use speech, they do not communicate meaningfully with adults. Eventually, infants discover simple sentences, such as [*me hungee >* meaning *I'm hungry*], then more complex sentences [*me hungee; eat num-num now!*] meaning *I'm hungry and want to eat some good food right now* !], and finally full discourse in standard English emerges. Adults provide a rich, helping environment and rarely correct grammar or pronunciation. Incrementally, infants independently reconstruct the language spoken by adults and eventually communicate with it.

First- and second-language acquisition follows a similar basic pattern. In a dated but nonetheless comprehensive study of second-language acquisition, Dulay and Burt (1974) recorded the English speech patterns of 145 children, ages 5 and 8, whose first language was Spanish and who were learning English as a second language. The researchers analyzed the speech samples for developmental and interference errors. Developmental errors are mistakes that most infants make when they are learning English as a first language. Interference errors are mistakes or habits that bilingual persons transfer from their first language to utterances in the second, such as the "foreign" accent of some bilinguals. Eighty-five percent of the errors were developmental; 10 percent were interference; the remainder were attributed to individual differences. The children were acquiring English much like children who acquire English as a first language.

The fundamental goal of language acquisition is communicative competence. Communicative competence refers to the ability of people to speak meaningfully so that native speakers of the language can understand the messages being sent and can respond with a meaningful message, that is, a person has communicative competence when speaking and can be understood by native speakers of the language. Competence refers to understanding and speaking a language; daily, thousands of people fill their basic needs without reading or writing because they accomplish their business affairs through speaking. Yet, some tasks require reading and writing abilities. The ideal goal of language acquisition is literacy, which refers to the ability to use the full range of the language arts, listening, comprehension, speaking, reading, and writing.

With bilingual students, the competency/literacy distinction is critically important. A bilingual's level of competence can have one of three effects on academic achievement: (1) additive bilingualism, which enhances academic achievement; (2) dominant bilingualism, which neither enhances nor retards academic achievement; or (3) subtractive bilingualism, which retards achievement. Additive bilinguals are equally competent and literate in two languages. They benefit from the linguistic and semantic flexibility that the two languages provide.

The additive bilingual has what Cummins (1979) calls Common Underlying Proficiency (CUP), which refers to the interdependence of the two languages. Once a concept is learned in one language it need not be learned in the second language. Dominant bilinguals are fully literate in their first language and are somewhat competent or literate in their second language. They are not affected in a positive or negative direction regarding academic achievement in their first language.

Subtractive bilinguals, unlike their additive peers, have not developed full literacy in their first language although they may have developed communicative competence in their two languages. They are able to function interpersonally in two languages (they are conversationally competent); they have not developed the higher level thinking skills necessary for full literacy. Because they have not developed higher levels of thinking skills in their first language, they do not have these skills to transfer to the second language. Consequently, subtractive bilinguals should develop full communicative competence and rudimentary literacy in their first language before being formally introduced to their second language.

Research Bases of Bilingual Instruction

The educational purpose of bilingual instruction is supposed to increase academic achievement by using the student's home language as the main communication medium (August & Hakuta, 1997). Bilingual instruction involves the use of two languages for instruction for part or all of the activities within the classroom. One language is English; the other language is the student's home language, that is, the language spoken in the home. English is taught as a second language. Many times the student's first significant introduction to English is when he or she enters school. In other instances, the student may begin school with minimum English language skills.

Moran and Hakuta (1995) analyzed and evaluated the efficacy of various approaches to bilingual instruction. For purposes of simplification, I have divided the various approaches into two types: *Maintenance of Native Language* (MNL) and *Transitional English as a Second Language* (TESL). The Maintenance Native Language methods uses the student's home language in all subject areas to begin instruction. After mastery in listening, speaking, reading, and writing, the student is introduced to English. The method's supposition is that native language literacy should be achieved before the student is introduced to the English language arts. Having achieved native language literacy, the student should have no difficulty transferring to English.

The second method, Transitional English as a Second Language, is sometimes called the direct method. TESL teaches the student immediate English language skills. The TESL pull-out system takes the student out of the classroom daily for instruction in the English language arts. The student returns to the regular class for instruction in other subjects. The TESL intensive system immerses the student in the English language arts for extended time periods. When the student learns to speak the language, then reading in English is introduced. When the student reads English, he or she is returned to the monolingual English classroom.

The bilingual education debate of the 1980s and 1990s centered on this question: Which method (MNL or TESL) best teaches English to the non-English speaker? The MNL camp reasoned that this method is effective because it builds a solid linguistic foundation in the student's native language before it attempts to teach the second language. This foundation provides a solid base from which the second language can be learned. However, the MNL methods take longer than does the TESL method. The MNL method requires the student to develop almost full literacy in the first language before attempting to learn the second language.

The TESL supporters identified the time factor as the critical flaw with the MNL method. Given the highly mobile nature of U.S. society, and given the possibility that linguistic minority students change schools quite often, the TESL camp argued that the MNL method was not a practical way of teaching English to highly mobile populations. Rather, the more direct TESL method is preferable because it provides the student with an immediate introduction to English, thereby ensuring an opportunity to learn it.

The weight of the research evidence tips the scale in favor of the MNL method because long-range academic achievement and educational development are its demonstrable outcomes (August & Hakuta, 1997; Chamot & O'Malley, 1994; Swain & Lapkin, 1981). In terms of learning English, speaking, reading, and writing—as well as learning other subjects, such as mathematics and the social sciences—the MNL method has demonstrated its efficacy. Willig's (1985) meta-analysis of 23 studies on the effectiveness of MNL conducted between 1968 and 1980 rendered the following results:

> Participation in bilingual education programs consistently produced small to moderate differences favoring bilingual education for tests of reading, language skills, mathematics, and total achievement when the tests were in English, and for reading, language, mathematics, writing, social studies, listening comprehension, and attitudes toward school or self when tests were in other languages. (p. 270)

On a short-range basis, the TESL method more quickly teaches students to speak, read, and write English at a functional level. Yet, the TESL method only provides students a minimum of lower-level literacy skills in speaking, reading, and writing. For the sake of efficiency or expediency, the TESL method does not attend to deep structure cognitive abilities, such as the skills required for critical thinking—hypothesizing, predicting, and inferring.

The results of both the MNL and TESL methods are predictable given their respective operating assumptions. The TESL method assumes its purposes to be compensatory; that is, the student's ability to use English is viewed as a deficiency that must be compensated for through a submersion into English-only instruction. Another assumption is that the student's first language is a liability that interferes with the development of English. Therefore, according to this assumption, the student's first language must be ignored, if not extinguished. By diminishing the value of the student's first language, and by ignoring or attempting to extinguish it, teachers using the TESL method create in their students a kind of subtractive bilingualism, that is, the students are not given the chance to develop fully in their first language. The short-range effect of the TESL method does produce English speakers who have superficial control of English and of their first language primarily because they have not developed the deep structure cognitive abilities attributed to full language literacy within a language.

The MNL method assumes its purpose to be enrichment. The student's inability to use English is viewed as a temporary condition, which can be ameliorated by fostering the enrichment and development of the student's first language. A corollary assumption is that the student's first language is worthy of development. What happens is that the MNL method, by valuing and developing full literacy in the first language, provides student's deep structure cognitive abilities that transfer to the second language, that is, additive bilingualism.

Global Stakes of Effective
Cross-Cultural Communications

We must begin to think in new ways about language education. It has often been used as a weapon for cultural imperialism and to promote the economic or political interests of sundry elite groups. Various religions, social classes, multinational corporations, and nations have all used language education to promote their self-interests. We should think of *language education as a means to achieve cultural understanding.*

Effective cross-cultural communications—interacting well with people from other cultures—is achieved by knowing and understanding people from other cultures. Contact with other people is essential. As commonsensical as this may sound, interacting with people from other cultures is the quickest, most effective way to learn about other peoples and their cultures. By working, socializing, and interacting with people who are culturally different, individuals can develop an understanding of how to communicate effectively across cultures. Also, cross-cultural contact can be achieved through travel or guided experiences, such as serving in a community center in a part of town that differs in cultural orientation from one's own culture.

Another way to develop cross-cultural communication abilities is through education. That is, one can know about other groups by studying another group's history, literature, art, or music. Yet, contact is still essential. Through the Internet, telecommunications, and/or videotapes, indirect contact with people from other cultures is possible. I am familiar with teachers who promote intercultural communications with their students via the Internet. Their U.S. students work on research projects with students from other countries, or with students in other communities, regions, or states within the United States. I am also familiar with teachers who use videotape exchanges produced by their students as a means to facilitate cultural sharing with students from other nations and from other communities in the United States. Given the wealth of communication technologies in our society, the possibilities for making contact across cultures are vast.

Whether one travels, uses guided experiences, or simply studies other cultures, these three fundamental principles can serve as guides when one is involved in the dynamics of cross-cultural communication:

1. *One should understand the nature of culture.* A culture is like an iceberg. Nine-tenths of an iceberg is submerged and out of sight. The visible one-tenth is important because it signals its location, but the overwhelming mass of the iceberg is unknown—its overall shape, density, and volume hidden from view. Only one-tenth of a person's culture is apparent. The visible signs of a culture, the material culture—clothing, foods, arts, music, religion, and language, for example—consists of about one-tenth of the culture's substance. The overwhelming mass of a culture is unconscious—assumptions about truth, beauty, worth, love, value, respect, and trust—and generally not conscious to an individual. It is hidden in the recesses of one's mind. When cultural conflict occurs, it usually occurs at the unconscious, implicit level, where people tuck away their ideologies, biases, beliefs, and attitudes that have formed from their life experiences.

2. *One should understand how culture filters one's world-view.* Social psychologists refer to the unconscious level of culture as one's *schemata*—a frame of reference that provides structure and organization for new experiences and that one uses to interpret social interactions and social events. We all view and interpret the world through our own unique schemata. From a strictly existential viewpoint, no one can truly know someone else's culture, primarily because an individual's culture is an aggregation of largely unconscious experiences unique to the individual. Yet, in general ways, we can know the cultures of others. Humans are more alike than they are different. We should not forget there is only one human race, and we all share in common the experience of being human on the same planet, drinking the same water, and breathing the same air. As we attempt to communicate with each other across cultures, we should not forget that we have much in common, and that it is the differences in culture that make life exciting and interesting. Still, cultural differences can impede communication, although they need not block communications entirely. For example, in Vietnamese culture, a person's head is considered sacred. It is viewed as the temple that holds one's soul. Touching the top of a person's head is frowned on within Vietnamese culture. In U.S. classrooms, a teacher might pat a student's head, or ruffle the student's hair, as a nonverbal sign of approval for a job well done. If the student is Vietnamese, the same gesture of support may offend the student by touching "the sacred temple of his soul"—even though the teacher's intent was to praise the student. If there is trust between the student and the teacher, the student may likely dismiss the teacher's gestures as 'benign ignorance.' If the student distrusts the teacher, the student may take offense. Minimally, empathy toward others should be developed (i.e., develop the knack of projecting oneself into the place of others). The better one understands the language and culture of others, the better one should be able to infer the underlying meaning of nonverbal cues.

3. *One develops relationships with individuals rather than with groups.* For effective cross-cultural communications, keep in mind that relationships are developed by individuals. One does not develop a relationship with a cultural group. One may study another cultural group, and one may become thoroughly familiar with the materials and intangible aspects of another culture, but relationships require that individuals interact with each other as individuals—not as members of this or that cultural group.

Effective cross-cultural communications occurs when individuals from different cultures understand each other, which comes through interaction. Genuine cross-cultural understandings occur when individuals from differing cultures are in sustained contact with each other working on common goals. As they interact, attempting to achieve their common goals, they develop empathy toward each other, a crucial element in cross-cultural understandings. Communication failures occur when people do not understand each other's cultures.

Benchmarks for Linking Language and Culture in Education

Teachers, school administrators, citizens, and school board members have the authority and legal power to implement a policy of linguistic pluralism in their schools. This policy would foster the knowledge of second languages and cultures; it would also foster respect for the languages and dialects spoken by other people within the United States and throughout the world. A policy of linguistic pluralism could be simply written, to read:

> It is the policy of the ['Sally Forward County Schools'—insert the name of the school district here] to foster the study of English in its various American dialects as well to study other languages of the world for the purpose of promoting effective cross-cultural communications.

The policy should provide parameters so that teachers can accommodate linguistic differences while teaching any subject, teach about linguistic diversity while teaching English, and teach languages other than English. To form and implement a pluralistic policy the following five benchmarks are suggested.

Benchmark 1: A Concise Statement Supportive of Linguistic Pluralism Should Be Made

School-English ethnocentrism—the attitude that school English is superior to other dialects and languages—is the nexus of the problem. The policy statement would foster mastery of American English and foster proficiency in other languages. The statement would have three major dimensions: (1) mastery of American English, (2) developing proficiency in other languages, and (3) teaching about linguistic diversity, while fostering a climate of respect for linguistic differences.

Benchmark 2: Teachers Should Be Cognizant of Their Linguistic Biases against the Dialects or Languages of Linguistically Different Students

Again, linguistic ethnocentrism is at the nexus of the problem. Primarily, respect for the student's home dialect should be fostered. Rather than viewing the home dialect as defective, teachers should view the dialect as a source of strength. Students do not enter school speaking a substandard dialect; they may enter school speaking non-school-standard English or a different language. The position that youngsters speak a substandard version of English is an imposition of school English as the only English dialect capable of use for learning.

Benchmark 3: Instructional Strategies Should Accommodate Linguistically Different Students

Linguistically different students should not be placed in special language programs that segregate them from the regular classroom. In fact, positive intercultural experiences can be fostered in linguistically diverse classrooms. When there are a large number of non-English speakers of the same language, a bilingual teacher is feasible. However, if possible, monolingual English-speaking students should be incorporated into this otherwise linguistically segregated arrangement. With students who use Ebonics, or other non-school English dialects, standard school-English should be taught as an alternate dialect necessary for broader social interactions. All students need to learn to understand, read, and write in standard English. Therefore, the linguistic resources of linguistically different students should be maximized to teach basic English literacy.

Benchmark 4: Curriculum Materials Should Reflect the Linguistic Diversity in the United States and the World

This benchmark requires that the curriculum be permeated with multilingual materials. Teachers should use every opportunity to incorporate nonschool English dialects and languages into all their curriculum materials. Examples I've seen work in the classroom include:

1. Learning to count in Spanish, French, German, or some other language.
2. Learning that people call their neighborhoods by different names, *ghetto* (Italian origin), *barrio* (Spanish for neighborhood).
3. Learning to read the Chinese calendar.
4. Using the Internet to communicate with other students in their native languages.
5. Using the Internet: exchanging folklore, stories, and music with students from other parts of the United States or world.
6. Using the Internet: collaborating on research projects with students from other parts of the United States or world.

The list is endless and the approach feasible. Incorporating linguistic diversity into curriculum materials adds variety to otherwise routine learning activities.

Benchmark 5: Schools Should Implement Second-Language Programs for All Students

When they graduate from high school, students should be fully literate in American English and in one or more other languages. For too long we have coddled the minds of our young people, wasting their time with elementary school language arts programs that have muted rather than empowered them to achieve full literacy in American English and in other languages. Yet, millions of children throughout the world have acquired second-language proficiencies, often without the benefits of educational programs. Now that the English language arts are being integrated into the teaching of other subjects, such as the sciences and social studies, there is room in the elementary school curriculum to incorporate second-language learning and literature.

Summary

Learning is a holistic phenomenon in which language and cognitive development dynamically interact. Literacy, that is, the ability to think, speak, read, and write language, should be approached as a holistic manifestation of learning. Consequently, the methods used for teaching first- or second-language literacy should reflect the holistic nature of learning literacy. Language learning should occur within the context in which the language is to be used.

Language, identity, culture, and education are inextricably intertwined. The issue of what language or dialect should be taught in school should be put to rest. The debate is over cultural identity and political power and should focus on what is best for the students. All students should be taught Standard American English. Furthermore, all students should expect that teachers will respect the dialects used by them in their homes. When possible, teachers should use the student's native language or dialect as a means to teach the student's cultural heritage, identity, and Standard American English. The search for the one best way to teach students Standard American English is futile and in some instances can be detrimental to the formative growth of students.

Most nations have a formal or informal language policy that fosters a national language standard. The policy of the United States is assimilation. English as spoken and written in the United States is well established as the nation's language. Even though English is not designated as the nation's official language, it has a powerful designation that ensures its status as the nation's unofficial official language—the designation granted by more than 200 years of tradition and usage. It is—and will remain—the language of opportunity in the United States. Yet, we are being nudged toward a policy of linguistic pluralism by the forces of global interdependence. Our students should be taught the languages and dialects of other people if they are to become true citizens of the global village.

REFERENCES

Anyon, J. (1980). Social Class and the Hidden Curriculum of Work. *Journal of Education, 162*(1), 67–92.

August, D., & Hakuta, K. (Eds.) (1997). *Improving Schooling for Language Minority Children: A Re-* *search Agenda.* Washington, DC: National Academy Press.

Burns, S. M., & Snow, C. E. (Eds.) (1999). *Starting Out Right: A Guide to Promoting Children's*

Reading Success. Washington, DC: National Academy Press.

California Education Code. (1999). Section 300–311.

Chamot, A. U., & O'Malley, J. M. (1994). *The CALLA Handbook: Implementing the Cognitive Academic Language Learning Approach.* Reading, MA: Addison-Wesley.

Committee on Appropriations. (1997). *EBONICS— A Hearing before the Committee on Appropriations.* U.S. Senate, 105th Congress, First Session. Washington, DC: U.S. Government Printing Office.

Crawford, J. (2000). Language Politics in the United States. In C. Ovando & P. McLaren (Eds.), *The Politics of Multiculturalism and Bilingual Education* (pp. 106–125). Boston: McGraw-Hill.

Cummins, J. (1979). Linguistic Interdependence and the Educational Development of Bilingual Children. *Review of Educational Research, 49,* 222–251.

Dulay, H. C., & Burt, M. K. (1974). A New Perspective on Creative Construction Processes in Child Second Language Acquisition. *Language Learning, 24,* 253–278.

Ferguson, C., & Heath, S. B. (Eds.). (1981). *Language in the USA.* New York: Cambridge University Press.

Fishman, J. (1966). *Language Loyalty in the United States.* London: Mouton Press.

Garcia, R., & Diaz, C. (1992). The Status and Use of Spanish and English among Hispanic Youth in Dade County, 1989–1991. *Language and Education, 6*(1), 13–32.

Geffert, H., Harper, R., Sarmiento, S., & Schember, D. (1975). *Current Status of US Bilingual Legislation.* Arlington, VA: Center for Applied Linguistics.

Good, T. L. (1981). Teacher Expectations and Student Perceptions: A Decade of Research. *Educational Leadership, 38*(5), 122–128.

Hoijer, H. (1951). Cultural Implications of Some Navajo Linguistic Categories. *Language, 27,* 111–120.

Holloway, J. (1990). *Africanism in American Culture.* Bloomington: Indiana University Press.

Joint Committee for Languages. (1992). *Official Language States.* Pamphlet. Washington, DC: Author.

Lau v. Nichols. (1974). 414 U.S. 563, 1974.

Martin Luther King Jr., Elementary School Children, et al. v. Ann Arbor School District Board, United States District Court, East District, Michigan. 1979 Civil Action No. 7–71861.

Moran, C., & Hakuta, K. (1995). Bilingual Education: Broadening Research Perspective. In J. Banks & C. A. M. Banks (Eds.), *Handbook of Research on Multicultural Education* (pp. 445–464). New York: Macmillan.

National Council for Languages and International Studies. (1992). *Language Competence and Cultural Awareness in the United States.* Pamphlet. Washington, DC: Author.

Nielsen, D. (1998). *Second Language Acquisition and Its Effects on the Social and Emotional Development of Immigrant Teens in a Small Midwestern Middle School. A Dissertation.* Lincoln: University of Nebraska.

Ogbu, J. (1988). Class Stratification, Racial Stratification, and Schooling. In L. Weis (Ed.), *Race, Class, and Schooling* (pp. 163–182). Albany: State University of New York Press.

Ovando, C., & Collier, P. (1998). *Bilingual and ESL Classrooms* (2nd ed.). New York: McGraw-Hill.

Perry, T., & Delpit, L. (eds.). (1998). *The Real Ebonics Debate: Power, Language, and the Education of African American Children.* Boston: Beacon Press.

Saussure, F. (1983). *Course in General Linguistics.* London: Duckworth & Company.

Shumway, N. (1986). Should English Be Made Official? Yes. As Recorded in the *Congressional Record,* pp. E2046–E2047.

Simpson, D. (1986). *The Politics of American English, 1776–1850.* New York: Oxford University Press.

Smitherman, G. (2000). *Talkin That Talk: Language, Culture and Education in African America.* New York: Routledge.

Swain, M., & Lapkin, S. (1981). *Bilingual Education in Ontario: A Decade of Research.* Toronto: Ontario Institute for Studies in Education.

U.S. English. *States with Official English Laws.* http://www.us-english.org/states.htm, Wednesday, August 4, 1999.

Williams, R. L. (Ed.). (1975). *Ebonics: The True Language of Black Folks.* St. Louis: Institute of Black Studies.

Willig, A. (1985). A Meta-Analysis of Selected Studies on the Effectiveness of Bilingual Education. *Review of Educational Research, 55,* 269–317.

Willis, P. (1977). *Learning to Labor.* New York: Columbia University Press.

CHAPTER

15 Reducing Prejudice in Students: Theory, Research, and Strategies

We cannot reduce racial prejudice unless we acquire an understanding of its causes. First, however, we need to define prejudice. The literature on race relations is replete with efforts to define *prejudice.* Even though the definitions differ to some extent, most suggest that prejudice is a set of rigid and unfavorable attitudes toward a particular group or groups that is formed in disregard of facts. Prejudiced individuals respond to perceived members of these groups on the basis of preconceptions, tending to disregard behavior or personal characteristics that are inconsistent with their biases. Brown (1995) provides a helpful definition of prejudice:

> Prejudice…is any or all of the following: the holding of derogatory social attitudes or cognitive beliefs, the expression of negative effect, or the display of hostile or discriminatory behaviour toward members of a group on account of their membership of that group. (p. 8)

Although social scientists have attempted for years to derive a comprehensive and coherent theory of prejudice, their efforts have not been totally successful (Young-Bruehl, 1996). A number of theories explain various components of prejudice, but none sufficiently describes its many dimensions. Social scientists have rejected some of the older, more simplistic theories of prejudice; other theories are too limited in scope to be helpful to educators. Still others are extremely useful in explaining certain forms of prejudice directed toward specific groups but fail to account for its other facets. A serious study of the theories of prejudice reveals the complexity of this configuration of attitudes and predispositions; thus, simplistic explanations of prejudice only hinder our understanding of it.

Theories of Prejudice

Simpson and Yinger (1985) describe a number of factors that result in prejudice. One factor is the personality requirements of the individual. As a result of both constitutional and learned needs, some people develop personalities that thrive on prejudices and irrational responses. This theory has been offered by a number of other writers and researchers. This chapter later discusses some research on which it is based. During the 1940s and 1950s, this theory was a prominent one in social psychology.

An individual may also develop prejudices based not on personality needs but on the way society is structured. The power structure of society is especially important to this concept. Simpson and Yinger point out that individual behavior takes place within a social, political, and cultural context.

Another genesis of prejudice is the culture itself. Write Simpson and Yinger (1985, p. 108), "Prejudice is a deep-rooted part of American culture, a vital part of the adjustment system of most individuals, a weapon in economic and political conflict…a significant part of the stream of tradition that brings the influences of the past into the present and puts them to use in contemporary conflicts." Simpson and Yinger emphasize that multiple explanations are needed to account for the complexity of prejudice and discrimination.

Personality Theories of Prejudice

In their discussion of the theories of prejudice, Simpson and Yinger describe personality explanations. They cite the individual's personality needs as one basic cause of prejudice. Many researchers during the 1940s and 1950s considered personality the most important variable in the formation of prejudice and discrimination. They attributed different types of personalities to differences in child-rearing practices, some of which were thought to produce personalities intolerant of different races and groups, whereas others helped develop racial tolerance and acceptance in the child. Else Frenkel-Brunswik (1948) and her associates conducted the pioneering research on the role of personality in the formation of prejudice.

In one of a series of studies, Frenkel-Brunswik (1948) compared the racial attitudes and personality characteristics of 1,500 children. Interviews were conducted with the subjects and their parents; both personality and attitude tests were administered. Frenkel-Brunswik concluded that there were significant differences in the personalities of prejudiced and unprejudiced children. She found that prejudiced children evidenced more rejection of out-groups, a blind acceptance of the in-group, a greater degree of aggression, and a strong rejection of persons perceived as weak. The more prejudiced children also displayed a greater resentment of the opposite sex and an admiration for strong figures. They were more willing to submit to authority, more compulsive about cleanliness, and more moralistic. The unprejudiced children were "more oriented toward love and less toward power than the ethnocentric child…and more capable of giving affection" (p. 305). In summarizing her study, Frenkel-Brunswik notes, "It was found that some children tend to reveal a stereotyped and rigid glorification of their own group and an aggressive rejection of outgroups and foreign countries" (p. 296).

Frenkel-Brunswik and her associates also studied the relationship between personality and prejudice in adults (Adorno et al., 1950). They concluded that certain individuals, because of their early childhood experiences, have insecure personalities and a need to dominate and to feel superior to other individuals. These individuals possess an *authoritarian personality,* which is manifested not only in racial prejudice but also in their sexual behavior and religious and political views.

Flaws in Personality Research

Even though the research by Frenkel-Brunswik and her associates contributed greatly to the literature on the origins of prejudice, other researchers have severely criticized it because of its methodological flaws and weak theoretical base. They discuss the theory on which the research is based and review a number of its methodological weaknesses.

Simpson and Yinger (1985) have written one of the most perceptive critiques. They point out that the inadequate attention given to sampling techniques limits the generalizability of the findings. The research is also weakened by heavy reliance on the subjects' memories of childhood; the inadequate control of variables, such as education and group membership; and the low reliability of the measuring instruments. The F Scale used by the researchers measured many variables simultaneously, failing to measure well any one variable. However, Simpson and Yinger conclude that the flaws in the research do not substantially diminish its importance in race relations theory and research.

Social Structure Theories of Prejudice

Blumer (1966) seriously questions attempts to attribute prejudice and discrimination to personality variables. He almost completely dismisses the role of attitudes in influencing behavior. Blumer asserts that the *social setting* rather than *racial attitudes* is the prime determinant of behavior. In trying to understand discrimination against minority groups, he contends that we should analyze social settings and norms instead of the personal attitudes of the individual. Blumer reviews a number of studies indicating the frequently occurring discrepancy between an individual's verbalized attitudes and actual behavior.

Saenger and Gilbert (1950) found that prejudiced individuals will patronize a racially mixed store when their desire to shop exceeds their antipathy toward African Americans. Research by Blalock (1956) suggests that discrimination is not always a correlate of racial prejudice. In certain situations, prejudiced individuals may not discriminate; the prevailing norms may affect their behavior more than their personal attitudes. Merton (1949) presents a useful typology for illustrating the relationship between prejudice and discrimination. He identifies four ideal-types:

1. The unprejudiced nondiscriminator.
2. The unprejudiced discriminator.
3. The prejudiced nondiscriminator.
4. The prejudiced discriminator.

Blumer (1966) summarizes an important study by Lohman and Reitzes (1952):

> In a study of race relations in a large city…the same set of whites behaved entirely differently toward [African Americans] in three situations—working establishment, residential neighborhood and shopping center; no prejudice or discrimination was shown in the working establishment where the whites and [African Americans] belonged to the same labor union, whereas prejudice and discrimination toward [African Americans] by the same whites was pronounced in the case of residential neighborhood. (pp. 112–113)

Blumer (1966) seriously underestimates the role of attitudes and personality as determinants of racial discrimination and prejudice. *An adequate theory of prejudice must take into account both personality variables and the social structure.* Explaining prejudice and discrimination as totally a product of a disorganized personality ignores the facts that humans are social beings and that their reactions in a social setting reflect not only their individual idiosyncrasies and biases but also the prevailing norms and expectations. Thus, bigoted teachers will be less inclined to manifest their true attitudes toward African American students when African American parents are visiting the classroom than when they are alone with their students.

However, social setting alone cannot completely explain racial discrimination; neither can it, as Blumer implies, totally diminish the importance of racial attitudes. If the same bigoted teachers were transferred to an all-African American school in which there was little tolerance for racial discrimination, their behavior would probably become more consistent with the dominant norms of the new setting, but their attitudes would most likely be revealed to their students in subtle ways and perhaps affect them just as profoundly. *The most equalitarian social setting cannot cause an intense bigot to exhibit behavior identical to that of a person free of racial prejudice.*

Much of the research Blumer relies on to support his hypothesis is subject to serious criticism, particularly the study by Lohman and Reitzes (1952). These authors found that their White subjects behaved *"entirely differently toward [Blacks] in different social settings"* [emphasis added] and showed "no prejudice toward them at work" (cited in Blumer, 1966, p. 112). However, I seriously question whether the African American factory workers would have endorsed these conclusions, believing instead that they most likely could have cited examples of discrimination directed against them by their White coworkers. It is highly unlikely that persons who are so bigoted that they would exclude African Americans from their neighborhoods could treat them with full equality at work or indeed in any other setting.

The *social setting* explanation of prejudice and discrimination presents other difficulties. In trying to explain an individual's reactions in a given situation, we must consider not only the group norms but also the importance the individual attaches to the group and setting. Research suggests that a group or situation must be important to an individual before he or she accepts its norms and values. Pearlin (1954) classified a random sample of 383 college students into "acceptors" and "rejectors" on the basis of their attitudes toward African Americans. A majority of the subjects who accepted African Americans in different situations had broken their own close family ties and developed identifications with campus groups.

The more prejudiced individuals indicated that they had maintained close ties with their families and developed few associations with campus groups. Students who became more racially liberal as a result of their college experience considered college group norms more important than their parents' attitudes, whereas the more prejudiced subjects deemed family norms more important. Thus, simply placing individuals in new settings with different norms and values does not necessarily change their behavior and attitudes.

The social setting hypothesis also fails to consider that individuals collectively determine the group norm. Whether a group sanctions racial discrimination or racial tolerance thus depends on the attitudes of its members. Clearly, then, we must consider both *individual attitudes* and *institutional and social norms* when attempting to explain the genesis and perpetuation of racial discrimination and prejudice.

Social Identity Theory: The Minimal Group Paradigm

Social identity theory, or the minimal group paradigm, is one of the modern social psychological theories of prejudice and discrimination (Rothbart & John, 1993). This theory states that whenever in-groups and out-groups form stereotypes, prejudice and discrimination develop. The minimal group paradigm indicates that when mere categorization develops, individuals favor the in-group over the out-group and discriminate against the out-group (Rothbart & John, 1993; Smith & Mackie, 1995). This can occur in situations without prior historical conflict and animosity, competition, physical differences, or any kind of important difference. Writes Tajfel (1970), "Whenever we are confronted with a situation to which some form of intergroup categorization appears directly relevant, we are likely to act in a manner that discriminates against the outgroup and favors the ingroup" (pp. 98–99). Language, for example, can become such a categorization when some students speak Spanish and others do not.

In a series of studies, Tajfel and his colleagues (Billig & Tajfel, 1973; Tajfel, 1970) produced considerable evidence to support the idea that individuals are likely to evaluate the in-group more favorably than the out-group and to treat the in-group more favorably even when the differences between the groups are minimal, contrived, and insignificant. This series of studies indicate the power of *categorization.* In one group of experiments, Tajfel (1970) told a group of public school boys in Bristol that he had divided them into two groups based on whether they had under- or overestimated the number of dots projected on a screen. The subjects were then given a series of tasks in which they could provide rewards to two anonymous students. When the students were in the same groups as the students giving the awards, they divided the awards equally. However, the students giving the rewards favored the in-group when one student was an out-group member and the other an in-group member. The experimenter contrived the groups. The assignment of the groups was random and was not based on the estimation of the dots by the subjects.

The minimum group paradigm, also known as *social identity* theory, is in some ways more helpful in explaining the development of in-group–out-group boundaries than in suggesting practices to reduce them. One implication of social identity theory is that to increase positive intergroup contact the salience of group characteristics should be minimized and a *superordinate group* to which students from different racial, cultural, ethnic, and language groups can become identified should be constructed. In a classroom characterized by language diversity, group salience is likely to be reduced to the extent that all students become competent in the same languages. For example, in a classroom with both Anglos and Latinos, group salience is increased if only the Latino students speak Spanish. However, if both Latino and Anglo Americans student become competent in both English and Spanish, bilingual competency can be the basis for the formation of a superordinate group to which all of the students belong.

The Causes of Prejudice.   The personalities of the individuals, the social structure and culture into which they are socialized, and group identity and categorization are all important factors that contribute to the development of prejudice and discrimination. The factors that cause prejudice are multiple and interact in complex ways. The factors are summarized in Figure 15.1.

Micro Approaches to Prejudice Reduction

Personality characteristics, the social structure of institutions, the national culture, and group identity and categorization influence the degree to which individuals are prejudiced and the extent to which they act on their prejudices, that is, *discriminate.* However, few researchers have studied the effects of changes in social structure on the racial attitudes of students (Brewer & Brown, 1998). Most researchers have examined the effects of particular components of the school, such as materials, films, interracial contact, and special units on the racial attitudes of students. It

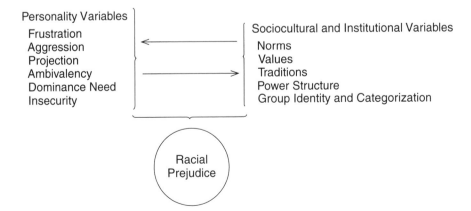

FIGURE 15.1   **Variables That Cause Racial Prejudice**

is very difficult to identify and manipulate all of the major variables within an institution, such as a school, in an experimental situation.

Studies that have been conducted using materials, interracial contact, and special units on minority groups indicate that children's racial attitudes can be modified by school experiences specifically designed for that purpose (Stephan, 1999). One of the most frequently cited studies on the effects of teaching materials on children's racial attitudes is the study by Trager and Yarrow (1952). Their curricula had significant effects on children's racial feelings. All changes were in the expected directions. Children exposed to a democratic curriculum expressed more positive racial attitudes; those exposed to an ethnocentric curriculum developed more negative racial feelings. Trager and Yarrow summarize their study:

> The changes achieved in the experiment demonstrate that democratic attitudes and prejudiced attitudes can be taught to young children. The experiment contributes to an understanding of some of the important conditions which are conducive to learning attitudes. Furthermore, it is apparent that children learn prejudices not only from the larger environment but from the content of the curriculum and its value. If democratic attitudes are to be learned they must be specifically taught and experienced. (p. 341)

Research by Johnson (1966) and by Litcher and Johnson (1969) confirms the Trager and Yarrow findings. Both studies support the postulate that teaching materials affect children's racial attitudes toward ethnic groups and themselves. Johnson (1966) studied the effects of a special program in Black history on the racial attitudes and self-concepts of a group of African American children. The course had a significant effect on the boys' attitudes. However, the effect on the girls' attitudes and self-perceptions was not significant.

Litcher and Johnson (1969) investigated the effects of multiethnic readers on the racial attitudes of White elementary students. On all posttest measures, the children who had studied multiethnic as opposed to all-White readers expressed significantly more positive racial feelings toward African Americans. The authors write: "The evidence is quite clear. Through the use of a multiethnic reader, white children developed markedly more favorable attitudes toward [African Americans]" (p. 151).

Katz and Zalk (1978) studied the effects of four short-term intervention techniques for modifying the racial attitudes of White elementary school children. The techniques were (1) increased positive racial contact, (2) vicarious interracial contact, (3) reinforcement of the color black, and (4) perpetual differentiation of minority group faces. The children were posttested after two weeks and again four to six months later. The authors conclude:

> Results revealed a significant short-term reduction in prejudice for all experimental groups on combined measures. Vicarious contact and perceptual approaches were more effective than the other two. Some interaction effects with grade and race of examiner were found. Long-term treatment effects were less pronounced,

although some gains were maintained in the vicarious contact and perceptual differentiation groups. (p. 447)

In a comprehensive review of the literature on changing intergroup attitudes
and behaviors, Stephan (1985) concluded that several techniques and approaches
are effective in reducing racial prejudice. A number of the studies he reviewed indicate that cooperation in multiethnic groups is one of the most effective ways to
help students attain more positive racial attitudes. Workshops—especially when
they help Whites understand the discrepancies between the reality and the ideals
related to race in the United States—can help adults attain more positive racial attitudes. The use of multiethnic school curricula has resulted in the reduction of prejudice in seven studies reported by Stephan, including those by Leslie, Leslie, and
Penfield (1972) and those by Yawkey and Blackwell (1974). Several studies discussed by Stephan reported that students developed more positive racial attitudes
when they took the role of people from other racial groups. Stephan (1985) derived
the following thirteen tentative principles about ways to reduce prejudice:

1. Cooperation within groups should be maximized and competition between
   groups should be minimized.
2. Members of the in-group and the out-group should be of equal status both
   within and outside the contact situation.
3. Similarity of group members on nonstatus dimensions (beliefs, values, etc.)
   appears to be desirable.
4. Differences in competence should be avoided.
5. The outcomes should be positive.
6. Strong normative and institutional support for the contact should be
   provided.
7. The intergroup contact should have the potential to extend beyond the immediate situation.
8. Individuation of group members should be promoted.
9. Nonsuperficial contact (e.g., mutual disclosure of information) should be
   encouraged.
10. The contact should be voluntary.
11. Positive effects are likely to correlate with the duration of the contact.
12. The contact should occur in a variety of contexts with a variety of in-group
    and out-group members.
13. Equal numbers of in-group and out-group members should be used. (p. 643)

In their important study of adolescent prejudice, Glock, Wuthnow, Piliavin,
and Spencer (1975) found that youths who are *cognitively sophisticated* exemplify
less prejudice and discrimination than do students who lack cognitive sophistication. By cognitive sophistication Glock et al. mean the ability to think clearly about
prejudice, to reason logically about it, and to ask probing questions. They write:

The findings suggest that the best way for the schools to combat prejudice is
simply for them to do their fundamental job of education more effectively. This at

least appears to be the message of the consistent finding that the most effective armor against prejudice is cognitive sophistication. Presumably, if the general level of cognitive sophistication were raised, without necessarily any specific instruction about prejudice, the incidence of prejudice would be reduced. (p. 174)

Although subject to the limitations of the research, a number of guidelines can be derived from the research on changing children's racial attitudes, some of which is reviewed above. The research suggests that students' racial attitudes can be modified if the school designs specific objectives and strategies for that purpose and if it increases students' cognitive sophistication. Most research studies indicate that specific instructional objectives must be clearly formulated; incidental teaching of race relations is usually not effective. Also, clearly defined teaching strategies must be structured to attain the objectives. Attitude changes induced by experimental intervention will persist through time, although there is a tendency for modified attitudes to revert to the pre-experimental ones.

However, the effects of the experimental treatment do not completely diminish. This finding suggests that intergroup education programs should not consist of one-shot treatments. *Systematic experiences must be structured to reinforce and perpetuate the desired attitudes.* Cooperative rather than competitive cross-ethnic situations should be fostered. A multicultural curriculum will enhance the possibility for students to develop more positive attitudes toward different racial and ethnic groups, as will equal-status contact situations.

Visual materials such as pictures and films greatly enhance the effectiveness of attempts to change racial attitudes (Cooper & Dinerman, 1951). Contact with minority groups does not in itself significantly affect children's racial attitudes. The prevalent attitude toward different races and groups in the social situation is the significant determinant of children's racial feelings. The attitudes and predispositions of the classroom teacher are important variables in a program designed to foster positive racial feelings (Banks, 1972). Students who are able to reason at a high level and to think critically tend to show less prejudice than do students who reason at lower levels and think less critically.

Macro Approaches to Prejudice Reduction

Most approaches to the reduction of prejudice in the schools have focused on limited factors in the school environment, such as instructional materials and cooperative learning (Slavin, 1995), and on aspects of the formalized curriculum, such as courses and increasing levels of cognitive sophistication (Gabelko & Michaelis, 1981). Although it is necessary to focus on these aspects of the school environment, this approach is clearly insufficient because the school is an interrelated social system, each part of which shapes and influences the racial attitudes and behavior of students. The social structure of institutions has a cogent impact on the racial attitudes, perceptions, and behavior of individuals. Thus, intervention designed to reduce prejudice among students should be institutional and comprehensive in scope. It is necessary to use multicultural instructional materials to increase the cognitive sophistication of students; but to focus exclusively on instructional materials and on increasing the cognitive sophistication of students is too narrow and will not substantially reduce institutional prejudice and discrimination.

To reduce prejudice, educators should attempt institutional or systemic reform of the total school and should try to reform all of its major aspects, including institutional norms, power relationships, the verbal interactions between teachers and students, the culture of the school, the curriculum, extracurricular activities, attitudes toward minority languages, and the counseling and testing programs. The latent or hidden values within an institution like a school often have a more cogent impact on students' attitudes and perceptions than does the formalized course of study. Educators who have worked for years in curriculum reform know that helping teachers attain new skills and then placing them in an institutional environment whose norms contradict and do not support the teachers' use of those newly acquired skills frequently lead to frustration and failure. Thus, any approach to school reform that is likely to succeed must focus on each major element of the school environment identified in Chapter 3 (in Figure 3.4).

Prejudice among students is reinforced by many aspects of the student's environment, including the school. Cortés (2000) uses the concept of the "societal curriculum" to describe the societal factors that influence and shape students' attitudes toward different ethnic and racial groups, such as television, newspapers, and popular books.

Often the negative images of ethnic groups that children learn in the larger society are reinforced and perpetuated in the school. Rather than reinforcing children's negative feelings toward ethnic groups, the school should counteract children's negative societal experiences and help them develop more positive attitudes toward a range of ethnic and racial groups. It is not possible for the school to avoid playing a role in the ethnic education of students. This is so because many children come to school with stereotypes of different racial and ethnic groups and negative attitudes toward these groups. Either the school can do nothing deliberate to intervene in the formation of children's racial attitudes (which means that the school would unwittingly participate in the perpetuation of racial bias), or it can attempt to intervene and influence the development of children's racial attitudes in a positive direction.

To take this latter course, it is imperative that the school do more than merely devise a few units or teaching strategies to reduce prejudice and focus on the histories and cultures of ethnic groups on particular days or weeks of the school year. Specialized units and teaching strategies are clearly insufficient. Teaching about ethnic groups only at particular times of the school year may do more harm than good because these kinds of activities and rituals may reinforce the idea that ethnic groups, such as Asian Americans and Native Americans, are not integral parts of U.S. society.

The school environment consists of both a manifest and a hidden curriculum. The manifest curriculum consists of such discernible environmental factors as curriculum guides, textbooks, bulletin boards, and lesson plans. These aspects of the school environment are important and must be reformed in order to create a school environment that promotes positive attitudes toward diverse ethnic and racial groups. However, the school's latent or hidden curriculum is often a more cogent factor than is its manifest or overt curriculum. The latent curriculum has been defined as the curriculum that no teacher explicitly teaches but that all students learn. It is the powerful part of the school experience that communicates to students the school's attitudes toward a range of issues and problems, including how the school views them as human beings and its attitudes toward diverse racial and ethnic groups.

How does the school communicate its cogent, latent messages to students? These messages are communicated to students in a number of subtle but powerful ways, including the following six:

1. By the kind of verbal and nonverbal interactions teachers have with students from different racial and ethnic groups; by the kinds of statements teachers make about different ethnic groups; and by teachers' nonverbal reactions when issues related to ethnic groups are discussed in class. Research by Gay (1974), Rist (1970), and the U.S. Commission on Civil Rights (1973) indicates that teachers often have more positive verbal and nonverbal interactions with middle-class, Anglo students than with students of color and lower-income students.

2. How teachers respond to the languages and dialects of children from different ethnic and racial groups. Some research suggests that teachers are often biased against the languages and dialects of children who are members of particular ethnic and racial groups (August & Hakuta, 1997).

3. Grouping practices used in the school. Research by Mercer (1989) and Oakes (1985) indicates that members of some ethnic groups in the United States are disproportionately placed in lower ability groups because of their performance on IQ and other standardized aptitude tests that discriminate against these groups because they are normed on middle-class Anglo-Americans.

4. Power relationships in the schools. Often in schools, most of the individuals who exercise the most power belong to dominant ethnic groups. Students acquire important learning by observing which ethnic groups are represented among the administrators, teachers, secretaries, cooks, and bus drivers in the school.

5. The formalized curriculum also makes statements about the values the school has toward ethnic diversity. The ethnic groups that appear in textbooks and in other instructional material teach students which groups the school considers important and unimportant.

6. The learning styles, languages, motivational systems, and cultures promoted by the school express many of the school's important values toward cultural differences. The educational environments of most schools are more consistent with the learning patterns and styles of mainstream students than with those of ethnic minority students, such as African Americans, Native Americans, and Puerto Ricans. In their classic study, Ramírez and Castañeda (1974) found that Mexican

American youths tend to be more field-sensitive than field-independent in their cognitive styles. Anglo-American students tend to be more field-independent. Field-sensitive and field-independent students differ in a number of characteristics and behavior. Field-sensitive students tend to work with others to achieve a common goal and are more sensitive to the feelings and opinions of other people than are field-independent students. Field-independent students prefer to work independently and to compete and gain individual recognition. Students who are field-independent are more often preferred by teachers and tend to get higher grades, although learning style is not related to IQ.

An Interdisciplinary Conceptual Curriculum

It is essential that educators take an *institutional approach* to school reform when intervening to reduce prejudice in students; the formalized curriculum is a vital element of the school. Hence, curriculum reform is imperative. The curriculum within a school designed to help reduce prejudice in students should be interdisciplinary, focus on higher levels of knowledge, and help students view events and situations from diverse ethnic and national perspectives.

Many ethnic studies units, activities, and programs emphasize factual learning and the deeds of ethnic heroes. These types of experiences use ethnic content but traditional teaching methods. Isolated facts about Martin Luther King, Jr., do not stimulate the intellect or help students increase their levels of cognitive sophistication any more than do discrete facts about George Washington or Thomas Jefferson. The emphases in sound multicultural programs must be on *concept attainment, value analysis, decision-making,* and *social action* (Banks, 1997). Facts should be used only to help students attain higher-level concepts and skills. Students need to master higher-level concepts and generalizations in order to increase their levels of cognitive sophistication.

Concepts taught in the multicultural curriculum should be selected from several disciplines and, when appropriate, be viewed from the perspectives of such disciplines and areas as the various social sciences, art, music, literature, physical education, communication, the sciences, and mathematics. It is necessary for students to view events and concepts from the perspectives of several disciplines because any one discipline gives them only a partial understanding of problems related to ethnicity. When students study the concept of culture, they can attain a global perspective of ethnic cultures by viewing them from the perspective of the various social sciences and by examining how they are expressed in literature, music, dance, art, communication, and foods. The other curriculum areas, such as science and mathematics, can also be included in an interdisciplinary study of ethnic cultures.

Concepts such as *culture* can be used to organize interdisciplinary units and activities. Other concepts, such as *communication* and *interdependence,* can also be analyzed and studied from an interdisciplinary perspective (see Figure 15.2). However, it is neither possible nor desirable to teach each concept in the curriculum from the perspectives of several disciplines and curricular areas. Such an attempt would

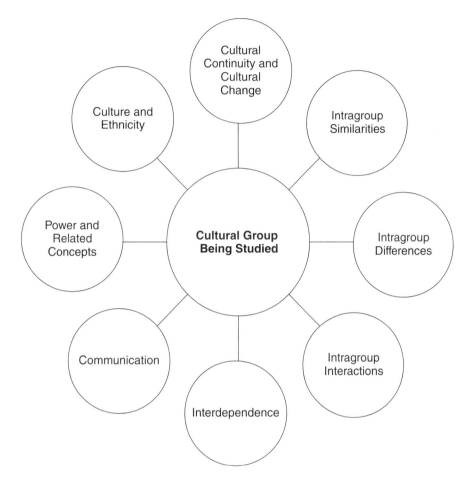

FIGURE 15.2   Interdisciplinary Concepts for Studying Cultural Groups

result in artificial relationships and superficial learnings by students. However, the many excellent opportunities that exist within the curriculum for teaching concepts from an interdisciplinary perspective should be fully explored and used.

Interdisciplinary teaching requires the strong cooperation of teachers in the various content areas. Team teaching will often be necessary, especially at the high school level, to organize and implement interdisciplinary units and lessons.

The Role of the Teacher in Prejudice Reduction

Teachers are human beings who bring their own cultural perspectives, values, hopes, and dreams to the classroom. They also bring their own prejudices, stereotypes, and misconceptions (Dilg, 1999; Howard, 1999; Rist, 1970). The teacher's values and perspectives mediate and interact with what they teach and influence how messages are communicated to and perceived by their students. Because the teacher mediates the messages and symbols communicated to the students through the curriculum, it is important for teachers to understand their own personal and cultural values and identities in order for them to help students from diverse racial, ethnic, and cultural groups to develop clarified identities and relate positively to each other. Research by Rubin (1967) indicates that increases in self-acceptance are associated with a reduction in prejudice.

Effective teachers in a multicultural society must have (1) democratic attitudes and values, (2) a multicultural philosophy, (3) the ability to view events and situations from diverse ethnic perspectives and points of view, (4) an understanding of the complex and multidimensional nature of diversity in Western societies, (5) knowledge of the stages of cultural identity and their curricular and teaching implications, and (6) the ability to function increasingly at higher stages of cultural identity. Figure 15.3 summarizes these characteristics.

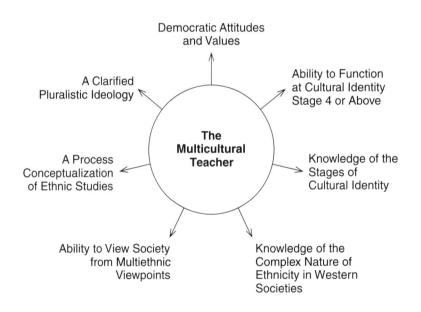

FIGURE 15.3   Characteristics of Effective Teachers in a Multicultural Society
To function effectively in ethnically pluralistic environments, the teacher must have democratic attitudes and values, a clarified pluralistic ideology, a process conceptualization of ethnic studies, the ability to view society from diverse ethnic perspectives and points of view, knowledge of the stages of cultural identity, knowledge of the complex nature of ethnicity in Western societies, and the ability to function at Cultural Identity Stage 4 or above. Reformed teacher-education programs should be designed to help teachers acquire these attitudes, conceptual frameworks, knowledge, and skills.

Changing Teacher Attitudes and Behaviors

What can teachers do to change their racial attitudes, perceptions, and behaviors? Even though researchers have amply documented the nondemocratic attitudes and interactions teachers frequently have with students of color and low-income students, little work has been done on effective techniques that can be used to change teachers' racial attitudes and behavior. Smith (1947) concluded that the racial attitudes of adults can be significantly modified in a positive direction by contact with and involvement in minority group cultures. Bogardus (1948) found that a five-week intergroup education workshop, which consisted of lectures on racial problems, research projects, and visits to community agencies, had a significantly positive effect on the participants' racial attitudes.

An extensive review of the research suggests that changing the racial attitudes of adults is a difficult task (Banks, 1972; Stephan, 1985). To maximize the chances for successful intervention programs, experiences must be designed specifically to change attitudes. Courses with general or global objectives are not likely to be successful. Courses that consist primarily or exclusively of lecture presentations have little impact. Diverse experiences, such as seminars, visitations, community involvement, committee work, guest speakers, videotapes, multimedia materials, and workshops, combined with factual lectures, are more effective than is any single approach. Community involvement and cross-cultural interactions (with the appropriate norms in the social setting) are the most cogent techniques. Psychotherapy is also promising. Individuals who express moderate rather than extreme attitudes are the most likely to change. This is encouraging since few individuals exemplify extreme prejudice.

A Multicultural Philosophy

Teachers need to clarify their own philosophical positions regarding the education of students of color and to endorse an ideology consistent with the multiple acculturation and structural pluralism that characterize Western societies. Teachers should be aware of the major ideologies related to ethnic pluralism and be able to examine their own philosophical positions and explore the policy and teaching implications of alternative ideologies. Teachers with an assimilationist ideology will most likely teach a unit on the American Civil War differently than will teachers with a multicultural ideology. Effective multicultural teachers should embrace a philosophical position that will facilitate their effectiveness in culturally and racially diverse educational environments. Teachers who endorse a multicultural ideology as defined in Chapter 6 respect and value the cultural characteristics of students of color but also believe these students need to acquire the values, skills, attitudes, and abilities needed to function successfully within the mainstream culture.

Effective teachers in the multicultural classroom must endorse what Chapter 6 describes as the multicultural ideology. This ideology derives from the complex and multidimensional nature of ethnicity and culture in modern Western societies.

However, because most classroom teachers were socialized within a society, schools, and teacher-education institutions that had mainstream-centric norms and were assimilationist oriented, many teachers are therefore likely to embrace an assimilationist ideology and to view pluralistic ideologies as radical and unpatriotic. It is very difficult for individuals to change their philosophical orientations or even to question their currently held ideological beliefs. Most people have a great deal of affective and intellectual commitment to their ideological orientations and values. These ideologies are deeply held and result from years of informal and formal socialization.

Teachers should first examine their currently held ideological positions related to race, ethnicity, and culture. If they feel they need to change their ideological orientations in order to become effective multicultural teachers, they should enroll in courses and seek other educational experiences related to race, ethnicity, and culture. Vicarious as well as direct experiences with other cultures, if they are open to these experiences, will help teachers examine their philosophical beliefs. The caveats about cross-cultural functioning discussed later in this chapter should be studied by teachers who seek cross-cultural experiences as a way to help them examine their philosophical beliefs. With these kinds of cross-cultural experiences, teachers will have opportunities to interact with individuals with widely differing ideologies and value positions about pluralism and race.

Teachers should also examine the *possible consequences* of embracing various philosophical beliefs. They should discuss how different philosophical orientations toward race and ethnic group life may influence their behavior in the classroom and the academic achievement and emotional growth of students from diverse groups. A number of researchers have observed that African American students tend to be more action-oriented and expressive in their learning styles than are Anglo-American students (Boykin, 1994; Gay, 2000, Lee, 1998). Mexican American and Anglo youths tend to differ in their learning styles (Ramírez & Castañeda, 1974). Mexican American students also tend to be less individually competitive than are Anglo students (Vasquez, 1979). The ideological positions and commitments of teachers, whether conscious or unconscious, influence how they respond to the different cultural learning styles and characteristics of African American and Mexican American students. Teachers who are strong assimilationists are likely to regard these different behaviors of African Americans and Mexican American students as negative characteristics that should be eradicated. Teachers who are more multicultural in their philosophical orientations are more likely to perceive these behaviors of African Americans and Mexican American students as legitimate and functional cultural behaviors that they should build on and use when planning and teaching (Ladson-Billings, 1994).

The Teacher and the Stages of Cultural Identity

To work successfully with students from diverse cultural, ethnic, and language backgrounds, teachers should be knowledgeable about the cultural characteristics of their students. Students differ in their ethnic identities and characteristics just as they differ in their cognitive and affective development (Kohlberg & Mayer, 1972; Piaget, 1968). Consequently, the teacher should make some attempt to individualize multicultural experiences for students.

These three hypothetical students might need somewhat different curricular experiences related to race and ethnicity. Juan was socialized within a rather conservative Mexican American community in the Southwest. Jessie Mae, who is African American, spent Saturday afternoons during her early years in an Afro-centric school. John is an Anglo-American student who has never had any first-hand experiences with persons of color. These students are now in the same eighth-grade social studies class. The teacher is beginning a unit on race relations in the United States. Each student will need some unique experiences tailored to his or her complex and emerging ethnic identities. Chapter 7 presents a typology that outlines the basic stages of the development of ethnic and cultural identity among individuals that teachers can use as a guide when trying to identify the ethnic and cultural characteristics of students.

To become more effective multicultural educators, teachers should try to determine their own stage of cultural identity and become sensitive to their ethnic and cultural behaviors and characteristics. Teachers should not only try to help students function at higher stages of cultural identity but should also try to function at higher stages of cultural identity themselves. Teachers who are functioning primarily at Stages 1 and 2 cannot realistically be expected to help students develop positive racial attitudes toward different ethnic and racial groups or to help students to function at higher stages of cultural identity. Once teachers are aware of their own ethnic and cultural attitudes, behaviors, and perceptions, they can begin an action program designed to change their behavior if necessary. Such a program may consist of individual readings, taking courses at a local college or university, or participating in cross-cultural experiences either in their own country or in other nations.

Cross-Cultural Experiences: Problems and Promises

Teachers who plan to have cross-cultural experiences should be aware of both the problems and promises of functioning in a different culture. Functioning cross-culturally, in the final analysis, is usually rewarding and personally revealing. Because enculturation into our own cultures is primarily a subconscious process, we can learn a great deal about our norms, values, behaviors, and perceptions by functioning in other cultural communities.

To acquire the maximum benefits from cross-cultural functioning, individuals must be able to interpret their experiences accurately and develop a sophisticated level of *cross-cultural awareness.* Despite its positive long-range outcomes, individuals functioning within another culture frequently experience cultural shock and confusion and make embarrassing cultural mistakes. All individuals are likely to experience cultural shock during their first experiences in another culture (Stewart &

Bennett, 1991). The greater the differences between the new culture and their own ethnic and/or national culture, the greater the cultural shock individuals are likely to experience.

People in the United States can experience cultural shock within ethnic cultures in their nation as well as in other nations. Anglo-Americans who have had few experiences with African American culture and have not traveled outside the United States are likely to experience cultural shock when they first visit a traditional African American Baptist Church as well as when they first visit a nation such as Mexico.

Some preparation before experiencing another culture may help reduce cultural shock and enable the individual to function more successfully within it. Such preparation may consist of readings, (especially literary works because literature often conveys the nuances and subtleties of a culture), viewing films and videotapes, and interacting with individuals socialized within the culture. However, no amount of preparation will totally eliminate cultural shock and cultural mistakes during an individual's first experience with a culture. If teachers are knowledgeable about the rewards as well as the problems of cross-cultural functioning, they will be better able to interpret their cross-cultural experiences accurately and will therefore benefit more from them in the long run.

Hypotheses Regarding Cross-Cultural Behavior

I have developed some hypotheses regarding cross-cultural behavior based on my own functioning in other cultures (such as Guam, Mexico, Japan, and the United Kingdom, and different ethnic cultures within the United States), on my observations of and conversations with other individuals who have functioned cross-culturally, and on my reading of the literature related to cross-cultural functioning (Stewart & Bennett, 1991). These hypotheses should be helpful to teachers who are planning cross-cultural experiences and to individuals who are trying to interpret their own cross-cultural interactions and behaviors or the cross-cultural behaviors of others.

■ The weaker the boundaries are between cultures, the more likely cross-cultural functioning will occur between these cultures.

■ The weaker the boundaries between cultures, the easier cross-cultural functioning will be for individuals in those cultures. Individuals who have weak cultural characteristics and identities are more likely to participate in cross-cultural behavior than are individuals with strong cultural characteristics and identities.

■ Psychological discomforts and confusion are so potentially high in cross-cultural functioning that cross-cultural behavior will occur only when motivation is high for functioning cross-culturally and the potential rewards are substantial.

■ Subethnic boundaries (within an ethnic group) are often distinct and tight. Consequently, individuals who are socialized within one subethnic culture may experience problems and conflicts when functioning within another subethnic culture within his or her ethnic group.

■ As an individual becomes more competent in functioning within an outside culture, his or her personal ethnicity and ethnic behavior changes and/or reduces in intensity.

■ The response to the individual who is functioning cross-culturally by the outside ethnic group influences the depth and nature of his or her cross-cultural behavior and his or her psychological interpretation of his or her cross-cultural behavior.

Summary

Major goals of the multicultural curriculum should be to reduce prejudice and to help students acquire more democratic racial attitudes and values. This chapter discusses theories that explain the causes of prejudice. Various theories focus on the personality of the individual, on group norms, on the social structure, and on group identity and categorization as the primary cause of prejudice. A comprehensive theory that incorporates each variable is needed to explain the complex nature of prejudice in contemporary societies.

Research reviewed in this chapter suggests that the school can help students become less prejudiced and acquire more democratic attitudes, values, and behaviors. However, instruction must be designed specifically for this purpose and must take place in a social environment that has a number of identifiable characteristics, including the promotion of cooperation rather than competition, a multicultural curriculum, and situations in which students experience equal status. The teacher is an important variable in a curriculum that fosters democratic attitudes and values. The final part of this chapter describes the characteristics of the effective teacher in a multicultural society.

R E F E R E N C E S

Adorno, T. W., Frenkel-Brunswik, E., Levinson, D. J., & Sanford, R. N. (1950). *The Authoritarian Personality.* New York: Harper and Row.

August, D., & Hakuta, K. (Eds.). (1997). *Improving School for Language-Minority Children: A Research Agenda.* Washington, DC: National Academy Press.

Banks, J. A. (1972). Racial Prejudice and the Black Self-Concept. In J. A. Banks and J. D. Grambs (Eds.), *Black Self-Concept: Implications for Education and Social Science* (pp. 5–35). New York: McGraw-Hill.

Banks, J. A. (1997). *Teaching Strategies for Ethnic Studies* (6th ed.). Boston: Allyn and Bacon.

Billig, M., & Tajfel, H. (1973). Social Categorization and Similarity in Intergroup Behavior. *European Journal of Social Psychology, 3,* 27–52.

Blalock, H. (1956). Economic Discrimination and Negro Increase. *American Sociological Review, 21,* 584–588.

Blumer, H. (1966). United States of America. In *Research on Racial Relations* (pp. 87–133). New York: UNESCO.

Bogardus, E. S. (1948). The Intercultural Workshop and Racial Distance. *Sociology and Social Research, 32,* 798–802.

Boykin, A. W. (1994). Harvesting Culture and Talent: African American Children and Educational

Reform. In R. Rossi (Ed.), *Schools and Students at Risk* (pp. 116–138). New York: Teachers College Press.

Brewer, M. B., & Brown, R. J. (1998). Intergroup Relations. In D. T. Gilbert, S. T. Fiske, & G. Lindzey (Eds.). *The Handbook of Social Psychology* (4th ed.), Vol. 2, (pp. 554–594). New York: McGraw-Hill.

Brown, R. (1995). *Prejudice: Its Social Psychology.* Cambridge, MA: Blackwell.

Cooper, E., & Dinerman, H. (1951). Analysis of the Film 'Don't Be a Sucker': A Study of Communication. *Public Opinion Quarterly, 15,* 243–264.

Cortés, C. E. (2000). *The Children Are Watching: How the Media Teach about Diversity.* New York: Teachers College Press.

Dilg, M. (1999). *Race and Culture in the Classroom: Teaching and Learning through Multicultural Education.* New York: Teachers College Press.

Frenkel-Brunswik, E. (1948). A Study of Prejudice in Children. *Human Relations, 1,* 295–306.

Gabelko, N., & Michaelis, J. U. (1981). *Reducing Adolescent Prejudice: A Handbook.* New York: Teachers College Press.

Gay, G. (1974). *Differential Dyadic Interactions of Black and White Teachers with Black and White Pupils in Recently Desegregated Social Studies Classrooms: A Function of Teacher and Pupil Ethnicity.* Washington, DC: National Institute of Education.

Gay, G. (2000). *Culturally Responsive Teaching: Theory, Research, and Practice.* New York: Teachers College Press.

Glock, C., Wuthnow, R., Piliavin, J. A., & Spencer, M. (1975). *Adolescent Prejudice.* New York: Harper and Row.

Harley, D. (1968). Prejudice in Whites. Unpublished paper, Michigan State University.

Howard, G. R. (1999). *We Can't Teach What We Don't Know: White Teachers, Multiracial Schools.* New York: Teachers College Press.

Johnson, D. W. (1966). Freedom School Effectiveness: Changes in Attitudes of Negro Children. *The Journal of Applied Behavioral Science, 2,* 325–330.

Katz, P., & Zalk, S. R. (1978). Modification of Children's Racial Attitudes. *Developmental Psychology, 14,* 447–461.

Kohlberg, L., & Mayer, R. (1972). Development as the Aim of Education. *Harvard Educational Review, 42,* 449–496.

Ladson-Billings, G. (1994). *The Dreamkeepers: Successful Teachers of African American Children.* San Francisco: Jossey-Bass.

Lee, C. D. (1998). Culturally Responsive Pedagogy and Performance-Based Assessment. *The Journal of Negro Education, 67*(3), 268–279.

Leslie, L. L., Leslie, J. W., & Penfield, D. A. (1972). The Effects of a Student Centered Special Curriculum upon the Racial Attitudes of Sixth Graders. *Journal of Experimental Education, 41,* 63–67.

Litcher, J., & Johnson, D. (1969). Changes in Attitudes toward Negroes of White Elementary School Students after Use of Multiethnic Readers. *Journal of Educational Psychology, 60,* 148–152.

Lohman, J., & Reitzes, D. C. (1952). Note on Race Relations in Mass Society. *American Journal of Sociology, 58,* 241–246.

Mercer, J. R. (1989). Testing and Assessment Practices in Multiethnic Education. In J. A. Banks (Ed.), *Education in the 80's: Multiethnic Education* (pp. 93–104). Washington, DC: National Education Association.

Merton, R. K. (1949). Discrimination and the American Creed. In R. M. MacIver (Ed.), *Discrimination and the National Welfare* (pp. 99–126). New York: Harper and Row.

Oakes, J. (1985). *Keeping Track: How Schools Structure Inequality.* New Haven, CT: Yale University Press.

Pearlin, L. I. (1954). Shifting Group Attachments and Attitudes toward Negroes. *Social Forces, 33,* 41–47.

Piaget, J. (1968). *Six Psychological Studies.* New York: Random House.

Ramírez, M. III, & Castañeda, A. (1974). *Cultural Democracy, Bicognitive Development and Education.* New York: Academic Press.

Rist, R. C. (1970). Student Social Class and Teacher Expectations: The Self-Fulfilling Prophecy in Ghetto Education. *Harvard Educational Review, 40,* 411–451.

Rothbart, M., & John, O. P. (1993). Intergroup Relations and Stereotype Change: A Social-Cognitive Analysis and Some Longitudinal Findings. In P. M. Sinderman, P. E. Tetlock, & E. G. Carmines (Eds.), *Prejudice, Politics, and the American Dilemma* (pp. 32–59). Stanford, CA: Stanford University Press.

Rubin, I. (1967). The Reduction of Prejudice through Laboratory Training. *Journal of Applied Behavioral Science, 3,* 29–50.

Saenger, G., & Gilbert, E. (1950). Customer Reactions to Integration of Negro Sales Personnel. *International Journal of Opinion and Attitude Research, 4,* 57–76.

Simpson, G. E., & Yinger, J. M. (1985). *Racial and Cultural Minorities: An Analysis of Prejudice and Discrimination* (5th ed.). New York: Plenum Press.

Slavin, R. (1977). How Student Learning Teams Can Integrate the Desegregated Classroom. *Integrated Education, 15,* 56–58.

Slavin, R. (1995). Cooperative Learning and Intergroup Relations. In J. A. Banks & C. A. M. Banks (Eds.), *Handbook of Research on Multicultural Education* (pp. 628–634). New York: Macmillan.

Smith, F. T. (1947). An Experiment in Modifying Attitudes toward the Negro. Summarized in A. M. Rose, *Studies in the Reduction of Prejudice* (p. 9). Chicago: American Council on Race Relations.

Smith, E. R., & Mackie, D. M. (1995). *Social Psychology.* New York: Worth Publishers, Inc.

Stephan, W. G. (1985). Intergroup Relations. In G. Lindzey & E. Aronson (Eds.), *The Handbook of Social Psychology,* Vol. 2 (3rd ed.) (pp. 599–658). Hillsdale, NJ.: Lawrence Erlbaum Associates.

Stephan, W. G. (1999). *Reducing Prejudice and Stereotyping in Schools.* New York: Teachers College Press.

Stewart, E. C., & Bennett, M. J. (1991). *American Cultural Patterns: A Cross-Cultural Perspective* (rev. ed.). Yarmouth, ME: Intercultural Press, Inc.

Tajfel, H. (1970). Experiments in intergroup discrimination. *Scientific American, 223*(5), 96–102.

Trager, H. G., & Yarrow, M. R. (1952). *They Learn What They Live.* New York: Harper.

U.S. Commission on Civil Rights. (1973). *Teachers and Students. Differences in Teacher Interaction with Mexican American and Anglo Students.* Washington, DC: U.S. Government Printing Office.

Vasquez, J. A. (1979). Bilingual Education's Needed Third Dimension. *Educational Leadership, 38,* 166–168.

Yawkey, T. D., & Blackwell, J. (1974). Attitudes of 4-year-old Urban Black Children toward Themselves and Whites Based upon Multiethnic Social Studies Materials and Experiences. *Journal of Educational Research, 67,* 373–377.

Young-Bruehl, E. (1996). *The Anatomy of Prejudices.* Cambridge, MA: Harvard University Press.

16 Curriculum Guidelines for Multicultural Education

Three major factors make multicultural education a necessity: (1) ethnic pluralism is a growing societal reality influencing the lives of young people; (2) in one way or another, individuals acquire knowledge or beliefs, sometimes invalid, about ethnic and cultural groups; and (3) beliefs and knowledge about ethnic and cultural groups limit the perspectives of many and make a difference, often a negative difference, in the opportunities and options available to members of ethnic and cultural groups. Because ethnicity, race, and class are important in the lives of many individuals in the United States, it is essential that all members of our society develop multicultural literacy, that is, a solidly based understanding of racial, ethnic, and cultural groups and their significance in U.S. society and throughout the world. Schools cannot afford to ignore their responsibility to contribute to the development of multicultural literacy and understanding. Only a well-conceived, sensitive, thorough, and continuous program of multicultural education can create the broadly based multicultural literacy so necessary for the future of the United States and world.

The guidelines presented in this chapter are predicated on a democratic ideology in which ethnic and cultural diversity is viewed as a positive, integral ingredient. A democratic society protects and provides opportunities for ethnic and cultural diversity and at the same time has overarching values—such as equality, justice, and human dignity—that all groups accept and respect. Ethnic and cultural diversity is based on the following four premises:

1. Ethnic and cultural diversity should be recognized and respected at individual, group, and societal levels.
2. Ethnic and cultural diversity provides a basis for societal enrichment, cohesiveness, and survival.
3. Equality of opportunity should be afforded to members of all ethnic and cultural groups.
4. Ethnic and cultural identification should be optional for individuals.

The Role of the School

The societal goals stated in this chapter are future oriented. In effect, they present a vision of our society that recognizes and respects ethnic and cultural diversity as compatible with national and societal unity rather than one that seeks to reduce ethnic and cultural differences. Further progress in that direction is consistent with the democratic ideals—freedom, equality, justice, and human dignity—embodied in our basic national documents. By respecting ethnic and cultural differences, we can help to close the gap between our democratic ideals and societal practices. Such practices are too often discriminatory toward members of marginalized ethnic and cultural groups.

It follows, therefore, that schools need to assume a new responsibility. Their socialization practices should incorporate the cultural and ethnic diversity that is an integral part of the democratic commitment to human dignity. At the same time, however, schools must help socialize youth in ways that will foster basic democratic ideals that serve as overarching goals for all individuals in the United States. The schools' goal should be to help attain a delicate balance of diversity and unity—one nation that respects the cultural rights and freedoms of its many peoples. As schools embark on educational programs that reflect multiculturalism, they must demonstrate a commitment to:

1. recognize and respect ethnic and cultural diversity;
2. promote societal cohesiveness based on the shared participation of ethnically and culturally diverse peoples;
3. maximize equality of opportunity for all individuals and groups;
4. facilitate constructive societal change that enhances human dignity and democratic ideals.

The study of ethnic and cultural diversity should not consist of a narrow promotion of ethnocentrism or nationalism. Personal ethnic identity and knowledge of others' ethnic identities are essential to the sense of understanding and the feeling of personal well-being that promote intergroup and international understanding. Multicultural education should stress the process of self-identification as an essential aspect of the understanding that underlies commitment to the dignity of humankind throughout the world community.

Curriculum Guidelines

1.0   Ethnic and cultural diversity should permeate the total school environment.
Effective teaching about U.S. ethnic and cultural groups can best take place within an educational setting that accepts, encourages, and respects the expression of ethnic and cultural diversity. To attain this kind of educational atmosphere, the total school environment—not merely courses and programs—must be reformed. Schools' informal or "hidden" curricula are as important as their formalized courses of study.

Teaching about various ethnic and cultural groups in a few specialized courses is not enough. Content about a variety of cultural and ethnic groups should be incorporated into many subject areas, preschool through twelfth grade and beyond. Some dimensions of multicultural education, however, have higher priority in some subject areas than in others. Five dimensions of multicultural education are described in Chapter 1 (*content integration, the knowledge construction process, prejudice reduction,* an *equity pedagogy,* and *an empowering school culture*). In social studies, the humanities, and the language arts, content integration is often the first and most important concern. In physics, however, developing pedagogies that will help students of color and female students to excel academically might be of greater concern than content integration (Belenky et al., 1986). Students can examine how knowledge is constructed in each discipline.

Multicultural education clearly means different things in different disciplines and areas of study. To interpret or attempt to implement multicultural education the same way in each discipline or area of study will create frustration among teachers and build resistance to the concept. Nevertheless, teachers in each discipline can analyze their teaching procedures and styles to determine the extent to which they reflect multicultural issues and concerns. An equity pedagogy exists when teachers modify their instruction in ways that facilitate the academic achievement of students from diverse racial, cultural, gender, and social-class groups. This includes using a variety of teaching styles and approaches that are consistent with the wide range of learning styles found in various cultural, ethnic, and gender groups.

To permeate the total school environment with ethnic and cultural diversity, students must have readily available resource materials that provide accurate information on the diverse aspects of the histories and cultures of various racial, ethnic, and cultural groups. Learning centers, libraries, and resource centers should include a variety of resources on the history, literature, music, folklore, views of life, and art of different ethnic and cultural groups.

Ethnic and cultural diversity in a school's informal programs should be reflected in assembly programs, classrooms, hallway and entrance decorations, cafeteria menus, counseling interactions, and extracurricular programs. School-sponsored dances that consistently provide only one kind of ethnic music, for example, are as contrary to the spirit and principles of multicultural education as are curricula that teach only about mainstream U.S. ideals, values, and contributions.

Participation in activities—such as cheerleading, booster clubs, honor societies, and athletic teams—should be open to all students; in fact, the participation of students from various racial, ethnic, and cultural backgrounds should be solicited. Such activities can provide invaluable opportunities not only for the development of self-esteem, but also for students from different ethnic and cultural backgrounds to learn to work and play together, and to recognize that all individuals, whatever their ethnic identities, have worth and are capable of achieving.

2.0   School policies and procedures should foster positive multicultural interactions and understandings among students, teachers, and the support staff.

School governance should protect the individual's right to (1) retain esteem for his or her home environment, (2) develop a positive self-concept, (3) develop empathy and insight into and respect for the cultures of others, and (4) receive an equal educational opportunity.

Each institution needs rules and regulations to guide behavior so as to attain institutional goals and objectives. School rules and regulations should enhance cross-cultural harmony and understanding among students, staff, and teachers. In the past, school harmony was often sought through efforts to "treat everyone the same." Experience in multiethnic settings, however, indicates that the same treatment for everyone is unfair to many students. Instead of insisting on one ideal model of behavior that is unfair to many students, school policies should recognize and accommodate individual and cultural group differences. This does not mean that some students should obey school rules and others should not; it means that cultural and ethnic groups' behaviors should be honored as long as they are not inconsistent with major school and societal goals. It also means that school policies may have to make allowances for cultural and ethnic traditions. For example, customs that affect Jewish students' food preferences and school attendance on certain religious days should be respected.

Equal educational opportunity should be increased by rules that protect students from procedures and practices that relegate them to low-ability or special education classes simply because of their low scores on standardized English reading and achievement tests.

It is especially important for educators to consider equity issues related to testing because many groups and individuals are pushing for the establishment of state tests. Unless significant changes are made within schools and society that will enable low-income students and students of color to perform well on state tests, these students will become double victims—victims of both a poor educational system and of state tests that relegate them to inferior jobs and deny them opportunities for further education (Mercer, 1989). If developed, state tests should be constructed and used in ways that are consistent with the principles of ethnic pluralism and multicultural education described in these guidelines.

Guidance and other student services personnel should not view students stereotypically regarding their academic abilities and occupational aspirations, and students must be protected from responses based on such views. Counselors should be cautioned to counsel students on the basis of their individual potentials and interests as well as their ethnic needs and concerns. Counselors will need to be particularly aware of their own biases when counseling students whose cultures and ethnicity differ from theirs (Ponterotto et al., 1995; Sue, 1995).

Schools should recognize the holidays and festivities of major importance to various ethnic groups. Provisions should be made to ensure that traditional holidays and festivities reflect multicultural modes of celebration. For example, the ways in which some American Indian tribes celebrate Thanksgiving, Orthodox Greeks celebrate Easter, and Jews celebrate Hanukkah can be appropriately included in school programs.

3.0   A school's staff should reflect the ethnic and cultural diversity within the United States.

Members of various ethnic and cultural groups must be part of a school's instructional, administrative, policymaking, and support staffs if the school is truly multiethnic and multicultural. School personnel—teachers, principals, cooks, custodians, secretaries, students, and counselors—make contributions to multicultural environments as important as do courses of study and instructional materials.

Students learn important lessons about ethnic and cultural diversity by observing interactions among racial, ethnic, cultural, and gender groups in their school, by observing and experiencing the verbal behavior of the professional and support staffs, and by observing the extent to which the staff is ethnically and racially mixed. Therefore, school policies should be established and aggressively implemented to recruit and maintain a multiethnic school staff, sensitive to the needs of a pluralistic democratic society.

In addition, students can benefit from positive and cooperative interactions with students from various racial, ethnic, and cultural groups (Slavin, 1995; Cohen, 1994). When plans are made to mix students from diverse groups—whether through school desegregation, exchange programs and visits, or program assignment—extreme care must be taken to ensure that the environment in which the students interact is a positive and enhancing one. When students from different ethnic and racial groups interact within a hostile environment, their racial antipathies are likely to increase (Stephan, 1999).

4.0   Schools should have systematic, comprehensive, mandatory, and continuing staff development programs.

A teacher is an important variable in a student's formal learning environment. Attention should be devoted to the training and retraining of teachers and other members of the professional and support staff to create the kind of multicultural school environment recommended in these guidelines. Sound materials and other instructional program components are ineffective in the hands of teachers who lack the skills, attitudes, perceptions, and content background essential for a positive multicultural school environment. An effective staff development program must involve administrators, librarians, counselors, and members of the support staff such as cooks, secretaries, and bus drivers. This is necessary because any well-trained and sensitive teacher must work within a supportive institutional environment to succeed. Key administrators, such as principals, must set by example the school norms for ethnic and cultural differences. The need to involve administrators, especially building principals, in comprehensive and systematic staff development programs cannot be overemphasized.

Effective professional staff development should begin at the preservice level, continue when educators are employed by schools, and focus on helping the staff members (a) clarify and analyze their feelings, attitudes, and perceptions toward their own and other racial, ethnic, and cultural groups; (b) acquire knowledge about and understanding of the historical experiences and sociological characteristics of ethnic and cultural groups in the United States; (c) increase their instructional skills within multicultural school environments; (d) improve their intercultural communications skills; (e) improve their skill in curriculum development as it relates to ethnic and cultural diversity; and (f) improve their skill in creating, selecting, evaluating, and revising instructional materials. Staff development for effective multicultural schools is best undertaken jointly by school districts, local colleges and universities, and local community agencies. Each group bears a responsibility for training school personnel, at both the preservice and in-service levels, to function successfully within multicultural instructional settings.

Effective staff development programs must be carefully conceptualized and implemented. Short workshops, selected courses, and other short-term experiences may be essential components of such programs, but these alone cannot constitute an entire staff development program. Rather, sound staff development programs should consist of a wide variety of program components, including needs assessments, curriculum development, peer teaching, and materials selection and evaluation. Lectures alone are insufficient. Ongoing changes should be made to make staff development programs more responsive to the needs of practicing professionals.

5.0   The curriculum should reflect the cultural learning styles and characteristics of the students within the school continuity.

Students in a school responsive to ethnic and cultural diversity cannot be treated identically and still be afforded equal educational opportunities. Some students have unique cultural and ethnic characteristics to which the school should respond deliberately and sensitively. Research indicates that the academic achievement of African American and Latino students increases when cooperative teaching techniques such as the jigsaw are used (Aronson & Gonzalez, 1988). Moreover, *all* students develop more positive racial and ethnic attitudes when teachers use cooperative, rather than competitive, learning activities (Aronson & Gonzalez, 1988).

Research indicates that many students of color, especially those from low-income families, often have value orientations, behaviors, cognitive styles, language characteristics, and other cultural components that differ from those of the school's culture (Delpit, 1995; Deyhle, 1986; Fordham, 1996; Fordham & Ogbu, 1986; Gay, 2000; Heath, 1983; Shade, Kelly, & Oberg, 1997). These components often lead to conflict between students and teachers. By comparison, most middle-class mainstream youths find the school culture consistent with their home cultures and are, therefore, much more comfortable in school. Many students, though, regardless of their racial, ethnic, or cultural identity, find the school culture alien, hostile, and self-defeating.

A school's culture and instructional programs should be restructured and made to reflect the cultures and learning styles of students from diverse ethnic and social-class groups (Banks & Banks, 1995). Research indicates that the instructional strategies and learning styles most often favored in the nation's schools are inconsistent with the cognitive styles, cultural orientations, and cultural characteristics of some groups of students of color (Aronson & Gonzalez, 1988; Fordham, 1996). This research provides important guidelines and principles that educators can use to change schools to make them more responsive to students from diverse cultural groups. Educators should not ignore racial and ethnic differences when planning instruction; nor should they dismiss the question of racial and ethnic differences with the all-too-easy cliché, "I don't see racial differences in students and I treat them all alike." Research on cognitive styles and language and communication characteristics of ethnic groups suggests that if all students are treated alike, their distinctive needs are not being met and they are probably being denied access to equal educational opportunities (Heath, 1983; Lee, 1998; Perry & Delpit, 1998; Philips, 1983).

Although differences among students are accepted in an effective multicultural school, teaching students to function effectively in mainstream society and in social settings different from the ones in which they were socialized, and helping them learn new cognitive styles and learning patterns, must also be major goals. The successful multicultural school helps students become aware of and able to acquire cultural and cognitive alternatives, thus enabling them to function successfully within cultural environments other than their own.

6.0   The multicultural curriculum should provide students with continuous opportunities to develop a better sense of self.

The multicultural curriculum should help students to develop a better sense of self. This development should be an ongoing process, beginning when the student first enters school and continuing throughout the student's school career. This development should include at least three areas:

1. Students should be helped to develop accurate self-identities. Students must ask questions such as, Who am I? and, What am I? in order to come to grips with their own identities.

2. The multicultural curriculum should help students develop improved self-concepts. Beyond considering such questions as who they are and what they are, students should learn to feel positively about their identities, particularly their cultural and ethnic identities. Positive self-concepts may be expressed in several ways. The multicultural curriculum, for example, should recognize the varying talents of students and capitalize on them in the academic curriculum. All students need to feel that academic success is possible. The multicultural curriculum should also help students develop a high regard for their home languages and cultures.

3. The multicultural curriculum should help students develop greater self-understanding. Students should develop more sophisticated understandings of why they are the way they are, why their ethnic and cultural groups are the way they are, and what ethnicity and culture mean in their daily lives. Such self-understanding will help students to handle more effectively situations in which ethnicity and culture may play a part.

Students cannot fully understand why they are the way they are and why certain things might occur in their future until they have a solid knowledge of the groups to which they belong and the effects of group membership on their lives. Multicultural education should enable students to come to grips with these individual and group relationships in general and with the effects of ethnicity and culture on their lives in particular.

Looking at group membership should not undermine a student's individuality. Rather, it should add a dimension to the understanding of a student's unique individuality by learning the effects of belonging to groups. Neither are students to be assigned and locked into one group. Instead, students should be aware of the many groups to which they belong, both voluntarily and involuntarily, and recognize that at various moments one or more of these groups may be affecting their lives.

The multicultural curriculum should also help students understand and appreciate their personal backgrounds and family heritages. Family studies in the school can contribute to increased self-understanding and a personal sense of heritage, as contrasted with the generalized experiences presented in textbooks. They can also contribute to family and personal pride. If parents and other relatives come to school to share their stories and experiences, students will become increasingly aware that ethnic groups are a meaningful part of our nation's heritage and merit study by all of us so that we can better understand the complexity of the nation's pluralistic experiences and traditions.

7.0 The curriculum should help students understand the totality of the experiences of ethnic and cultural groups in the United States.

The social problems that ethnic and cultural group members experience are often regarded as part of their cultural characteristics. Alcoholism, crime, and illiteracy, for example, are considered by many people cultural characteristics of particular racial or ethnic groups. Ethnicity is often assumed to mean something negative and divisive, and the study of ethnic groups and ethnicity often becomes the examination of problems such as prejudice, racism, discrimination, and exploitation. To concentrate exclusively on these problems when studying ethnicity creates serious distortions in perceptions of ethnic groups. Among other things, it stereotypes ethnic groups as essentially passive recipients of the dominant society's discrimination and exploitation. Although these are legitimate issues and should be included in a comprehensive, effective multicultural curriculum, they should not constitute the entire curriculum.

Although many ethnic group members face staggering sociopolitical problems, these problems do not constitute the whole of their lives. Nor are all ethnic groups affected to the same degree or in the same way by these problems. Moreover, many ethnic groups have developed and maintained viable life-styles and have made notable contributions to U.S. culture. The experiences of each ethnic group are part of a composite of human activities. Although it is true that each ethnic group has significant unifying historical experiences and cultural traits, no ethnic group has a single, homogeneous, historical-cultural pattern. Members of an ethnic group do not conform to a single cultural norm or mode of behavior, nor are ethnic cultures uniform and static.

Consequently, the many dimensions of ethnic experiences and cultures should be studied. The curriculum should help students understand the significant historical experiences and basic cultural patterns of ethnic groups, the critical contemporary issues and social problems confronting each group, and the dynamic diversity of the experiences, cultures, and individuals within each ethnic group.

A consistently multifaceted approach to teaching benefits students in several major ways. It helps them to become aware of the commonalities within and among ethnic groups. At the same time, it helps counteract stereotyping by making students aware of the rich diversity within each ethnic group in the United States. It also helps students develop more comprehensive and realistic understandings of the broad range of ethnic group heritages and experiences.

8.0   The curriculum should help students understand the totality of the experiences of ethnic and cultural groups in the United States.

Traditionally, students in U.S. public schools have been taught a great deal about the ideals of our society. Conflicts between ideals, however, are often glossed over. Often values, such as freedom in the U.S. democracy, are treated as attainable ideals, and the realities of U.S. society have been distorted to make it appear that they have, indeed, been achieved. Courses in U.S. history and citizenship especially have been characterized by this kind of unquestioning approach to the socialization of youth (Banks, 1997). This form of citizenship education, termed "passing down the myths and legends of our national heritage," tends to inculcate parochial national attitudes, promote serious misconceptions about the nature of U.S. society and culture, and develop cynicism in youth who are aware of the gaps between the ideal and the real.

When ethnic studies emerged from the civil rights movement of the 1960s, there was a strong and negative reaction to the traditional approach to citizenship education. A widely expressed goal of many curriculum reformers was to "tell it like it is and was" in the classroom. In many of the reformed courses, however, U.S. history and society were taught and viewed primarily from the viewpoints of specific ethnic groups. Little attention was given to basic U.S. values, except to highlight gross discrepancies between ideals and practices of U.S. society. Emphasis was often on how ethnic groups of color had been oppressed by Anglo-Americans.

Both the unquestioning approach and the tell-it-like-it-is approach result in distortions. In a sound multicultural curriculum, emphasis should be neither on the ways in which the United States has "fulfilled its noble ideals" nor on the "sins committed by the Anglo-Americans" (or by any other group of Americans). Rather, students should be encouraged to examine the democratic values that emerged in the United States, why they emerged, how they were defined in various periods, and to whom they referred in various eras. Students should also examine the extent to which these values have or have not been fulfilled and the continuing conflict between values, such as freedom and equality, and between ideals in other societies.

Students should also be encouraged to examine alternative interpretations of the discrepancies between ideals and realities in the life and history of the United States. From the perspectives of some individuals and groups, there has been a continuing expansion of human rights in the United States. Others see a continuing process of weighing rights against rights as the optimum mix of values, none of which can be fully realized as ideals. Many argue that basic human rights are still limited to U.S. citizens who have certain class, racial, ethnic, gender, and cultural characteristics. Students should consider why these various interpretations arose and why there are different views regarding conflicts between the ideals and between the ideals and realities of U.S. society.

9.0 The multicultural curriculum should explore and clarify ethnic and cultural alternatives and options in the United States.

Educational questions regarding students' ethnic and cultural alternatives and options are complex and difficult. Some individuals, for a variety of complex reasons, are uncomfortable with their ethnic and cultural identities and wish to deny them. Some individuals are uncomfortable when their own ethnic groups are discussed in the classroom. Teachers need to handle these topics sensitively; they must not ignore them.

The degree of a class's resistance when studying ethnic or cultural groups is influenced by the teacher's approach to the study of diversity. Students can sense when the teacher or other students in the class are intolerant of their particular group or of some of its characteristics. Students often receive such messages from nonverbal responses. The teacher can minimize students' resistance to studying their own heritage by creating a classroom atmosphere that reflects acceptance and respect for ethnic and cultural differences. Most important, teachers need to model their own acceptance of and respect for ethnic, racial, and cultural diversity.

Teachers should help students understand the options related to their own ethnic and cultural identity and the nature of ethnic and cultural alternatives and options within the United States. Students should be helped to understand that, ideally, all individuals should have the right to select the manner and degree of identifying or not identifying with their ethnic and cultural groups. They should learn, however, that some individuals, such as members of many White ethnic groups, have this privilege while others, such as most African Americans, have more limited options. Most persons of European ancestry can become structurally assimilated into the mainstream U.S. society. When they become highly assimilated, they can usually participate completely in most U.S. economic, social, and political institutions. On the other hand, no matter how culturally assimilated or acculturated members of some ethnic groups become, they are still perceived and stigmatized by the larger society on the basis of their physical characteristics.

Students should also be helped to understand that although individualism is strong in the United States, in reality many people in the United States, such as American Indians and Chinese Americans, are often judged not as individuals but on the basis of the racial or ethnic group to which they belong. While teachers may give American Indian or Chinese American students the option of examining or not examining their ethnic heritage and identity, such students need to be helped to understand how they are perceived and identified by the larger society. Educators must respect the individual rights of students; at the same time, however, they have a professional responsibility to help students learn basic facts and generalizations about the nature of race and ethnicity in the United States.

10.0 The multicultural curriculum should promote values, attitudes, and behaviors that support ethnic pluralism and cultural diversity as well as build and support the nation-state and the nation's shared national culture. E pluribus unum should be the goal of the schools and the nation.

Ethnicity and cultural identity are salient factors in the lives of many U.S. citizens. They help individuals answer the question, Who am I? by providing a sense of peoplehood, identity, and cultural and spiritual roots. They provide a filter through which events, life-styles, norms, and values are processed and screened. They provide a means through which identity is affirmed, heritages are validated, and preferred associates are selected. Therefore, ethnicity and cultural identity serve necessary functions in many people's lives. Ethnicity and cultural identity are neither always positive and reinforcing, nor always negative and debilitating, although they have the potential for both. An effective multicultural curriculum examines all of these dimensions of ethnicity and cultural identity.

The curriculum should help students understand that diversity is an integral part of life in the United States. Ethnic and cultural diversity permeate U.S. history and society. Demographic projections indicate that the United States will become increasingly multiethnic and multicultural in the future. Consequently, schools should teach about ethnic and cultural diversity to help students acquire more accurate assessments of history and culture in the United States. Major goals of multicultural education include improving respect for human dignity, maximizing cultural options, understanding what makes people alike and different, and accepting diversity as inevitable and valuable to human life.

Students should learn that difference does not necessarily imply inferiority or superiority, and that the study of ethnic and cultural group differences need not lead to polarization. They should also learn that although conflict is unavoidable in ethnically or racially pluralistic societies, such conflict does not necessarily have to be destructive or divisive. Conflict is an intrinsic part of the human condition, especially so in a pluralistic society. Conflict is often a catalyst for social progress. Multicultural education programs that explore diversity in positive, realistic ways will present ethnic conflict in its proper perspective. Such programs will help students understand that there is strength in diversity, and that cooperation among cultural and ethnic groups does not necessarily require identical beliefs, behaviors, and values.

The multicultural curriculum should help students understand and respect ethnic diversity and broaden their cultural options. Too many people in the United States learn only the values, behavioral patterns, and beliefs of either mainstream society or their own ethnic groups, cultural groups, or communities. Socialization is, in effect, encapsulating, providing few opportunities for most individuals to acquire more than stereotypes about ethnic and cultural groups other than their own. Therefore, many people tend to view other ethnic groups and life-styles as abnormal or deviant. The multicultural curriculum can help students correct these misconceptions by teaching them that other ways of living are as valid and viable as their own.

The multicultural curriculum should also promote the basic values expressed in our major historical documents. Each ethnic group should have the right to practice its own religious, social, and cultural beliefs, albeit within the limits of due regard for the rights of others. There is, after all, a set of overarching values that all groups within a society or nation must endorse in order to maintain societal cohesion. In our nation, these core values stem from our commitment to human dignity and include justice, equality, freedom, and due process of law. Although the school should value and reflect ethnic and cultural diversity, it should not promote the practices and beliefs of any ethnic or cultural group that contradict the core democratic values of the United States. Rather, the school should foster ethnic and cultural differences that maximize opportunities for democratic living. Pluralism must take place within the context of national unity. *E pluribus unum*—out of many, one—should be our goal.

Although ethnic and cultural group membership should not restrict an individual's opportunity and ability to achieve and to participate, it is sometimes used by groups in power to the detriment of less powerful groups. Individuals who do not understand the role of ethnicity often find it a troublesome reality, one extremely difficult to handle. Multicultural curricula should help students examine the dilemmas surrounding ethnicity as a step toward realizing its full potential as an enabling force in the lives of individuals, groups, and the nation.

11.0 The multicultural curriculum should help students develop their decision-making abilities, social participation skills, and sense of political efficacy as necessary bases for effective citizenship in a pluralistic democratic nation.

The demands on people to make reflective decisions on issues related to race, ethnicity, and culture are increasing as the nation's ethnic texture deepens. When people are unable to process the masses of conflicting information—including facts, opinions, interpretations, and theories about ethnic groups—they are often overwhelmed.

The multicultural curriculum must enable students to gain knowledge and apply it. Students need a rich foundation of sound knowledge. Facts, concepts, generalizations, and theories differ in their capability for organizing particulars and in predictive capacity; concepts and generalizations have more usefulness than do mere collections of miscellaneous facts. Young people need practice in the steps of scholarly methods for arriving at knowledge—identifying problems; formulating hypotheses; locating and evaluating source materials; organizing information as evidence; analyzing, interpreting, and reworking what they find; and making conclusions. Students also need ample opportunities to learn to use knowledge in making sense out of the situations they encounter.

When curricular programs are inappropriate, teaching is inept, or expectations are low for students of some ethnic groups, and especially for those who are low-income, the emphasis in class is likely to be on discrete facts, memorization of empty generalizations, and low-level skills. Even if the names, dates, and exercises in using an index are drawn from ethnic content, such an emphasis is still discriminatory and inconsistent with the basic purpose of multicultural education. All young people need opportunities to develop powerful concepts, generalizations, and intellectual abilities when studying content related to ethnic and cultural diversity (Banks & Banks, with Clegg, 1999).

Students must also learn to identify values and relate them to knowledge. Young people should be taught methods for clarifying their own values relating to ethnic and cultural diversity. Such processes should include identifying value problems (their own and others'), describing evaluative behaviors, recognizing value conflicts in themselves and in social situations, recognizing and proposing alternatives based on values, and making choices between values in light of their consequences.

Determining the basic ideas, discovering and verifying facts, and valuing are interrelated aspects of decision-making. Ample opportunity for practice in real-life situations is necessary; such practice frequently requires interdisciplinary as well as multicultural perspectives. Decision-making skills help people assess social situations objectively and perceptively, identify feasible courses of action and project their consequences, decide thoughtfully, and then act.

The multicultural curriculum must also help students develop effective social and civic action skills because many students from ethnic groups are overwhelmed by a sense of a lack of control of their destinies. These feelings often stem from their belief that, as in the past, they and other people of color have little influence on political policies and institutions (Ogbu, 1990). The multicultural curriculum should help students develop a sense of political efficacy and become active and effective in the civic life of their communities and the nation. With a basis in strong commitments to such democratic values as justice, freedom, and equality, students can learn to exercise political and social influence responsibly to influence societal decisions related to race, ethnicity, and cultural freedom in ways consistent with human dignity.

The school, in many ways, is a microcosm of society, reflecting the changing dynamics of ethnic group situations. The school can provide many opportunities for students to practice social participation skills and to test their political efficacy as they address themselves to resolving some of the school's racial and ethnic problems. Issues such as the participation of ethnic individuals in school government, the uneven application of discriminatory disciplinary rules, and preferential treatment of certain students because of their racial, ethnic, cultural, and social-class backgrounds are examples of problems that students can help to resolve. Applying social action skills effectively, students can combine knowledge, valuing, and thought gained from multicultural perspectives and experiences to resolve problems affecting racial, ethnic, and cultural groups.

By providing students with opportunities to use decision-making abilities and social action skills in the resolution of problems affecting ethnic, racial, and cultural groups, schools can contribute to more effective education for democratic citizenship.

12.0 The multicultural curriculum should help students develop the skills necessary for effective interpersonal, interethnic, and intercultural group interactions.

Effective interpersonal interaction across ethnic group lines is often difficult to achieve. The problem is complicated by the fact that individuals bring to cross-ethnic interaction situations attitudes, values, and expectations that influence their own behavior, including their responses to the behavior of others. These expectations are sometimes formed on the basis of what their own groups deem appropriate behavior and what each individual believes he or she knows about other ethnic groups. Much knowledge about ethnic groups is stereotyped, distorted, and based on distant observations, scattered and superficial contacts, inadequate or imbalanced media treatment, and incomplete factual information. Attempts at cross-ethnic interpersonal interactions, therefore, are often stymied by ethnocentrism.

The problems created by ethnocentrism can be at least partially resolved by helping students recognize the forces operating in interpersonal interactions and how these forces affect behavior. Students should develop skills and concepts to overcome factors that prevent successful interactions, including identifying ethnic and cultural stereotypes, examining media treatment of ethnic groups, clarifying ethnic and cultural attitudes and values, developing cross-cultural communication skills, recognizing how attitudes and values are projected in verbal and non-verbal behaviors, and viewing the dynamics of interpersonal interactions from others' perspectives.

One goal of multicultural education should be to help individuals function easily and effectively with members of both their own and other racial, ethnic, and cultural groups. The multicultural curriculum should provide opportunities for students to explore lines of cross-cultural communication and to experiment with cross-ethnic and cross-cultural functioning. Actual experiences can be effective teaching devices, allowing students to test stereotypes and idealized behavioral constructs against real-life situations and make the necessary adjustments in their frames of reference and behaviors. In the process, they should learn that ethnic group members, in the final analysis, are individuals, with all of the variations that characterize all individuals, and that ethnicity is only one of many variables that shape their personalities. Students will be forced to confront their values and make moral choices when their experiences in cross-ethnic and cross-cultural interactions produce information contrary to previously held notions. Thus, students should broaden their ethnic and cultural options, increase their frames of reference, develop greater appreciation for individual and ethnic differences, and deepen their own capacities as human beings.

13.0 The multicultural curriculum should be comprehensive in scope and sequence, should present holistic views of ethnic and cultural groups, and should be an integral part of the total school curriculum.

Students learn best from well-planned, comprehensive, continuous, and interrelated experiences. In an effective multicultural school, the study of ethnic and cultural content is integrated into the curriculum from preschool through twelfth grade and beyond. This study should be carefully planned to encourage the development of progressively more complex concepts and generalizations. It should also involve students in the study of a variety of ethnic and cultural groups.

A comprehensive multicultural curriculum should also include a broad range of experiences within the study of any group: present culture, historical experiences, sociopolitical realities, contributions to the nation's development, problems faced in everyday living, and conditions of existence in society.

Students should be introduced to the experiences of persons from widely varying backgrounds. Although the study of ethnic and cultural success stories can help students of an ethnic group develop pride in their own group, the curriculum should include study of ethnic peoples in general, not just heroes and success stories. In addition, those outside of an ethnic group can develop greater respect for that group by learning about these heroes and successes. Moreover, in establishing heroes and labeling people as successes, teachers should move beyond the standards of the dominant society and consider the values of each ethnic group and the worth of each individual life. An active contributor to an ethnic neighborhood may be more of a hero to the local community than a famous athlete; a good parent may be more of a success than a famous politician.

For optimum effectiveness, the study of ethnic and cultural group experiences must be interwoven into the total curriculum. It should not be reserved for special occasions, units, or courses, nor should it be considered supplementary to the existing curriculum. Such observances as African American History or Brotherhood Week, Hanukkah, Cinco de Mayo, St. Patrick's Day, and Martin Luther King, Jr.'s, birthday are important and necessary, but insufficient in themselves. To rely entirely on these kinds of occasions and events, or to relegate ethnic content to a marginal position in the curriculum is to guarantee a minimal influence of the multicultural content.

The basic premises and organizational structures of schools should be reformed to reflect the nation's multicultural realities. The curriculum should be reorganized so that ethnic and cultural diversity is an integral, natural, and normal component of educational experiences for all students, with ethnic and cultural content accepted and used in everyday instruction, and with various ethnic and cultural perspectives introduced. Multicultural content is as appropriate and important in teaching such fundamental skills and abilities as reading, thinking, and decision-making as it is in teaching about social issues raised by racism, dehumanization, racial conflict, and alternative ethnic and cultural life-styles.

14.0 The multicultural curriculum should include the continuous study of the cultures, historical experiences, social realities, and existential conditions of ethnic and cultural groups, including a variety of racial compositions.

The multicultural curriculum should involve students in the continuous study of ethnic groups of different racial compositions. A curriculum that concentrates on one ethnic or cultural group is not multicultural. Nor is a curriculum multicultural if it focuses exclusively on European ethnics or exclusively on ethnic groups of color. Every ethnic group cannot be included in the curriculum of a particular school or school district—the number is too large to be manageable. The inclusion of groups of different racial compositions, however, is a necessary characteristic of effective multicultural education.

Moreover, the multicultural curriculum should include the consistent examination of significant aspects of ethnic experiences influenced by or related to race. These include such concepts as racism, racial prejudice, racial discrimination, and exploitation based on race. The sensitive and continuous development of such concepts should help students develop an understanding of racial factors in the past and present of our nation.

15.0 Interdisciplinary and multidisciplinary approaches should be used in designing and implementing the multicultural curriculum.

No single discipline can adequately explain all components of the life-styles, cultural experiences, and social problems of ethnic groups. Knowledge from any one discipline is insufficient to help individuals make adequate decisions on the complex issues raised by racism, sexism, structural exclusion, poverty, and powerlessness. Concepts such as racism, anti-Semitism, and language discrimination have multiple dimensions. To delineate these dimensions requires the concepts and perspectives of the social sciences, history, literature, music, art, and philosophy.

Single-discipline or monoperspective analyses of complex ethnic and cultural issues can produce skewed, distorted interpretations and evaluations. A promising way to avoid these pitfalls is to use consistently multidisciplinary approaches in studying experiences and events related to ethnic and cultural groups. For example, *ethnic protest* is not simply a political, economic, artistic, or sociological activity; it is all four of these. Therefore, a curriculum that purports to be multicultural and is realistic in its treatment of ethnic protest must focus on its broader ramifications. Such study must address the scientific, political, artistic, and sociological dimensions of protest.

The accomplishments of the United States are due neither to the ingenuity and creativity of a single ethnic or cultural group, nor to accomplishments in a single area, but rather to the efforts and contributions of many ethnic groups and individuals in many areas. African American, Latino, American Indian, Asian American, and European immigrant group members have all contributed to the fields of science and industry, politics, literature, economics, and the arts. Multidisciplinary analyses will best help students to understand them.

16.0 The multicultural curriculum should use comparative approaches in the study of ethnic and cultural groups.

The study of ethnic and cultural group experiences should not be a process of competition. It should not promote the idea that any one ethnic or cultural group has a monopoly on talent and worth, or incapacity and weakness, but, instead, the idea that each individual and each ethnic group has worth and dignity. Students should be taught that persons from all ethnic groups have common characteristics and needs, although they are affected differently by certain social situations and may use different means to respond to their needs and to achieve their objectives. Furthermore, school personnel should remember that realistic comparative approaches to the study of different ethnic and cultural group experiences are descriptive and analytical, not normative or judgmental. Teachers should also be aware of their own biases and prejudices as they help students to use comparative approaches.

Social situations and events included in the curriculum should be analyzed from the perspectives of several ethnic and cultural groups instead of using a monoperspective analysis. This approach allows students to see the subtle ways in which the lives of different ethnic group members are similar and interrelated, to study the concept of universality as it relates to ethnic groups, and to see how all ethnic groups are active participants in all aspects of society. Studying such issues as power and politics, ethnicity, and culture from comparative, multicultural perspectives will help students to develop more realistic, accurate understandings of how these issues affect everyone, and how the effects are both alike and different.

17.0 The multicultural curriculum should help students to view and interpret events, situations, and conflict from diverse ethnic and cultural perspectives and points of view.

Historically, students have been taught to view events, situations, and our national history primarily from the perspectives of mainstream historians and social scientists sympathetic to the dominant groups within our society. The perspectives of other groups have been largely omitted in the school curriculum. The World War II Japanese American internment and the Indian Removal Act of 1830, for example, are rarely studied from the points of view of interned Japanese Americans or the American Indians forced to leave their homes and move west.

To gain a more complete understanding of both our past and our present, students should look at events and situations from the perspectives of the mainstream and from the perspectives of marginalized groups. This approach to teaching is more likely to make our students less ethnocentric and more able to understand that almost any event or situation can be legitimately looked at from many perspectives. When using this approach in the classroom, the teacher should avoid, as much as possible, labeling any perspective "right'" or '"wrong." Rather, the teacher should try to help students understand how each group may view a situation differently and why. The emphasis should be on understanding and explanation and not on simplistic moralizing. For example, the perceptions that many Jewish Americans have of political events in the United States have been shaped by memories of the Holocaust and of anti-Semitism in the United States.

Ethnicity and cultural diversity have strongly influenced the nature of intergroup relations in U.S. society. The way that individuals perceive events and situations occurring in the United States is often influenced by their ethnic and cultural experiences, especially when the events and situations are directly related to ethnic conflict and discrimination or to issues such as affirmative action and busing for school desegregation. When students view a historical or contemporary situation from the perspectives of one ethnic or cultural group only—whether majority or minority—they can acquire, at best, an incomplete understanding.

18.0 The multicultural curriculum should conceptualize and describe the development of the United States as a multidirectional society.

A basic structural concept in the study and teaching of U.S. society is the view that the United States has developed mainly from east to west. According to this concept, the United States is the product of the spread of civilization from Western Europe across the Atlantic Ocean to the east coast of what is today the United States and then west to the Pacific. Within this approach, ethnic groups appear almost always in two forms: as obstacles to the advancement of westward-moving Anglo civilization or as problems that must be corrected or, at least, kept under control.

The underlying rationale for this frame of reference is that the study of U.S. history is, for the most part, an account of processes within the national boundaries of the United States. In applying this frame of reference, however, educators have been inconsistent, including as part of the study of the United States such themes as pre-United States geography, the pre–United States British colonies, the Texas revolution, and the Lone Star Republic. In short, the study of the United States has traditionally included phenomena outside the boundaries of the political United States.

Yet, while including some non–United States themes as part of the traditional study of the United States, school programs have not adequately included study of the Native American, Hispanic, and Mexican societies that developed on land that ultimately became part of the United States. Nor has sufficient attention been devoted to the northwesterly flow of cultures from Africa to the United States, the northerly flow of cultures from Mexico, Latin America, and the Caribbean, the easterly flow of cultures from Asia, and the westerly flow of latter-day immigrants from Eastern, Central, and Southern Europe.

Multicultural education, from the early years of school onward, must redress these intellectually invalid and distorting imbalances by illuminating the variety of cultural experiences that compose the total U.S. experience. Multicultural education must consistently address the development of the entire geocultural United States—that area which, in time, was to become the United States and the peoples encompassed by that area. Moreover, the flow of cultures into the United States must be viewed multidirectionally.

19.0 Schools should provide opportunities for students to participate in the aesthetic experiences of various ethnic and cultural groups.

The study of ethnic and cultural groups should be based on more than the social sciences. Although incorporating statistical and analytical social science methodologies and concepts into the study of ethnic and cultural groups is valuable, an overreliance on these methods lacks an important part of the multicultural experience—participation in the experiences of ethnic and cultural groups.

A number of teaching materials can be used. Students should read and hear past and contemporary writings of members of various ethnic and cultural groups. Poetry, short stories, folklore, essays, plays, and novels should be used. Ethnic autobiographies offer special insight into what it means to be ethnic in the United States.

Ethnic music, art, architecture, and dance—past and contemporary—provide other avenues for experiential participation, interpreting the emotions and feelings of ethnic groups. The arts and humanities can serve as excellent vehicles for studying group experiences by focusing on these questions: What aspects of the experience of a particular ethnic group helped create these kinds of musical and artistic expressions? What do they reveal about these groups?

Studying multiethnic literature and arts, students should become acquainted with what has been created in local ethnic communities. In addition, members of local ethnic communities can provide dramatic "living autobiographies" for students; invite them to discuss their viewpoints and experiences with students. Students should also have opportunities for developing their own artistic, musical, and literary abilities, even to make them available to the local community.

Role playing of various ethnic and cultural experiences should be interspersed throughout the curriculum to encourage understanding of what it means to belong to various ethnic groups. The immersion of students in multiethnic experiences is an effective means for developing understanding of both self and others.

20.0 The multicultural curriculum should provide opportunities for students to study ethnic group languages as legitimate communication systems and to help them develop literacy in at least two languages.

A multicultural curriculum recognizes language diversity and promotes the attitude that all languages and dialects are valid communicating systems for some groups and for some purposes. The program requires a multidisciplinary focus on language and dialect.

Concepts about language and dialect derived from disciplines such as anthropology, sociology, and political science expand students' perceptions of language and dialect as something more than correct grammar. For example, the nature and intent of language policies and laws in the United States can be compared to those in bilingual nations. Students can also be taught sociolinguistic concepts that provide a framework for understanding the verbal and nonverbal behavior of others and themselves. Critical listening, speaking, and reading habits should be nurtured with special attention to the uses of language.

Research indicates that a school's rejection of a student's home language affects the student's self-esteem, academic achievement, and social and occupational mobility. Conversely, a school's acceptance and use of a student's home language improves the student's self-esteem, academic achievement, and relationships among students in a school (U.S. Commission on Civil Rights, 1975). In a multicultural curriculum, students are provided opportunities to study their own and others' dialects. They become increasingly receptive to the languages and dialects of their peers. Such an approach helps students develop concepts in their own vernaculars whenever necessary and at the same time promotes appreciation of home-language environments.

Literacy in U.S. English is a time-honored goal of schools and should be maintained. Another important goal of the multicultural curriculum, however, is to help all students acquire literacy in a second language. Second-language literacy requires students to understand, speak, read, and write well enough to communicate effectively with native speakers of the second language. Equally important, students should study the cultures of the people who use the second language. Ultimately, effective communication in the second language requires an understanding of its people and their culture.

Some students come to school speaking two languages. These students should be provided the opportunity to develop full literacy in their native language. In turn, these students and their parents can be used as resources for helping other students acquire a second language proficiency.

Second-language literacy complements other areas of the multicultural curriculum. For example, approaches for studying the culture of other people are described in several of the above guidelines. As students are learning a second language, they can also learn skills in interpersonal and intercultural communications. Further, because these guidelines encourage multidisciplinary approaches, second-language literacy can be achieved while other areas of the language arts and the social studies are taught.

21.0 The multicultural curriculum should make maximum use of experimental learning, especially local community resources.

An effective multicultural curriculum includes a study of ethnic and cultural groups not only nationally, but locally as well. An effective multicultural curriculum must expand beyond classroom walls. Teachers should use the local community as a laboratory in which students can develop and use intellectual, social, and political action skills. Planned field trips and individual or group research projects are helpful. Continuous investigation of the local community can provide insights into the dynamics of ethnic and cultural groups. Such investigation can create greater respect for what has been accomplished. It can promote awareness of and commitment to what still needs to be done to improve the lives and opportunities of all local residents.

Every member of the local community, including students' family members, is a valuable source of knowledge. There are no class, educational, or linguistic qualifications for participating in the U.S. experience, for having culture or society, for having family or neighborhood traditions, for perceiving the surrounding community, or for relating experiences. Teachers should invite local residents of various ethnic backgrounds to the classroom to share their experiences and views with students, relate their oral traditions, answer questions, offer new outlooks on society and history, and open doors of investigation for students. Special efforts should be made to involve senior citizens in school multicultural programs both to help them develop a higher sense of self-worth and to benefit the students and the school community.

It is important that students develop a sensitivity to ethnic differences and a conceptual framework for viewing ethnic differences before interacting with ethnic classroom guests or studying the local ethnic communities. Otherwise, these promising opportunities may reinforce, rather than reduce, ethnic stereotypes and prejudices.

In study projects, students can consider such topics as local population distribution, housing, school assignments, political representation, and ethnic community activities. Older students can take advantage of accessible public documents, such as city council and school board minutes, minutes of local organizations, and church records, for insight into the community. To separate the local community from the school is to ignore the everyday world in which students live.

22.0 The assessment procedures used with students should reflect their ethnic and cultural experiences.

To make the school a truly multicultural institution, major changes must be made in the ways in which we test and ascertain student abilities. Most of the intelligence tests administered in the public schools are based on a mainstream conformity, mono-ethnic model. Because many students socialized within other ethnic and cultural groups find the tests and other aspects of the school alien and intimidating, they perform poorly and are placed in low academic tracks, special education classes, or low-ability reading groups (Oakes, 1985). Research indicates that teachers in these kinds of situations tend to have low expectations for their students and often fail to create the kinds of learning environments that promote proficiency in the skills and abilities necessary to function effectively in society (Page, 1991).

In the final analysis, standardized intelligence testing frequently serves to deny some youths equal educational opportunities. The results of these tests are often used to justify the noneducation of students of color and of low-income students and to relieve teachers and other school personnel of accountability (Deyhle, 1986; Mercer, 1989). Novel assessment devices that reflect the cultures of ethnic youths need to be developed and used. Moreover, teacher-generated tests and other routine classroom assessment techniques should reflect the cultures of students from diverse cultural and ethnic groups. It will, however, do little good for educators to create improved assessment procedures for students unless they also implement multicultural curricular and instructional practices.

23.0 Schools should conduct ongoing, systematic assessment of the goals, methods, and instructional materials used in teaching about cultural and ethnic diversity.

Schools should formulate attainable goals and objectives for multicultural education. To evaluate the extent to which these goals and objectives are accomplished, school personnel must judge—with evidence—what occurs in their schools in three broad areas: (1) school policies and governance procedures; (2) everyday practices of staff and teachers; and (3) curricular programs and offerings, academic and nonacademic, preschool through twelfth grade. These guidelines and the checklist in the Appendix will help school practitioners to assess multicultural outcomes.

Many sources of evidence should be used. Teachers, administrators, support staff, parents, students, and others in the school community ought to participate in providing and evaluating evidence.

Assessment should be construed as a means by which a school, its staff, and students can improve multicultural relations, experiences, and understandings. Assessment should be oriented toward analyzing and improving, not castigating or applauding, the multicultural components of the school.

REFERENCES

Aronson, E., & Gonzalez, A. (1988). Desegregation, Jigsaw, and the Mexican-American Experience. In P. A. Katz & D. A. Taylor (Eds.), *Eliminating Racism: Profiles in Controversy* (pp. 301–314). New York: Plenum Press.

Banks, J. A. (1997). *Educating Citizens in a Multicultural Society.* New York: Teachers College Press.

Banks, J. A., & Banks, C. A. M. (Eds.). (1995). *Handbook of Research on Multicultural Education.* New York: Macmillan.

Banks, J. A., & Banks, C. A. M., with Clegg, A. A., Jr. (1999). *Teaching Strategies for the Social Studies: Decision-Making and Citizen Action* (5th ed.). New York: Longman.

Belenky, M. E., Clinchy, B. M., Goldberger, N. R., & Tarule, J. M. (1986). *Women's Ways of Knowing: The Development of Self, Voice and Mind.* New York: Basic Books.

Cohen, E. G. (1994). *Designing Groupwork: Strategies for the Heterogeneous Classroom* (2nd ed.). New York: Teachers College Press.

Delpit, L. D. (1995). *Other People's Children: Cultural Conflict in the Classroom.* New York: The New Press.

Deyhle, D. (1986). Success and Failure: A Micro-Ethnographic Comparison of Navajo and Anglo Students' Perceptions of Testing. *Curriculum Inquiry, 16,* 365–389.

Fordham, S. (1996). *Blacked Out: Dilemmas of Race, Identity, and Success at Capital High.* Chicago: The University of Chicago Press.

Fordham, S., & Ogbu, J. U. (1986). Black Students' School Success: Coping with the Burden of 'Acting White.' *The Urban Review, 18,* 176–206.

Gay, G. (2000). *Culturally Responsive Teaching: Theory, Research, and Practice.* New York: Teachers College Press.

Heath, S. H. (1983). *Ways with Words: Language, Life and Work in Communities and Classrooms.* New York: Cambridge University Press.

Lee, C. D. (1998). Culturally Responsive Pedagogy and Performanced-Based Assessment. *The Journal of Negro Education, 67*(3), 268–279.

Mercer, J. R. (1989). Alternate Paradigms for Assessment in a Pluralistic Society. In J. A. Banks & C. A. M. Banks (Eds.), *Multicultural Education: Issues and Perspectives* (pp. 289–304). Boston: Allyn and Bacon.

Oakes, J. (1985). *Keeping Track: How Schools Structure Inequality.* New Haven, CT: Yale University Press.

Ogbu, J. U. (1990). Overcoming Racial Barriers to Equal Access. In J. I. Goodlad & P. Keating (Eds.), *Access to Knowledge: An Agenda for Our Nation's Schools* (pp. 59–89). New York: The College Board.

Page, R. N. (1991). *Lower-Track Classrooms: A Curricular and Cultural Perspective.* New York: Teachers College Press.

Perry, T., & Delpit, L. (Eds.). (1998). *The Real Ebonics Debate: Power, Language, and the Education of African-American Children.* Boston: Beacon Press.

Philips, S. U. (1983). *The Invisible Culture: Communication in Classroom and Community on the Warm Springs Indian Reservation.* New York: Longman.

Ponterotto, J. G., Casas, J. M., Suzuki, L. A., & Alexander, C. M. (Eds.). (1995). *Handbook of Multicultural Counseling.* Thousand Oaks, CA: Sage Publications.

Shade, B. J., Kelly, C., & Oberg, M. (1997). *Creating Culturally Responsive Classrooms.* Washington, DC: American Psychological Association.

Slavin, R. E. (1995). Cooperative Learning and Intergroup Relations. In J. A. Banks & C. A. M. Banks (Eds.), *Handbook of Research on Multicultural Education* (pp. 628–634). New York: Macmillan.

Stephan, W. G. (1999). *Reducing Prejudice and Stereotyping in Schools.* New York: Teachers College Press.

Sue, D. W. (1995). Toward a Theory of Multicultural Counseling and Therapy. In J. A. Banks & C. A. M. Banks (Eds.), *Handbook of Research on Multicultural Education* (pp. 647–659). New York: Macmillan.

U.S. Commission on Civil Rights. (1975). *A Better Chance to Learn: Bilingual-Bicultural Education.* Washington, DC: Author.

A P P E N D I X

Multicultural Education Program Evaluation Checklist

	Rating			Guidelines
Strongly ◄———► Hardly at all				

Guidelines

1.0 Does ethnic and cultural diversity permeate the total school environment?

   1.1 Are ethnic content and perspectives incorporated into all aspects of the curriculum, preschool through 12th grade and beyond?

   1.2 Do instructional materials treat racial and ethnic differences and groups honestly, realistically, and sensitively?

   1.3 Do school libraries and resource centers offer a variety of materials on the histories, experiences, and cultures of many racial, ethnic, and cultural groups?

   1.4 Do school assemblies, decorations, speakers, holidays, and heroes reflect racial, ethnic, and cultural group differences?

   1.5 Are extracurricular activities multiethnic and multicultural?

2.0 Do school policies and procedures foster positive interactions among the various racial, ethnic, and cultural group members of the school?

   2.1 Do school policies accommodate the behavioral patterns, learning styles, and orientations of those ethnic and cultural group members actually in the school?

   2.2 Does the school provide a variety of instruments and techniques for teaching and counseling students of various ethnic and cultural groups?

   2.3 Do school policies recognize the holidays and festivities of various ethnic groups?

   2.4 Do school policies avoid instructional and guidance practices based on stereotyped and ethnocentric perceptions?

Rating				Guidelines
Strongly ← → **Hardly at all**				

				2.5 Do school policies respect the dignity and worth of students as individuals *and* as members of racial, ethnic, and cultural groups?
				3.0 Is the school staff (administrators, instructors, counselors, and support staff) multiethnic and multiracial? 3.1 Has the school established and enforced policies for recruiting and maintaining a staff made up of individuals from various racial and ethnic groups?

				4.0 Does the school have systematic, comprehensive, mandatory, and continuing multicultural staff development programs?
				    4.1 Are teachers, librarians, counselors, administrators, and support staff included in the staff development programs?
				    4.2 Do the staff development programs include a variety of experiences (such as lectures, field experiences, and curriculum projects)?
				    4.3 Do the staff development programs provide opportunities to gain knowledge and understanding about various racial, ethnic, and cultural groups?
				    4.4 Do the staff development programs provide opportunities for participants to explore their attitudes and feelings about their own ethnicity and others'?
				    4.5 Do the staff development programs examine the verbal and nonverbal patterns of interethnic group interactions?
				    4.6 Do the staff development programs provide opportunities for learning how to create and select multiethnic instructional materials and how to incorporate multicultural content into curriculum materials?

				5.0 Does the curriculum reflect the ethnic learning styles of students within the school? 5.1 Is the curriculum designed to help students learn how to function effectively in various cultural environments and learn more than one cognitive style?

(continued)

Rating					Guidelines
Strongly ◄────► Hardly at all					

5.2 Do the objectives, instructional strategies, and learning materials reflect the cultures and cognitive styles of the various ethnic and cultural groups within the school?

6.0 Does the curriculum provide continuous opportunities for students to develop a better sense of self?
　6.1 Does the curriculum help students strengthen their self-identities?
　6.2 Is the curriculum designed to help students develop greater self-understanding?
　6.3 Does the curriculum help students improve their self-concepts?
　6.4 Does the curriculum help students to better understand themselves in light of their ethnic and cultural heritages?

7.0 Does the curriculum help students understand the wholeness of the experiences of ethnic and cultural groups?
　7.1 Does the curriculum include the study of societal problems some ethnic and cultural group members experience, such as racism, prejudice, discrimination, and exploitation?
　7.2 Does the curriculum include the study of historical experiences, cultural patterns, and social problems of various ethnic and cultural groups?
　7.3 Does the curriculum include both positive and negative aspects of ethnic and cultural group experiences?
　7.4 Does the curriculum present people of color both as active participants in society and as subjects of oppression and exploitation?
　7.5 Does the curriculum examine the diversity within each group's experience?
　7.6 Does the curriculum present group experiences as dynamic and continuously changing?
　7.7 Does the curriculum examine the total experiences of groups instead of focusing exclusively on the "heroes"?

Rating				Guidelines
Strongly ←——→ Hardly at all				
				8.0 Does the curriculum help students identify and understand the ever-present conflict between ideals and realities in human societies?
				8.1 Does the curriculum help students identify and understand the value conflicts inherent in a multicultural society?
				8.2 Does the curriculum examine differing views of ideals and realities among ethnic and cultural groups?
				9.0 Does the curriculum explore and clarify ethnic alternatives and options within U.S. society?
				9.1 Does the teacher create a classroom atmosphere reflecting an acceptance of and respect for ethnic and cultural differences?
				9.2 Does the teacher create a classroom atmosphere allowing realistic consideration of alternatives and options for members of ethnic and cultural groups?
				10.0 Does the curriculum promote values, attitudes, and behaviors that support ethnic and cultural diversity?
				10.1 Does the curriculum help students examine differences within and among ethnic and cultural groups?
				10.2 Does the curriculum foster attitudes supportive of cultural democracy and other unifying democratic ideals and values?
				10.3 Does the curriculum reflect ethnic and cultural diversity?
				10.4 Does the curriculum present diversity as a vital societal force that encompasses both potential strength and potential conflict?
				11.0 Does the curriculum help students develop decision-making abilities, social participation skills, and a sense of political efficacy necessary for effective citizenship?
				11.1 Does the curriculum help students develop the ability to distinguish facts from interpretations and opinions?
				11.2 Does the curriculum help students develop skills in finding and processing information?

(continued)

Rating					Guidelines
Strongly ⬅➡ **Hardly at all**					

11.3 Does the curriculum help students develop sound knowledge, concepts, generalizations, and theories about issues related to ethnicity and cultural identity?

11.4 Does the curriculum help students develop sound methods of thinking about issues related to ethnic and cultural groups?

11.5 Does the curriculum help students develop skills in clarifying and reconsidering their values and relating them to their understanding of ethnicity and cultural identity?

11.6 Does the curriculum include opportunities to use knowledge, valuing, and thinking in decision-making on issues related to race, ethnicity, and culture?

11.7 Does the curriculum provide opportunities for students to take action on social problems affecting racial, ethnic, and cultural groups?

11.8 Does the curriculum help students develop a sense of efficacy?

12.0 Does the curriculum help students develop skills necessary for effective interpersonal and intercultural group interactions?

12.1 Does the curriculum help students understand ethnic and cultural reference points that influence communication?

12.2 Does the curriculum help students participate in cross-ethnic and cross-cultural experiences and reflect on them?

13.0 Is the multicultural curriculum comprehensive in scope and sequence, presenting holistic views of ethnic and cultural groups, and an integral part of the total school curriculum?

13.1 Does the curriculum introduce students to the experiences of persons of widely varying backgrounds in the study of each ethnic and cultural group?

13.2 Does the curriculum discuss the successes and contributions of group members within the context of that group's values?

13.3 Does the curriculum include the role of ethnicity and culture in the local community as well as in the nation?

Rating				Guidelines
Strongly ⟷ Hardly at all				
				13.4 Does content related to ethnic and cultural groups extend beyond special units, courses, occasions, and holidays?
				13.5 Are materials written by and about ethnic and cultural groups used in teaching fundamental skills?
				13.6 Does the curriculum provide for the development of progressively more complex concepts, abilities, and values?
				13.7 Is the study of ethnicity and culture incorporated into instructional plans rather than being supplementary or additive?
				14.0 Does the curriculum include the continuous study of the cultures, historical experiences, social realities, and existential conditions of ethnic groups with a variety of racial compositions?
				14.1 Does the curriculum include study of several ethnic and cultural groups?
				14.2 Does the curriculum include studies of both White ethnic groups and ethnic groups of color?
				14.3 Does the curriculum provide for continuity in the examination of aspects of experience affected by race?
				15.0 Are interdisciplinary and multidisciplinary approaches used in designing and implementing the curriculum?
				15.1 Are interdisciplinary and multidisciplinary perspectives used in the study of ethnic and cultural groups and related issues?
				15.2 Are the approaches used authentic and comprehensive explanations of ethnic and cultural issues, events, and problems?
				16.0 Does the curriculum use comparative approaches in the study of racial, ethnic, and cultural groups?
				16.1 Does the curriculum focus on the similarities and differences among and between ethnic and cultural groups?
				16.2 Are matters examined from comparative perspectives with fairness to all?
				17.0 Does the curriculum help students view and interpret events, situations, and conflict from diverse ethnic and cultural perspectives and points of view?

(continued)

Rating				Guidelines
Strongly ←——→ **Hardly at all**				

				17.1 Are the perspectives of various ethnic and cultural groups represented in the instructional program?
				17.2 Are students taught why different ethnic and cultural groups often perceive the same historical event or contemporary situation differently?
				17.3 Are the perspectives of each ethnic and cultural group presented as valid ways to perceive the past and the present?
				18.0 Does the curriculum conceptualize and describe the development of the United States as a multidirectional society?
				18.1 Does the curriculum view the territorial and cultural growth of the United States as flowing from several directions?
				18.2 Does the curriculum include a parallel study of the various societies that developed in the geocultural United States?
				19.0 Does the school provide opportunities for students to participate in the aesthetic experiences of various ethnic and cultural groups?
				19.1 Are multiethnic literature and art used to promote empathy for and understanding of people from various ethnic and cultural groups?
				19.2 Are multiethnic literature and art used to promote self-examination and self-understanding?
				19.3 Do students read and hear the poetry, short stories, novels, folklore, plays, essays, and autobiographies of a variety of ethnic and cultural groups?
				19.4 Do students examine the music, art, architecture, and dance of a variety of ethnic and cultural groups?
				19.5 Do students have available the artistic, musical, and literary expression of the local ethnic and cultural communities?
				19.6 Are opportunities provided for students to develop their own artistic, literary, and musical expression?

Rating Strongly ←——→ Hardly at all					Guidelines
					20.0 Does the curriculum provide opportunities for students to develop full literacy in at least two languages? 20.1 Are students taught to communicate (speaking, reading, and writing) in a second language? 20.2 Are students taught about the culture of the people who use the second language? 20.3 Are second-language speakers provided opportunities to develop full literacy in their native language? 20.4 Are students for whom English is a second language taught in their native languages as needed? 21.0 Does the curriculum make maximum use of local community resources? 21.1 Are students involved in the continuous study of the local community? 21.2 Are members of the local ethnic and cultural communities continually used as classroom resources? 21.3 Are field trips to the various local ethnic and cultural communities provided for students? 22.0 Do the assessment procedures used with students reflect their ethnic and community cultures? 22.1 Do teachers use a variety of assessment procedures that reflect the ethnic and cultural diversity of students? 22.2 Do teachers' day-to-day assessment techniques take into account the ethnic and cultural diversity of their students? 23.0 Does the school conduct ongoing, systematic evaluations of the goals, methods, and instructional materials used in teaching about ethnicity and culture? 23.1 Do assessment procedures draw on many sources of evidence from many sorts of people? 23.2 Does the evaluation program examine school policies and procedures?

(continued)

		Rating		Guidelines
Strongly ⟷ **Hardly at all**				
				23.3 Does the evaluation program examine the everyday climate of the school?
				23.4 Does the evaluation program examine the effectiveness of curricular programs, both academic and nonacademic?
				23.5 Are the results of evaluation used to improve the school program?

INDEX